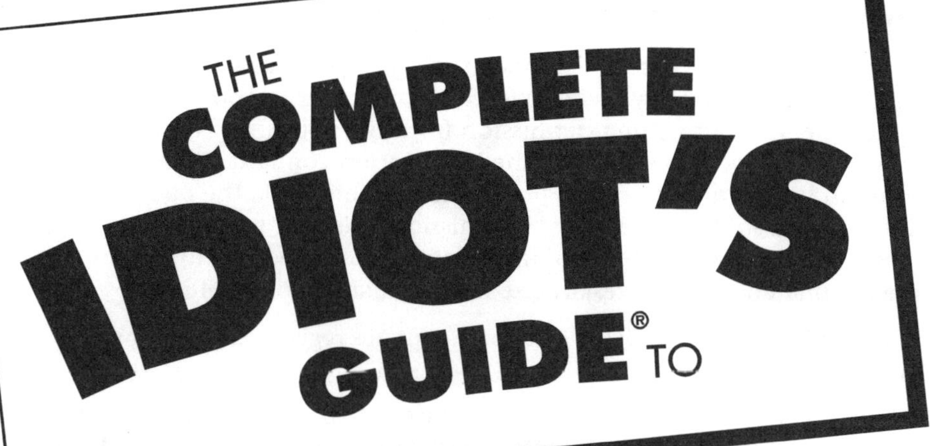

Making Home Videos

by Steven Beal

alpha books

Macmillan USA, Inc.
201 West 103rd Street
Indianapolis, IN 46290

A Pearson Education Company

To my wife, Debra, and my son, Benjamin. I couldn't be luckier ...

Macmillan Publishing books may be purchased for business or sales promotional use. For information please write: Special Markets Department, Macmillan Publishing USA, 1633 Broadway, New York, NY 10019.

International Standard Book Number: 0-02-863606-6
Library of Congress Catalog Card Number: 99-068237

02 01 00 4 3 2 1

Interpretation of the printing code: the rightmost number of the first series of numbers is the year of the book's printing; the rightmost number of the second series of numbers is the number of the book's printing. For example, a printing code of 00-1 shows that the first printing occurred in 2000.

Printed in the United States of America

Publisher
Marie Butler-Knight

Product Manager
Phil Kitchel

Associate Managing Editor
Cari Luna

Acquisitions Editors
Randy Ladenheim-Gil
Amy Gordon

Development Editor
Matthew X. Kiernan

Production Editor
Mark Enochs

Copy Editor
Anne Owen

Editorial Researcher
Roderick A. Beltran

Line Art
Mark Lee

Cover Designer
Mike Freeland

Photo Editor
Richard H. Fox

Illustrator
Brian Mac Moyer

Designer
Scott Cook and Amy Adams of DesignLab

Indexer
Marianne Huff

Layout/Proofreading
Svetlana Dominguez
Mary Hunt
Donna Martin
Gloria Schurick

Contents at a Glance

Contents

Appendixes

Foreword

The most frequently used buzzwords these days include: Internet, e-commerce, broadband, fiber optics, hdtv, and streaming audio and video, but to understand what these words are all about, you have to start at the beginning ... the motion picture camera.

I began my professional career when film was the only way to gather moving images and audio. Now we have videotape, chips and soon bubble memory. But whatever it is, we all see it through someone else's lens. I say that as a way to start the discussion about the video camera. When that great piece of pre-millenium technology became a reality, our lives changed! Now, anyone who can shoot a family video, can shoot for Dateline NBC.

But if you want to do it right, you've got to have a solid background in the basics, and that's what you get with *The Complete Idiot's Guide to Making Home Videos*. Steven Beal has pulled together everything you need to know, plus a few tricks of the trade, and written a manual that will surely outlive whatever equipment you own today.

This book belongs in every school that teaches filmmaking and certainly belongs on the bookshelf of everyone who owns a video camera. So, before you shoot your first frame or your next one ... read this book.

Jennifer Wiesenfeld
Assistant to Frank Radice, VP
NBC Advertising & Promotion, East Coast

Introduction

The camcorder is one of the most powerful devices in human history. That's a pretty bold statement to make when you take into account all of the amazing computerized devices that recent technology has brought into our lives. But at no other time have we been able to record our own reality and events that take place around us with such stunning accuracy and detail. And as TV and camcorder sales continue to explode into the new millennium, more and more people will have the opportunity to explore this booming technology, opening up a world of unlimited creative freedom and pure archival power.

But once you buy a camcorder, what exactly do you do with it? Will you record birthday parties, graduations, and vacations? Or will you take it a step further and put together little mini-movies and other entertaining programs for your family and friends? It's hard to believe that such an amazing device will probably see the light of day only for the most special occasions. But it's true… the majority of camcorders can be found sitting on a closet shelf coated with dust and with the rechargeable batteries decomposing in their hard plastic shell.

The stereotypes, which continue to discourage most home videographers, can be blamed on only one thing. Most people who use a camcorder have never taken the time to learn how to properly shoot video. The resulting home movies are enough to send potential audiences running for the hills at the prospect of having to watch. We've all been spoiled by Hollywood films and network TV shows that utilize multi-million dollar budgets to wow audiences. The typical home movie is ten times as shaky as any show on MTV, devoid of special effects or editing and are often unbearably long. How can you compete?

Here's the deal. Most people turn to television these days as a major source of information and entertainment. Modern camcorders are perfectly capable of delivering broadcast-quality images, and with a little creativity and a basic knowledge of shooting and editing, you're perfectly capable of keeping your friends and family entertained for years to come. You hold the power of TV in the palm of your hand … . It's time to take back the tube!

How to Use This Book

Using a camcorder can be little more than a special interest, or it can become a serious hobby, even a career. Just like anything else in life, the more you put into it, the more you'll get out of it. If you simply want to record life's precious moments, all you really have to do is point and shoot. Camcorders are complex machines but as automatic features become more advanced, they're incredibly simple to operate. On the other hand, if you're interested in exploring the creative possibilities a camcorder can open up to you, then you'll be well served to read on.

This book will take you through the home video experience, from buying a camcorder to editing your footage together into programs that people will want to watch. If you've already got a camcorder and have some experience shooting, the information is presented in such a way that you'll have no problem jumping in wherever you see fit.

If you have access to the Internet, you'll also be happy to note that I've made this book very Web-friendly. Not only is video gaining more a presence on the World Wide Web in the form of online programming and streaming video, there are all kinds of resources available to home moviemakers. Whether you want to buy a camcorder or join a discussion on home video, you'll find the Internet will welcome you with open arms.

This book contains five separate parts. Each part covers a different aspect of home video.

Part 1, "Buying Your Camcorder," walks you through the very basics of how a camcorder works. This will ultimately help you make a decision on what features, gadgets and gizmos you're going to need. You'll also figure out how to choose between a few of the more common camcorder manufacturers. Once you've chosen a camcorder it's hard to resist all of those tempting video-extras. From a camcorder bag to external microphones, this part will help you decide what you really need.

Part 2, "Pre-Production," takes you through a checklist of things you need to consider before commencing with your production. You'll learn how to write a script, scout a location, and plan and set up for lighting and sound. You'll also learn how to prepare and pull off different shot angles that will give your audience a unique perspective on your subject matter.

Part 3, "Lights, Camera, Action!" This is the part of the book where you learn to become a jack of all trades! As captain of the ship, you're responsible for choosing and directing people to star in your home movies. As camcorder operator, this is the part of the book where you'll learn how to take the shake out of your shots. There are also a few suggestions for getting children to participate in the video activities, as well as a few tips on how to get out from behind the camcorder in order to enjoy the event.

Part 4, "Video Perfection—Rescued in the Edit," helps you figure out what to do with your footage after you're done shooting. Whether it's basic editing with your camcorder and VCR, or nonlinear editing on your home computer, you'll learn how to operate the simple tools of post-production and some tips and tricks to putting together some really cool programs.

Part 5, "Round Up the Gang ... It's Showtime!" Now that you've finished making your home movies, it's time to share them with your family and friends. In this part you'll learn how to hold a video-screening, and other various ways to distribute your video to the general public including the Internet and CD-ROM. You'll also get a few tips on videotape care and storage, and a quick rundown of some additional creative camcorder uses.

Keep an Eye Out ...

As you travel through the pages of this book, you'll see special bits of information signified by little pictures to guide you. They'll give you a little extra help in navigating your way through the numerous and varied concepts you're trying to convey to your kids.

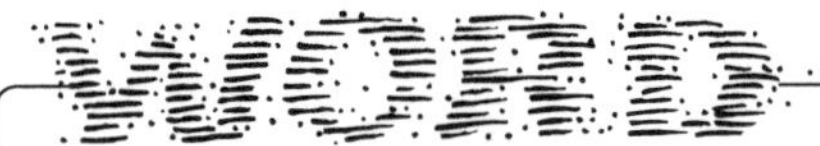

Blurred Word

The video industry is chock-full of confusing jargon, words and phrases. Here you'll find simple, easy to understand definitions and explanations.

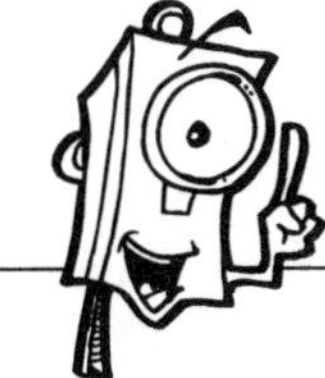

Candid Camera

Video-insider tips and tricks of the trade or additional information like a phone number or Web site.

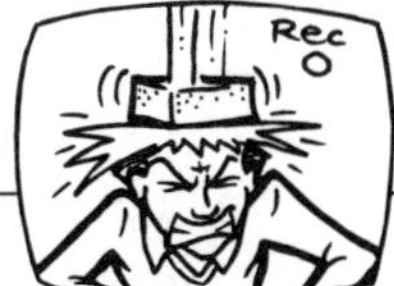

Blooper

Video no-no's and other things that you should avoid along the way.

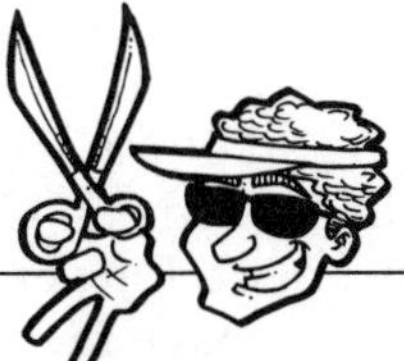

Director's Cut

Bet-you-didn't-know advice or comments from actual industry professionals.

Special Thanks to the Technical Reviewer

The Complete Idiot's Guide to Making Home Videos was reviewed by an expert who double-checked the accuracy of what you learn here, to help us ensure that this book gives you everything you need to know about home video. Special thanks are extended to David Preisman.

David Preisman is a Director in the New Media department at Showtime Networks, Inc. He brings with him a wealth of experience working with the Internet, as an on-air TV producer, animator, and video editor. David's extensive production experience includes working on short films, music videos, TV shows, commercials and network promotions. In addition, his work in the past as a video instructor for teens provided practical insight for this book. David is currently conquering the next generation of television that will combine the computer and TV into one super-appliance coming soon to a living room near you.

Acknowledgments

I'd like to thank my mom and dad for providing me with the love, support and a solid foundation to conquer such a huge task. My sister, a bright future and Ben Ben's biggest fan. My grandmother who is grinning broadly in a better place. My mother- and father-in-law whose love and generosity transcend anything that can be described in words. Joy ... If imitation is a form of flattery, then this book is your greatest compliment! G-Rock, there would be no words on this page if not for a certain conversation on waiter hill. To David Preisman, whose undying dedication to this project led to the most rewarding collaboration of my career. Uncle Onion, Pammy-Mammy, and Dango123, my best friends in the world and lifelong partners in crime. Jesse and Cole, my favorite niece and nephew and an endless source of home video footage. The Neilerator for an entire summer of wakeboarding. To the people who were instrumental in launching my career: Harvey Beal, Glenda Forest, Matty G., Taz, Jon Chironna, Chris Ward, Che Che, Irene, and especially Elaine M. Brown for giving me an early start. Mitch for that extra push! And the rest of the gang ... Nancy, Jon, Camrin, Karen, Kinney, Bardsley, Harley, Eileen, Bob, Nan, Heath, Steph, Chris, Elise, Blick, Houslin, Alberto, Rob, the Rock, Mark Lee, Leone, Pascal, Joachim, Namibian, Cynthia, Maria, and Argis. To Glenda Heron for taking great care of my boy boy. Roderick for taking all of my late night phone calls and rambling e-mails! A special thanks to Helmit, Richie, and LT for a lifetime of great friendship and footage! Camp Delaware for forever plotting the course of my life. And most of all to Debra and Ben who make life worth living.

I also thank the many talented staff members at Alpha/Macmillan. Thanks to Acquisitions Editor Jessica Faust for giving me the opportunity to write this book, and Randy Ladenheim-Gil for helping me to see it through, Development

Editor Matthew X. Kiernan for injecting a new life into this project, Copy Editor Anne Owen, an incredible wordsmith and fellow Zaboomafoo fan, Production Editor Mark Enochs for his patience and perseverance, and to everyone else behind the scenes for all of their hard work.

Trademarks

Part 1

Buying Your Camcorder

Thinking about buying a camcorder? Your timing is impeccable. Camcorders are cheaper than ever, and with the introduction of MiniDV and other consumer-grade digital video formats into the marketplace, the image quality of home video has hit an all time high.

But here's the problem: trying to buy a camcorder can be just as confusing and frustrating as buying a car! Instead of Ford, Chevy, Honda, or Chrysler, you've got to choose from Sony, Canon, Panasonic, Hitachi, JVC, and Sharp to name a few. And you've also got that pesky salesperson problem to deal with. If you don't have any idea how a camcorder works or if you haven't done your research, it's easy to get hoodwinked by one of these quirky characters.

And then you've got all of the cool extras to weed through. From a camcorder bag to a tripod, microphone, or lighting kit, if you don't have an idea of what you plan to shoot, you could easily set yourself back a few grand.

By the time you finish this part of the book, you'll know what kind of camcorder you need, where to buy it, approximately how much you're going to spend, and what extras you're going to need. You'll even learn how to buy and pack a camcorder bag to safely tote around your new toy.

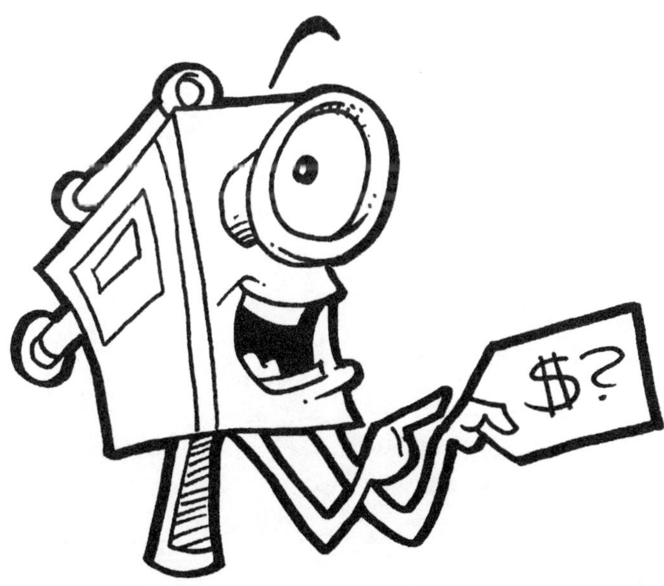

Chapter 1

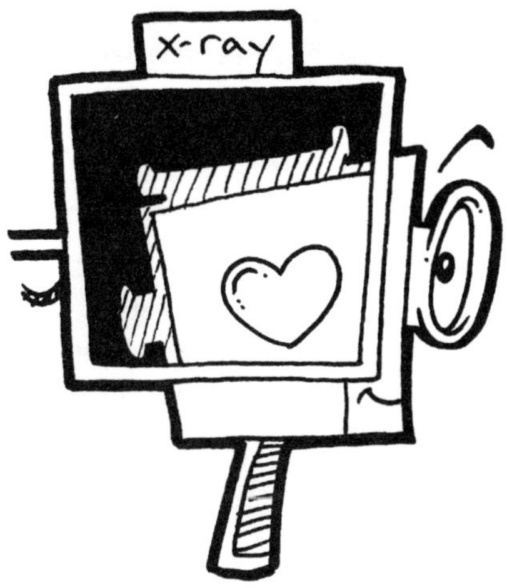

What Makes a Camcorder Tick?

In This Chapter

- Learning about lenses
- Look into the "eye" of your camcorder
- Exposure basics
- On-board microphones
- Recording to tape
- The recipe for camcorder soup

Imagine coming home after work to discover that your house has been robbed. Everything is gone: the computer you use to log onto the Internet, the wide-screen TV set in the living room, and the surround-sound home-theater stereo system that was hooked up to it. Electronic appliances (like the notebook computer I'm writing this with) are such a big part of our everyday lives that sometimes we forget they are all miracles of modern science.

Your camcorder is no exception. Believe it or not, hidden in that sleek outer shell lives some of the most sophisticated circuitry available to consumers today.

Let's take a few minutes to crack open a camcorder and take a quick tour of what's going on inside. (Don't try this at home!) It's not possible to cover every nut, bolt, and circuit—just the main features and advanced systems that make the camcorder an amazing appliance.

In this chapter you'll get an overview of what makes a camcorder tick. Having a basic knowledge of the camcorder's features and functions will help you become an informed buyer; it will also prepare you to deal with all the confusing buttons and switches that, if you don't know what they do, can drive you absolutely mad.

Focusing on the Lens

Let's start with one of the camcorder's most visible external features: the lens. Just like its cousin, the still camera, a video camera uses a lens to let the outside world in. Even though most camcorder lenses are small, they still perform the photographic miracle of capturing light rays so they can be transformed into pictures.

Think of light rays as cars trying to leave a parking lot. Drivers, anxious to leave, are randomly zipping up and down the aisles, looking for the fastest way out. But as the cars approach the exit, they take their places in line and leave in an orderly manner. That's pretty much how a lens captures and directs light. Light rays called protons bounce off your subject at, you guessed it, the speed of light, zipping all over the place with no intention of pulling over for your camcorder. The curved lens miraculously redirects the rambunctious protons and aims them onto a single surface called the CCD, or Charged Coupled Device, (defined in the section "The Eye of Your Camcorder: The CCD") where the video image is formed.

The lens is one of the most vital elements in image gathering. If it is dirty, scratched, or cheaply constructed, the final product will inevitably suffer. Different camcorders have different lenses, depending on the format and how much you're willing to spend. Some of the smallest cameras have tiny plastic lenses that work almost as well as their glass counterparts. Some of the higher-end cameras come with removable lenses that can be changed depending on the need of the shot.

Zoom In, Zoom Out

The camcorder's zoom feature has come a long way in recent years. I have a few ancient film cameras I often use when I need a realistic film-look in my projects. My old Super-8 movie camera can zoom in and out, but I have to do it myself with a little lever, often resulting in choppy, uneven zooms. My wind-up Bolex 16mm movie camera can't zoom at all. What you see is what you get.

When I look into the lens of my camcorder and zoom in on myself, I can see what looks like a smaller lens behind the outer lens moving away from me. What's happening is a tiny motor deep inside the camcorder changes the "focal length" of the lens, increasing or decreasing the field of vision.

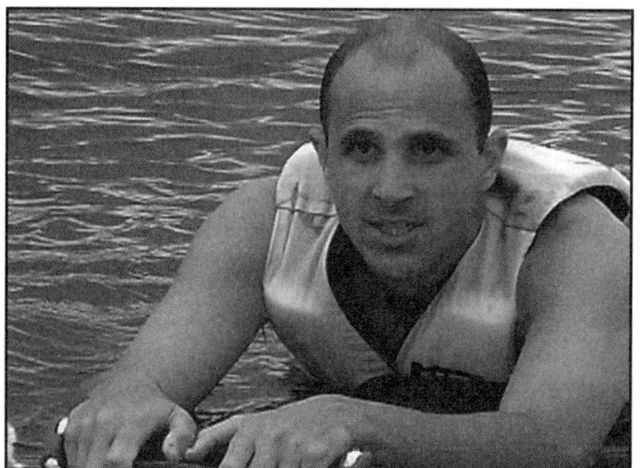

Camcorder zoomed in.

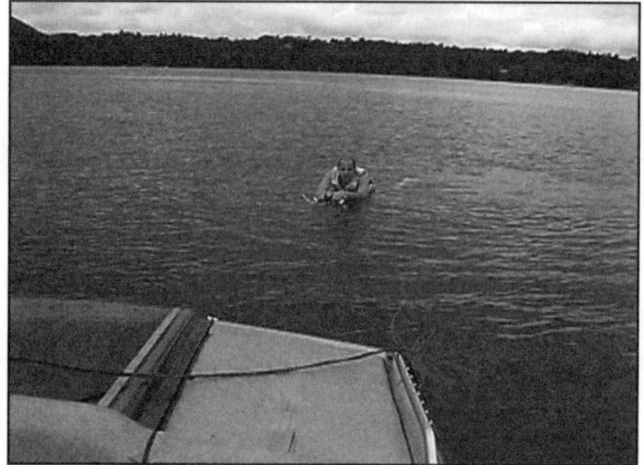

Camcorder zoomed out.

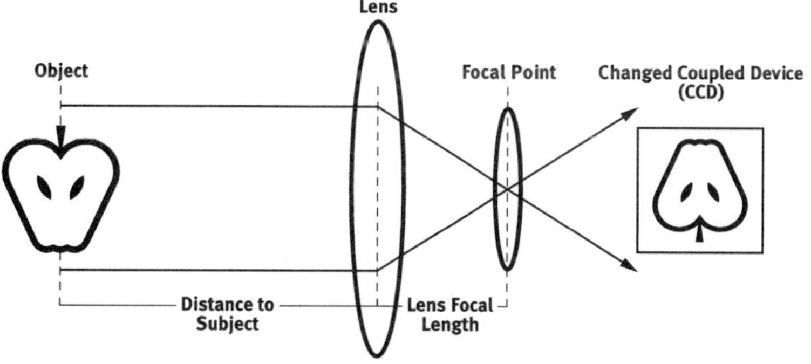

Lens basics.

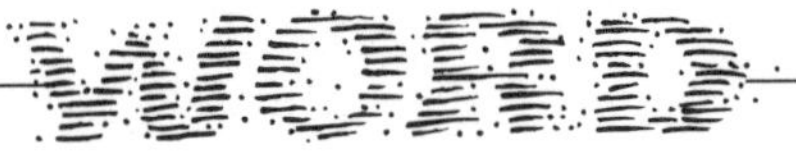

Blurred Word

The **focal point** refers to the exact point in the lens where light converges. **Focal length** is the distance from the focal point in the lens to the imaging surface of the CCD or the Charged Coupled Device.

Finding the Right Focus

Most people cringe when they hear the word *focus*. That's because an out-of-focus lens is responsible for many ruined video shots and photographs. Even with the best lighting, cameras, and sound gear, I can't count how many of life's greatest moments I watched pass while fumbling with the focus ring. Simply put, focusing is one of the most crucial systems that light encounters on its accelerated journey from the outside world to videotape.

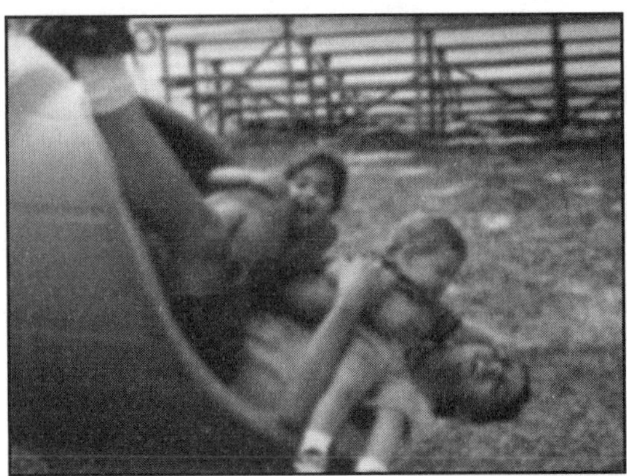

Out of focus.

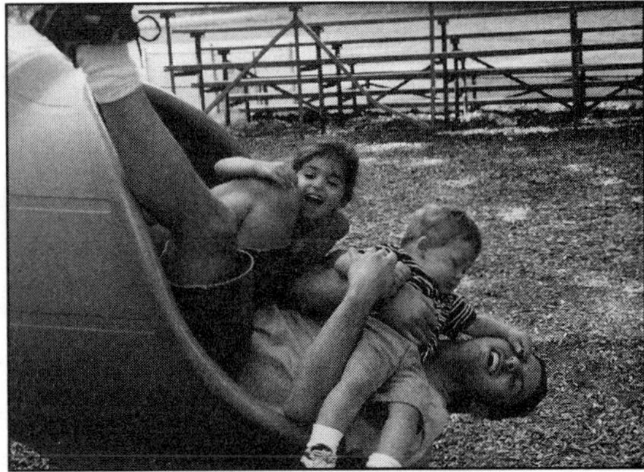

In focus.

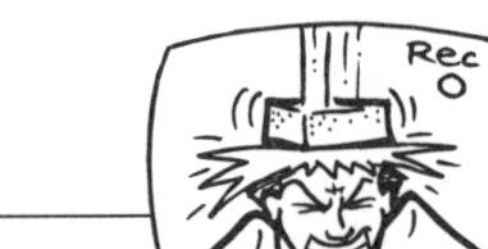

Blooper

Your camcorder's Auto-Focus will frantically move back and forth if there are people or objects (such as cars) moving between your intended subject and the lens. If you rely on this feature, it's best to keep things front and center and to avoid too much movement in your shots.

In some situations, you can count on your camcorder's Automatic Focus to keep things looking sharp. When this feature is working correctly it's such a smooth, natural process that you forget that it's working at all. In theory, it's a ground-breaking procedure in which your camcorder takes control of the focus by determining the distance to the centermost object in the frame. But in practice, Auto-Focus has a long way to go. Among this feature's many drawbacks is that it's often slow to respond and has trouble finding a subject in low light. Auto-Focus can also go haywire when your subject moves from the middle of the picture.

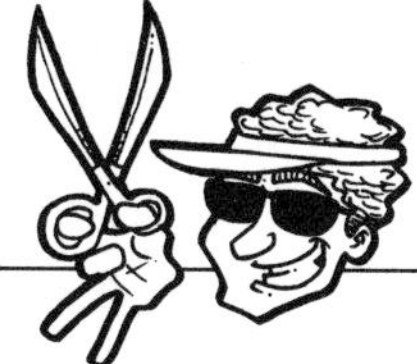

Director's Cut

For a cleaner look, try switching your camcorder into Manual Focus. Once you're out of Auto-Focus, zoom in as close as possible to your subject and focus there. Then zoom out to the desired distance, and you'll find that your picture remains in crisp focus.

The Eye of Your Camcorder: The CCD

Using a camcorder without a CCD, or Charged Coupled Device, would be like trying to drive a car without an engine. The CCD doesn't look like much—just a tiny silicon chip—but it is actually the most sophisticated piece of electronics inside a camcorder.

The CCD has been in action only since the early 1980s in video cameras and has had a profound effect on the way video is recorded. Before CCD technology emerged, video cameras were huge and often relied on external videocassette recorders that the videographer had to sling over a shoulder. The older cameras also used vacuum tubes to capture light and interpret images, and the final picture quality was far from perfect. It wasn't until very recently that camcorders emerged into the compact, technological marvels of today.

The CCD is to the camcorder what a microchip is to a computer. On the surface there is a tiny jungle of electronics and light sensors. The CCD's main function is to collect the light that passes through the lens and turn it into an electronic video signal that is later recorded to tape by an electromagnetic drum. What's even more incredible is that it happens fast—60 times per second to be exact! It is an intricate process, but you don't have to be a nuclear physicist to understand the basics of how it works.

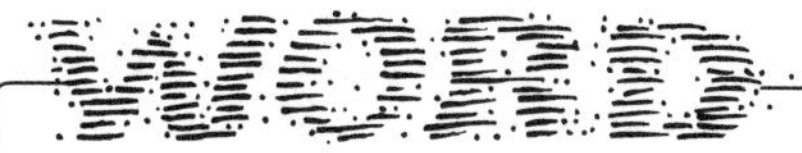

Blurred Word

Charged Coupled Device (CCD) is a silicone chip behind the lens that reads and transforms light rays into electronic signals that later become moving pictures.

Rays of light pass through the lens and fall on the surface of the CCD.

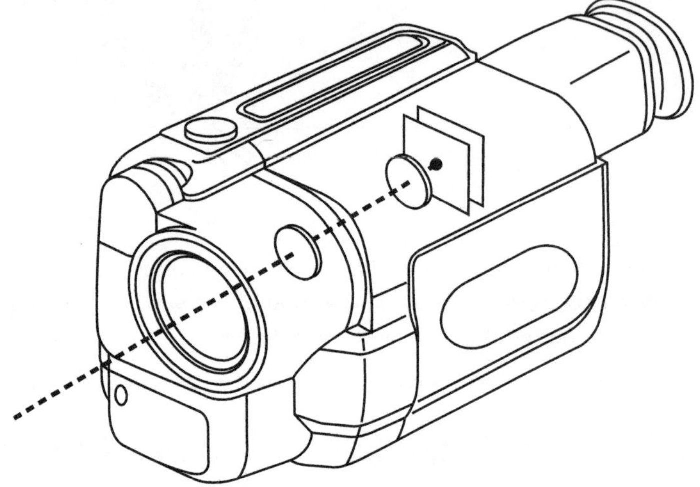

CCD's are relatively inexpensive, extremely sensitive to light, use little power, and can be squeezed into very small spaces. As soon as CCDs hit the scene, businesses and government agencies such as NASA recognized the potential and now cash in on the technology. CCDs can be found on-board space shuttles, the Hubble Space Telescope, and have even been to Mars!

1-Chip vs. 3-Chip Cameras

I own a high-end digital video camera called the Canon XL-1. It is considered one of the best prosumer cameras on the market. It's a 3-chip camera, which means that it has three separate CCDs, each one dedicated to its own primary color in the light spectrum. This creates sharper images and more realistic colors than 1-chip cameras.

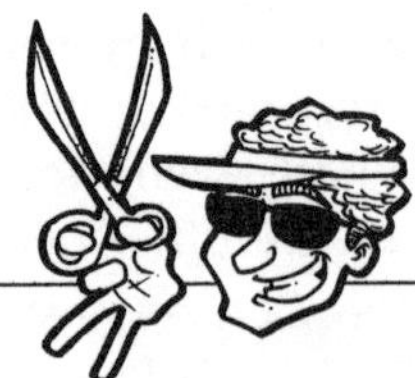

Director's Cut

Prosumer camcorders differ from *consumer* camcorders in that they are marketed toward semi-professional and professional videographers who may shoot weddings, breaking news, or low-budget films/documentaries. For the average camcorder user, the prices of these cameras are high, but for serious shooters who don't want to spend tens of thousands on high-end professional cameras, prosumer gear is the way to go, delivering near-professional quality at a fraction of the price.

Camcorder developers really had their thinking caps on when they invented 3-chip technology. It's an amazing process in which the light separates after passing though the lens and is split in three. Light separation and redirection can be achieved in a couple of ways. In some 3-chip cameras, tiny prisms are placed just behind the lens, and when light passes through, the rays are broken up into their "primary" colors—red, green, and blue (commonly referred to as RGB)—and then directed to the respective CCD. In other camcorders, precision mirrors are used to break up the light, achieving the same effect.

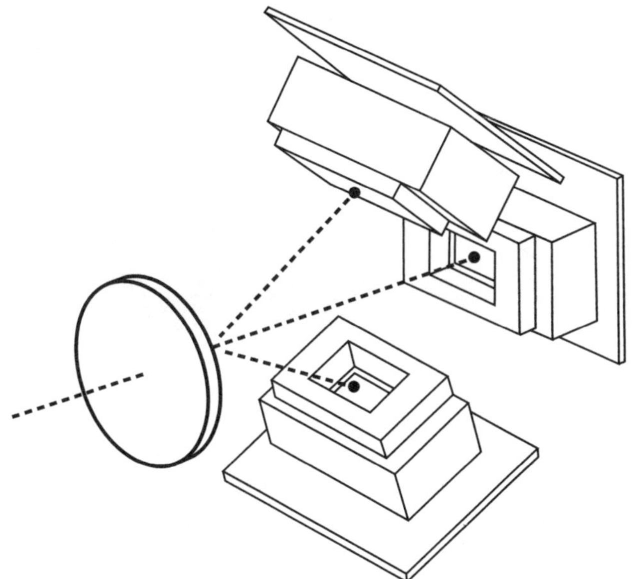

Light passing through the lens of a 3-chip camcorder is separated into its "primary" colors—red, green, and blue (RGB)—and sent to the respective CCD.

Some experts argue that despite their superior image and color quality, 3-chip cameras don't shoot as well in low-light situations. Because light encounters additional obstacles (prisms and mirrors) after it passes the through the lens, a more intense light source is needed to maintain realistic color and brightness.

Easy Does It! The Lowdown on Image Stabilization

Image Stabilization is an elegant technology that has forever changed the face of home video. My old Canon Hi8 camcorder was one of the first on the scene with Optical Image Stabilization or OIS. Sony and a few other camcorder manufacturers countered with Electronic Image Stabilization or EIS.

Imagine yourself walking to a table holding a cup of coffee. Even though your body is bouncing up and down when you walk, your brain sends messages to your hand telling it to keep the cup steady, eliminating spillage. Your camcorder steadies images in the same way. Optical Image Stabilization is a process that takes place in the lens of the camcorder. If the system senses a sudden movement or shake (the calling card of most home videos), it sends an instant message to precision lens parts to recenter the image on the CCD, counter-balancing the movement.

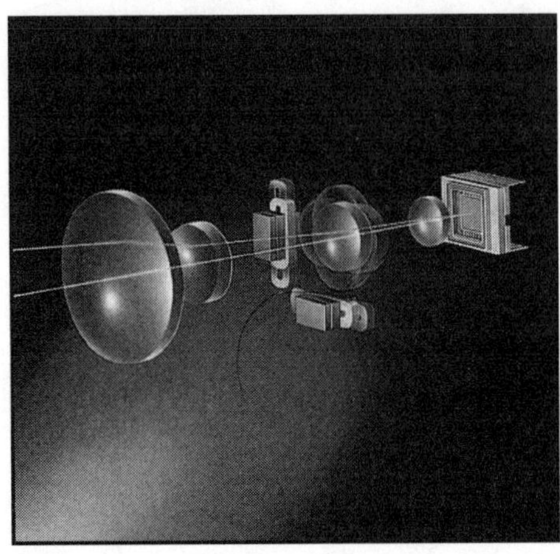

The process of Optical Image Stabilization.

(Courtesy of Canon USA, Inc.)

Electronic Image Stabilization is a digital technology that is greatly dependent on the imaging capabilities of the CCD. It functions by zooming in on the CCD, leaving an outer edge that digitally compensates when it senses a camcorder shake.

Think of a tiny rectangle with an even smaller rectangle drawn inside. The inner rectangle functions as the imaging surface. The outer rectangle acts as a buffer.

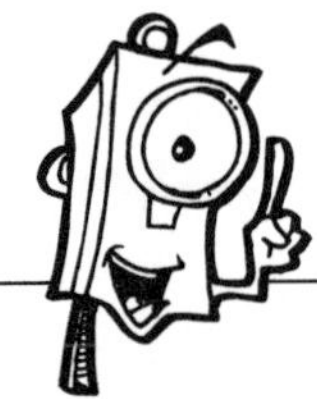

Candid Camera

When Electronic Image Stabilization is turned on (this is default in most camcorders), image quality is slightly compromised because the entire surface of the CCD is not being utilized. On the consumer level, however, the benefits of this feature far outweigh the negatives.

More Than Just an Open-and-Shut Case: Exposure Basics

What happens when a doctor examines your eye by shining a bright flashlight into it? Your pupil gets really small, protecting the delicate optics inside your eye from excessive light rays.

Since people began taking pictures and shooting video, camera manufacturers have borrowed nature's elegant design for regulating light. The camcorder's ultra-sensitive CCD requires a specific amount of light to form a good video image. The exposure system controls two things to regulate the light hitting the CCD: the iris and the shutter. A lot of people get the two mixed up, but here's the lowdown.

The iris is an opening or diaphragm that controls the amount of light that passes through the lens. On a still camera, the shutter is the mechanism that actually opens and lets light in for the brief moment it takes to capture a photograph. On a camcorder, there's no physical shutter, so the CCD electronically simulates the effect of a shutter by regulating the amount of time it processes the light.

We know that the CCD works super-fast, so there's no time to spare if there's too much or too little light coming in.

When a manual shutter adjustment is made, the CCD continues capturing and releasing images at 60 times per second. The only thing that has changed is how long the CCD holds on to those 60 images before releasing.

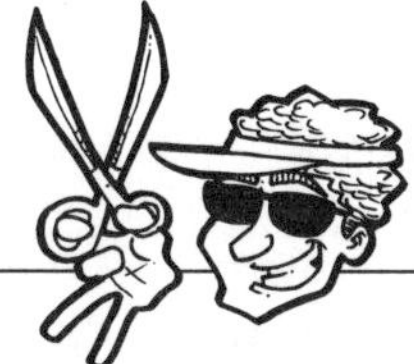

Director's Cut

Video is recorded at 30 frames per second. A *frame* is simply a picture, or video snapshot. Thirty *snapshots* equal one second of moving video (29.97 frames to be exact).

At a low shutter speed, say $\frac{1}{60}$ of a second, the CCD is getting more light, so the resulting image is brighter. This is perfect for poorly lit scenes such as a school play or rock concert. At a higher shutter speed, say $\frac{1}{1000}$ of a second, the CCD gets less light, resulting in a darker image. A fast shutter speed is helpful when you're shooting brightly lit action scenes.

My Hi8 camcorder has an option for manual shutter, but there is no control for the iris. When I change the shutter speed, the iris is automatically adjusted. Most camcorders on the market don't let you directly control the iris.

The Ears of the Camcorder: On-Board Microphones

It takes more than pictures to tell the whole story.

With microphone technology advancing by leaps and bounds, your home video has the potential to sound closer to real life than you ever could have imagined.

Unfortunately, in the world of home video, sound is often an afterthought. Not that the everyday videographer needs to become an audio recording engineer, but a basic working knowledge of how sound and video coexist will greatly improve the overall quality of your work.

Most microphones can be found somewhere in the front of the camcorder, usually underneath or above the lens, giving it the best possible opportunity to retrieve sounds. Most microphones that come standard with camcorders are *omni-directional*, meaning sounds from all directions are picked up with the loudest sound being favored.

Sound waves take a pretty incredible journey from the outside world to videotape. First, they are converted into electrical signals by the microphone. These signals are extremely weak, so they're sent to a "pre-amp" for amplification, significantly boosting the signal in order for it to be audible upon playback. This is a crucial stage because a level too low or too high will result in either tape noise or distortion.

Another useful automatic feature found in most camcorders is Automatic Gain Control or AGC. This system scans the incoming audio levels and compares them to a predetermined internal reference point. If the incoming levels are below or above this point, the overall level is adjusted accordingly. One of the main drawbacks to Automatic Gain Control is that it tries to raise even the lowest sound to the ideal preset level. So when there's a lull in the audio, the system searches for even the slightest sounds, which can leave your audio track sounding like a scratched vinyl record from the 1960s. Some top-shelf camcorders have VU meters (Volume Unit Meters) that allow you to visually measure the incoming audio levels. Unfortunately, most consumer camcorders do not.

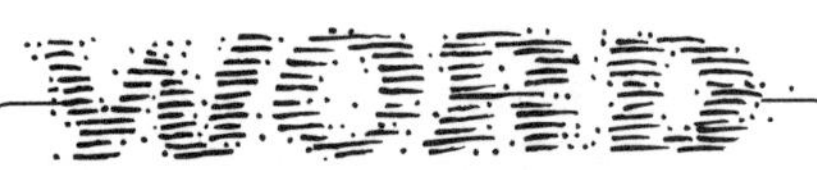

Blurred Word

VU meter or **volume unit meter** measures audio signals with a bouncing needle or LED. VU meters are the best way to monitor your audio track because you can actually see how your incoming levels compare to optimal level points on

How Do Audio and Video Stick to the Tape?

Videotape recording is quite a mind-boggling process, but you only need to know the basics to understand the miracle of home video. Did you ever wonder what happens to a cassette after you pop it into the camera and close the door?

Actually, once the videocassette is inserted, tiny mechanical arms inside the camcorder poke and prod at the cassette, and precisely thread the tape around a rotating electromagnetic drum. The tape is coated with tiny metal particles that are magnetized by a record head with the necessary information needed to reproduce a video and audio signal when the tape is played back. As it turns out, your camcorder is actually a pint-sized VCR as well as an image gatherer.

The Recipe for Camcorder Soup

Camcorder manufacturers add functions and features to a camcorder the way a gourmet chef adds ingredients to soup. There are literally hundreds of them packed into your camcorder, so it's easy to get confused and frustrated when you're learning how to shoot with it.

Following is the recipe for camcorder soup.

Record

It's the bright red button that switches the camera into record mode.

Record/Review

Pressing this button allows you to play back in the viewfinder the scene you just recorded.

Record Indicator Light

It's usually a blinking red light in the front of the camcorder that alerts the general public that you are recording. Some camcorders have the capability to turn this off.

Standby

This feature is intended to help you conserve precious battery life by switching the camcorder into a sleep or low power mode. This way, the camcorder can "wake up" faster than turning it on from scratch. Some camcorders go into standby mode automatically after several minutes of inactivity.

Viewfinder Controls

Most viewfinders can be adjusted like your TV set. You can adjust the color, contrast, and brightness settings.

Viewfinder Diopter Switch

If you wear glasses, you're going to love this feature! It allows you to shoot with your glasses off by compensating for near- and far-sightedness.

Video Insert

This feature allows you to insert a section of video on the tape without recording over the existing sound.

Audio Dub

This is similar to video insert, except you overwrite the audio track without disturbing the picture.

Digital Video Effects (DVEs)

These are cool features that let you add special effects to your video, such as strobe, mosaic, paint, smear, solarize, and so on. You can also add digital transitions between shots, such as dissolves, wipes, and fades.

Electronic Enhancers

Features that allow you to digitally enhance controls such as zoom and image brightness.

Titler/Character Generator

When activated, this feature utilizes other buttons on the camcorder, such as record, rewind, fast forward, and so on, to allow the user to enter letters of the alphabet that can be displayed on screen. On most models with this feature, you can store titles you create in the camera's memory.

Program Auto-Exposure

This is a nice feature that automatically adjusts the iris and shutter for specific shooting scenarios. Settings often include Sports, Sand and Sunlight, Portrait, and Spotlight.

Most camcorders come standard with the following:

- Rechargeable battery
- A/C power supply/battery charger
- Threaded tripod socket
- Audio/video output jacks

As you can see, the streamlined appearance of a camcorder can be deceiving. Even though a camcorder can do a great many things and handle a vast array of shooting situations, it can be a puzzling device. It's a good idea to spend a little time familiarizing yourself with the functions and features that are common to all camcorders before setting out on the journey of choosing one to buy. And once you own one, give the owner's manual a once-over.

The Least You Need to Know

- Don't be fooled by the camcorder's sleek, compact appearance. It is truly a technological marvel that should be understood before deciding which one to purchase.
- Your camcorder's lens is vital in image gathering.
- Electronic zoom can make your lens either wide-angle or telephoto.
- The CCD is the "eye" that allows your camcorder to see the outside world.
- The Auto-Exposure system automatically adjusts the camcorder's iris and shutter.
- Your camcorder functions as a video camera and tiny VCR.

Chapter 2

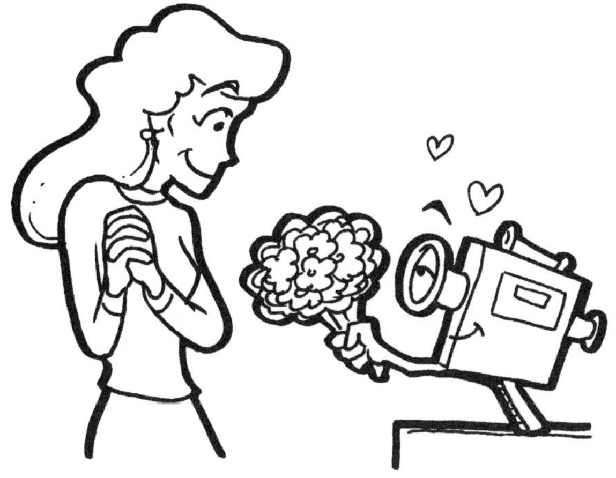

The Right Camcorder for You

In This Chapter

- Determining your needs
- A quick list of must-have features
- Which video format should you choose?
- Unraveling the mystery of digital video

Ever been to the camcorder section of an electronics store? It's like being the center of attention at a national press conference. With hundreds of video lenses focused on you, choosing a camcorder that best suits your needs can be a little scary. They come in all different shapes, sizes, and videotape formats, and there are hundreds of features and functions to choose between. This chapter will help you understand the features that make it easier to shoot great-looking video and give you an idea of where you can find their corresponding buttons on the camcorder. You'll also get some tips on choosing the right video format and a quick lesson in digital video (DV).

Determining Your Needs

Whether I'm taking the train to work, I'm on vacation, or I'm walking down the street with my family, there's a good chance that I've got at least one camcorder in my possession. Not only do I get a huge amount of satisfaction shooting and editing fun programs for my friends and family, but I also use my digital camcorder and editing gear to make money producing and editing documentaries, TV shows, music videos, and short- and feature-length films.

As you can probably guess, I have pumped tens of thousands of dollars into film and video equipment. For me, it's been an investment in my career. But most home videographers don't plan on making a dime shooting and producing video.

So, it's important to figure out a few things before spending any money on video equipment:

- What are you going to shoot with your camcorder?
- Are you going to use your camcorder often?
- Do you plan to edit the raw footage into programs?
- Are you going to use your camcorder to shoot material you might try to sell in some way or possibly enter into film and video festivals?

You can do a million and one things with a camcorder. The possibilities are as unlimited as your imagination. Having an answer to some of these questions can greatly influence which camcorder you buy. If you plan on shooting strictly for family and personal entertainment, you can pick up a camera that delivers great picture quality for less than $500. But if you plan to get more serious about video, toss a few extra bucks into the pot, and you can get a camcorder that's loaded with professional features and capable of producing unbelievably sharp images.

Features You Can't Live Without

The evolution of the camcorder has been fast and furious. It has gone from a bulky enclosure of scrap metal and vacuum tubes to a technologically complex little marvel.

Whatever the future has in store for the ever-evolving camcorder, right now there are a few basic features that are essential in helping you shoot quality video.

If you can find a camcorder that has all of the following features in your price range, you're on the road to home video perfection:

- Image Stabilization
- Auto/Manual Focus
- Optical Zoom
- Manual White Balance
- Manual Exposure
- LANC/Control-L
- Date and Time
- Color Viewfinder

Keep It Steady, Will Ya!

As with any battery-powered electronic device, people want to be able to pop it into their pocket when it's not in use. So, just like cell phones, computers, and even TVs, it was just a matter of time before the camcorder began to shrink.

Even though most compact, lightweight camcorders had the ability to produce beautiful images and were unbelievably convenient to tote around, home videographers found themselves faced with a major challenge: They couldn't hold the camcorders steady while shooting.

Sudden camera jolts and shakes work well on MTV and in Woody Allen movies, but when you don't know how to tastefully pull it off, you can irritate viewers in a hurry. Camcorder makers needed to come up with a solution, and they needed to do it fast!

Image Stabilization hit the scene just a few short years ago and has quickly become the camcorder industry's crowning achievement. Without question, it's top on the list of must-have features. If you haven't had the chance to see image stabilization in action, stop by your local electronics store and check it out. It's very subtle, but it really works!

Image Stabilization can easily be turned on with the flick of a button. Both of my camcorders have Optical Image Stabilization, and I can honestly say that I've never had a reason to turn it off.

Maybe You Need Glasses; Maybe You Don't!

Rule #1: Never have too much confidence in your camcorder's Auto-Focus feature. Sooner or later, it will let you down. That's why it's important to make sure that your camcorder has the ability to shift into Manual Focus.

While automatic features are instrumental in making home videography more idiot-proof, it's essential for any videographer to understand that there are times when you need to take away the reigns from your camcorder. Manual Focus is essential when there are objects, moving or still, in the foreground that can potentially distract the Auto-Focus system. Let's say you're videotaping someone running in a race. If your subject is in second place, your camera may decide to focus on the runner in first place, ruining your shot. Manual Focus is a simple technique and with a little practice, even the most novice videographer can become an expert.

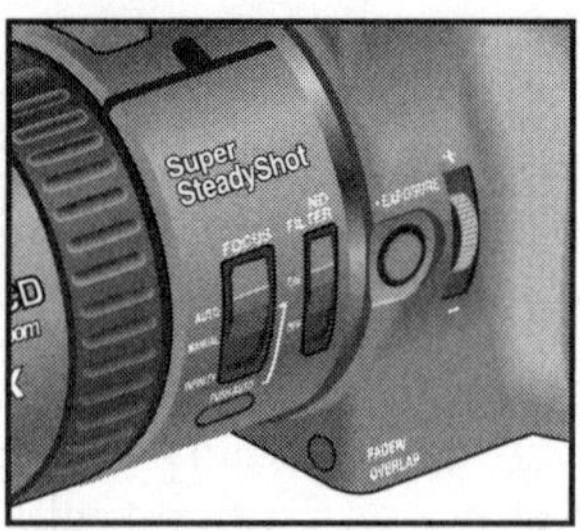

Auto-Focus On/Off—focus ring.

Most camcorders have a simple switch to turn Auto-Focus on or off. On my Canon Hi8, I first have to flip the camcorder out of automatic mode, and then I hit the AF On/Off button. There's a tiny dial close by that allows me to focus manually. It's in a convenient location, but sometimes I have a hard time finding the right focus with such a small dial. My DV camcorder has a large Manual Focus ring around the lens that is more intuitive and effective to use, because I've been focusing my 35mm still camera in a similar way for decades. If possible, search for a camcorder with a focus ring around the lens.

A "Balanced" Palate

Most people have never even heard are the phrase "White Balance," but if this function on your camcorder is out of whack, your video will look like someone dipped the lens into a bucket of multi-colored paint. Even though most cameras perform White Balance automatically, it's helpful to understand how it works.

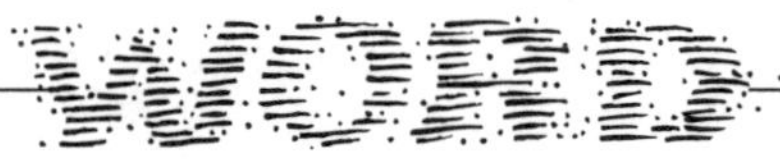

Blurred Word

White Balance is a feature that determines how your camcorder "sees" and records the colors of the environment in which you're shooting. In automatic mode, the camera automatically reads the white levels and adjusts accordingly. On some camcorders this function can be performed manually.

Basically, when a camcorder is "White Balanced," the camera's perception of color is forced into equilibrium with the scene that's being shot. This is useful when shooting outdoors because sunlight can often record with a blue tint. Similarly, some indoor lights can record with a yellowish-green tint. A White Balance helps you avoid recording these funky looking colors by teaching the camcorder what the color white is supposed to look like in the current shooting situation so it can adjust the rest of the colors accordingly.

It's also important to note that if you have White Balanced your camcorder for shooting indoors and then walk outside to record some more footage, you'll need to re-White Balance for the new shooting environment. In general, you should make sure that your camcorder is White Balanced every time you begin to shoot.

Catch the Action!

If possible, find a camcorder that will let you make your own shutter adjustments. You'll be glad you did. Taking charge of shutter speed is essential when shooting bright, outdoor action scenes. At low shutter speeds, moving images tend to blur together. At high shutter speeds, they are crisper and easier to make out, especially when played back in slow motion.

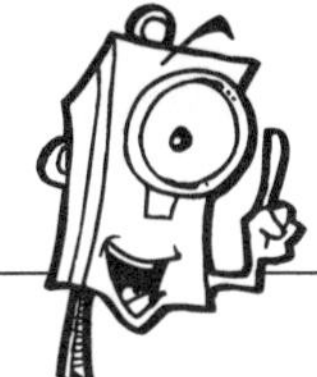

Candid Camera

Look for a camcorder that has the ability to override Auto-White Balance. A Manual White Balance is easy to do and is usually more accurate than Automatic White Balance. In a well-lit area, simply place a white card or piece of paper (there's a tear-out card for White Balancing in the front of this book) and place it close to your shooting subject. Simply hit the White Balance or "WB" button and whammo! Your camcorder's now in sync with the rest of the world!

Most camcorders come with Auto-Exposure (AE) or Program Auto-Exposure. Auto-Exposure is a wonderful thing 90 percent of the time because it takes a lot of practice to effectively make manual light adjustments while concentrating on shooting. There are a million other things to worry about such as focus, shot composition, audio, and so on.

There are times, however, when Auto-Exposure freaks out, forcing you to make a manual shutter adjustment if you want to save the shot. Very much like the Auto-Focus feature, Auto-Exposure has no idea what portion of the video frame you want to see, so the subject of the shot can easily end up incorrectly exposed. This can be annoying, especially when you're shooting an event where the lighting changes from room to room like a birthday party or even following a child around the house with a camcorder.

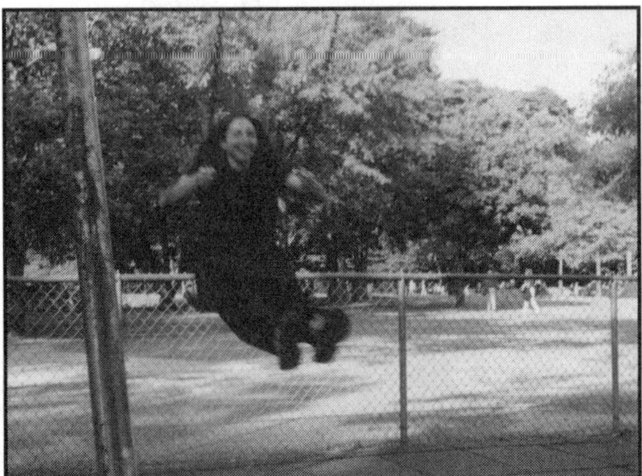

Low shutter speed.

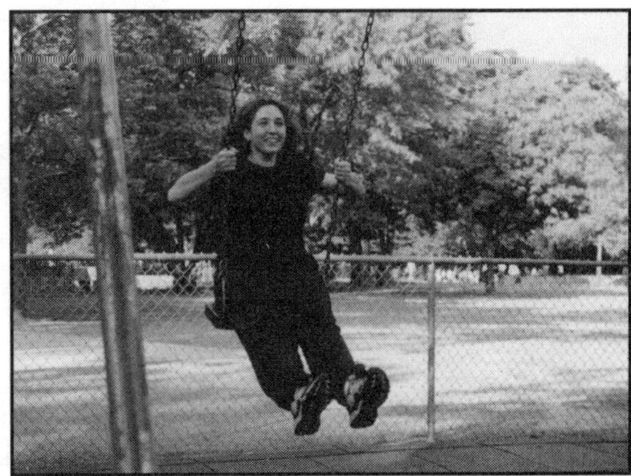

High shutter speed.

On some cameras, there is a button you can hit called Backlight that partially overrides the camera's Auto-Exposure, letting more light into the lens. This is very useful when your subject in the foreground is being washed out by a strong light source in the background like a window. Or, if your camcorder doesn't have this feature, you can manually override the auto exposure yourself, or you can move your subject away from the light source.

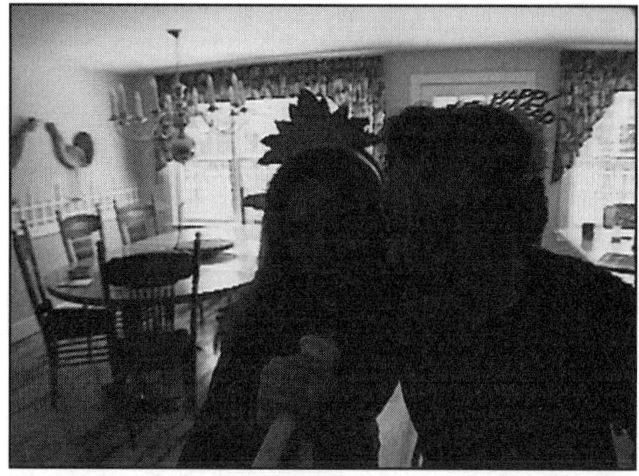

Auto-Exposure with a strong light source in the background.

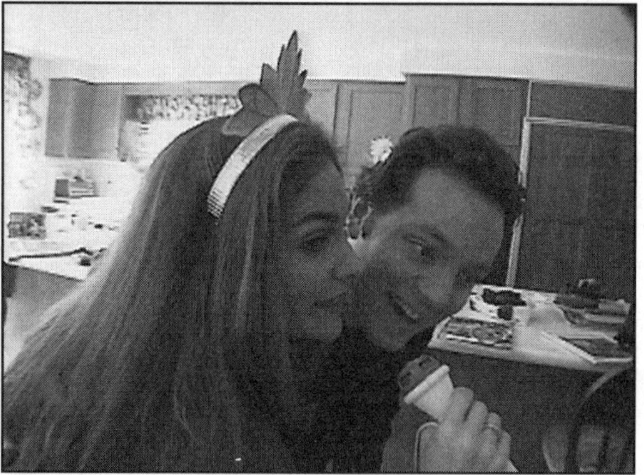

Auto-exposure with subject moved away from the strong light source.

On higher-end cameras, you can counter-balance this problem by adjusting the iris. Unfortunately, most of the consumer grade cameras don't have controls for manual iris.

On some camcorders, there's a digital solution worth mentioning. You can use the Gain switch to electronically pump up light levels in a dark environment. This should be used only in emergency situations when there's almost no picture visible in the viewfinder. Video that has been processed by the camera's digital "gain" will often result in a harsh, grainy look.

Some Sony camcorders also have a feature called NightShot that lets the camcorder "see" in almost total darkness by using a built-in infrared system. Keep in mind that you won't have perfect image quality and the colors may be a washed out, but just the fact that you can record an image at all in dark conditions is an incredible feat. Rumors flew when NightShot came out that you could use your camcorder to see through clothing during the daytime. After much trial and error, I can honestly say that the x-ray capabilities don't even come close to working!

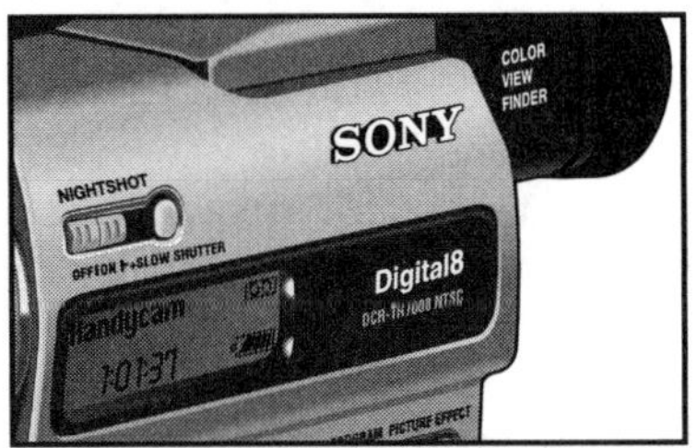

Sony's Nightshot feature.

Taking Control with LANC/Control-L Connections

LANC or Control-L is a useful feature, but most people don't have the slightest clue as to what it means.

Developed by Sony, LANC/Control-L is an editing protocol that has become the standard in most consumer camcorders. This feature allows your camcorder to be hooked up to LANC-compatible editing controllers and PC/Mac-based software. The ability to edit video is the best way to take the "home" out of home video by nuking unwanted scenes and re-ordering sequences so they play with a natural flow. (For more on editing, see Part 4.)

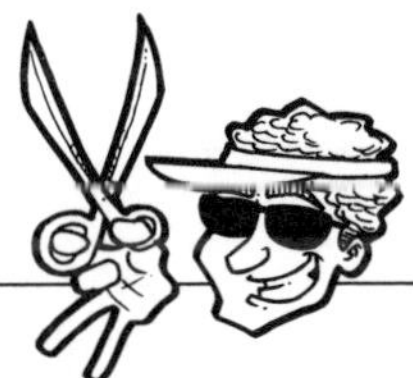

Director's Cut

You don't need LANC/Control-L to have the ability to edit video. It's just an easy, convenient way to begin editing without shelling out money for high-end editing systems. Other editing protocols you might come across are Control-P and Control-M. They work pretty much the same way as LANC/Control-L.

Make a Date to Stamp Your Video

For people like me who shoot almost as much video as there are hours in a day, the ability to superimpose the time and date is extremely useful. It's also a great habit to get into because if you ever forget to label a tape, you can always shuttle back through your footage and find out when it was shot.

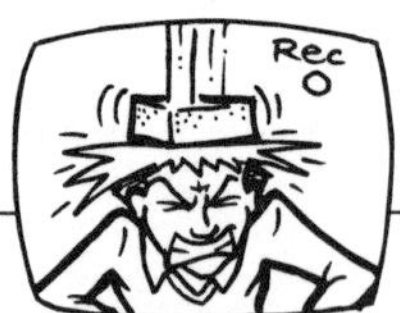

Blooper

Never leave the date and time up constantly throughout your video without turning it off! Your video will look something like amateur tornado footage that you'd see on a Discovery Channel program. I suggest marking the very beginning of your video with the time and date, but be careful not to leave it on during key moments.

What You See Is What You Get

Camcorder viewfinders have come a long way since the early days of television when the camera operator had to squint through a tiny tube. Now, peering through a viewfinder is similar to looking through the periscope of a submarine. You are fed all kinds of information like elapsed recording time, automatic and color settings, even remaining battery life. Above all, you get to see what you're shooting in amazing color and detail. In fact, the picture quality of some viewfinders is better than most early television sets!

Many of the newer camcorders have a traditional viewfinder and a flip-out LCD screen. This allows you to shoot from all sorts of weird angles and still be able to see what you're doing. It's great when you want to get an extreme shot from above or below; you can twist the screen in any direction you need. And because they are comparatively large in size to traditional viewfinders (2 to 4 inches), you can move the camera far away from yourself and still monitor your shot. You can even "spy" around corners or over walls using your pop-out screen.

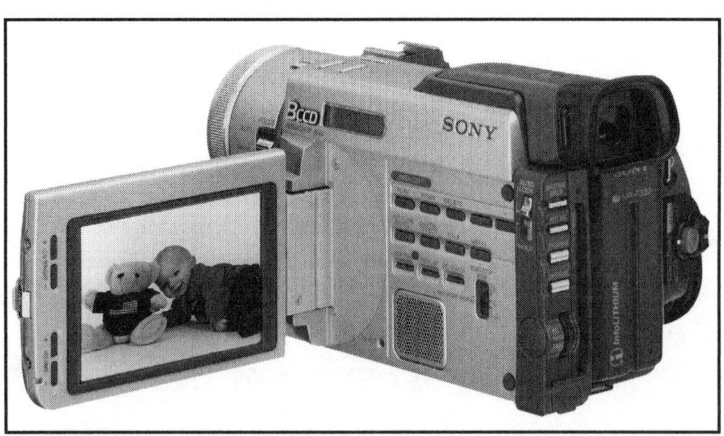

Sony camcorder with pop-out LCD viewfinder.

Taking a Closer Look

Some camcorders are advertised as having both an Optical Zoom and a Digital Zoom. It can be misleading because Digital Zoom (which can be as high as 100×) and Optical Zoom are totally different.

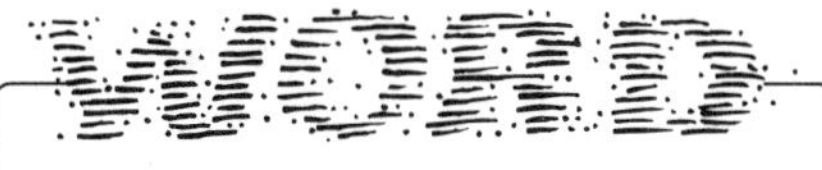

Blurred Word

LCD or **Liquid Crystal Display** is a screen composed of tiny crystals that, when "excited" by electricity, form moving video images.

One great thing about my Canon Hi8 camera is that it has a 20× Optical Zoom. This feature was perfect for when my wife and I were on our honeymoon in Italy. Whether we were videotaping the ceiling of the Sistine Chapel (I almost got thrown out!) or scanning the cliffs of the Amalfi Coast, I was able to zoom in with great accuracy and sharpness.

If I were using a camera with a Digital Zoom for these shots, my footage would look much different, and definitely not for the better.

Digital Zooming works very much like Electronic Image Stabilization. When you hit the zoom button, the camcorder begins to expand its focal length until it hits its optical focal limit. Then the digital mechanism kicks in. The camera electronically enlarges the image by zooming in on the pixels of the CCD, simulating an increased focal length. The closer you zoom in, the more resolution you lose. If the Digital Zoom is deep enough (100× to 200×), the image eventually looks like a bunch of fuzz, similar to the blurry boxes when a TV station tries to cover a nude scene or obscure someone's face.

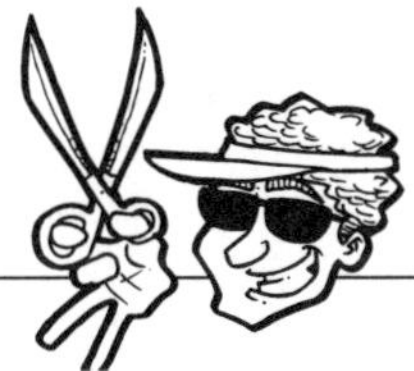

Director's Cut

When Digital Zoom and Electronic Image Stabilization technology emerged, video purists were outraged! They felt camcorder makers were misleading users and tricking them into degrading their picture with the promise of perfectly still video and the ability to see a bug on a tree two blocks away. However, when used in moderation digital enhancement features are OK because manufacturers compensate for image degradation by using CCDs that are slightly more sensitive.

Choosing Between Common Videotape Formats

The format battles that began in the late 1970s mushroomed into an all-out war by the mid-1980s. Remember the famous clash between Sony Betamax and VHS? Even in today's world of digital video, it seems that we just can't break the vicious cycle. MiniDV, DV-CAM, DVC-PRO: The formats just keep on coming! And as new video formats are developed, manufacturers constantly battle over which one should be the industry standard. In the meantime, some people buy the new format, while others condemn it. And with the emergence of consumer Digital Video technology, the misinformation is worse than ever.

Choosing a video format is the most important decision you make when buying a camcorder. But before that pushy salesperson convinces you to make a purchase, ask yourself a few questions:

- Will the format you choose be around for more than a few years?
- Will you easily be able to watch the footage on your TV?
- Will you be able to edit your videos?
- Is the new format capable of delivering the image quality that best suits your needs?

Consumer videotape formats.

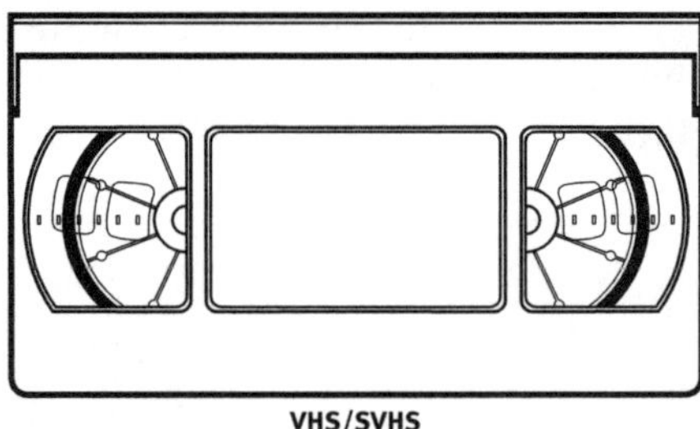

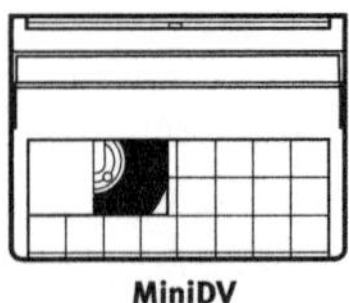

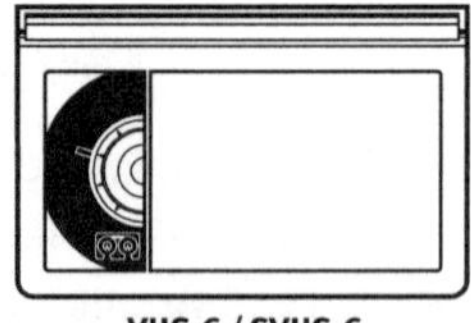

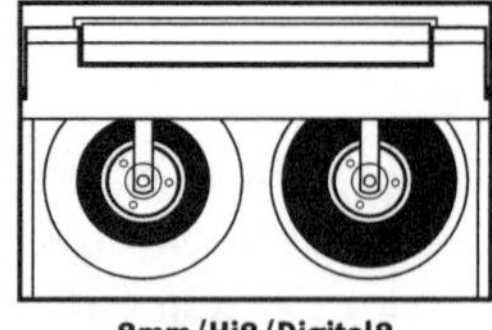

Right now there are about eight consumer videotape formats on the market:

- VHS
- VHS-C
- 8mm

- SVHS
- SVHS-C
- Hi8
- MiniDV
- Digital8

VHS

This is the format that started the home video revolution and won the war in a very big way! In fact, VHS has had the longest shelf life of any dominant video format in television history.

Full-size VHS camcorders use the familiar cassettes that you record your favorite TV shows on. Unfortunately, the format's biggest bonus is also its biggest drawback. While it's incredibly convenient to shoot video and then pop it into your home VHS VCR, the camcorders are big and heavy due to the large size of the VHS cartridge.

The Lowdown on VHS	
Cassette Size	7.4 × 4.1 × .98 inches (188 × 104 × 25mm)
Tape Size:	½ in.
Resolution:	250 horizontal lines

VHS also set the home video standard with about 250 lines of resolution. If you look closely at the TV screen or watch a movie where a TV screen has been filmed, you can make out the horizontal lines that compose a video picture. The larger the number of lines of resolution, the sharper the image.

How much more wind does VHS have in its sails? Only time will tell. If you walk into any video store these days, you'll often see big boxes where previously viewed movies are being sold for just a few dollars. There's a very good reason for that. With the arrival of DVD, video store owners are preparing for the oncoming onslaught of digital movie home rentals.

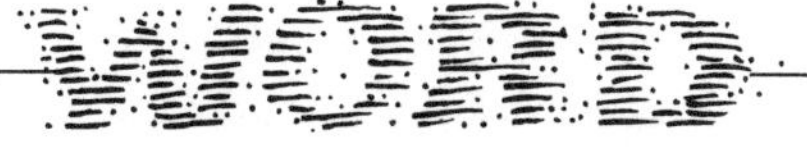

Blurred Word

DVD stands for **Digital Versatile Disk.** It is the same thickness (1.2mm) and diameter (120mm/4.7 in.) to a regular Compact Disc. The first generation of DVDs, however, have seven times the storage capacity of a CD, with a 4.7 gigabyte capacity on a single side/single layer. That's room enough for a 133-minute movie.

VHS-C

VHS-C is a VHS format, but it's packaged in a much smaller cartridge. This has eliminated the size problems of its larger VHS cousin, resulting in much smaller camcorders. However, when you cram a large format tape (½ in.) into a small container, you quickly run into a space problem, resulting in shorter record times of 40 minutes or less. You can get longer record times from VHS-C using EP (Extended Play), but the image quality suffers.

VHS-C can be played in regular VHS VCRs using a battery powered adapter cartridge. VHS-C tapes are generally more expensive than regular VHS tapes.

The Lowdown on VHS-C	
Cassette Size	5.6 × 2.2 × .87 in. (92 × 58 × 22mm)
Tape Size	½ in.
Resolution	250 horizontal lines

8mm

8mm was born after a rare cease-fire in the video wars when manufacturers decided to agree on a single format. 8mm was extremely well received and is still widely used today. Consumers love the compact size of both the cassette and 8mm camcorders, and the fact that they can record two hours of home video on a single tape!

The only drawback is that you have to plug an Audio/Video (A/V) cable into your TV or VHS VCR from your 8mm camcorder to see the video. (Some TVs now come with A/V plugs in the front designed specifically for camcorders.)

The Lowdown on 8mm	
Cassette Size	3.7 × 2.5 × 0.6 in. (95 × 62.5 × 15mm)
Tape Size	8mm (⅓ in. wide)
Resolution	250 horizontal lines

SVHS/SVHS-C/Hi8

SVHS/SVHS-C and Hi8 are considered to be "high-band" formats. This means that they are capable of producing an impressive 400 to 420 lines of resolution, making them a viable choice for video-hobbyists, semi-professionals and even professional videographers.

The respective cassette sizes of these formats are exactly the same as their low-band counterparts, but they deliver close to twice the resolution with hi-fi stereo sound and cost about twice as much.

One of the nice things about the "high-band" formats is that they are "backward compatible," which means that you can play an 8mm tape in a Hi8 camcorder. Similarly, you can play a VHS in an SVHS camcorder, or VHS-C in an SVHS-C camcorder. Backward compatibility allows you to continue to enjoy your current library while beginning a new library of better quality videos.

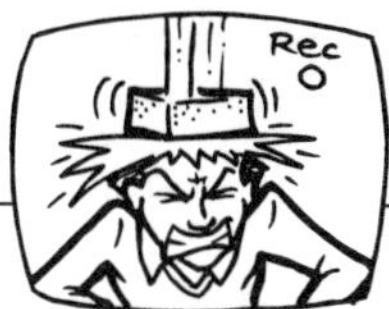

Blooper

There are a few catches with "high-band" formats you should be aware of: If you play a "low-band" format in a "high-band" deck, you don't gain the extra resolution of SVHS/SVHS-C and Hi8. Also, higher resolution formats work best on higher resolution TV sets that have S-Video (Y/C) inputs. You can still play the high-resolution tapes on low-resolution TVs, but the extra lines of resolution can not be fully appreciated.

MiniDV

When Digital Video (DV) hit the consumer scene, a lot of confusion was generated after multiple formats under the DV heading were announced. It seemed as though every manufacturer was spinning off in different directions.

Now that some of the smoke has cleared, MiniDV has caught fire among consumers! It's truly an amazing advancement, and in my opinion, the second revolution in home video has begun!

Blurred Word

Digital video is recorded to tape in the language of computers (0s and 1s). This enabled manufacturers to develop **FireWire,** also known as IEEE 1394 or i.LINK which is a transfer protocol that allows you to digitally "copy" your video from one tape to another or from tape to your computer's hard drive without any signal loss. All DV cameras equipped with a Firewire port also have traditional analog outputs.

Simply put, MiniDV delivers truly amazing picture and color quality. What's more, when you make a digital copy of a MiniDV cassette using Firewire (IEEE 1394), the copy looks exactly the same as the original without losing any image quality. Technology that once belonged only to high-end video professionals is now in the hands of the home videographer!

MiniDV is capable of 500 lines of resolution; that's exactly twice the resolution of traditional VHS and 25 percent higher than SVHS or Hi8! It's also capable of recording CD quality audio (44.1 kHz), which makes your home video sound more like a home movie!

The Lowdown on MiniDV	
Cassette Size	2.6 × 1.9 × 0.5 in. (66 × 48 ×12.2mm)
Tape Size	6.35mm tape (¼ in.)
Resolution	500 horizontal lines

Digital8

Digital8 is the newest of the DV formats, and it shifts the concept of "backward compatibility" into high gear! Developed and launched by Sony in early 1999, the new Digital8 camcorders use special technology to record DV quality pictures and sound (up to 500 lines of resolution) onto regular 8mm and Hi8 tapes. And here's the best part: You can still play back your old 8mm/Hi8 movies! This is the perfect gateway into the digital future, with the option to enjoy your favorite analog moments.

All of these format choices can be overwhelming, and you can be sure that manufacturers will bring more to the table as time goes on. If your main concern is price and backward compatibility with your existing home videos, then any of the high band formats will suit your needs just fine. But if near-picture-perfect image quality and tape durability is your main concern, or if you plan to edit your footage later on with a personal computer, DV is the way to go.

The Least You Need to Know

- Figure out what you're going to do with a new camcorder before you buy it.
- Don't waste money on features you don't need. Look for a camcorder that excels at the things you absolutely need.
- Don't let a salesperson talk you into a video format. Do your homework!

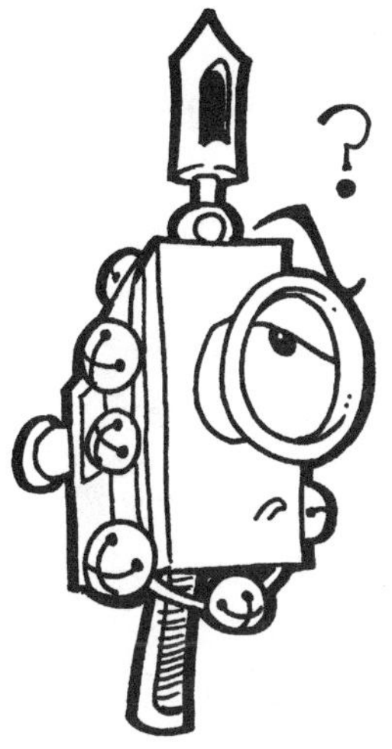

Chapter 3

Cool Extras ... Do You Need the Bells and Whistles?

In This Chapter

- Locking down your video with tripods
- Wide-angle/telephoto converters
- Lens filter basics
- Using external microphones
- Lighting accessories

For me, a trip to a video superstore like B & H Photo/Video in New York City is like Augustus Gloop walking into Willy Wonka's Chocolate Factory for the first time! Not only is the place jam-packed with camcorders, but also there are hundreds of accessories at your fingertips to choose from, and there are just as many salespeople who are more than willing to point you in the right direction. But instead of letting a salesperson spend your money for you, take a quick tour of some of the cool extras that commonly entice camcorder buyers so you can decide for yourself what you need.

3 Legs Are Better Than 2

A tripod is one of the most needed, but least purchased, video accessories. Even if you're broke after buying a camcorder, think about scraping up a few more bucks for a tripod. It would be a solid move. Even the cheap ones will greatly stabilize your home video and give it a professional feel. A tripod is also essential if you're interested in exploring some of the techniques and simple show ideas you'll find in later chapters. Here's a quick breakdown of a tripod's components.

Common tripod.

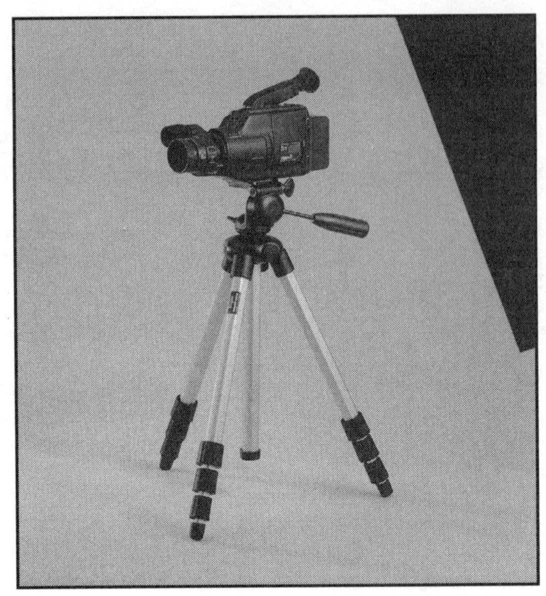

Level Headed!

Even the best tripods can't help your home videos unless you've got the camera on straight! Most tripods consist of a base (three legs), a neck, and a head. Similar to a human body, the tripod's neck keeps the head level. More expensive models use a handy "ball leveling" system that's incredibly easy to use and extremely accurate in centering the picture in your viewfinder. With a twist of a screw, the tripod's head becomes loose in a socket. Leveling is as easy as maneuvering a tiny ball into a fluid-filled circle. On cheaper tripods you actually have to adjust the length of the tripod's legs to level the camcorder.

The Brain of the Tripod

Most of the functionality takes place in the head of the tripod. You can twist and turn in all directions, and on most models there's a little lever allowing you to quick-release your camcorder for those unexpected handheld shots. Almost all tripods come with a handle that lets you take control of several functions, including panning from side to side and tilting up and down. Some handles also allow you to adjust panning tension by screwing it clockwise or counterclockwise. Tripods with high-quality heads also allow the user to raise and lower the entire platform, which can be locked down at any height.

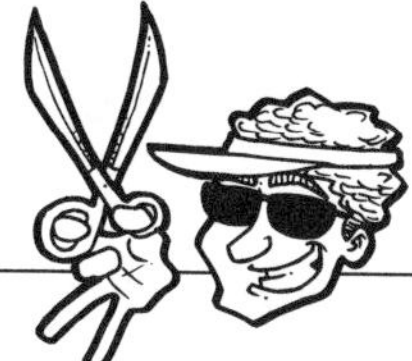

Director's Cut

When shopping for a tripod, insist that your salesperson attach a camcorder for you to test the control and stability. (Make sure it's screwed in super-tight!) Here's a quick to-do list:

- Extend and lock down the tripod's legs at full length.
- Pan the camcorder from side to side, and tilt it up and down.
- Adjust the tension and test the pan and tilt again.
- Raise the head-platform to full height and test the overall stability of the tripod.
- Check stability as you zoom the camcorder in and out and hit the record start-stop button (a sturdy tripod won't reveal your movements).

How Much Should It Cost?

Be prepared to dole out at least $70 for even the cheapest tripod. The prices go up from there, depending what features you choose. You can find a list of most of the major tripod manufacturers, their addresses, Web addresses, and phone numbers in Appendix C, "Camcorder and Accessory Manufacturers." Most of these companies make their complete product lines available for viewing (or even purchasing) on the Web, or by U.S. mail. It's always a good idea to have a basic familiarity with the product line before heading off to your local retailer. Or after you buy a tripod, it might be helpful to have this information handy in case you have a question or problem.

Contacts for Your Camcorder: Wide-Angle/Telephoto Lens Converters

When you hear the words *telephoto* or *wide-angle,* you instantly say to yourself, "Now that's something I've gotta get!" But before you bust out your wallet, remember that your camcorder has both a telephoto and wide-angle lens! This is possible thanks to one of the camcorder's most entertaining yet potentially distracting features: electronic zoom. But if you just can't get that tight shot of the neighbor's ear from the backyard next door, or if you want to squeeze both cliffs of the Grand Canyon into your viewfinder, a lens converter may be for you.

Most lens converters either slip over or screw into threaded sockets in front of your camcorder's built-in lens, making them easy to install and remove. This is perfect when you're out in the field and you need to quickly expand or decrease the focal capabilities of your camcorder.

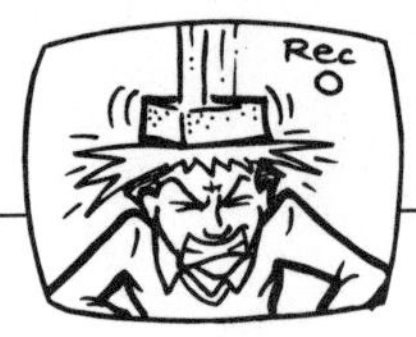

Blooper

Keep in mind that by using lens converters, you are slightly decreasing the amount of light that reaches the CCD. This can affect the camcorder's auto-exposure system. If you are manually controlling exposure, be sure to keep an eye on your image in the viewfinder and adjust the shutter or iris to compensate if it looks too dark.

Why Shoot Wide-Angle?

When you zoom the camcorder's lens back as far as it can go, the camcorder is in its deepest wide-angle mode. Add a wide-angle converter, and you'll be able to cram even more into your shot.

I've got a postcard hanging in my office of a beautiful lake in New York's Adirondack mountains. The shot was obviously taken with a very deep wide-angle lens because the photographer was miraculously able to pack about five square miles of beautiful blue water and colorful fall foliage into a single photograph.

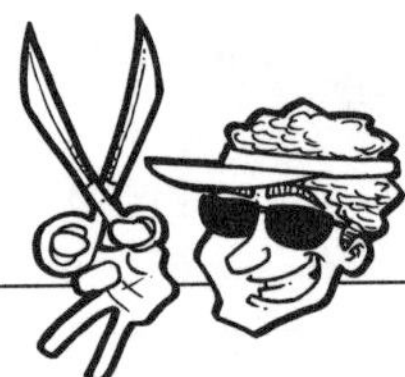

Director's Cut

When to use wide-angle:

- ➤ While hiking in the mountains, walking through a large city, or anywhere else with a breathtaking view, a wide-angle converter will help make the scenery look larger than life.
- ➤ If you're shooting in a tiny room or small set, you can squeeze more of the scene into the shot.

When to avoid wide-angle:

- ➤ If your subject is even slightly self-conscious, he or she can gain as much as 10 to 20 pounds on TV!
- ➤ When you are squeezing too much scenery into the shot, details can become fuzzy.

Time for Telephoto?

When you zoom all the way in on a subject, you have lengthened the focal distance between the lens and the CCD, placing the lens into extreme telephoto mode. This setting is invaluable, especially if you shoot sporting events, wildlife, live performances, or even surveillance video.

Telephoto lens converters work great for me when I videotape my friends and family waterskiing. I usually sit in the back of the boat with my camera latched to a tripod and zoom as close as I can get! When shooting telephoto, the tripod is vital because the slightest camera movement is intensified in telephoto mode. Without a tripod, the slightest bounce in the boat would send my subject right off the screen!

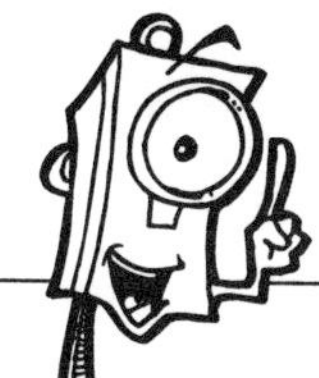

Candid Camera

Unlike wide-angle, the telephoto lens removes any feeling of depth from a video frame, creating a flat, picture-like image.

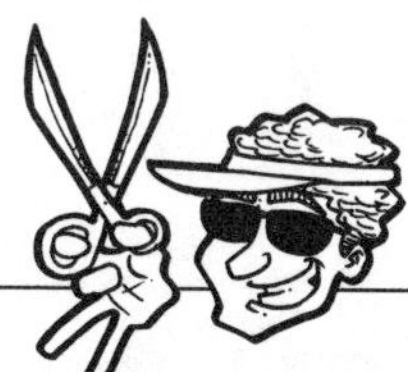

Director's Cut

When to use telephoto:

- ➤ When you're far away from the action.
- ➤ If you want to eliminate distracting background elements.

When to avoid telephoto:

- ➤ When you don't have a tripod or something to steady the camcorder.
- ➤ If you need to record clean audio, telephoto mode often leaves you too far from the subject for the camcorder microphone.

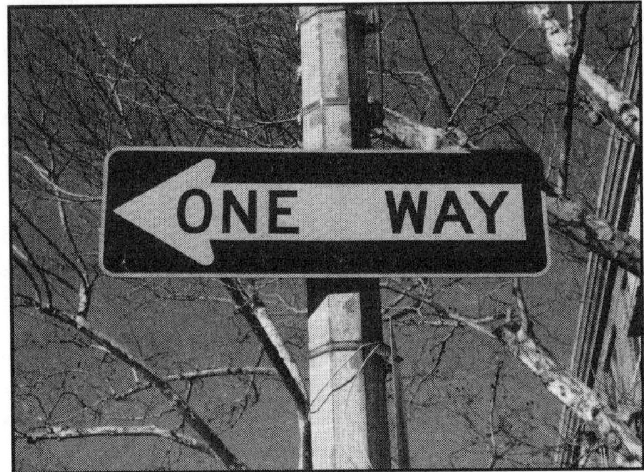

Telephoto mode.

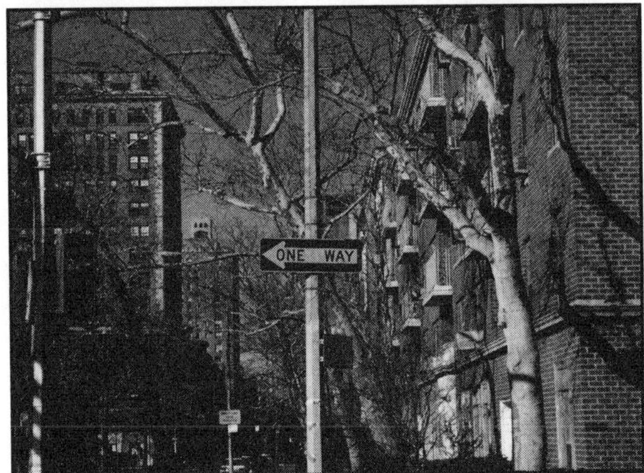

Wide-angle mode.

Focal length is usually measured in millimeters. Larger focal lengths refer to telephoto. Smaller focal lengths refer to wide-angle.

Knowing and understanding the basics of wide-angle/telephoto will greatly affect the way you shoot and will open up a world of creativity in your home video.

Shooting Through Rose-Colored Glasses: Lens Filters

From simple lens protection to serious image manipulation, lens filters have a ton of uses and are a valuable and cheap tool for any videographer. They attach to your camcorder in very much the same way that lens converters do. You can either screw them in or mount them in a "matte box" that attaches to the front of the camcorder.

The following are types of lens filters you can buy:

- U/V (ultra-violet)
- Neutral-density (ND)
- Polarizing
- Diffusing
- Colored
- Special effects

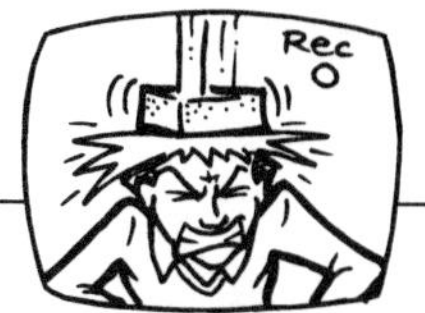

Blooper

This is one extra you don't want to skimp on. If something scratches the lens, you'd much rather replace an inexpensive U/V filter than your camcorder's lens itself. Don't be caught without protection!

U/V (Ultra-Violet)

Sometimes referred to as U/V (ultra-violet) or clear filter, it's an absolute must-have for any camcorder. Besides protecting your images from the unwanted effects of the haze and glare of ultra-violet light, you can keep it on your camera permanently to protect your lens from dust, dirt, and scratches.

Nine out of ten times, U/V filters are the first thing that salespeople (both video and still-amera) will push you to purchase. They're usually $20 or less, making them a great investment in protecting your delicate lens.

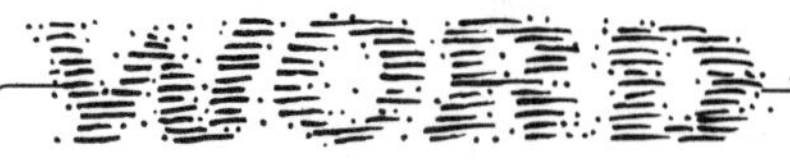

Blurred Word

Depth of field is the portion of your picture in which all objects at different distances from the lens appear in focus. This range can be altered with lens hardware, camcorder aperture settings, and neutral density (ND) lens filters.

Neutral-Density (ND)

When you're shooting in extremely bright sunlight, a neutral-density or "ND" filter will help to reduce overexposure. Also, an ND filter works in conjunction with your camcorder's iris to regulate the amount of light that enters the lens without affecting the color quality of your video. This is especially useful for reducing depth of field in your shot without having to resort to a telephoto converter.

ND filters are great for any well-lit action scenes that have a lot of movement in the background. Just pop it on your lens and manually open the iris, or let the camcorder do it automatically for you. With a decreased depth of field, your viewers will be able to better focus on the subject of the shot. ND filters are a bit more expensive than UV filters, but it's not a bad idea to have both in your video arsenal. Expect to or pay at least $25 to $30 for a decent ND filter.

Polarizing

Using a polarizing filter is like or outfitting your camera with high-quality sunglasses. It sharpens the clarity of your shots and is perfect for reducing unwanted glare from sunlight on any reflective surface like water, glass, sand, and ice. I usually swap between this filter and a U/V (ultra-violet), but I find that polarizing filters give my video a sharper look, especially when shooting outdoor sports.

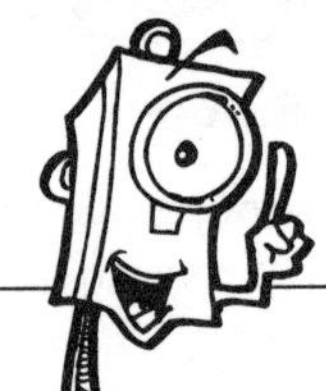

Candid Camera

Some cameras (like my Canon XL-1) have a built-in neutral-density feature that can be accessed by flipping a switch on the lens. The result is exactly the same as using an external ND filter.

Diffusing

A diffusing filter is sometimes referred to as a "face-saver" because it has been known to mask a wrinkle or two on close-up shots. It simulates a soft-focus by adding a subtle "fuzz," which reduces the harshness of raw video. I use this filter often when interviewing for documentaries and whenever I plan to transfer the video to film or use a computer-generated "film look." A diffusing filter on its own can give video a subtle film look.

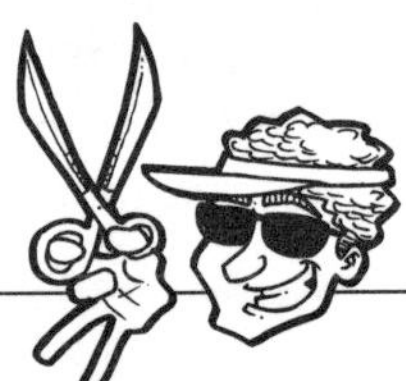

Director's Cut

I sometimes use a light colored stocking which I stretch over and attach to the front of my lens. This gives me a similar effect as using a diffusing filter.

Colored

These filters are fun to use but can also get you into a lot of trouble. Basically, colored filters allow you to tint your video any color of the rainbow: red, green, yellow, blue, and everything in between. But don't forget that colored filters tint the entire picture, and once you've tinted it, there's no way to reverse it!

The only time I've ever used a colored filter is when I needed to create a purplish moving background for a credit roll at the end of a program. It worked very well. These kinds of filters are commonly used in the TV industry for graphic design and for creating moods in movies and documentaries.

Special Effects

These wacky filters really set your creative juices in motion and open up a world of stylistic opportunities in your video. You can defy reality and add sparkle to your shot with star shapes, fisheye lens, lines, dots, streaks—you name it! Special effects filters accomplish their magic with surface grooves that redirect your image in funky directions.

These filters are perfect for spicing up any video where there is a lot of similar looking footage, like in a wedding video or a birthday party. They help your viewers focus in on certain parts of the frame while distorting the outer edges.

Lens Accessory Manufacturers

Shopping for lens accessories can easily become "what you see is what you get." Many retailers only carry products from one or two manufacturers, and these choices may not be right for your camcorder. In Appendix C, you'll find a complete list of lens accessory manufacturers, phone numbers, and Web addresses to help you hone in on the perfect filters for you.

Turn Up the Volume! External Microphones

You may ask yourself why waste money on another microphone when your camcorder already comes with one? Because your camcorder's on-board microphone was built for one purpose: to capture every single sound that can be heard. And when it can't hear anything, it automatically pumps up the overall recording volume until it picks up a sound, often creating unwanted background noise.

For some home videographers, the on-board microphone is all they will ever need. But if you plan to get a little more creative, or if you're looking for semi-professional or even professional quality audio, put an external microphone on your shopping list.

But before making an impulse purchase, you should figure out which type of external mic best suits your needs. As mentioned in Chapter 1, "What Makes a Camcorder Tick?" most built-in camcorder mics are omni-directional, which means that they generally pick up sound from every direction, with a slight emphasis on the direction that it's pointing. So if you're interviewing Aunt Jenny in the kitchen for that family documentary you learned how to produce reading later chapters in *The Complete Idiot's Guide to Making Home Videos,* your audio track might also include a conversation between Uncle Glenn and Aunt Pam in the living room. You might even hear a car passing outside, or even the distant whistle of a freight train. Here's where an external microphone really makes a difference.

If You Can Hold It, You Can Hear It!

Flick on the tube at about 6:00 P.M. for the nightly news and within two minutes, you'll see at least ten handheld microphones in action. These versatile microphones are most common in newscasts, street interviews, and press conferences, and they are also very useful for home and consumer/prosumer applications.

Handheld mics can't be beat when you have to get a lot of people talking on camera and you don't have time to properly set up for sound. They're also great for speeches, narration, and any type of on-the-spot interviews. And you can pick up a decent one for between $30 and $100.

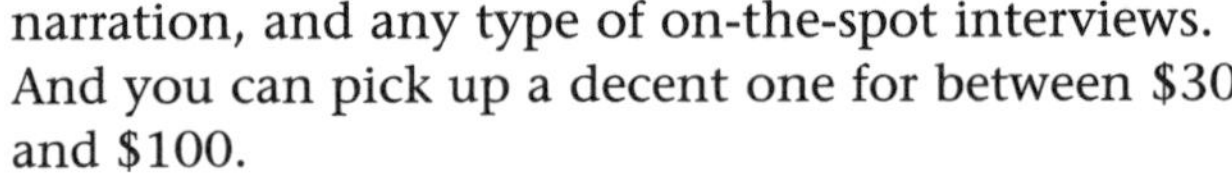

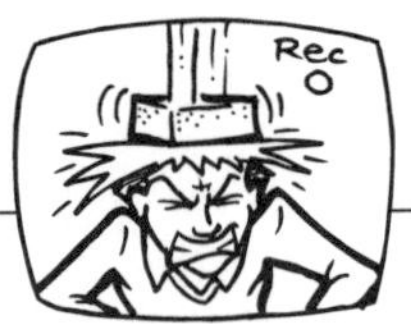

Blooper

One complaint that videographers have with handheld mics is that they draw attention away from the subject. When conducting interviews, try to hold the mic below the field of your camcorder's vision.

Shotgun

These mics look more like weapons than serious audio gear, but they are widely used by prosumers and professionals thanks to their ability to record sound from great distances. Unlike built-in camcorder mics, shotguns are "directional" microphones, which means that they filter out sound from the sides and pick up mostly in the direction they're pointed. These mics are perfect for wildlife photography, live concerts, or any situation where you need to record from a distance.

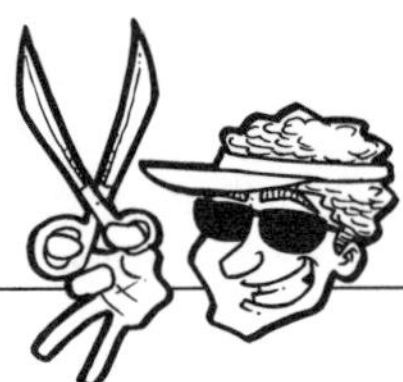

Director's Cut

There are a couple of shows on The Learning Channel that take full advantage of shotgun microphones (and MiniDV camcorders!): *Trauma: Life in the E.R.* and *Paramedics.* If you've ever seen these shows, you know that the videographers are busy chasing stretchers around and following doctors into operating rooms, so they don't have any time to pay attention to sound. Shotguns are perfect in these emergency situations because they record clean sounding interviews from variable distances and they also record the "natural sound" of the scene that's being shot with incredible accuracy.

Lavalier ("Lav")

A lavalier (commonly referred to as a "lav") is the ultimate interview microphone. Small in size yet super sensitive, a lav can easily be attached to your interview subject's collar, tie, or shirt for clean and close-up audio. The best part about these little over-achievers is that they can be completely hidden from view without any distracting clips or wires. You can also find wireless versions of the lav that record clean sound from great distances, but they are expensive, starting at a few hundred dollars.

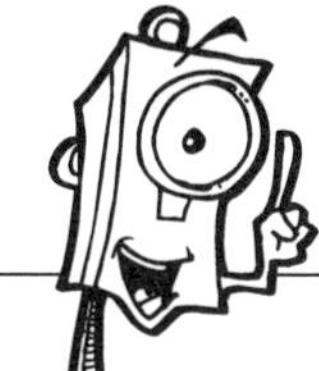

Candid Camera

A lavalier microphone ("lav") clips on close to your subject's mouth for super-clean interview audio.

Cast Some Light on the Matter!

An external light may be the last thing on your video shopping list, but before you flick the switch on deciding whether to buy one, consider this: Lighting is the single most important element in your home videos. If your lighting is bad, your video is bad. End of story.

Good lighting is both an art form and a technical skill. In fact, on major Hollywood movie sets, setting up for a lighting design is one of the most time-consuming processes in filmmaking. Good lighting can set a mood, fill in shadows, add depth, or simply brighten colors. Like many of the topics covered in these chapters, an entire book can be written on lighting alone. The subject is covered more thoroughly in Chapter 9, "Cast Some Light on the Matter," but here's a brief rundown of some lighting accessories you may want to consider.

Simple Shiners: Clip-On Lights

Clip-on lights that mount on top of your camcorder are the cheapest and most basic lighting accessory money can buy. They're perfect for low-light emergencies when there's almost no hope of recording any visible picture. Keep in mind, however, that because these lights are mounted front and center on a camcorder, they usually cast harsh shadows on your subject. One way to get rid of this "mug-shot" effect is by

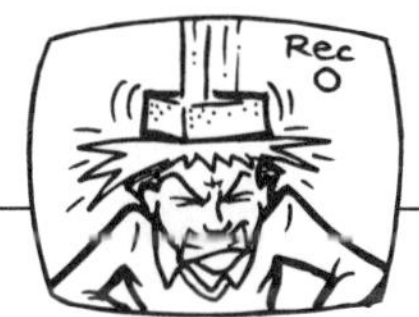

Blooper

Clip-on lights can be very unflattering to your subject. They tend to cast harsh shadows that can play cruel tricks with facial features.

mounting the light on a special diagonal offset bracket that directs the rays on an angle, resulting in less distracting shadows. (You can pick one up at your local video retailer.) Clip-on lights also work in the brightest daylight; these lights can help your subject pop out on screen. Clip-on lights are self-powered, which means that they have their own batteries and don't drain the camcorder of precious power. They're also quite cheap, starting at around $90.

Redirecting Rays

Another great item for the beginner's bag of tricks is the reflector. They look like the huge silver shields that a Roman gladiator would wield. But they fold up neatly and are an invaluable source of energy-free illumination out in the field. They even work indoors to help fill shadows or brighten a room. Reflectors offer inexpensive illumination that you don't have to plug in; you can buy one starting at around $30. How can you go wrong?

Higher-End High Beams

If you think that down the line you might want to get a little more creative, it might be in your best interest to drum up a few hundred dollars and invest in a lighting kit. Many kits come with at least three lights and three light stands, which will be perfect for pulling off the "three-point lighting" technique (more on this in Chapter 9). You can also choose kits that include other useful lighting extras like gel filters, umbrellas, lightbanks, and softboxes. These accessories can help you master the art and science of lighting.

Lighting kits are anything but cheap! They start at close to $400, and the prices go up quickly as you add extras. Lighting kits are a great value if you add up how much all the components would cost if you bought them separately.

Lighting Equipment Manufacturers

You can find a complete list of lighting equipment manufacturers in Appendix C. Many of these companies have electronic versions of their catalogues on the web, giving you a better idea of what's out there.

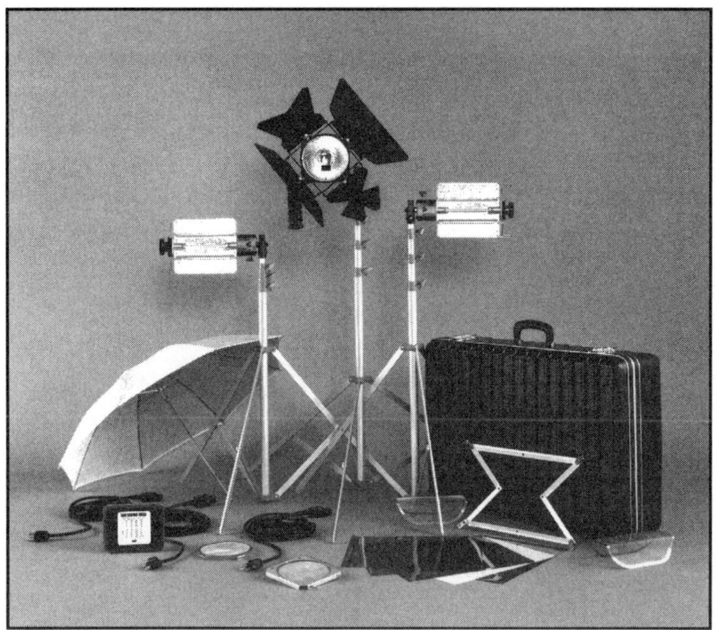

Lighting kit.

(Courtesy of Lowel)

The Least You Need to Know

- Tripods are the most effective way to achieve steady shots, giving your home video a professional feel.
- Wide-angle/telephoto lens converters are easy to attach and can greatly expand or decrease the focal length of your camcorder.
- Lens filters not only protect your lens, they can also sharpen, color, and distort your image.
- External microphones can significantly improve the sound track of your home movies.
- From simple illumination to setting a mood, lighting accessories are invaluable tools in home video production.

Chapter 4

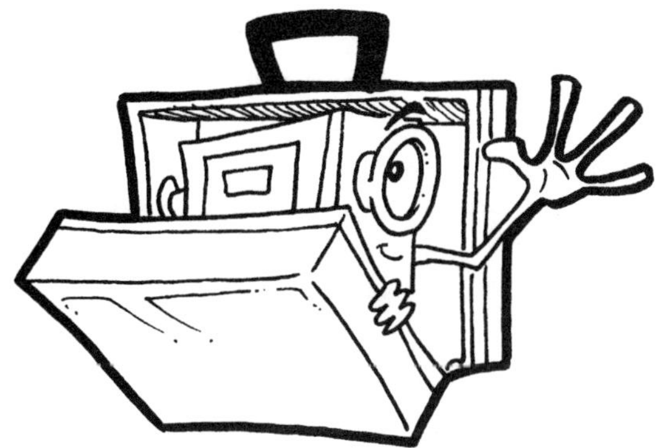

Camcorder Bag Basics

In This Chapter

- Choosing a camcorder case
- Got any spare batteries?
- Extra videotape
- Cables, connectors, and converters
- Bionic ears: headphone basics
- Camcorder care

If you think about it, there's a good chance you'll spend more time lugging your camcorder around than actually shooting with it. Whether you travel by car, bus, plane, train, taxi, or even the space shuttle (NASA sends their astronauts up with small Sony DV camcorders), your camcorder is going to get smashed, bashed, thrown, stacked, chucked, dropped, and possibly even tossed. And that kind of roughhousing calls for heavy-duty protection. In this chapter, you'll learn where and how to shop for the right camcorder bag that best protects your valuable investment. And because they're designed to hold a lot more than your camcorder, you'll get a rundown of all the bag essentials that help keep you up and running, and that help protect and care for your camcorder.

Taking on the Case

Recently I bought a bag for my notebook computer that is made out of the same material as a bulletproof vest. Now, whenever I leave the house, I'm confident that my computer's safe and travelling in style. I also have similar armored car-like cases for my camcorders. We're talking about delicate electronics here. If they get banged around, you're going to be left with a pile of plastic, silicon chips, and wires.

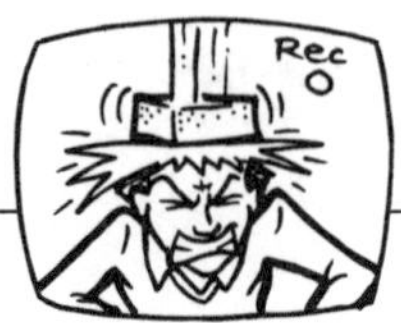

Blooper

It's tempting when you're buying a new camcorder to get all the accessory purchasing out of the way in one shot, but don't let a salesperson pressure you into buying a "bargain-bag" that you're not absolutely sure you want or need. If you haven't researched the product in advance, don't be afraid to tell the salesperson, "No thanks."

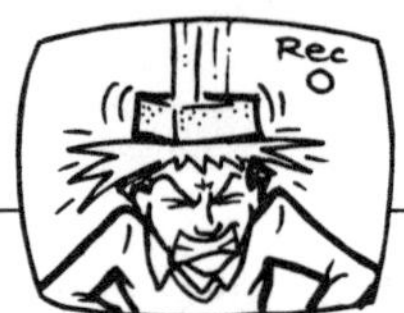

Blooper

Camera cases can handle a lot of cargo, but if you cram more accessories in than the case is designed for, you will compromise the safety of your equipment.

Choosing a camcorder bag isn't as hard as you might think. There are many different brands out there, but if you have an idea of what size and features you're looking for, the decision comes down to quality and craftsmanship.

There are two types of camcorder cases to choose between: hard shell and soft case. Hard shell cases offer the best protection from the elements and are convenient when you're travelling or shipping your video equipment. They're made of indestructible plastic with foam padding inside that tightly cradles your gear. Many high-end camcorders come with cases of their own with custom notches and shelves so everything fits perfectly. After-market hard shell cases come with foam pieces that can be cut out to fit your camcorder and all the extras.

In the past few years, soft cases have grown steadily in popularity. First of all, they're much lighter than their hard-shell counterparts, making them perfect for family outings and vacations. They also offer good protection, easy access, and they are a snap to custom-configure with Velcro dividers that can be positioned anywhere to match the size of your camcorder and accessories. A quality case may cost you more, but throughout the life of your camcorder, it's a great investment because it will provide years of service and protection.

Check out Appendix C, "Camcorder and Accessory Manufacturers," for a list of camera bag manufacturers and their addresses, Web addresses, and phone numbers. You may want to check out the dimensions and look at a few pictures of camcorder cases before buying.

Jump Start Your Camcorder with Spare Batteries

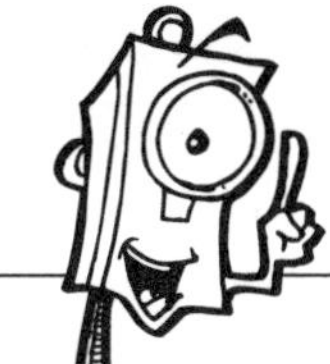

Candid Camera

Batteries are like peanut M&Ms. You can't stop at just one. Keep as many extras in your camcorder bag as possible without bogging yourself down with too much weight.

There you are, videotaping your son in the living room. Right now, he's grasping on to the coffee table, but yesterday he let go and balanced himself for a few seconds. Something amazing is about to happen. You can feel it! You move in closer. Junior is curious. As his hand slips away from the coffee table, a battery warning starts flashing in the viewfinder. Oh, no! Not now! But it's too late. The camera flickers, takes its last breath, and Junior's image fades into darkness. Junior, unaware that he is reaching a major childhood milestone, has cleared the coffee table and slowly but surely takes his first steps toward his exasperated dad and a dead camcorder.

It's a scene that any videographer can relate to. There's nothing that can halt your production quicker than a dead battery. And it's one of the emptiest feelings you'll experience as a videographer.

One day, maybe all camcorders will use tiny solar panels for power, and the bulky external powerhouses that we know and love will be a distant memory. But until then, we're stuck shelling out big bucks for batteries. And the more you buy, the longer you'll keep yourself on the air because every little zoom, start/stop, auto-focus, and image stabilization draws power from the battery. If you have three or more, you can have two simmering on the charger while shooting with the third. This way, you'll never run into a power outage.

Different generations of video cameras use different types of batteries. Here's a rundown of the most common types of batteries found in today's camcorders.

Lead Acid Batteries

If you shoot infrequently, lead acid batteries are a good choice because they retain their charge for long periods of time. They are also the least expensive rechargeable batteries. But because they contain lead, you pay the price in added weight. If you've got three or four of these in your video toolkit, it's time to strap on your weightlifting belt.

As you use lead acid batteries, their power will decline in a slow, steady stream. Since most camcorders that use lead acid batteries are older and don't have a running battery gauge in the viewfinder, this makes it easy to determine exactly how much power is left. Once you've shot with these batteries for a while, it becomes second nature to predict their remaining power.

Nickel Cadmium (NiCad) Batteries

If you use your camcorder often, Nickel Cadmium (NiCad) batteries are the way to go. Even though they cost more than lead acid batteries, NiCads are surprisingly lightweight and have a large power capacity. They also can be recharged anywhere between 300 to 500 times and work very well with "quick-chargers." NiCads are still in demand, especially for replacements on older cameras, but are quickly being replaced by lithium-ion batteries as the industry standard.

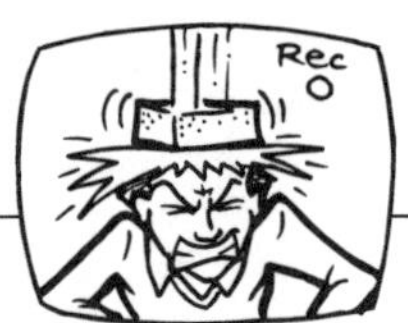

Blooper

Recharge your lead acid batteries immediately after use. If left uncharged, sensitive components inside the battery can quickly decompose, hurting the overall battery life.

Despite their versatility, NiCads have a few disadvantages. The first major one is that they do not hold up very well in extreme weather conditions. So if you wanted to shoot your son snowboarding or catch the winning touchdown of that late January football game, your NiCad may not provide you with the power it does in warmer temperatures. Another thing to keep in mind: NiCads don't have the same longevity when dormant as lead acid batteries do. They lose about 2 percent of their charge every day of inactivity. After a couple of months on the shelf, the battery could be completely dead.

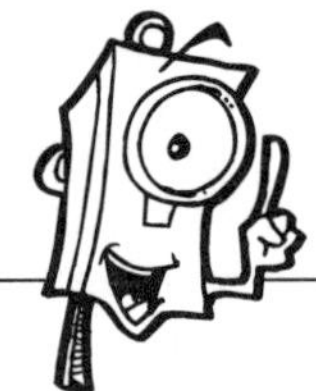

Candid Camera

When your NiCad or lead acid battery is permanently out of gas, you can't just toss it in the trash. Key ingredients of these batteries like cadmium and lead are considered environmental hazards, so they must be recycled. Some electronic stores will trash old batteries for you. You can also call the Rechargeable Battery Recycling Corporation at 1-800-822-8837, or visit them on the Web at www.rbrc.com to locate a recycler near you.

Another infamous NiCad problem is "memory." This happens when you charge a battery, use it for a short time, charge it up again, and after repeating this process several times, the battery "forgets" that it is capable of holding a full charge, decreasing its overall capacity significantly. While some experts argue that NiCad "memory" is a myth, they recommend buying "memory free" batteries and discharging fully before recharging.

Nickel Metal Hydride NiMH Batteries

Nickel metal hydride batteries are very similar to NiCads, but they supply approximately 20 percent more power. And if you let these batteries sit idle, they wont lose power as fast as NiCads. The better performance will cost you a bit more than NiCads, however.

Lithium-Ion Batteries

Lithium-ion is the battery of the future. In fact, the notebook computer that I'm writing this on is powered by a $200 lithium-ion battery that gives me almost three hours of operation on the road (and trust me, this computer is power hungry). Lithium-ion camcorder batteries are lightweight, fully recharge in about an hour, and in some of the newer cameras have as much as an incredible 10 to 15 hours per charge! The only problem with these batteries is that right now they are pretty expensive. This poses a big problem if you're looking to pick up a few extras. For the 10- to 15-hour variety, you're looking at anywhere from $150 to $200. Almost all of the newer camcorders are shipping with lithium-ion batteries.

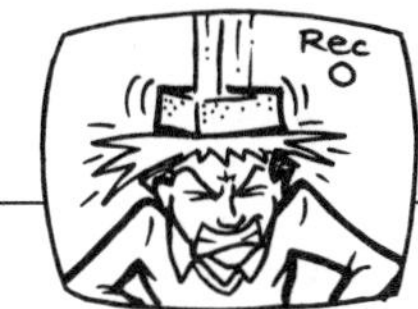

Blooper

Be careful not to bang your NiCad around. Even the slightest bumps and bruises can wreak havoc on the battery's internal structure.

Where Do I Get Them?

Before purchasing extra batteries, make sure you know exactly what kind of battery you need. It's important to remember that you can't just buy any battery for any camcorder. If your camcorder came with a NiCad battery, you can't just replace it with a new lithium-ion battery. When shopping for a battery, make sure you tell your salesperson your camcorder's make and model number. Or you can call the camcorder's manufacturer, and they will be more than happy to send you a replacement for premium dollars. I'd recommend buying from any of the major mail order houses (see Chapter 5, "Meandering the Maze of Manufacturers"), or these days the World Wide Web is a great place to buy batteries. If you're not comfortable giving your credit card number out over the Internet, all of the major Web dealers have toll-free numbers you can call.

MJM Electronic
www.mjmelectronic.com
1-888-226-4606

The Battery Bank
www.batterybank.com
1-800-229-9449

Atbatt.com
www.atbatt.com
1-877-4AT-BATT

Aardvark Batteries & Accessories
www.aardvarkbat.com
1-888-883-4937

Go Battery
www.gobattery.com
1-888-GO-Battery

Batteries Direct
www.batteriesdirect.com
1-888-320-1212

E-Battery
www.e-battery.com
1-877-BATT2GO

Extra Tapes

This is a no-brainer, but you'd be surprised by how many productions have been stopped dead because someone forgot to pack extra videotapes in the bag. Depending on the length of tape you're shooting with (consumer videocassettes come in lengths of 30, 60, 90, and 120 minutes), you should have at least one spare in your bag. If possible, use 120-minute tapes, which gives you an incredible two hours of record time. In fact, I used only two 120-minute Hi8s on my two-week honeymoon, but I carried around two extras in my camera bag just in case.

In videography as in life, there's a general rule that should always be followed: Travel light! Depending on the physical size of the cassettes you're using, you can easily fit two or three in the sack without feeling a big difference in weight, especially if it's 8mm, VHSC, or MiniDV. But if you're using full-size VHS, you may have to bust out that weightlifting belt again.

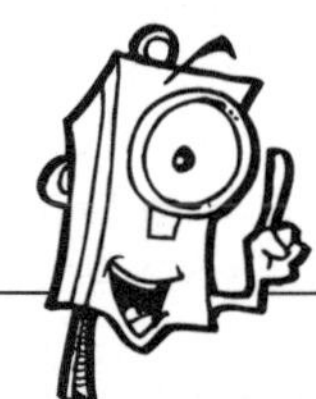

Candid Camera

Most formats of videotape are very easy to find when you're on vacation or travelling. Take a look in any convenience, camera, or drug store for 8mm, VHS, and VHSC. However, I've had problems tracking down hi-band formats like Hi8, SHVS, and MiniDV in local drug stores. A good place to buy these tapes is back at the camera or photo store or by mail order.

Cables, Connectors, and Converters—Oh My!

Cables, connectors, and converters are the links that let your camcorder talk to the rest of your audio/video equipment. From top to bottom, your camcorder has all kinds of inputs and outputs, and in order to make a lot of them work, you need to pack the proper cables in your bag! The video and audio inputs enable you to connect your camcorder to your TV, monitor, or editing equipment. The control jack enables you to trigger a wide range of VCR functions, making remote editing a snap. Some camcorders have A/V inputs and outputs that enable you to dub from any source to your camcorder, or to use your camcorder as either a source or record deck for editing.

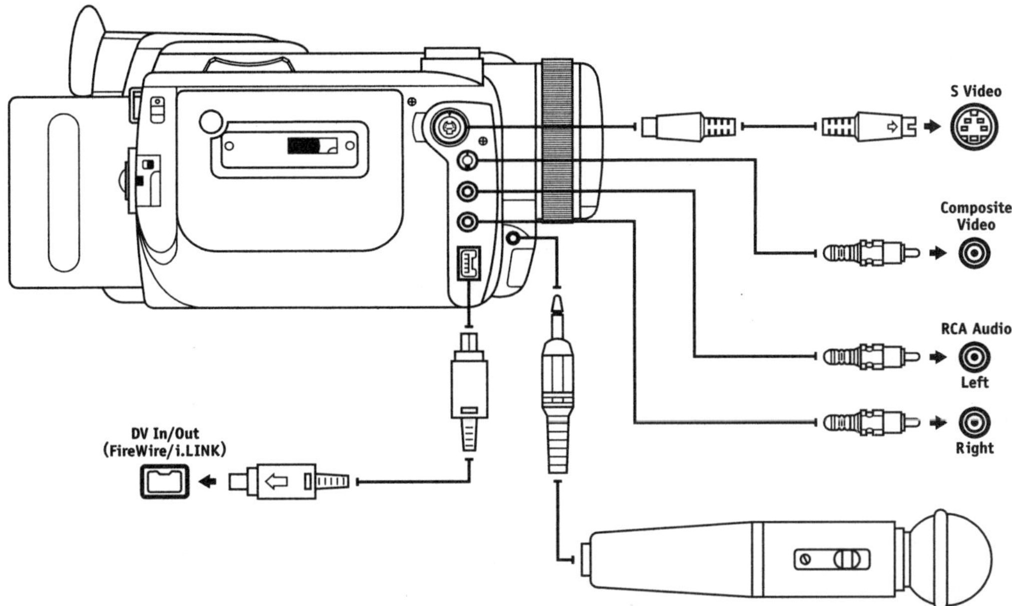

Camcorder connections.

Composite Video Jack

Composite video is achieved when all the "components" of video are channeled into one signal. This includes luminance and chrominance. Usually an RCA-type connection, the composite video jack carries both the luminance and the chrominance in one signal. On most camcorders and VCRs, this connection is yellow. This is the most common type of analog video output jacks found on camcorders.

Y/C Jack

Sometimes referred to as an S-VHS or S-Video connector, the Y/C jack splits the luminance and chrominance into two signals, resulting in superior image quality. This is one way to enjoy the "hi-band" of formats such as SVHS, Hi8, and MiniDV. The analog output from a Y/C jack is noticeably better than a composite (RCA) jack.

IEEE 1394 (FireWire/i.LINK) Port

The IEEE 1394 (FireWire or i.LINK) port lets you plug into your DV camcorder's digital video interface. This allows you to copy video in the language of computers (0s and 1s) to another digital tape or your computer's hard drive without any loss of the video quality. To date, FireWire is the best option for videographers since it is a digital connection as opposed to analog.

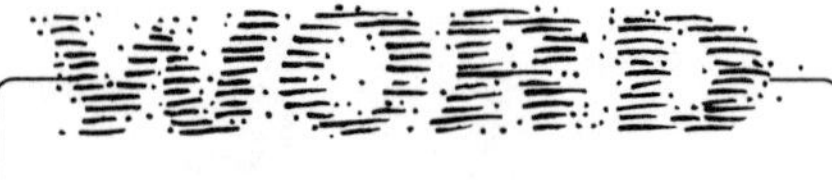

Blurred Word

Luminance carries the black-and-white portion of video signal This is usually represented by the symbol "Y."

Chrominance carries the color information (hue and saturation). This is usually represented by the symbol "C."

FireWire cables are still quite expensive but you usually get one for free when you buy a camcorder or editing system that utilizes FireWire.

Audio Jacks

On most camcorders, there are two RCA audio jacks, one for each stereo channel. Red is usually for the right channel, and white is for the left. These are the same jacks you use to hook up a CD player to your home stereo system. Commonly included with a new camcorder is the "3-wire" RCA cord that has a yellow wire for composite video, and a red and white wire for the audio. These wires are usually six feet or longer, allowing you to hook up your camcorder to a TV or editing system from far away.

RF Jack

This connector, a screw or push-on type with a central wire, carries both video and audio signals. Though transmission is not as high quality as that of RCA or Y/C cables, an RF connector is useful for sending the signal directly to a monitor or TV set.

Edit Control Jack

This enables your camcorder to be "taken over" by an edit control system. Control-P type jacks communicate commands to the VCR section of the camcorder. Control-L and Control-M communicates tape position and function mode information back to the edit controller. An edit controller can either be a stand-alone unit or a personal computer running the proper software.

Headphone Jack

This is the jack you plug your headphones into. Headphones are invaluable tools in monitoring the exact sound that is going to end up on tape. (See "Never Leave Home Without Your Phones!" later in this chapter)

External Microphone Jack

An external microphone jack enables you to replace the camcorder's on-board microphone with an external mic that better serves the need of the shoot. When an external mic is plugged into this jack, the on-board mic is automatically disabled.

AC Power/Battery Recharge Jack

This jack is where you connect your camcorder's power adapter. On some models when you have your camcorder plugged into the wall with a battery attached, the battery automatically recharges.

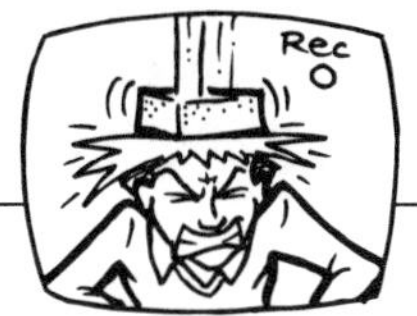

Blooper

Because external mics connect to your camcorder with consumer grade "mini-plugs" (the same as headphones on a "Walkman"), it is vitally important to monitor your audio with headphones because the connections tend to jiggle around causing unwanted interference.

Never Leave Home Without Your Phones!

Suppose that you're shooting more interviews for your family documentary project. This time you're able to lure Uncle Dan outside on the back porch. You neatly hide the lavalier microphone well enough so that only the very end is peering out from beneath his button-down shirt. You feel a slight breeze over your shoulder, but you don't give it a second thought as you fire one question after another at him. After an hour, Uncle Dan calls it quits. Later, when you playback the Uncle Dan interview, you make a horrible discovery. That slight breeze that you decided to ignore sounds like a tornado whipping against the microphone. Uncle Dan's voice can barely be heard. The audio track is completely unusable.

In video, disastrous situations like this one come up all the time, and headphones are the only way to protect your delicate audio track. By wearing them, you are privy to the exact soundtrack of your video, without any outside distractions. Without them, the human ear doesn't have the capacity to differentiate what sounds are going to be recorded and what sounds are going to be left out.

In the Uncle Dan interview, for instance, you would have discovered in the first few seconds that the breeze was too strong, and you could have either popped a windshield on the microphone or repositioned Dan with his back to the wind.

It's easy to get caught up in the visual end of home video, but sound plays an equally important role. As you can see, headphones can be a videographer's best friend.

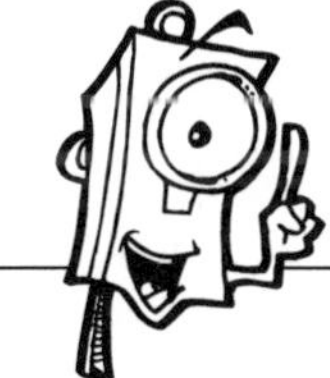

Candid Camera

When buying headphones, look for quality manufacturers such as Sony, Beyerdynamic, Audio-Technica, and Sennheiser. They cost anywhere from $15 to $300.

If You Take Care of Your Camcorder, Your Camcorder Will Take Care of You

When you walk into a camcorder repair shop, the owner is licking his chops. He knows that whatever the problem is, it's going to cost you $75 for an estimate (before any work is done!) and after that $100 dollars an hour for labor. He's hoping that the recording heads are blown, or the lens is scratched beyond repair. Add another $300 to $400 to your bill.

This is a person you don't want to meet. All it takes is a few of the essential camcorder-care accessories in your bag of tricks, and chances are, you'll never see the inside of a repair shop.

Head Cleaners

Every so often, your camcorder's tape transport mechanism and record heads need to be wiped free of dust, dirt, and particles that can be left over by videotape. It would be nice to pop open the camcorder's shell and clean everything by hand, but manufacturers have no intention of letting consumers fiddle around inside the camera. There are too many things that can come loose and break. Or, if you carelessly opened up the camcorder with the power on, you could end up with one hair-raising shock!

Head-cleaning cassettes can be used to take care of camcorder housekeeping. You can use either the "wet" or "dry" varieties. They work equally well. It only takes a few minutes to run a cleaning cycle, and because it's only as large as a regular videocassette, head cleaners don't take up much real estate in your camcorder bag. If you're shooting frequently, clean your camcorder's heads often. You can check your owner's manual for manufacturer's recommendation.

Lens Care

We know that the camcorder's lens is a delicate piece of hardware that should rarely come into contact with the outside world. That's because the surface of the lens is coated with clear chemicals that can dissolve when exposed to finger oils, dust, dirt, even water. If you destroy this delicate coating, your image quality will have a defocused, smudgy look that can't be wiped away. As I mentioned earlier, the best way to protect your lens is to use a clear (U/V) or polarized filter. But if you're not using a filter and your lens becomes soiled in any way, follow these steps:

➤ If there's dust or dirt on the lens, try blowing it off or use compressed air. It's a good idea to have on hand a small can of compressed air.

- Use a photo accessory that combines a little brush that's connected to a rubber blower (see the following figure). This combines a blast of air and soft bristles to clean off your lens.
- If all else fails, you should use a mild lens solution and lens tissue.

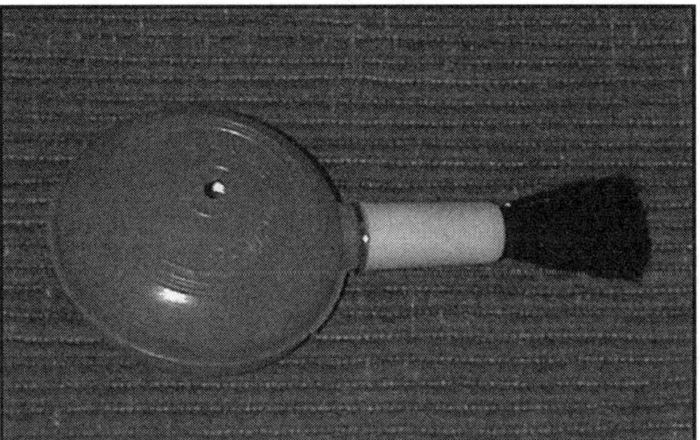

Brush-blower lens accessory.

You can purchase all of these accessories at any photo/video or camera store. Lens cleaner, tissue, compressed air, and the brush-blower accessory are inexpensive and should always be permanent residents of your camcorder bag.

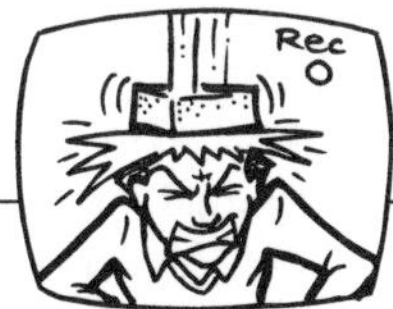

Blooper

Never use your shirt or any other fabric that is not specifically designed to clean your lens. It can cause microscopic scratches that, over time, can destroy your lens. You should use the same care to clean lens filters as you would for your lens alone.

Pop-Out LCD Viewfinder Care

From time to time, you may find that your viewfinder or pop-out LCD screen may become dirty. The LCD screens are easier to clean because they are much larger and have a less-delicate surface. Simply wipe the offending matter off with a cottony cloth or lens tissue.

The viewfinder is a little trickier to clean because it's tiny and there are deep corners that are tough to reach. Wrap a soft cloth or lens tissue around your pinky and try to fit it in there. If that doesn't work, soak the end of a Q-tip in lens solvent and with small circular motions, try to wipe away the dirt.

Some camcorders have an inner screen that can be exposed by flipping up the eyepiece. This can be cleaned in the same manner as the large pop-out LCD screen.

Miscellaneous Camcorder Bag Cargo

There are a few more items worth mentioning that will help make your video experience hassle-free. Again, the goal here is to keep your camcorder bag payload as manageable as possible, but the following items take up little to no space.

- **Pen.** It's a great idea to get into the habit of labeling your tapes as you shoot. There's nothing more confusing than having to scroll back through tapes in order to see what's on them. It's also a good way to avoid accidentally shooting over tapes that already have material on them.
- **White-Balance Card.** This is a stark white piece of paper or cardboard that can be folded up and placed in your bag's side pocket. (You can find a tear-out white-balance card in the front of this book.) Performing a manual white balance is the best possible way to get your camcorder in synch with the colors in the scene you are shooting. See Chapter 2, "The Right Camcorder for You," for more on white balancing.
- **Extension Cords.** These may take up a little more room than you planned for, but extension cords are worth their weight in gold. From lighting to audio gear, extension cords are a necessity on any shoot.
- **Wire Ties.** If you are using many wires and/or extension cords on your shoot, the last thing you want is to have people tripping all over the place. You can use almost anything to tie wires together. I often pack rubber-bands, garbage bag ties, hair-bands (for pony and pig-tails), and even string.

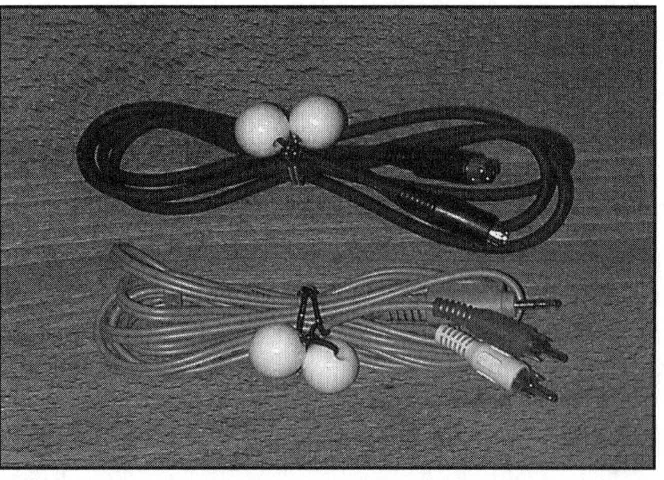

Hair-band ties are perfect for neatly wrapping A/V wires.

The Least You Need to Know

- A good camcorder case is the best way to protect your valuable investment.
- Don't get caught out in the cold. Bring extra videotapes!
- Carrying the right cables, connectors, and converters in your camcorder bag gives you the freedom to hook up with all kinds of audio/video equipment.
- If you want your audio track to sound good, wear you headphones!
- With the right accessories in your bag, it's easy to take care of your camcorder in just a few minutes.

Chapter 5

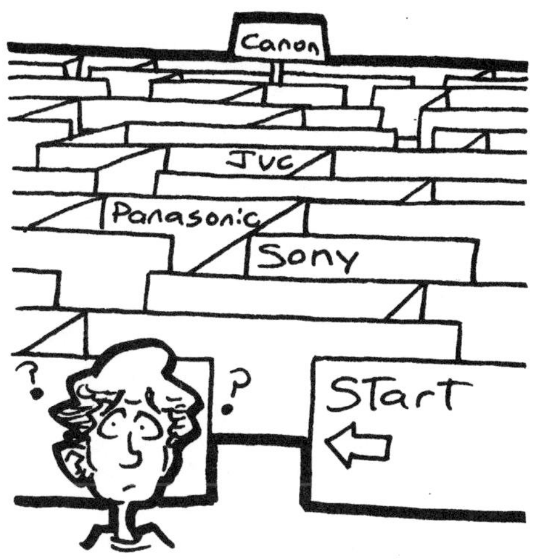

Meandering the Maze of Manufacturers

In This Chapter

- Sony
- Canon
- Panasonic
- JVC
- Sharp
- Hitachi

At this point, you probably have a pretty good idea of what features you're looking for in a camcorder, but picking one out is like trying to choose a brand of ice cream from your grocer's freezer. They all look so good! Whether you choose Ben and Jerry's, Breyers, or Häagen Daz, you're going to go home a happy camper.

Camcorder shopping is no different. It's not easy choosing between Sony, Canon, Panasonic, JVC, Sharp, and Hitachi. The names are familiar, and you have grown to trust their other numerous electronic and entertainment products. To help you narrow down the choices, here's a breakdown of each manufacturer and a sampling of a few brand new camcorders that show off cutting-edge design, use of technology, and creative implementation of the functions and features you've learned about.

Sony

Glance up from wherever you are in the world, and you have a 95 percent chance of seeing the word "Sony" on something or another. They make everything but the kitchen sink. From music, movies, and movie theaters to computing, wireless, and home and professional electronics, Sony does it all. And when it comes to home video, they have really made shooting and editing a joy, not a chore.

In 1985 Sony Electronics introduced the 8mm format that made it possible for the average consumer to get involved in home video. The new 8mm camcorders were comparatively compact, lightweight, easy to use, and delivered good video quality. Today, over 500 million 8mm tapes have been sold worldwide.

In 1989 the line between home and professional video began to blur when Sony developed the Hi8 format. Sony Handycam camcorders were well on their way in helping families enjoy high-quality home recording as a part of everyday life. Then in 1995, Sony pioneered consumer Digital Video with the introduction of the DCR-VX1000 MiniDV camcorder, a move that continued to close the gap between prosumers and professionals.

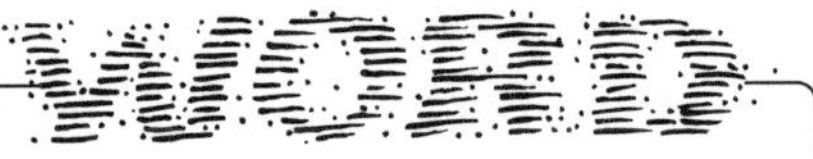

Blurred Word

i.LINK is Sony's way of saying **FireWire** (IEEE 1394), the digital interface developed by Apple that enables lossless digital transfers from camcorder to camcorder or from camcorder to PC.

In 1995, Sony began to build i.LINK (IEEE 1394/FireWire) interface into Handycam camcorders to facilitate the transfer of images to PCs and to enable editing with no generation loss.

1999 was another breakthrough year for Sony with their introduction of the new video format, Digital8, and a brand new line of Handycam camcorders that will lead the digital revolution into the next century. This backward-compatible format is expected to attract a large following of 8mm and Hi8 camcorder owners who have spent years building a home videotape library.

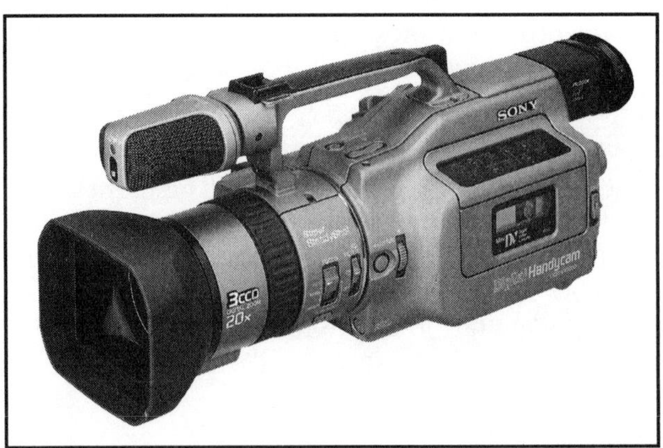

Sony DCR-VX1000.

In case you haven't seen it before, take a look at a living piece of home video history: the Sony DCR-VX1000. The first time somebody fired up this baby was like the shot heard around the world.

The first of its kind, this high-quality digital camcorder still survives as the choice of filmmakers, documentarians, and other video professionals. Its compact frame and overall portability help disguise this image grabbing monster, affording videographers permit-free shooting opportunities they could never get with huge professional cameras.

It's not as light as some of the newer MiniDV camcorders, but it's got a nice balanced feel when shooting, which helps to eliminate some of the handheld camera shake. It also has a rear LCD panel display that keeps you up to date on battery life, remaining tape, audio level, and videotape running time. It also has extensive menu functions, but the button is somewhat out of reach behind the battery bay door.

Following are the feature highlights of the Sony DCR-VX1000:

- MiniDV Camcorder
- 3⅓" CCDs 410,000 Pixels
- 500 Lines of Resolution
- 10× Optical/20× Digital Zoom
- Auto/Manual Focus/White Balance/Exposure
- Optical Image Stabilization
- Analog Video Outputs: Composite/Y/C
- i.LINK DV Interface (IEEE 1394)

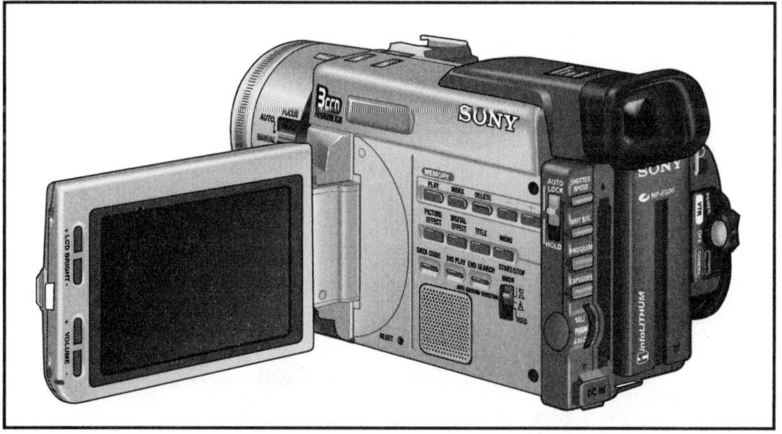

Sony DCR-TRV900.

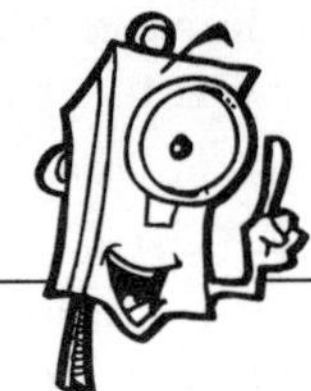

Candid Camera

When converting an analog video signal into a digital video signal, your picture isn't going to look any better than the original. In fact, your video has lost one generation. The main benefit, however, is that digital video has a much longer shelf-life than analog. Also, once you have made a copy, any other duplication or editing that you do from that point on is lossless.

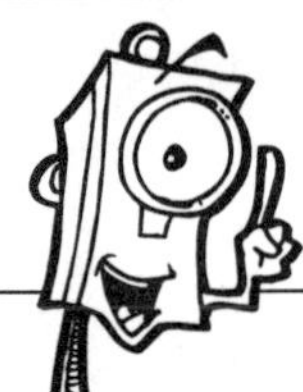

Candid Camera

The DCR-TRV900 has another older brother called the DSR-PD100. The two cameras look exactly the same, but the PD100 is considered a "professional" camcorder, and it can record to both MiniDV and the professional DVCAM format. The PD100 is more expensive, but it offers features that can't be found anywhere in a camcorder so small. Check Sony's Web site at www.sony.com for more info on their professional line of camcorders.

The DCR-TRV900 is one of Sony's "Prosumer Powerhouses," offering image quality that's almost indistinguishable to its older brother's, the DCR-VX1000. This is one of the tiniest 3 CCD camcorders available, offering a wealth of features and an ever-decreasing price tag.

With its huge 3.5" pop-out LCD screen, this camcorder is a force to be reckoned with. The record and zoom controls are intuitively positioned, and nearby there's a digital photo button that can be used to record digital still photos to tape. The TRV900 comes with an adapter that allows you to hook up a 3.5" floppy drive to the camcorder to download the digital stills. It also has a neat "End Search" feature that automatically finds the end of the last video you shot.

Another neat feature that helps you control the camcorder's auto-exposure is zebra striping. This feature forms a zebra-like pattern in the viewfinder wherever the picture is going to be overexposed.

In addition, the TRV900 has analog video inputs, which enables you to "feed" video into the camcorder from any other source like a Hi8 camcorder or VCR. This is a great way to archive older footage or to convert an analog source into a digital source.

The following are the feature highlights of the Sony DCR-TRV900:

- MiniDV Camcorder
- 3¼" CCDs with 380,000 Pixels
- Approx. 450 Lines of Resolution
- 12× Optical/48× Digital Zoom
- Auto/Manual Focus/White Balance/Exposure/Gain
- 9-hour INFOlithium Battery
- Digital Image Stabilization
- Analog Video Outputs: Composite/Y/C
- i.LINK DV Interface (IEEE 1394)

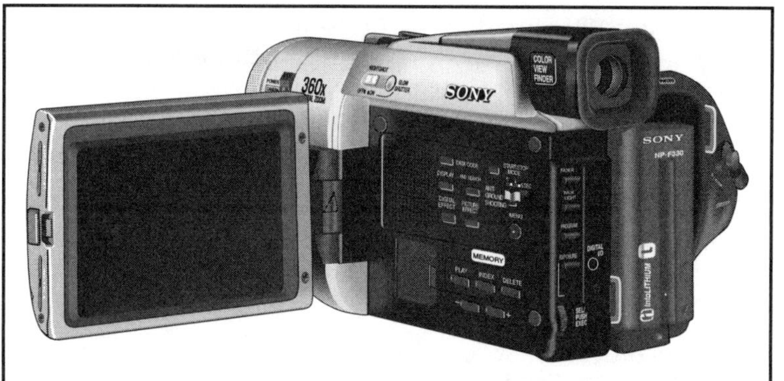

Sony DCR-TRV510.

The DCR-TRV510 is Sony's first is generation of the newest format to hit the scene, Digital8. Geared to the average consumer, this camcorder has all the is features and performance of a MiniDV, with an equally attractive low price tag.

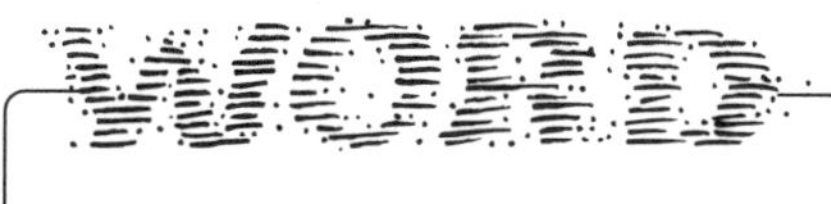

Blurred Word

Low Lux refers to any low light condition.

While it has only one chip, the TRV510 has a large 4-inch LCD viewfinder and is packed with useful features like a seven mode Program Auto-Exposure that includes Portrait Mode, Sports Lesson Mode, Spotlight Mode, Beach and Ski Mode, Sunset and Moon Mode, Landscape Mode, and Low Lux. This is a great way to take control of the camcorder's exposure system without getting into the nitty-gritty of the iris, shutter, and f-stop.

The following are the feature highlights of the Sony DCR-TRV510:

- Digital8 Camcorder
- ¼" CCD 460,000 Pixels
- 20× Optical/360× Digital Zoom
- Auto/Manual Focus/Exposure
- Digital Image Stabilization is
- i.LINK DV Interface (IEEE 1394)

Canon

Canon is one of the biggest players in the home video industry. Besides camcorders and other professional and consumer broadcast equipment, Canon is an industry leader in a wide array of products including cameras and lenses, copiers, color laser printers, calculators, and fax machines.

I own two Canon camcorders: a Canon A-1 still camera from the early '80s, and an old Canon Super8 film camera of 1960s vintage. I have gone with Canon again and again for several reasons, but mostly because they are world-famous for producing the finest photographic and video lenses, and I've found that image quality relies heavily on lens quality.

Canon is also the industry leader in optical imaging technology and Optical Image Stabilization. As mentioned in earlier chapters, digital methods of image stabilization tend to decay image quality by zooming in on the CCD's pixels. Canon's technique of subtle lens shifting has no effect on the image quality.

When it comes to building camcorders, their foresight and creative approach to design and use-of-technology has attracted thousands of consumers, prosumers, and professionals alike.

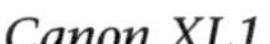

Canon XL1.

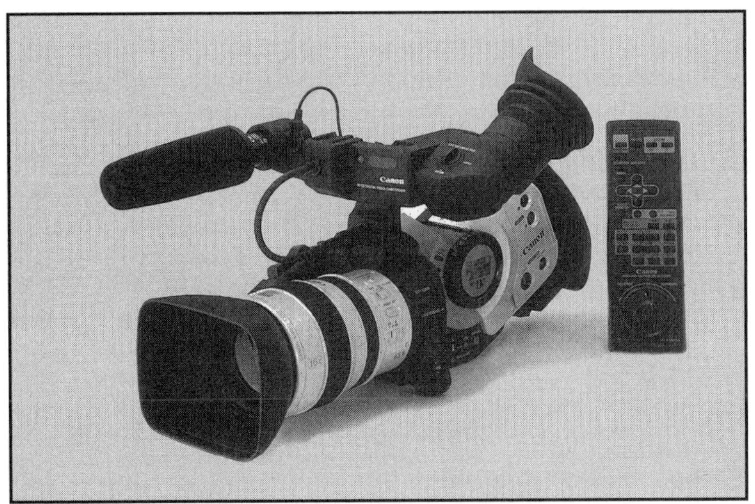

The XL1 is by far the funkiest looking 3-chip MiniDV camcorder ever invented. I've heard people say it looks like a guitar, and some say it looks like a chainsaw. But appearance aside, this is one amazing machine that's chock full of professional features and controls—the most noteworthy is the fact that it's the only prosumer camcorder that offers interchangeable lenses. Videographers get to choose from Canon's XL video lenses, which includes a 3× wide-angle lens or the collection of EOS 35mm still camera lenses.

The XL1 was introduced after the Sony DCR-VX1000, and Canon took its time tweaking some of the features like manual audio controls and the precision on-board microphone. Also unique to the XL1 is a conveniently located manual iris wheel that can be adjusted without even a second glance.

Following are the feature highlights of Canon XL1:

- 3 CCD MiniDV Camcorder
- 525 Lines of Resolution
- XL Interchangeable Lens System, Standard Lens 16× Optical Zoom/Optional 3× Extra Wide Angle Lens
- Auto/Manual Focus/White Balance
- Auto/Manual Iris/Shutter
- Digital Still Photo Feature
- Optical Image Stabilization
- Analog Video Output: Composite/Y/C
- Digital Video Input and Output: IEEE 1394 (FireWire)

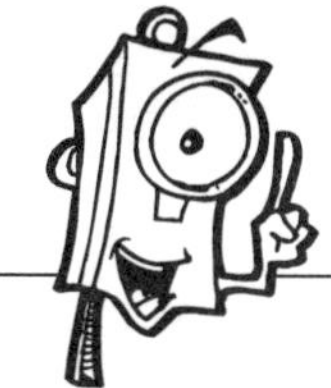

Candid Camera

Similar to Sony, Canon's Program Auto Exposure enables users in challenging shooting situations to control the camcorder's exposure system without manually adjusting the iris or the shutter. On Canon camcorders there is usually a dial where you can punch up any of the following exposure modes: Easy Recording Auto, Sports, Portrait, Spotlight, Sand and Snow, and Low Light.

Canon's brand new GL1 looks like a miniaturized version of the XL1. One of the main differences, however, is that interchangeable lenses are missing from the GL1, and this may make all the difference for serious hobbyists and semi-professionals. But before you write off this 3 CCD powerhouse, you should know that it has a professional-quality Fluorite lens (better than a glass lens). It is also packed with tons of other useful features including a pop-out LCD viewfinder (a major feature absent in the XL1), 3 shooting modes, and analog video input (also absent on the XL1) for making digital copies of your old home movies.

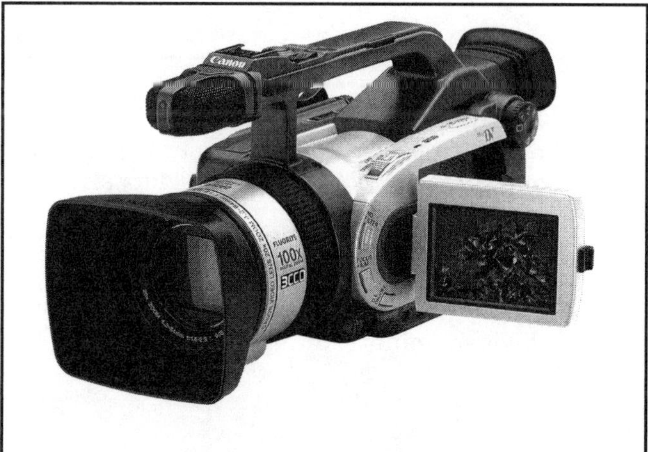

Canon GL1.

Following are the feature highlights of Canon GL1:

- 3 CCD MiniDV Camcorder
- 20x Zoom Lens with 100x Digital Zoom
- Auto/Manual Focus/White Balance
- Pop-Out LCD Color Viewfinder
- Auto/Manual Iris/Shutter
- Digital Still Photo Feature
- Optical Image Stabilization
- Analog Video Input/Output: Composite/Y/C
- Digital Video Input and Output: IEEE 1394 (FireWire)

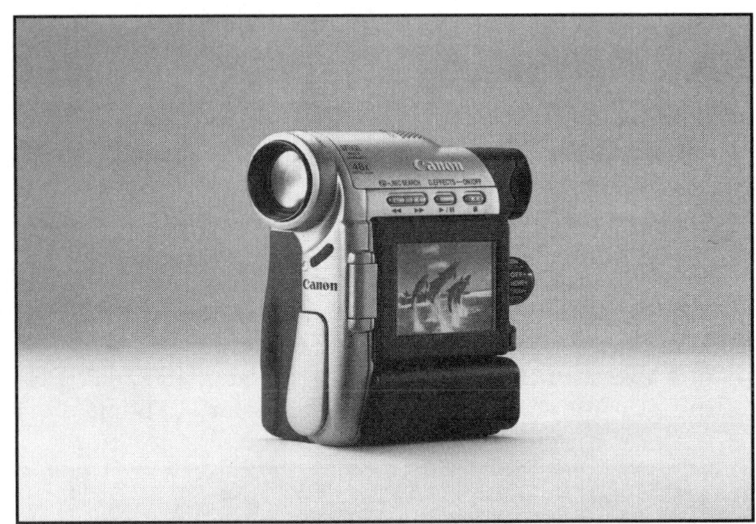

Canon Elura.

An amazing little camcorder that exudes the latest technologies, the Canon Elura functions as both a digital still camera and video camcorder. Besides Program Auto Exposure, a 12× optical zoom and Optical Image Stabilization, the Elura also features three shooting modes:

- **Video Mode.** For capturing smooth, full-motion video.
- **Photo Mode.** For capturing crystal clear digital still photos. You can store up to an incredible 500 photos on a single 60-minute MiniDV cassette.

- **Digital Motor Drive (Progressive Scan Movie Mode).** An amazing feature that produces superior high resolution, full frame digital stills of fast moving subjects. The Elura continuously records at 60 full frames per second (full motion video) as opposed to 60 fields per second. This extra clarity can help you capture a photo-finish at the races, facial expressions, and other magical moments that would otherwise pass by in normal video mode. The Elura performs three times faster than any professional 35mm still camera on the market.

Following are the feature highlights of the Canon Elura:

- 1 Progressive Scan CCD/MiniDV
- 1 Pound 4¾ Ounces
- Pop-Out Color LCD Viewfinder
- 12× Optical Zoom/48× Digital Zoom
- Auto/Manual Focus/White Balance/Shutter
- Optical Image Stabilization
- Analog Video Input and Output
- Digital Video Input/Output: IEEE 1394 (FireWire)
- PCM Digital Stereo Sound

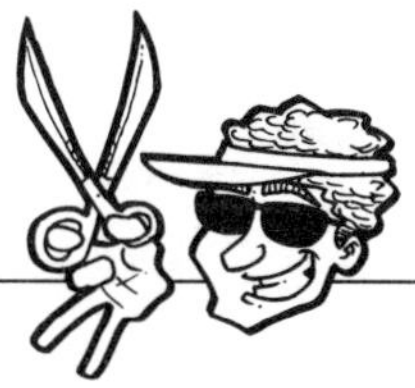

Director's Cut

A frame of video is made up of two fields that form a single image by blending (interlacing) together. In most camcorders the CCD captures and releases a partial video image (field) 60 times per second. A camcorder with a progressive scan CCD delivers impeccable image quality by capturing a full-frame video image 60 times per second.

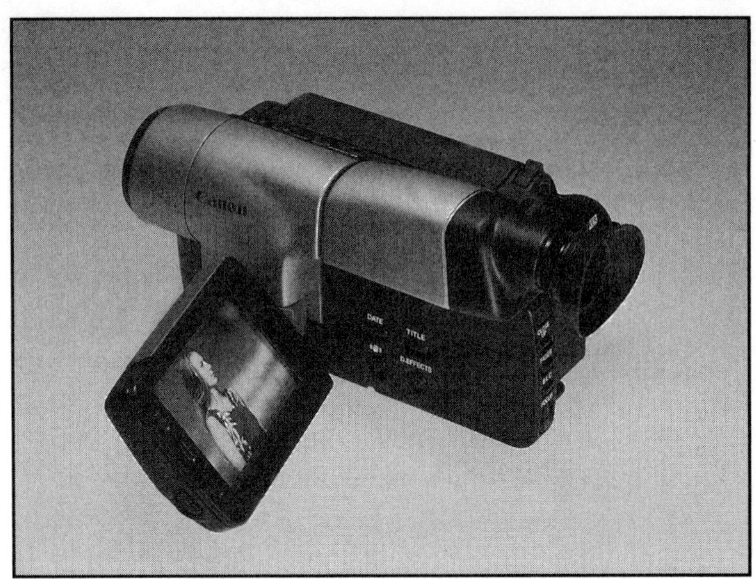

Canon ES7000V.

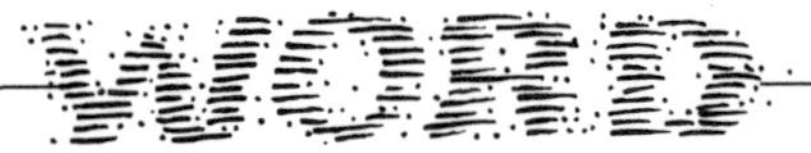

Blurred Word

NTSC (National Television Standards Committee) is a television standard used in the USA, Canada, Japan, and parts of South America and Asia. **PAL** (Phase Alternate Line) is the standard used in most of western Europe, Australia, India, China, Argentina, Brazil and most of Africa. **SECAM** (Sequential Color with Memory) is the standard used in France, parts of Russia, Eastern Europe, the Middle East and parts of Africa. Each of these standards are similar in picture quality, frame rate and lines of resolution.

One of the highest-end Hi8 consumer camcorders on the market, the ES7000V incorporates all of the optical imaging technology of its more expensive MiniDV cousins.

One neat feature exclusive to the ES7000V is that it can convert NTSC signals recorded on tape to PAL60 signals. You can view pictures even in Europe and Asia where the PAL TV system is used.

The following are the feature highlights of the Canon ES7000V:

- Hi8 Camcorder
- ¼" CCD 470,000 Pixels
- 1 Pound 15⅞ Ounces
- 16× Optical/72× Digital Zoom
- Additional Extra Long Digital 160× Zoom
- Auto/Manual Focus
- Backlight Compensation
- 3.5" Pop-Out Color ES7000V LCD Viewfinder

Panasonic

Another world leader in electronics and other appliances, Panasonic offers a full line of camcorders, broadcast audio/video equipment, VHS decks, hi-fi audio systems, home theater systems, DVD players, fax machines, TVs, and telephones to name a few. An early warrior in the digital video battles of the mid-1990s, Panasonic was the first to introduce a digital videocassette (DV) to the consumer market.

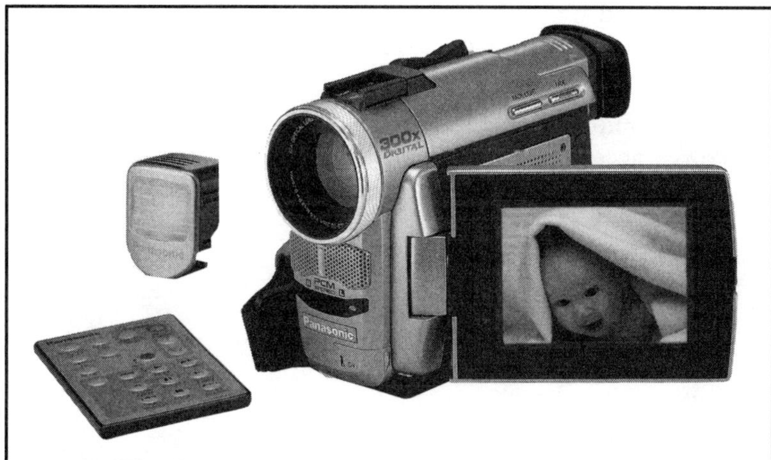

Panasonic PV-DV910.

One of the most affordable ways to kick off your DV career, the Panasonic PV-DV910 is a neat little camcorder that delivers great image quality and is light and easy to handle. It's perfect for the videographer who wants to spend less time fidgeting with camera controls and more time enjoying the video moments.

Not only does the PV-DV910 offer a full range of easy-to-use digital effects including wipes, dissolves, and fade-in/fade-outs, it also includes three White-Balance settings and five exposure presets.

Following are the feature highlights of the Panasonic PV-DV910:

- MiniDV Camcorder
- 1¼" CCD 307,200 Pixels
- 18× Optical/300× Digital Zoom
- Auto-Focus
- Digital Image Stabilization
- 5 Mode Program AE (Auto Exposure)
- 3" Color LCD Monitor
- FireWire IEEE 1394 Digital Interface

The Panasonic AG-EZ30U is one of the tiniest and lightest 3-CCD camcorders with a pop-out viewfinder to hit the MiniDV scene. One of its nicest features is accurate and smooth control over the zoom. You can easily finesse the speed of the zoom, and there's a comfortable rubber ring that's perfect for manual focusing.

The power and start/stop controls are both on one button that's easily accessible with your thumb. Manual controls are also easy to get to thanks to a nicely positioned dial. The AG-EZ30 also has many functions hidden in an easy-to-access menu system.

To cut down on camera weight and size, Panasonic came up with a cool docking station for the AG-EZ30 that has the Y/C (S-Video) and RCA Audio output connections for the camera.

Even though the AG-EZ30 is included in Panasonic's broadcast line of cameras, the price still makes the camcorder accessible to the average consumer.

Following are the feature highlights of the Panasonic AG-EZ30U:

- MiniDV Camcorder
- 3 ¼" CCDs
- 1.5 Pounds (Lightest 3-Chip Camcorder Available)
- Approx. 460 Lines of Resolution
- 12× Optical/30× Digital/120× Super Digital Zoom
- Auto/Manual Focus, Shutter, Gain, Iris, White Balance
- Digital Image Stabilization
- Time Code Generator
- Video Output: Composite, Y/C
- 2.5" Color Pop-Out LCD Viewfinder
- Zebra Pattern Function
- Digital Effects: Wipe, Mix, Strobe, Gain-Up, Black/White, Still
- Digital Still Shot Function

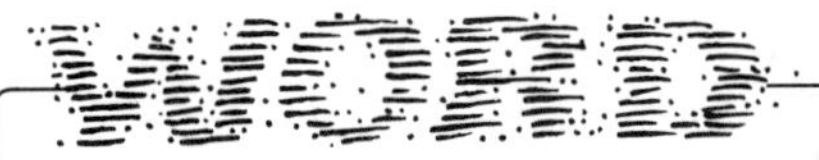

Blurred Word

Timecode is a series of 8 numbers displayed either on a camcorder or video editing deck that reveal the hours, minutes, seconds and frames related to each individual frame on a videotape. Suppose you're looking for a shot that was recorded at one hour, two minutes, five seconds and four frames into the tape. The timecode display would read 01:02:05:04. Timecode information is recorded onto the videotape itself.

JVC

Yet another major international electronics powerhouse, JVC also manufactures a vast array of products including A/V receivers, CD players, TVs, DVD players, digital still cameras, home theater, VCRs, satellite systems, and speakers.

In the world of home video, JVC is actually the inventor of the VHS format. Also the developers of the first compact DV camcorders available to consumers, JVC continues to set the pace with ultra user-friendly and portable designs.

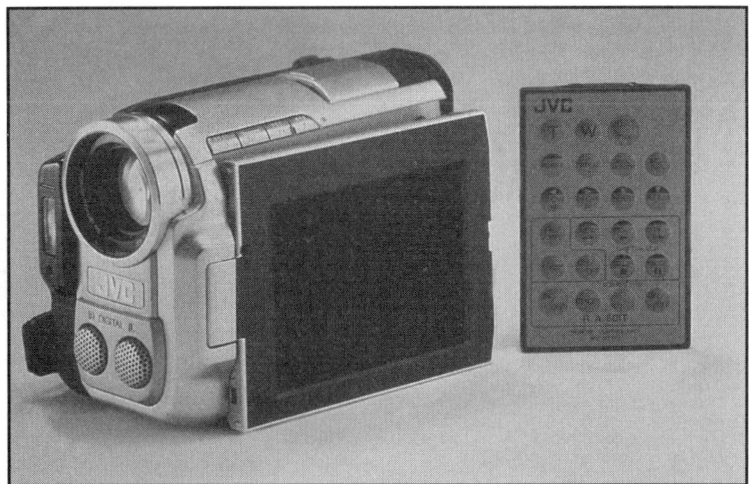

JVC GR-DVL9500.

Here's an impressive 1-chip camcorder that takes full advantage of the latest digital technology, offering image quality that's second to none in the 1-chip category.

The JVC GR-DVL9500 has many cool features in its arsenal, including a special editing feature that allows you to assemble up to eight video clips, transitions, and special effects inside the camera that can then be sent to another camcorder or VCR. This is one of the only ways I've seen so far that can make the complicated process of video editing completely idiot-proof.

The GR-DVL9500 uses a progressive scan CCD and is capable of a high-speed, 60 frame-per-second capture mode that is ideal for viewing clips in slow motion. There is also a built-in flash for digital snapshots. Effects such as wipes, fades, and dissolves are easy to custom configure, and special modes such as sepia, strobe, and black-and-white recording are available during capture or playback. This camera packs an incredible punch for a low price.

Following are the feature highlights of the JVC GR-DVL9500:

- MiniDV Camcorder
- $1\frac{1}{3}$" CCD, 360,000 Pixels

- 10× Optical/200× Digital Zoom
- 500 Lines of Resolution
- Digital Image Stabilization
- 9 Digital Effects and 11 Scene Transitions
- 3.8" Pop-Out LCD
- Auto-Focus
- i.LINK DV In/Out (IEEE 1394) Digital Interface

JVC GR-DVM50.

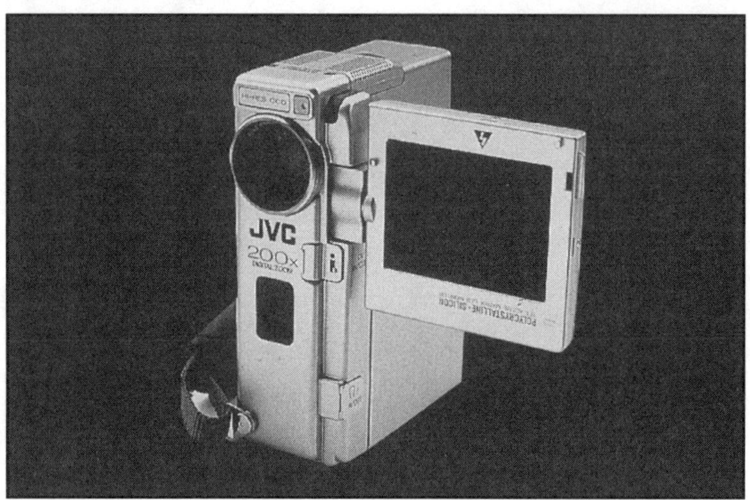

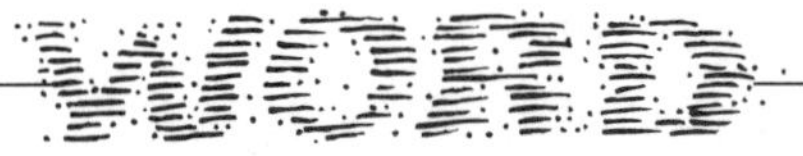

Blurred Word

Scene transition is a video editing term that refers to the method in which one scene ends and the other begins. The most common is a dissolve where one scene melts away into the next. You can also have wipes, a push or pull, spin, and so on. See Chapter 20, "Linear Editing: The Next Step," for more on transitions.

The GR-DVM50 is among the world's smallest digital video cameras. This is one way to hold the power of MiniDV in the palm of your hand, or even in your pocket. With a camcorder this tiny, you're ready to shoot high-quality video and digital stills as fast as you can remove the lens cap.

But this tiny digital performer packs a lot of punch. Besides a high-performance 680,000-pixel CCD, 10× optical/200× digital zoom, and 2.5" pop-out LCD viewfinder, the GR-DVM50 comes complete with a full line of powerful graphics and video editing software for Microsoft Windows 98 or 95.

I almost bought the GR-DVM50 before my last vacation, but my wife swiped my credit card before I could hit the cm store. I've already used up my camcorder budget for the next 10 years or so.

Following are the feature highlights of the JVC GR-DVM50:

- ➤ MiniDV Ultra-Compact Camcorder
- ➤ 1¼" CCD, 680,000 Pixels
- ➤ 10× Optical/200× Digital Zoom
- ➤ Auto-Focus, White Balance, Exposure
- ➤ Digital Image Stabilization
- ➤ 2.5" Pop-Out Color LCD Viewfinder
- ➤ 8 Digital Special Effects/12 Scene Transitions
- ➤ i.LINK DV In/Out (IEEE 1394) Digital Interface
- ➤ Docking Station with A/V Output

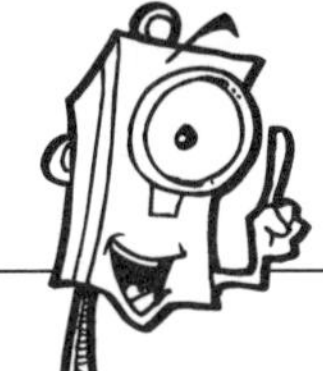

Candid Camera

Sony makes a similar designed camcorder to the JVC GR-DVM50 called the Sony DCR-PC1. I think either of these camcorders is perfect for anyone who has the desire to shoot high-quality video without worrying about lugging equipment or fussing with knobs and buttons.

Sharp

When someone said, "From Sharp Minds Come Sharp Products™," they must have been looking at the company's camcorder selection.

Sharp's huge catalogue of electronic equipment includes air conditioners, microwave ovens, vacuum cleaners, copiers, fax machines, TVs, DVD, VCRs, scanners, and printers. In the early 1970s, Sharp made their big contribution to camcorders: the LCD display, which also kicked off the LCD age of futuristic electronics.

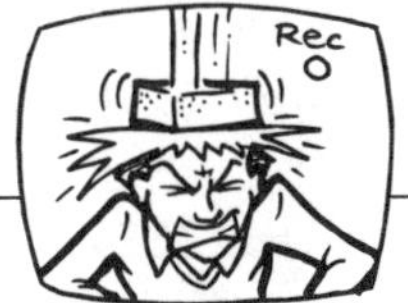

Blooper

As impressive as these tiny camcorders are, don't be fooled by salespeople saying that pint-size MiniDV camcorders deliver the same or better image quality of camcorders twice their size. In the world of camcorders, bigger is still better.

In 1992, Sharp's Viewcam VL-H100U was the world's first camcorder to incorporate a full-color, 4-inch LCD view screen. And since then, Sharp has never looked back. In 1998, they introduced the Digital Slimcam™, an incredibly thin and lightweight digital camcorder that featured yet another Sharp exclusive: Touch Screen Operation.

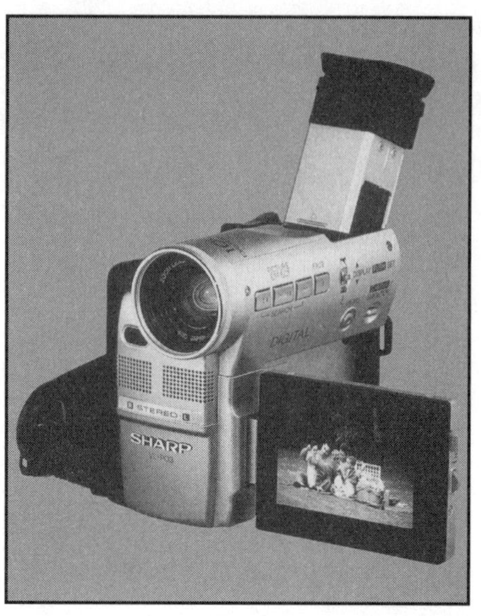

Sharp VL-PD3U.

The latest in their camcorder line, the Sharp VL-PD3U is one of the world's lightest digital camcorders and is designed to fit snugly in the palm of your hand. At just 17.7 ounces, it's ideal to tote around wherever you go.

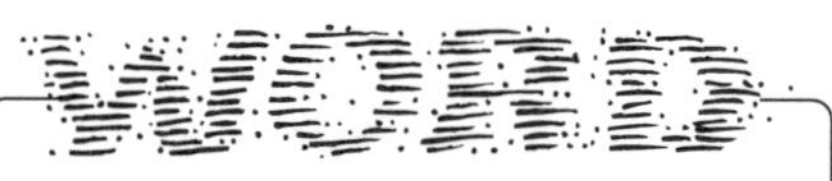

Blurred Word

Digital Gamma Brightness Correction is a form of exposure control that brightens the darker and more obscure portions of the image. It's another feature unique to Sharp camcorders. The brightness of a subject is maintained while minimizing background "washout," making the entire image significantly easier to see, even in extremely bright rooms.

Since Sharp invented the pop-out LCD viewfinder, you can bet that the VL-PD3U has one of the best on the market. Not only does it offer low-light reflectivity, but it also absorbs 99 percent of all reflective light, making for ideal viewing in all lighting conditions.

Following are the feature highlights of the Sharp VL-PD3U:

- MiniDV Camcorder
- 1 CCD/660,000 Pixels
- 2.5" Color LCD
- Digital Gamma Brightness Correction
- 17.7 Ounces
- 10× Optical/100× Digital Zoom

Hitachi

Add one more to a long list of world leaders in electronics. Hitachi also has an impressive lineup of quality products, including high-performance computer storage products, high-capacity hard drives, multimedia products, optical drives, digital multimedia recorders, handheld computers, and LCD projectors.

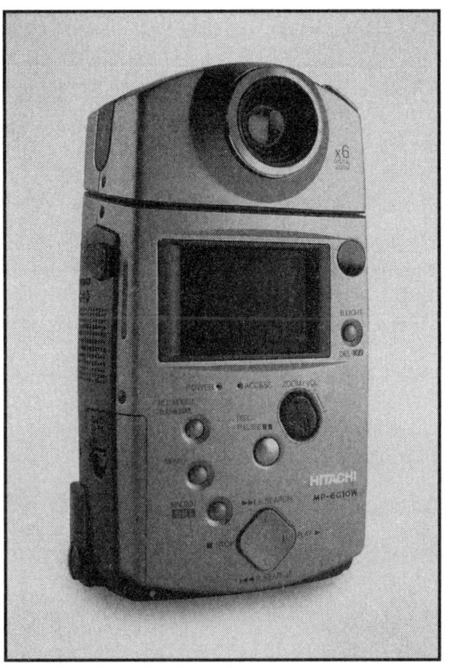

Hitachi MP-EG10W (M2).

When Hitachi released the MP-EG10W (M2), not only were they giving the public the opportunity to own the latest in multimedia technology, they were also giving us a unique glimpse into the future of the video and multimedia industries.

The MP-EG10W can record full-motion video, audio, and still images in MPEG-1 and JPEG codecs.

Digital files are compressed and stored on a removable 260-megabyte PC hard drive. Video and stills can be instantly played back on the LCD display, allowing you to choose what you want or delete unwanted media. The MP-EG10W can record 27 minutes of MPEG audio/video and 3,000 JPEG digital stills.

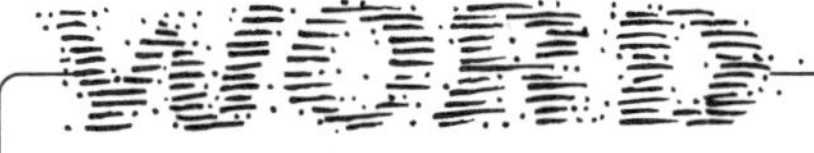

Blurred Word

Codec stands for "compression/decompression." It means that the video is compacted in an efficient way so that it doesn't lose any vital playback information but makes the file size small enough to handle with today's equipment. Upon playback, the video is instantaneously expanded for viewing. This is extremely useful in video editing, CD-ROM/DVD-ROM production, and Internet distribution.

Following are the feature highlights of the Hitachi MP-EG10W (M2):

- MPEG-1/JPEG Camcorder/Digital Still Camera
- 27 Minutes of MPEG Video Recording
- 3,000 JPEG Photographs
- 3× Optical/6× Digital Zoom
- 260 Megabyte Internal Hard Drive
- 1.8" Color LCD Viewfinder

The Least You Need to Know

- Sony is truly an innovator in the world of home video with a solid line of MiniDV, Hi8, Digital8, and 8mm.
- Canon specializes in precision lenses, and all of their camcorders have 'em.
- Panasonic was the first manufacturer to bring a digital videocassette to the consumer market and continues the tradition with a nice lineup of MiniDV camcorders.
- JVC invented the VHS format and now manufactures some of the lightest MiniDV camcorders.
- Sharp, the mastermind behind full-color LCD screens, utilizes LCD technology in their camcorders.
- Hitachi gives us a look into the digital future of camcorders with their unique MP-EG10W camcorder.

Chapter 6

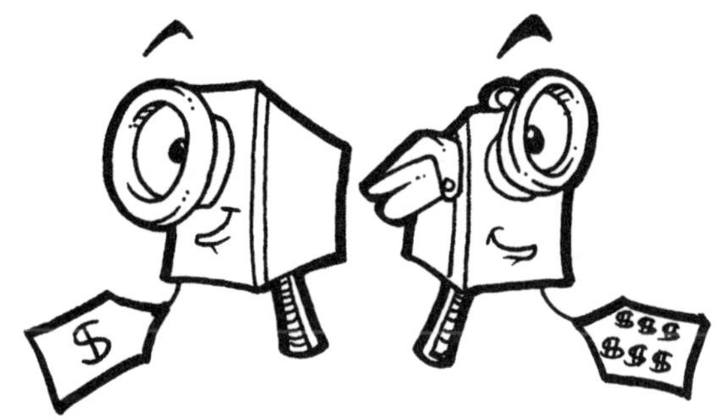

Searching for the Best Deal

In this Chapter

- Visiting your local electronics store
- Schmoozing the sales force
- Using direct mail to find the lowest price
- Buying a camcorder on the World Wide Web

You've done all the research, compared all the features, and weighed all the options. Now you're probably ready to buy your new camcorder. But buying a camcorder isn't like shopping for a shower curtain. Camcorders are expensive items, and there's nothing more frustrating than to see the one you bought last week selling for hundreds less than what you paid. Unfortunately, rapid depreciation is an inherent part of buying electronic equipment. Today's camcorder marketplace is teeming with amazing deals. In this chapter, you'll learn exactly where to look for them and how to protect yourself as a consumer.

Take a Test-Drive at Your Local Electronics Store

The next time you walk into an electronics store, pretend you're dropping a quarter into a Pac Man machine. Now watch all the little ghosts (better known as salespeople) as they gravitate toward you. If you don't get away fast, they're going to gobble you up.

Actually, salespeople aren't that bad. In fact, they can be quite helpful if you know how to handle them. The only way to get gobbled up in your quest for a camcorder is to starve yourself of precious product research in advance.

I'd strongly recommend checking out the latest video and camcorder magazines (see the sidebar later in this chapter) well in advance of your planned purchase. These magazines frequently have camcorder shootouts that compare features, functions, and prices. You can also get the latest camcorder information on the Web (see Appendix C, "Camcorder and Accessory Manufacturers") directly from the manufacturers or from other various video Web sites. At the very end of your home video study before stepping into the store, make a list of the features that are important to you and the camcorder models that you'd like to try out.

Now, if you've done your homework, the best tactic is to ward off salespeople completely at first. Let them know that you're there to look at camcorders, not to talk about them. At this point you may get a dirty look or even an attitude from the salesperson. Don't worry about it. Take some time to test-drive the camcorder you've been reading so much about. It's one thing to look at photos of a camcorder, but it's another to actually hold it in your hand, fire it up, and shoot.

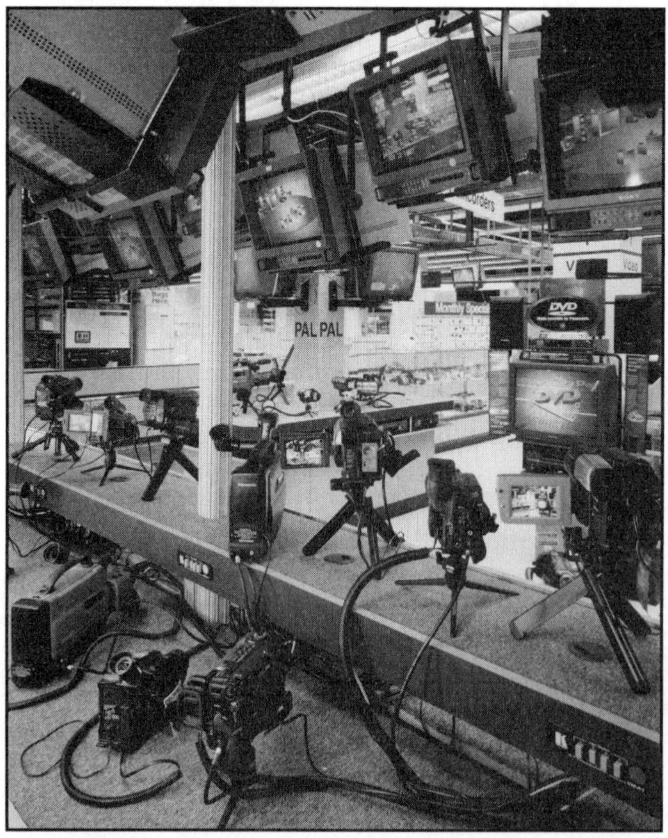

B&H photo/video interactive display.

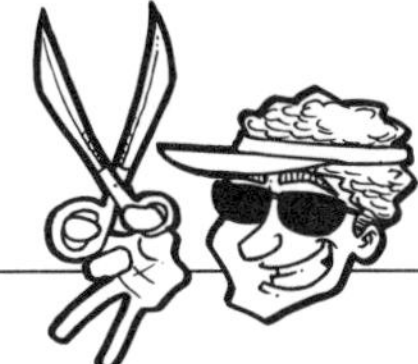

Director's Cut

"Whenever I shop for a camcorder, or any other electronic gadget for that matter, I've always got a pen and something to write on. Notes are a good thing because there are so many important details to remember when value shopping."
—Noah Lerner, Writer/Producer, HBO

Most electronics stores have hi-tech interactive displays where each camcorder is hooked up to its own professional TV monitor. Take advantage of the setup. Here's a quick rundown of things to do in the camcorder section:

- Get a sense of the feel and weight of the camcorder. Make sure it's something that's not too bulky or heavy to lug around with you.
- Look through the eyepiece and compare how the picture looks on the TV screen as compared to the viewfinder or Pop-Out LCD viewfinder.
- Test the camcorder's zoom.
- Determine how well the auto-focus works.
- Quickly locate and execute a few of the main controls like manual focus, program auto-exposure, and manual shutter.
- Make sure the controls are conveniently located and the camcorder feels comfortable in your hand. While holding the camcorder up to your eye, press the record start/stop button, and zoom in and out a few times. Is the camcorder still steady in your hand?
- If the camcorder has menus, scroll through for a quick feature tour.
- If the camcorder has Image Stabilization, give it a try. Slightly shake the camcorder while turning the feature on and off. Notice a difference? You probably will.

After you're done browsing, find a salesperson and ask as many questions as possible. Get a feel for the models that they are pushing and find out why. Take notes as needed. After you've got all the information, ask for prices and write them down. Forget about bargaining at this point; there'll be plenty of time for that later. Resisting any further temptation to strike a deal, purposefully place your notes in your pocket, thank the salesperson, and walk out of the store.

Schmoozing Your Salesperson

After careful research and price comparison in magazines, catalogs, and on the Web, you're ready to take on the video sales force. When you arrive back at the store, the battle usually begins with a few high-pressure pitches for whatever camcorder is the flavor of the day. Most salespeople have been through extensive training and are always ready to strike with a highly developed plan of attack. It's important to keep in mind that they are only interested in one thing: to sell you a camcorder right then and there, without any outside price or model comparison on your part. And the best way to do this is to get you charged up about a camcorder. When emotions run high, there is usually little or no negotiation that takes place. They are experts at creating the illusion that you're privy to an unbelievable deal that you couldn't get anyplace else.

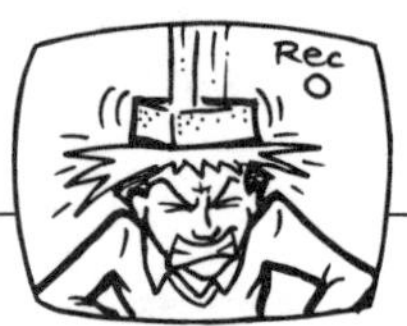

Blooper

Never buy a camcorder on impulse at the first store you check out. If you haven't had a chance to do any research, go to at least one or two other stores to get as much information as possible and the lowest price.

The salesperson is also aware of the fact that if you're not hooked right away, you're almost guaranteed to purchase elsewhere. Simply put, they are not terribly interested in establishing and maintaining any kind of long-term relationship with you, despite what might be said to the contrary. Hit and run is the game, and if you don't see it coming, you're going to get a crash course in camcorder chicanery.

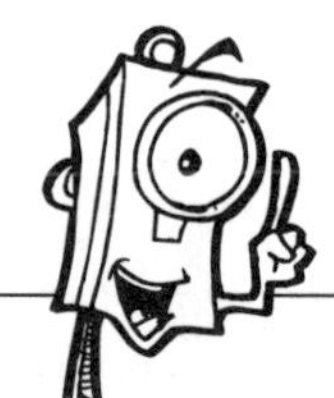

Candid Camera

If the salesperson is not willing to negotiate at all or doesn't move from the sticker price, say goodbye and walk out the door. This is a hard-line tactic, but if they're playing hardball, you're almost guaranteed to find a lower price elsewhere. If you find that they had the lowest price and return to the store to make a purchase, chances are nobody will remember you!

Here's how to schmooze your salesperson:

- Find the lowest prices for the models you're interested in and lower them by at least 10 percent. This is a good jumping off point for negotiation.
- In battle, never show signs of emotion. If you feel yourself becoming nervous, overly zealous, or even desperate, force yourself to mask it. Think of Mr. Spock shopping for a camcorder. *Stoic* is the word. Let your opponent think that at any moment you're ready to walk out the door.
- Wait for the salesperson to hit you with a counteroffer before allowing your own bid to be raised.
- Try to steer the counteroffers in tiny increments from your starting point. If the salesperson thinks you have one foot out the door, he or she is more likely to fold if there is too much negotiating taking place.

Catalog/Mail-Order Checklist

If you've lost the war at the electronics store, don't throw down your weapons just yet! You may be ready for direct mail. These colorful, hard-to-miss catalogs grace the back of every electronic, computer, and video magazine under the sun. Mail-order houses pride themselves on providing the lowest prices. They can do this because the mail-order business sells in bulk and isn't burdened with enormous overhead like electricity, rent, and excessive inventory.

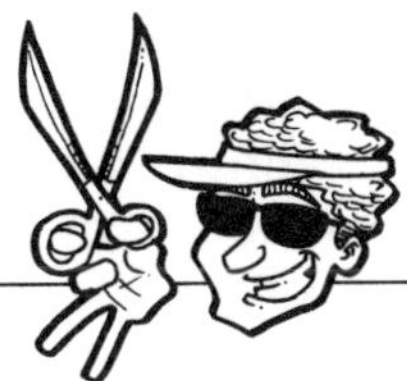

Director's Cut

Not only do these magazines have great articles and reviews on camcorders and home video, they also contain many mail-order ads to choose from:

Videographer
www.videographer.com
530-891-8410

Sound and Vision
www.soundandvisionmag.com
212-767-6000

DV
www.dv.com
415-905-2200

Videography
www.videography.com
212-378-0400

New Media
www.newmedia.com
650-573-5170

Camcorder & Computer Video
805-644-3824

Mail-order and Internet shopping have a few disadvantages, however. First, you don't get the instant gratification of purchasing a product you can hold in your hand and can take home that day. Second, mail-ordering has the potential to be a bit risky because the place of purchase is much less visible than if you were shopping at a huge electronics store. What happens if your credit card gets charged and your camcorder never shows up? Or what if the camcorder arrives in seven pieces?

Also, who pays for the return shipping? You or the company? If they pick up the shipping tab, it's a sure sign that they're serious about having and keeping you as a customer.

Thanks to the efforts of several major consumer advocacy groups like the Better Business Bureau, the Direct Marketing Association, and the Federal Trade Commission, mail order is much more of a viable option than it used to be.

The Direct Marketing Association has compiled a handy top-ten tip list to assist consumers with mail-order shopping:

1. **Make sure you know the company's return policy and satisfaction guarantee before you order.** Is there a "lifetime guarantee?" Can you only exchange for credit? Most catalogs have very liberal policies, but you should check before you buy.
2. **Keep a record of your order.** These facts are especially important to know: name of the company, company's phone number, item you ordered including size and color, method of payment, expected delivery date, and any confirmation number you may have been given.
3. **Know the expected delivery date of your package and find out the various shipping options.** Will you need to be home to sign for the package? Can the company deliver to a P.O. box? Is overnight or rush delivery available?
4. **Find out the total price of your purchase before you finalize the sale.** This includes sales tax, shipping and handling, and any other charges that may apply so there are no surprises when you receive your credit card bill.
5. **Catalogs often have services you may find useful.** Gift-wrapping and monogramming are just a few examples of services that may be available to you free of charge or for a minimal fee.
6. **If you need your order delivered in time for a holiday or special date, make sure the company can deliver in time.** Many catalogs have order deadlines during peak shopping times, such as the holiday season.
7. **If your order is a gift, make sure the person taking your order knows this.** Frequently, catalogs offer gift-wrapping, cards, or inclusion of personalized messages. You can also request that the price of the purchase be deleted from the packing slip.

8. **After you receive your merchandise, keep all receipts and product packaging until you are sure that you plan to keep your purchase.** Test the item immediately to make sure that it works and that you are satisfied with it.
9. **Contact the catalog company immediately if your merchandise arrives damaged.** The company will likely pick up the order at its expense and replace it immediately.
10. **If you are ever in doubt about a company's products, policies, or services, just ask.** Catalogs are known for providing exceptional service and will want to ensure that you are absolutely satisfied.

Here are a few of the major mail-order companies. Most of these companies have been advertising in magazines for several years, which is usually a good indication that the company isn't going to go bust while your order is pending:

- Abe's of Maine 718-998-6650
- Adorama 1-800-223-2500 (e-mail: adorama@aol.com)
- Armato's 1-800-628-6801 (www.armatos.com)
- B & H Photo/Video/Pro Audio 1-800-947-9925 (www.bhphotovideo.com)
- Beach Camera 1-800-634-1811 (www.beachcamera.com)
- Berger Bros. Camera and Video Exchange 1-888-262-4160 (www.berger-bros.com)
- CCI Camera City Inc. 1-800-837-8623 (e-mail: ccicam@aol.com)
- Camera Sound 1-800-477-0022 (www.camerasound.com)
- Camera World 1-800-729-8933 (www.cameraworld.com)
- DV Direct 1-888-383-8366 (www.dvdirect.com)
- Elite Video 1-800-468-1996 (www.elitevideo.com)
- Family Photo & Video 1-800-899-7468 (e-mail: familyph@aol.com)
- Marine Park 1-800-448-8811
- Tri-State Camera & Video (e-mail: tscamvid@aol.com)
- Worldwide Video Enterprises 1-800-617-4686

Speaking about mail-order companies going bust, check out this horror story. In 1992, I ordered a computer from a small mail-order house I saw in the back of *Computer Shopper Magazine*. They quoted my system at almost $100 lower than the lowest price I had found elsewhere. When the computer showed up, it wasn't working, and upon further inspection I discovered that the construction of the system seemed shoddy, and there was a silicon board that had come loose somewhere and was banging around inside. Enraged, I called the company and they issued an R.M.A. number (Return Merchandise Authority) and had me ship the computer back (at my expense).

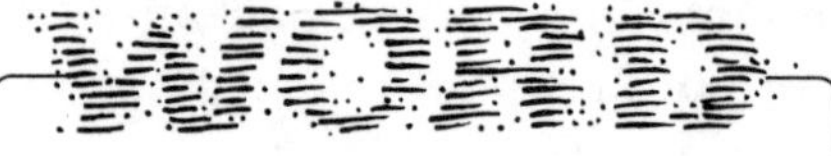

Blurred Word

Caveat Emptor is Latin for "Let the buyer beware." In other words, it's your responsibility to do all the relevant research before buying because if something goes wrong, the buck stops with you.

I never saw the computer again, and when I called the company, the number was disconnected! A few months went by, and I contacted the Attorney General's office and the Better Business Bureau, but there was little they could do to help. They had compiled a list of about 250 customers who had experienced similar rip-offs from the same company but were unwilling to speculate on any further action that was being taken.

After a year of fuming, I decided to chalk the $950 up to a lesson learned, but it still stings. The moral of the story: If the ad or the company seems suspicious to you in any way, it might be worth calling the Better Business Bureau or the state's Attorney General's office to see if any complaints have been filed against the company. Even still, there is no way to foresee this kind of disaster. The best thing you can do is to trust your instincts. If something seems fishy, it probably is. Never forget: when shopping for a camcorder it's Caveat Emptor!

Browsing the Web

Want to hear something incredible? According to Forrester Research Inc., by the year 2002, approximately $842.7 billion in commerce will be conducted via the Internet and by 2003, that figure will increase to approximately $1.3 trillion! Whether you like it or not, the Internet is taking over the way you conduct daily business. With the press of a button, you can buy groceries, airline and movie tickets, CDs, DVDs and books, or even purchase stock. The World Wide Web is a bargain-hunter's paradise that never closes!

Here are a few links to companies that sell camcorders over the Web:

- camcorder.com: www.camcorder.com
- AudioVideo.com: www.audiovideo.com
- bid.com: www.bid.com
- Source Electronic: www.electronics4sale.com
- Wolf Camera: www.wolfcamera.com
- Electro Buy Online: 1-800-electro.com/index2sony.html
- Focus Camera and Video: focuscamera.com
- Shopunet: www.shopunet.com
- Supreme Video and Electronics: www.supremevideo.com
- Digital Eye: www.1mall4all.com/digital_eye.htm

- cameraworld.com: www.cameraworld.com
- Circuit City Online: www.circuitcity.com
- 1-888-Camcorder: www.888camcorder.com/camcorder.htm
- Planet 3000: www.planet3000.com
- Camcorders4Sale.com: www.camcorders4sale.com
- Videodiscovery: www.videodiscovery.com

Online shopping can be as safe as conventional shopping if you take a few simple precautions. The Federal Trade Commission has provided a helpful checklist for Internet security, safety, and privacy:

- **Use a secure browser.** This is the software you use to navigate the Internet. Your browser should comply with industry security standards, such as Secure Sockets Layer (SSL) or Secure Electronic Transaction (SET). These standards encrypt or scramble the purchase information you send over the Internet, ensuring the security of your transaction. Most computers come with a browser already installed. You also can download some browsers for free over the Internet. In addition to a secure browser, make sure that the Web site you're connecting to is secure. Your browser will usually tell you when you have established a secure link.
- **Shop with companies you know.** Anyone can set up shop online under almost any name. If you're not familiar with a merchant, ask for a paper catalog or brochure to get a better idea of their merchandise and services. Also, determine the company's refund and return policies before you place your order.
- **Keep your password(s) private.** Be creative when you establish a password and never give it to anyone. Avoid using a telephone number, birth date, or a portion of your Social Security number. Instead, use a combination of numbers, letters, and symbols.
- **Pay by credit or charge card.** If you pay by credit or charge card online, your transaction will be protected by the Fair Credit Billing Act. Under this law, consumers have the right to dispute charges under certain circumstances and temporarily withhold payment while the creditor is investigating them. In the case of unauthorized use of a consumer's credit or charge card, consumers are generally held liable only for the first $50 in charges. Some cards may provide additional warranty or purchase protection benefits.
- **Keep a record.** Be sure to print a copy of your purchase order and confirmation number for your records. Also, you should know that the federal Mail or Telephone Order Merchandise Rule covers orders made via the Internet. This means that unless stated otherwise, merchandise must be delivered within 30 days, and if there are delays, the company must notify you.

- **Pay your bills online.** Some companies let you pay bills and check your account status online. Before you sign up for any service, evaluate how the company is securing your financial and personal information. Many companies explain their security procedures on their Web site. If you don't see a security description, call or e-mail the company and ask.
- **Keep your personal information private.** Don't disclose personal information—such as your address, telephone number, Social Security number, or e-mail address—unless you know who's collecting the information, why they're collecting it, and how they'll use it. If you have children, teach them to check with you before giving out personal or family information online.
- **Look for a company's online privacy policy.** Many companies with privacy practices post their privacy policy on their Web site. A company's privacy policy should disclose what information is being collected on the Web site and how that information is being used. Before you provide a company with personal information, check its privacy policy. If you can't find a policy, send an e-mail or written message to the Web site to ask about its policy and request that it be posted on the site.
- **Make choices.** Many companies give you a choice on their Web site as to whether and how your personal information is used. These companies allow you to decline—or "opt-out" of—having personal information, such as your e-mail address, used or shared with other companies. Look for this as part of the company's privacy policy.

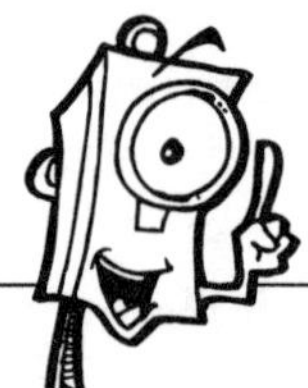

Candid Camera

When you order merchandise by mail, phone, or online, you are protected by the Federal Trade Commission, the United States Postal Service, and various state regulations and guidelines set for the industry by the Direct Marketing Association. Check Appendix C for organizations you can turn to if you can't resolve your problem or if you suspect fraud.

The Least You Need to Know

- Always give the camcorder you're interested in a test-drive at your local electronics store.
- Beat salespeople at their own game. Always do your research in advance.
- Direct mail is a viable option for finding the lowest camcorder prices.
- Don't worry about getting tangled in the World Wide Web. It's a great and safe place to shop for camcorders.

Part 2

Pre-Production

O.K. … so you've got your gear, and you're chomping at the bit to get started shooting. But before you begin, it's important to understand that even for the most basic production situations, if you do a little planning, it can make a huge difference in the final product. Whether it's a birthday party, graduation, wedding, or any other type of creative program that you conjure up, you have many things to take into account like a basic story line, location, lighting, sound, and even shot selection.

It sounds like a lot to digest, but it's really not. After you've been through the checklist once or twice, pre-production planning becomes second nature.

In this part you'll learn how to write a basic script for your home videos. This can be anything from a 120-page screenplay to a bunch of potential shots that you've scribbled in a notepad.

After that, you'll become a master at scouting and lighting your location. You'll also become an expert at recording the best sound possible in your programs, and how to angle your camcorder just right to get the most interesting and dynamic shots.

So read on … you're just about ready to kick off your home video production!

Chapter 7

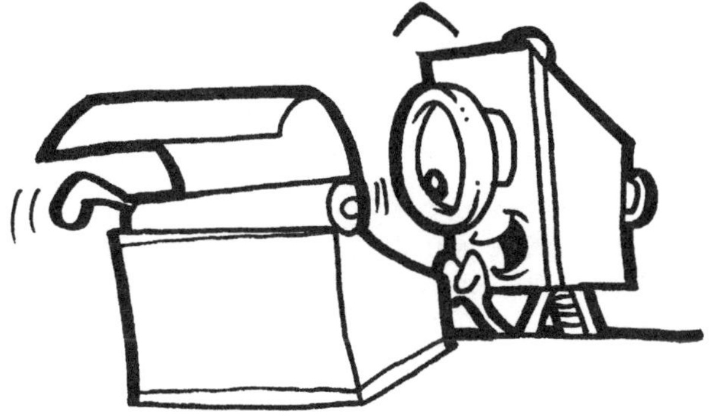

Scriptwriting 101

In This Chapter

- Deciding on a plan of action
- Flowing with the writing process
- Learning simple script formats and lingo
- Script ideas you can use at home

If you do it right, videography can be a creative, enriching experience. From the simplest vacation videos to feature length movies you can shoot with a camcorder, the possibilities are unlimited. Videography in its rawest form, however, isn't a streamlined art. If you don't have a plan, you will end up shooting hours and hours of "filler" video footage that will bore your audience to tears. In this chapter, you'll learn how to write basic scripts for your home videos. You'll also get a sampling of script terminology, a handful of simple scripts/programs you can create yourself, and the tools and software that can help you format scripts.

So, What's the Plan?

We've all seen those surveillance video cameras hanging from the ceilings of department stores and banks. Ever stop to think that there's probably a security guard planted in front of a TV screen in a back room somewhere monitoring the live footage all day long? It's a pretty mind-numbing thought. I'd rather watch a compilation program of all the bank robberies and shoplifting footage that the security cameras have captured over the years. All of a sudden, you've got an interesting program on your hands and the fuel for more than one TV series on Fox.

Now imagine being the producer of a bank robbery show. You've got years of footage to boil down into 20 minutes of programming after commercials. This is where a script is invaluable. You can't just edit all of the robberies together, put a title at the beginning, roll credits at the end of the show, and put it on the air. You need to tell a story and organize the footage in a manner that makes sense and is entertaining to the viewer. You need a master plan.

As you set out on your journey in producing creative home videos, think of a script as the backbone of your program. If you write before you shoot, a script will give your project structure, organization, direction, tone, and attitude. Your home videos will no longer look like monotonous surveillance footage.

Writing a script also forces you to think about and visualize your project in advance, which is the best way to solve problems you would have encountered while shooting or editing. And most video production problems arise from a lack of structure, so organizing your thoughts before the fact becomes even more attractive. The script is also the best way to communicate your ideas and direction to your video crew (if you're lucky enough to have one). Not only is scripting your home videos a great way to harness and direct your creativity, it will make shooting and editing a snap, and your final product will have a smooth, natural flow.

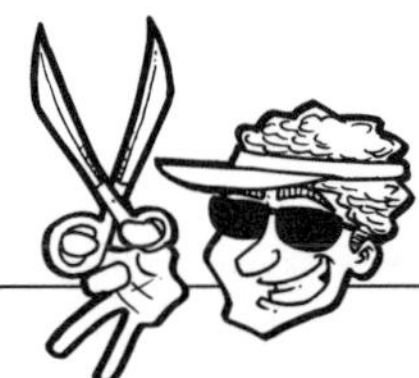

Director's Cut

"It only takes a second to click a remote, so it's very important to keep your audience glued to the set. One dull moment and they're off to surf the dozens of channels at their fingertips. Chances are they'll land on a show that's driven by a good script."
—Matt Ginsburg, Senior Producer, VH1

As you'll see, writing and formatting a script is easy and can be a lot of fun. Think of a script as a dynamic document that takes place in three dimensions. You've got sights and sounds that take place over time. Even if you have a short shot list or have taken a few notes on how you want to organize something, you've got a working script.

Sitting Down to Write

I've heard Billy Joel say in an interview that some of his best ideas come to him in dreams. Elton John can't do it all by himself, so he splits the responsibilities with Bernie Taupin. Stephen King can blurt out a novel almost as fast as he can think it. The writing process is a mystery, and everyone has different ways of channeling the random thoughts and ideas into sentences on the page.

Granted, you're probably not planning to pen the next pop hit or best-selling novel, but creative videography has its roots in creative writing. If your idea or story works on the page, it has a much better chance of working on the screen.

For me, the hardest part of any writing project is getting started. I used to fear the blank page. Now, as soon as I see one, I begin to fill it up with random thoughts and ideas—whatever comes to mind. I usually end up with countless pages of junk, but buried in that junk, I can usually find the gold nugget of an idea. It's a great way to get by that initial roadblock. The next time you sit down to write, give it a try. You'll be amazed by how many good ideas, thoughts, and turn-of-phrases are floating by in that active brain of yours.

Some Simple Script Ideas

In this early stage of pre-production, it's not a bad idea to start brainstorming on the types of programs you might be interested in putting together. Forget about editing, graphics, music, or any other production element at this point. Just concentrate on coming up with the ideas that are the core of any good script.

Here are a few ideas for scripts and projects that will make your home video stand out. By no means is this a complete list. Use it as a jumping off point.

- **Low Budget Thrillers:** Home movies on a shoestring budget.
- **Music Videos:** Choose a tune and script your video to the words or music.
- **Documentary/Mockumentary:** Choose your topic and plan on using elements such as narration, still photos, old film, and video. *Documentaries* are narratives that provide commentary on the subject. The *mockumentary* is a humorous form of a documentary.
- **News Magazine:** Watch any of the news magazine shows like *20/20*, *Dateline*, or *Eye on People*. A news magazine segment is usually 7 to 10 minutes long and employs many documentary production techniques.
- **Reality TV:** Ever watch *The Real World* on MTV? It's a brilliant combination of a soap opera and documentary that has spawned a new genre of television. All it takes is a camcorder and four or five interesting and unique characters. Any American family will do.

- **Surveillance Video:** Back to the idea of a bank robbery show ... You can probably think of a few things that you might encounter on a day-to-day basis that would be interesting enough to tie together in a story. If you're in the right place at the right time or come up with a great idea for a new series, there's a lot of money to be made. Ever wonder how much the videographer of the Rodney King beating footage made? More than you can imagine!
- **The Special Occasion Video:** If you've got a party planned, it's a perfect forum to screen a video. Besides being a lot of fun to write and produce, it's a great gift for someone because the kind of work that goes into the production is worth a lot more than dollars. You can structure a birthday video in the form of a documentary/mockumentary, music video, or you can simply clip together candid moments to music.

The Writing Process and Home Video Scripts

There's nothing more rewarding than taking a raw idea for a home video and making it work on TV. When it comes to making home movies, it's all about coming up with the idea, writing it down, transforming your idea into a working script, and then later into actual images and sounds on your television set. In theory, it sounds easy, but in practice, more people get hung up in the writing stage than at any other point. Putting pen to paper can be more of a stumbling block than a creative outlet.

From the seed of an idea, to actual words on paper, here's a timeline of the writing process as it relates to making home videos.

1. **Get an idea.** It sounds easy, but it's anything but. Once you've chosen a basic framework for your project (an event, activity, vacation and so on), try to come up with a unique and interesting hook that will make people want to watch. Sometimes an idea can hit you instantly, other times, you can wait weeks for inspiration. However it happens, your goal is to create a program that will leave your audience saying things like "Why didn't I think of that?" and "Wow, that was clever." The best ideas are usually the simplest, but they offer a unique twist or insight into a story, situation or event. Coming up with an idea can be hard work. That's why people in the TV business get paid big bucks for coming up with ideas.
2. **Brainstorm.** Once you have an idea in place, clear your mind of everything else and visualize how you think you would like your project to look and sound. Play scenes and/or possible situations again and again in your head until they take on a life of their own. Once you've got a general feel for the project, begin to think out your scenes in a sequence that makes sense. Don't worry about all the details; many of the holes will take care of themselves when you get deeper

into the writing stage. One of the most powerful tools in the world and your most valuable possession is your imagination. Use it to bring your video projects to life.

3. **Write it down.** Now it's time to start scratching this thing out. Writing is not an easy task, so don't expect to have a polished home video script on the first pass. Your objective at the very beginning is to get everything that's in your brain out on paper as quickly as possible. This will help you focus in on your idea, and help you visualize the kind of footage that you'll need to shoot later. If you feel that you're ready, you may want to map out a rough outline for your project. This way, if you're planning on writing a treatment (see "Simple Script Formats" later in this chapter), you'll have a roadmap to work from.

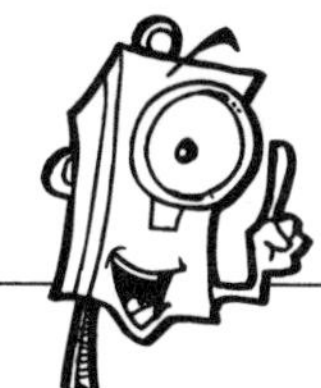

Candid Camera

Sometimes when you need to have an idea, your mind goes blank. This is writer's block. The best way to handle it is to walk away from the project and clear your mind completely of the problem at hand. Group discussions or "brainstorming meetings" are a great way to spark creativity and can help you capture an idea that's buried deep in the back of your brain.

Research, Research, Research

Depending on the project you choose to tackle, you may find yourself with a some research and pre-production legwork to do. On movie sets, Associate Producers and Production Assistants take care of this, but in your home movie you're flying solo. Suppose you're putting together a family documentary, an informational video for class, or even a corporate video. You've got some research to do. It's almost impossible to begin to think about writing a script for these kinds of projects without having all the facts in front of you. If you try to hop in without doing research you will find that your scripts will have gaps that are impossible to cover up, and the final product will most likely be inaccurate and boring.

If your project is based on the documentary format, you can start by pre-interviewing all parties involved. For example, if you are putting together a video for your grandmother's 86th birthday, start by asking your mom or dad for any information or materials that you can use in your piece. This can include childhood memories or stories about your grandmother, photographs and any film footage that you can easily have transferred to videotape at a photo-video store.

For more serious projects, research can be a painstaking process, but technology is making it easier. Just hop on the Internet and do a search, or pop an electronic encyclopedia into your CD-ROM. Newspapers and magazines also have archives you can access online. It's that simple.

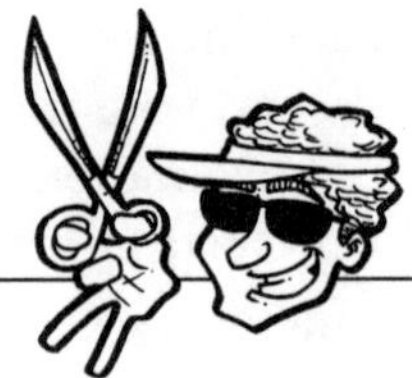

Director's Cut

Internet search engines can be invaluable researching tools. Here are a few of my favorites:

www.metacrawler.com

www.yahoo.com

www.infoseek.com

www.excite.com

www.thunderstone.com

www.lycos.com

Know Thy Audience

As creative videographers, sometimes we forget to do one very important thing: figure out who the audience is going to be and what they'll get out of your program. Like some infamous Hollywood directors, it's easy to get caught up in your personal creative vision and forget about everyone else, including the cast, crew, and audience. It's a horrible thing to present a project you've put a lot of time into only to watch your audience unbuckle their seatbelts and hop off the couch at the first commercial break.

When you first begin your foray into home video, you'll most likely find that your only audience is family and friends. This is not a bad thing because they will probably have the most patience for beginner's mistakes and unstructured videos that aren't made for a "mainstream" audience. This is great preparation if you have plans to delve into more challenging projects like music videos, short films, or family documentaries. Whether family, friends, colleagues, or just casual acquaintances are watching your videos, most audiences behave and react to things in predictable ways. (See Chapter 23, "Time to Show Off Your Video Masterpiece.") The more home movies that you make, the more moving, inspiring and entertaining they will become.

Simple Script Formats

There are several ways to skin a script, but what you should remember is that there is no right and wrong way to format one. It can be a properly formatted screenplay, a couple of paragraphs describing your video, or just a piece of paper with a list of shots that you want to shoot. Whatever works for you is the best way—as long as you are accomplishing the task of putting words on paper which tell a story.

But remember, writing a more formal script should be the final step in the creative process. If you haven't worked through and outlined your idea fully in your head and on paper, scriptwriting is going to be a very difficult and frustrating process for you. The writing may start out smoothly, but you'll suddenly find yourself faced with discontinuous story lines, plot roadblocks, and other various literary nightmares.

When you are finally ready to write, here are a few of the most common script formats. Feel free to make any adjustments to the formatting of these examples to fit your needs.

Treatment

Think of a treatment as scriptwriting in its rawest form. There is really no set format; it's simply a description of your production and can contain details as to how you plan to shoot it, and what it's going to look and sound like.

I've found that it works best to put together a treatment (whether it's for yourself or for a client) well in advance of shooting. This way, once production begins, you can focus on capturing footage that supports the main theme outlined in the treatment.

A treatment for a simple home video project can be as simple as this:

> For their 35th wedding anniversary, the incredibly generous Ellen and Artie Schloss took their extended family on a weeklong Caribbean cruise. To express their gratitude, their son Glenn and son-in-law Steve plan to put together a touching yet humorous video-memento of the journey.
>
> The program will include beauty shots and funny family moments from the various cruise locations including Jamaica, Mexico, St. Thomas, and the Cayman Islands. They plan to use quick soundbites from family members thanking mom and dad.
>
> In addition, they will record local residents and crew-members aboard the ship saying "Happy 35th anniversary Ellen and Artie." These will be sprinkled throughout the program to help move things along.

If you write a treatment like this before shooting, you've given yourself a plan of attack well in advance. You know that your agenda on the cruise includes shooting beauty shots, interviews with family members, and as many people as possible saying

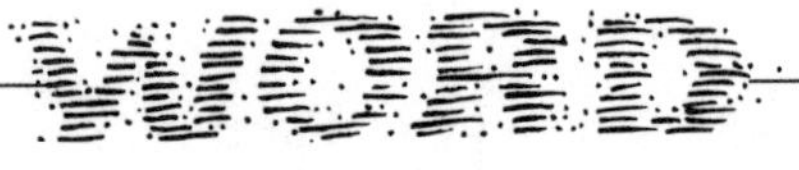

Blurred Word

Soundbites or **bites** are spoken words or phrases by anyone on camera. News reporters in the field design their interview questions to draw short, meaningful responses.

Beauty shots refer to any shot that shows off or highlights a person, place, or thing. Beauty shots are often used to establish location in a video project.

"Happy 35th anniversary, Ellen and Artie." Having a plan is a lot more efficient than editing random bits of cruise footage together into an awkward program.

On the other hand, you can also write a treatment for a program you plan to produce from previously recorded footage, but you'll find that the possibilities aren't as unlimited as starting from scratch. With a little creativity, however, you can easily leap over this hurdle.

For instance, last year, my buddy Rick called to tell me that he was engaged. I knew I had a great videomaking opportunity on my hands because over the years, I had collected hours and hours of footage of Rick and our other friends growing up. Before coming up with the concept for the video, I decided that the best thing to do was to collect all of the video that I had shot, and over the next several days I watched every bit of it and took careful notes. When I was finished I had a good idea of what footage I was interested in using, and it was easier for me to come up with a concept. Here's the treatment I came up with:

> BAREFOOTIN' THROUGH LIFE
>
> *A Mockumentary by Steven Beal*
>
> Richard William Krug, one of the world's finest water-skiers, once vowed to a group of his friends and family that he would never marry. Years later, Steve gets a phone call from his best friend saying that he's planning on taking the plunge. Pleasantly surprised, Steve decides that the best way to express his joy and amazement is to compile 10 years of raw video and film footage of Rick and the gang into a comprehensive program commemorating Rick's startling decision.
>
> Shortly thereafter, "Barefootin' Through Life" was born. A 15-minute comedic documentary on Rick's journey through life, the program will be narrated by Steve, and features interviews with Larry Tisdall and Chris Hadjandreas, Rick's life-long buddies. The story takes us on a wild ride from Rick's childhood through his meeting with his future wife, Kim. The soundtrack of this mockumentary will feature some of Rick's favorite music.

This is the short version of the "Barefootin' Through Life" treatment, but writing it first helped me create an overall vision for the project when I sat down to write the 15-page script.

Audio/Video (A/V) Script

Writing an Audio/Video script is a much more exact science than coming up with a treatment. Professionally, the A/V script is a favorite tool for producers of television commercials, documentaries, and corporate and training videos because it's simple to read and understand. I often use the A/V script for home video projects because it forces me to visualize exactly what elements I plan on using. I usually write my A/V script after I'm done shooting. This way, after watching my footage I can easily determine which shots I want to use.

An A/V script is usually split down the middle into two columns with the video on the left and the audio on the right. The video column contains descriptions of the shots, graphics, and any special effects. The audio column contains narration, dialog, sound effects, and music. If your script is carefully written after envisioning in your mind what you want the video to look and sound like, editing is as easy as following a recipe. Here's what the first page of an A/V script looks like.

"BAREFOOTIN' THROUGH LIFE"
Show Open

VIDEO	AUDIO
Various shots of Rick water-skiing and goofing around.	(STEVE) (Hard-Sell) FOR NEARLY 30 YEARS RICHARD WILLIAM KRUG VOWED HE WOULD NEVER MARRY…
Rick flipping on water ski. CUT to himself talking on-camera.	(RICK) "I just thought I would water-ski for the rest of my life."
SLO-MO shot of Steve looking amazed.	(STEVE) YET JUST A FEW SHORT WEEKS AGO CAME A STARTLING ANNOUNCEMENT …
Chris ON-CAMERA	(CHRIS) "Rick and Kim are engaged! I can't believe it! Finally!"
Shot of Rick walking from behind, he turns, pushes away camera.	(STEVE) NOW… IT'S THE STORY BEHIND THE STORY.
SLO-MO shot of Rick sitting in boat making Jim Carrey-like faces.	(STEVE) WHAT MADE THIS FREE-WHEELING JOKESTER, WILD-MAN-WATERSKIER DECIDE TO TAKE THE PLUNGE?
Kim ON-CAMERA	(KIM) "If he didn't ask me soon, I was getting ready to walk."

continues

Show Open (continued)

VIDEO	AUDIO
	(STEVE)
STILL PHOTO—Rick Childhood	EXPLORE HIS CHILDHOOD …
Shot of Rick fixing boat	DISCOVER HIS SECRETS …
Slow C/U PAN of Rick water-skiing	JOURNEY INTO THE HEART AND MIND OF ONE MAN …
GRAPHIC Title ________	(STEVE) RICKY KRUG … BAREFOOTIN' THROUGH LIFE.

In this case, after carefully screening all of my footage, it was easy to determine exactly what shots I was going to use. The only time I used any audio from the original footage is when there's a soundbite in the script. The soundtrack mainly consists of narration and music. (For more on narrating your home videos, see Chapter 12, "Your Supporting Cast.") With this type of video project, the only time you'll want to use original audio is when there's an interesting sound that can enhance the listening experience, such as water splashing and boat noises when someone is water skiing.

Here are some A/V formatting rules you can follow:

- Narration, camera instructions, locations, and other elements like sound effects, transitions, still photos, and graphics should be in all caps.
- Shot descriptions and sound bites should be in title case (initial cap).
- Try to align your supporting video shots as close as possible to the corresponding audio for easy reading.

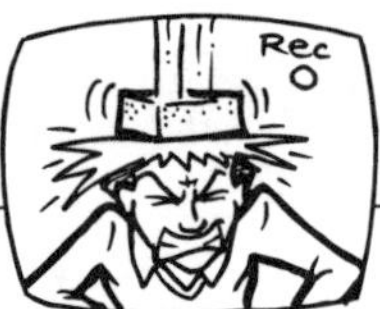

Blooper

An A/V script can be formatted easily using the "Tables" feature in any word processing program. But if you revise the script at all, watch out for the rest of the column falling out of alignment. There's nothing worse than printing out and trying to work from a misaligned A/V script.

Screenplay

Dramatic home movies are entertaining and one of the most popular ways to have fun and get the most out of your camcorder. And, if you're interested in filmmaking as a career, it's a great way to learn the ropes of movie making. If famous Hollywood directors like Robert Rodriguez and James Cameron began their careers shooting and editing home movies, you can, too.

Your mini-movie is simply a story that is shot and edited in Hollywood style. Hollywood also offers something else that home videographers can take advantage of: the screenplay script format. The screenplay packs together a ton of useful production information, and its uncluttered design lends itself to easy reading and understanding.

As the writer of a screenplay or mini-screenplay, you lay down the groundwork for many aspects of your movie, including action, scene location, characterization, and dialog. Screenplays are written as full-page documents, from margin to margin, and use upper-/lowercase characters to help differentiate between elements.

Here is a scene from a screenplay by William C. Martell called "Crash Dive." William has written 17 films for cable and video. (You can read all of his scripts at http://ourworld.compuserve.com/homepages/wcmartell.)

CRASH DIVE

FADE IN:

EXT. SUB COMMAND — DAY

A sign outside the building identifies it as: Submarine Command, Admiral A. J. Pendelton, East Coast Operations.

An aging sports car skids to a stop in front of a No Parking sign, and JAMES ALLEN CARTER climbs out, manila folder over flowing in one hand, a cup of coffee from home in the other.

Carter is USN, Ret. He's on the wrong side of 40 but still in shape. Unshaven, hair wind-blown, clothes look like he's slept in them. Coffee cup exclaims the joys of Bass Fishing. He jogs to the door, careful not to spill his coffee.

INT. SUB COMMAND, HALLWAY—DAY

Carter jogs down the hall, evading the occasional UNIFORM.

INT. PENDELETON'S OFFICE—DAY

ADMIRAL PENDELTON, a leonine man with a booming voice, is going over paperwork when the door bursts open.

CARTER

It was right there in the specs. The electromagnetic field was interfering with the missile's gyroscopic guidance system, and ...

Pendelton takes the folder from Carter, smiling.

PENDELTON

I'll read the report.

CARTER

(smiles)

No, you won't.

Pendelton flips through the paperwork, then looks at Carter.

PENDELTON

Had a team of MIT engineers on this for three weeks. You solved it in...

Carter looks at his "countdown watch".

CARTER

Twenty seven hours and twelve minutes.

(resets watch)

You have a check for me?

Pendelton hits his intercom, talks to his secretary.

Unlike the A/V script, a screenplay is usually written before it's shot. That's because most, if not all of the dialogue and action is written to be acted out by willing participants.

Here are some basic screenplay formatting rules that you can use as guidelines:

1. Action/Description: 1.5 inches on left, 1 inch on right.
2. Dialogue: 3 inches from left, 2 inches from right.
3. Character Names: 4 inches from left.
4. Parentheticals: 3.5 inches from left.
5. Page numbering: 1/2 inch from top of the page and 1 inch from right edge.
6. Characters are introduced in ALL CAPS.
7. Use abbreviations: INT. = Interior. EXT. = Exterior.
8. Single space in Action/Description and Dialogue.
9. Double space between Action and Dialogue.
10. Double space between different character's dialogue.
11. Double space between the "slug line" (INT. DOGHOUSE—DAY) and Action.
12. Try to keep Action blocks to 4 lines (or less) in length.
13. (OS) after dialogue means the character is Off Screen. (VO) after dialogue means it's a Voice Over narration.

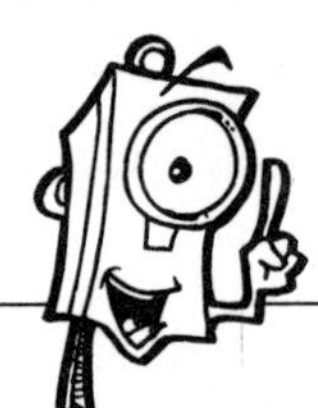

Candid Camera

Screenplay Lingo:

CU—Close-up
ECU—Extreme close-up
MCU—Medium close-up
EXT—Exterior
INT—Interior
SFX—Sound effects
V/O—Voice Over

Scriptwriting Glossary

Here's some vocabulary you can use to shape your home movie screenplay. Again, these are typical Hollywood terms. You can come up with any words that will make things the easiest for your productions.

- **CUT:** A transition between two shots where one shot instantly cuts to the next. This is the most common editing technique.
- **DIALOG:** Spoken words in the script between actors and actresses.
- **DISSOLVE:** A transition between two shots in which one shot melts away into the other.
- **ESTABLISHING SHOT:** Usually a wide-angle shot at the beginning of a scene that establishes place.
- **NARRATION:** Spoken voice over information that is relayed to the audience by a narrator or one of the actors/actresses.
- **PAN:** The side-to-side rotation of the camera. If the camera is following an actor as he walks by, it is considered to be panning.
- **SETTING:** The time and place of any given scene.
- **SHOT:** A single run of recorded film or video footage.
- **SOUND EFFECT (SFX):** Audible additions to the sound track to support or enhance action. SFXs can also be ambient. In other words, if an actress is walking on the beach and there is no sound recorded at the time of the shot, ambient ocean noise can be added.
- **TALENT:** Actors, actresses, or anyone else who appears on screen in your video or movie. The voice/over (V/O) artist is also considered talent.
- **TILT:** The up and down movement of the camera.
- **TRUCK:** Physically moving the camera forward or backward. The sideways movement of a camera. This can be done with a dolly.
- **ZOOM IN:** When the camera's focal length is brought from a wide-angle to a close-up.
- **ZOOM OUT:** When the camera's focal length is brought from a close-up to wide-angle.

For more information on scriptwriting, here is some recommended reading:

- *The Art of Dramatic Writing, Its Basis in the Creative Interpretation of Human Motives*, by Lajos Ergi
- *The Complete Book of Scriptwriting,* Revised and Expanded, by J. Michael Straczynski

- *The Complete Guide to Standard Script Formats, Part I: The Screenplay,* by Cole/Haag
- *Creating Unforgettable Characters, A Practical Guide to Character Development In: Films, TV Series, Advertisements, Novels and Short Stories,* by Linda Seger
- *How to Write a Movie in 21 Days: The Inner Movie Method,* by Viki King
- *Lew Hunter's Screenwriting 434, The Industry's Premier Teacher Reveals the Secrets of the Successful Screenplay*, by Lew Hunter
- *Making a Good Script Great,* 2nd Edition, by Linda Seger
- *Screenwriting: The Art, Craft and Business of Film and Television Writing,* by Richard Walter
- *The Screenwriter's Problem Solver, How to Recognize, Identify, and Define Screenwriting Problems,* by Syd Field
- *The Screenwriter's Workbook, Exercises and Step-by Step Instruction for Creating a Successful Screenplay,* by Syd Field
- *Story, Substance, Structure, Style, and the Principles of Screenwriting,* by Robert McKee
- *Writing the Script, A Practical Guide for Films and Television,* by Wells Root

Besides books, there are also numerous software titles that help you format your scripts and that can actually help you with story structure and plot by analyzing what you've got and offering suggestions.

- *Movie Magic™ Dramtica Pro:* Story development—Screenplay Systems Inc.
- *Write a Blockbuster:* Story development—truby's Writers Studio
- *IdeaFisher™:* Story development—Idea Fisher Systems Inc.
- *Write Pro®:* Story development—The Writepro Corporation
- *Fiction Master:* Story development—The Writepro Corporation
- *Three By Five:* Story development—B. C. Software Inc.
- *Storybuilder:* Story development—Seven Valleys Software
- *Plots Unlimited:* Story development—Ashleywilde Publishers
- *Writer's Blocks:* Story develoment—Ashley Software
- *ComedyWriter:* Story development—Ideascapes
- *FirstAid for Writers:* Story development—The Writepro Corporation
- *A Zillion Kajillion Rhymes & Cliche[as]s:* Rhyming dictionary /Cliché thesaurus
- *StoryCraft:* Story development—Storycraft
- *ScriptWizard™:* Script processing—Warren and Associates
- *Final Draft™:* Script processing—B. C. Software

- *SideBySide™:* Script processing—Simon Skill
- *ScriptThing™:* Script processing—Scriptperfection Enterprises
- *Movie Magic™ Screenwriter:* Script processing—Screenplay Systems Inc.
- *Scriptware®:* Script processing—Cinovations Inc.

Writing scripts for your home video projects, be it a special occasion shoot or a home-made mini-drama, can help you hash out your ideas well before you begin shooting. The most important thing to remember is that you don't have to be Hemingway to start putting words on paper. Your goal is to bring your ideas to life on the screen. So even if the script you write is a simple list of scenes or shots in the sequence that you want to shoot, pull out that pen and let it rip. One written word can be worth a thousand pictures.

The Least You Need to Know

- Having a plan in advance is the best way to tackle any home video project.
- Writing a script is easy and fun once you learn how to effectively put your thoughts on paper and stop writer's block in its tracks.
- There are many formatting rules in scriptwriting; find one that works best for you and alter it to fit your needs.

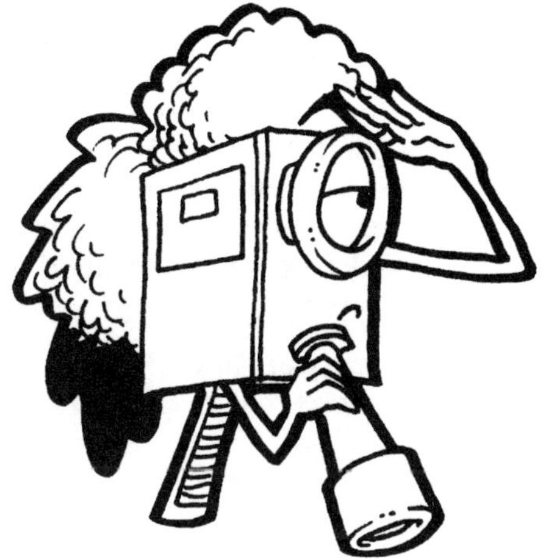

Chapter 8

Scouting Out Your Location

In this Chapter

- ➤ What are you going to need?
- ➤ Obtaining permission to shoot
- ➤ Predicting the weather on shoot day
- ➤ Potential outdoor pitfalls
- ➤ Livening up your set with props

Attempting any video production without scouting your location in advance is like trying to plan a wedding at a place that you've never seen. Whether you're going to videotape a birthday party, or make a training video for your business, you are committed to the location that you choose, and there are always potential pitfalls and challenges that need to be discovered and dealt with in advance.

If you don't have the time to scout, take a few minutes to visualize your location. Since scouting will invariably affect the look and sound of your video, this will be time well spent. From assessing your on-location equipment needs and obtaining permissions and shooting permits to predicting and planning around factors you can't control like the weather and lighting, you're going to have your stuff together way before you hit that record button.

Deciding What to Bring

There's nothing more frustrating than arriving the day you plan to shoot to discover that you've forgotten to pack an extra videotape, battery, or any other essential item or accessory. In the real world, travelling light is usually a good thing. In the world of serious videography if you don't need at least two people to carry your stuff it means you probably don't have enough equipment to pull off your production. Less is never more when you're on location. Missing equipment is the quickest way to ensure that you'll be back again to shoot the same thing until you get it right.

So take some time to consider what you'll need on the day of your shoot. Whether you're shooting indoors or outdoors, the following are questions that can be answered by a pre-production inspection.

- ➤ What are the lighting conditions like?
- ➤ Is it quiet, or is there a lot of external noise?
- ➤ Are there any power supplies available to you? Will you be able to plug in your lights, camcorder, and audio equipment?
- ➤ Will there be any other unusual circumstances that could affect the lighting, audio, or power on shoot day?

Answers to these questions will have a major impact on what kind and how much equipment you'll need.

The most difficult element that you have to control on a shoot is lighting, and it's a lot easier when you've got an on-board light, or even better, a lighting kit. (For more on working with lights see Chapter 9, "Cast Some Light on the Matter.") For any type of production a lighting kit is invaluable and makes your home video look like it was shot by a pro. You can also get pro results from available or natural light, but you may have to pack special lens filters, adapters or possibly collapsible light reflectors to make up for the difference.

Next is the audio. If you're going to be recording natural sound, the on-camera mike may be sufficient. But if you're shooting someplace like a museum or a theater, the omni-directional on-camera mike will pick up every sound, and not necessarily the one you were hoping for. That means you may want to bring a directional shotgun microphone, or if you're shooting interviews, bring a clip-on or lavalier microphone. If it's going to be noisy, headphones are perfect for monitoring your audio and blocking out distracting external noise.

So chances are you're probably going to be bringing a lot of stuff along with you. If you don't have a reliable power source, either a stockpile of spare batteries or an adequate power outlet that can handle everything you've got, you might as well just take the day off. You can never bring too many extension cords, adapters, cables, and converters. Especially if you're taking your production overseas, make sure to find out the power requirements of the specific country and purchase as many adapters as you can afford and carry. (They can be heavier than lead!) Radio Shack is a great place to find a power converter. If you are shooting indoors, locate the outlets and plot the paths of your extension cords in advance to avoid a spaghetti mess that people can trip over while you're shooting.

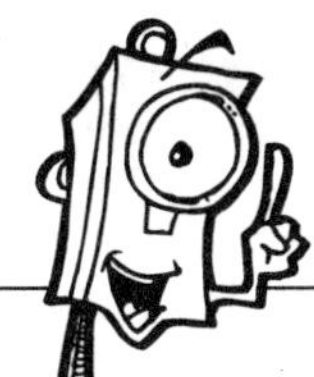

Candid Camera

There are several things you can do to increase your battery life. Never leave the camcorder on between shots, and if possible, flip it into manual mode. Auto focus and exposure suck the life out of your battery. Many camcorders have an "instant focus" feature that momentarily does an auto focus, then switches back to manual. This is a great way to lock focus without draining your battery.

Whether you're scouting your location in advance, or planning it in your head, here's a checklist which will help you sort through your equipment needs:

- **Spare Batteries:** Both for the camcorder, lights, and microphones.
- **Tons of Spare Videotapes:** This is the last thing you want to run out of!
- **Extension Cords/Power Strips/Adapters:** Wrap them around your arms and legs if you run out of carrying space.
- **Spare Light Bulbs:** On a bad day, these can blow as often as once an hour. On a good day, you'll definitely blow at least one.

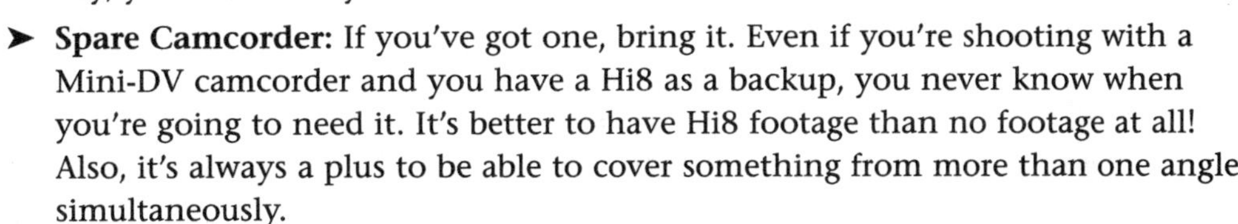

- **Spare Camcorder:** If you've got one, bring it. Even if you're shooting with a Mini-DV camcorder and you have a Hi8 as a backup, you never know when you're going to need it. It's better to have Hi8 footage than no footage at all! Also, it's always a plus to be able to cover something from more than one angle simultaneously.
- **Gaffer's/Duct/Electrical Tape:** These are great to have in your bag of tricks the day of the shoot. You can tie down wires to increase safety on the set, you can even hide a lavalier microphone with the stuff. There's not a movie set in the world that doesn't have at least 30 rolls of Gaffer's tape lying around.
- **Toolkit:** No matter what you're shooting, indoors or outdoors, bring a toolkit. If something breaks, you can pull out a screwdriver or even needle-nose pliers and fix it.
- **Battery Charger A/C power supply:** If you're shooting indoors and there are outlets available, there's no reason to rely on batteries unless you plan to be moving around a lot.

The Bare Minimum

The good news is newer MiniDV, SVHS, and Hi8 camcorders depend less on this bulky equipment in order to capture great-looking video. They use longer tapes (up to 120 minutes) and last longer than ever before on a single battery charge. In addition, these efficient image grabbers are designed to shoot well in all sorts of bad lighting environments, like in a school auditorium or in a basement. As camcorder technology continues to mature, CCDs are getting more sensitive to light and cutting-edge circuitry offer all kinds of digital solutions to low light situations. Cutting the lighting gear out of the video equation can certainly be a back-saver.

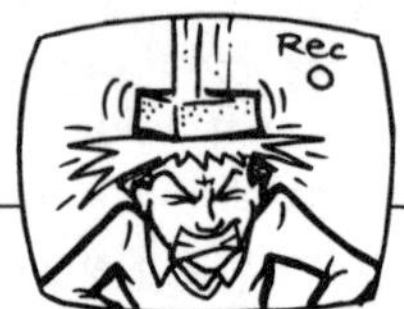

Blooper

Lighting gear is notorious for hogging up power in a single circuit. Familiarize yourself with the power requirements of your lights and try to dedicate one power hungry light to one circuit sector or zone. This may mean more and longer extension cords, but it's much better than blowing a fuse in the middle of a shot.

As you get more experienced, you'll find yourself in shooting situations where you can't avoid packing truckloads of gear that you'll need to hire a video crew to help you manage. However, in the beginning you're not going to want to tote much more than your camcorder and maybe a few essential items in your camera case. You also want to keep your personnel requirements to a minimum as well. You want to start yourself off slowly and work into higher profile and more interesting projects.

This is not to say that a lighting kit or a good hand-held or lavalier mic will not significantly add to the production value of your projects. But camcorder manufacturers, using technology to give personal productions a boost, are in turn allowing consumers unarmed with any video extras to begin to catch up to prosumers and professionals who have an arsenal of stuff at their disposal.

Be Polite! Don't Forget to Ask Permission

Ever had a run-in with the long arm of the law? You will if you try to shoot somewhere that prohibits the use of lights, camcorders, or microphones. You may be thinking, it's a free country, right? I should be able to videotape whatever I want, as long as I don't get in anybody's way or pose a threat to anyone.

Unfortunately, shooting on location isn't that simple. People in general become very curious when a movie or video is being shot. I live near N.Y.U. in Manhattan where moviemaking is one of the biggest rubbernecking events. A shoot can also interrupt traffic, both automotive and pedestrian. In fact, they shut down an entire block for the movie *Deep Impact* and filled it with fake cars and extras fleeing a giant tidal wave. (Incidentally, the filmmakers shot for three days, and the resulting sequence in the movie lasted for only four or five seconds!)

Depending on the location that you choose, the potential downsides of shooting is taken into account and restrictions are often placed. If you're shooting in a store, business, restaurant, shopping mall, etc. the specific organization reserves the right to decide whether or not they want you to shoot. You can usually get away with shooting on a street or any other public space as long as you're not interfering with traffic or risking public safety in any other way.

As a general rule, the less equipment that you have and the less people you have at your side, the better your chance of getting permission to shoot. If it's just you with a camera and a friend, wife, or child with a small bag of gear you may stand a better chance at getting permission because of the perceived small scale of your project.

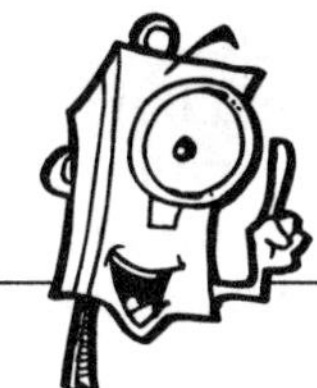

Candid Camera

Armed with a small Hi8 camcorder (or even better, a palm-sized MiniDV), you can get away with shooting professional quality video in the field without being hassled for a permit.

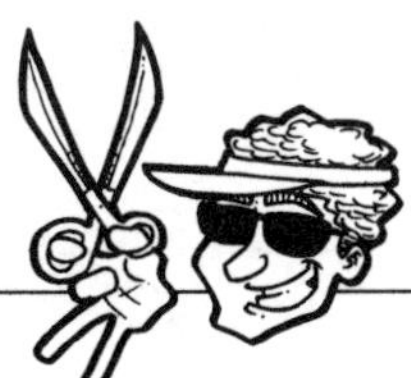

Director's Cut

If you're planning a shoot that requires a permit or involves the cooperation of public authorities or private property owners, it's a good idea to find a contact person at your location to help you organize the details of the shoot. A contact can also help you get permission to shoot, give you a personal tour, and help you figure out what you can expect from the location.

But if you've got a big-time project on your hands and you want to shoot in heavily populated areas like a city or crowded parking lot, you almost always need to get a permit from the town, city, organization, or business that owns the property. That means you need to find out if the locale has its own film commission and if it does, it's time to get the ball rolling on the stack of paperwork that needs to be filled out. If you hate paperwork, you might want to consider giving up higher-profile projects altogether because unfortunately, it's part of the game. Also, private property owners are concerned with the purpose of your project. Is it commercial, educational, or personal? This will impact whether they grant permission or not. (For example, a museum may let you shoot with a hand-held camera—no tripod—without specific permission; but if you want to bring in personnel and equipment, you need permission; and if it's for commercial purposes, there's a good chance they will ask for a fee if they grant permission.) If you are shooting in a national or state park, the Parks Commissioner or Supervisor can often grant you the rights. Depending on the size of your production, permit fees can get costly, so if your project isn't worth the money, consider choosing a new location.

Can Your Shoot Weather the Storm?

There's nothing worse than the feeling of icy cool raindrops dripping down the back of your neck. Imagine how your camcorder would feel if water somehow made its way into the sensitive electronics inside? One step short of cloud seeding, we have no way to control the weather. But as technology emerges and the Internet helps us disseminate information, we're definitely getting much better at predicting it.

But these days, who can you trust when it comes to weather forecasting? You've got a lot invested in your production. You don't want to be the victim of false predictions.

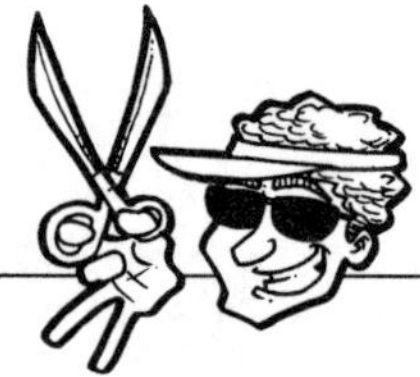

Director's Cut

"Weather forecasts are updated about every six hours with the first new report coming out around 5 a.m. Each new forecast is based upon new weather data, so by checking in regularly with radio or television weather reports on the day of your shoot, there should be no surprises from the sky above. Keep in mind that each season offers its own weather challenges depending upon your geographic location. The dreaded pop-up afternoon thunderstorm is a summer headache to forecast especially throughout the southern United States, while rain or snow squalls can appear quickly in winter time, most commonly in mountainous regions as well as across the Great Lakes and the Northeast. Spring can provide areas of severe weather throughout the Midwest. If your looking for predictability, look to fall when weather patterns usually offer no surprises, and you may find longer periods of dry weather."
—Nick Gregory, Meteorologist, Fox 5 News, New York

You can always start with the meteorologist on your local newscast. Most of the time, they can get you a pretty accurate prediction of what you can expect on the day of the shoot. They can't always tell you exactly when it's going to rain, but they get astonishingly close in letting you know what the chances of precipitation are, thanks to all kinds of weather satellites, radar, computer models and all sorts of other high-tech equipment. Counting on a prediction a day in advance is still risky because depending upon where you live, those sudden, unexpected storms can crop up and force you to close down for the day.

So what are your options? Depending on the size of your production, the more you're at the mercy of Mother Nature. If you're not shooting a specific function or event, it's always a good idea to build possible rain dates into your schedule. If you are shooting something like a sports event, plan for the worst case scenario even if the prediction is for sunny skies. You never know when a thunderstorm might be lurking around the corner.

Let's say you're shooting your cousin's wedding on a rainy day, and you need to get a shot of the bride and the groom walking down the steps to the limo as they leave for their honeymoon. The wedding video simply wouldn't be complete without this shot. The best thing to do to protect your camcorder from the downpour is to outfit it with raingear that you can find in most camera stores. Some are hard-shell like underwater housings. Others offer a soft, waterproof wrap with easy access to your camcorder's controls. As for yourself, you probably don't want to ruin that tuxedo, so don't forget to pack your rain parka. Golf and sporting goods stores sell all kinds of raingear. You should look for something light that can be folded away to almost nothing when not being used.

Here are a few places on the Internet where you can get up-to-the-minute weather reports:

- **Accuweather Inc.:** www.accuweather.com/weatherf/index_corp
- **America Online Inc.:** www.aol.com/mynews/weather/home.adp
- **CNN Interactive Weather:** www.cnn.com/WEATHER
- **EarthWatch, Inc.:** www.earthwatch.com
- **Intellicast:** www.intellicast.com
- **Massachusetts Institute of Technology:** www.mit.edu/weather
- **National Weather Service, NOAA:** www.nws.noaa.gov
- **Unisys Weather:** http://weather.unisys.com
- **The Weather Channel Enterprises Inc.:** www.weather.com/twc/homepage.twc
- **WeatherNex:** http://cirrus.sprl.umich.edu/wxnet
- **The Weather Underground Inc.:** www.wunderground.com

Planning a Shoot in the Great Outdoors

When you're planning to shoot indoors, you hardly have to worry about unstable lighting conditions, scarce power supplies or unpredictable weather. But when most

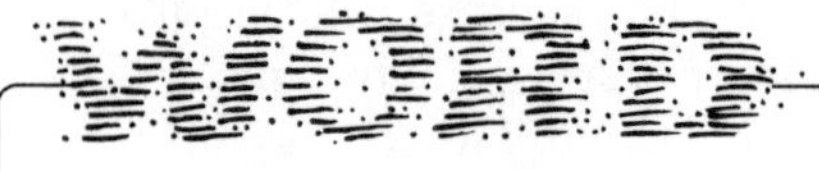

Blurred Word

In videography, **natural light** refers to sunlight. In many cases you can pull of your shoot in natural light without any additional lights.

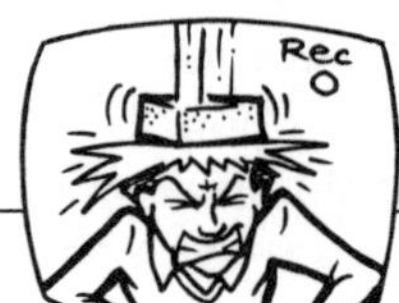

Blooper

Try to maintain continuity by shooting all shots in a scene at the same time of day under similar lighting conditions.

of your project will be shot outdoors, the slightest variation can really throw a monkey wrench into your plans.

Just as we can't control the weather, the same is true about the sunrise and sunset, or cloud cover. The only thing we can do is try to the best of our ability to plan around these unforeseeable events and hope for the best.

Relying on natural light, especially when you have a large production at stake, can be like waiting for your boss to give you a raise. It's a game of hit and miss. Sometimes luck takes over. Sometimes you go down in flames. Just hope that you get lucky on the projects that really count.

In the planning stage of your project, it's important to determine exactly how much of an impact the climate is going to have on your shoot. If you absolutely need sunny skies and a clear day, you can't really set a date in advance. You have much more flexibility if your shoot location is close to home, or if you can live with a little cloud cover in your videos. If you're shooting a wedding or any other event-specific project, you need to plan for any and all unforeseeable weather or climatic conditions.

Here Comes the Sun

Sunlight can help you paint beautiful pictures with your video if you time it right. I try to avoid mid-day shooting if possible because the sun is directly overhead and often casts unflattering shadows across my shots and the video tends to look too bright or blown out. For shots that I feel need a dramatic edge, I wait for "Golden Hour" when the sun is low on the horizon while either rising or setting. The deep-orange glow that floats in on an angle offers all kinds of artistic and dramatic opportunities. (See Chapter 9 for more on lighting.)

You Could Dew Without

Here's a sticky situation that comes up occasionally while shooting outdoors: condensation from excessive humidity. It happens to cold drinks and air conditioners; it can also happen to your camcorder.

On some camcorders, there's a warning light that alerts you to excessive moisture; on other camcorders, you might not ever know it's happening at all. But over time, it can wreak havoc on your camcorder's insides.

The only way to avoid the problem is to avoid exposing your camcorder to extreme temperature variations. Let's say you kept your camcorder in an air-conditioned hotel room all night. In the morning, you rush out to do a shoot in the Everglades. You will probably have a moisture problem.

The other way to help decrease temperature shifts is to wrap your camcorder in a towel to protect it from the elements. After about 20 minutes, your camcorder will adjust to the environment. If you get the warning light, bring the camcorder inside and pop open the tape door to help evaporate the condensation.

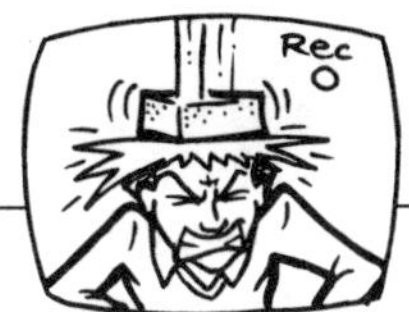

Blooper

Before you go painting your bedroom wall remember that the background only needs to be as big as you plan to frame your subject. If you are shooting close-ups, then your background doesn't need to be more than 5 feet × 5 feet.

Liven Up Your Location!

You arrive at your location to begin production. You turn your camera on and point it where you want to shoot—but something's wrong. The shot doesn't look half as good as you imagined it would. You move the camera up and down and back and forth for different perspectives, but nothing seems to work. The backdrop for your project looks distracting.

It's time for some simple set dressings. If your shot is going to stay in the same place for a while like during documentaries, shows, or performances, the easiest way to jazz things up is to introduce a new background into the shot. Good quality textured or painted backgrounds are expensive to buy, but easy and fun to put together by yourself. Combine these masterpieces with a colored lighting scheme, and you've got yourself a professional looking backdrop.

You can make a background out of anything, colored cardboard, plywood or an old sheet or blanket. If you're looking for a textured background, you can always find materials in a store where knitting, fabric or sewing supplies are sold. The background can be constructed simply by tacking or stapling the textured materials to the backdrop.

The easiest way is to use a combination of colored paint and colored lighting schemes to create a professional looking background. Shades of white and gray work best because when you aim colored light on the surface, you can have any color in the rainbow. It looks even cooler if you lightly add in a second color to add texture. You can get colored lights at any photo-video store. (See Chapter 9.)

If you don't have the time to mess with your background, you can easily liven up your shoot with props. An on-camera prop can be anything from a box of tissues to a telephone. If you're shooting indoors, the most common method of propping is to collect all of your best furniture and knick-knacks and use them to inconspicuously decorate the backdrop.

Recently, I shot a music video with Malik Yoba, star of the Fox TV series *New York Undercover*. We shot in a sound stage at the Chelsea Market (a *New York Undercover* favorite location). The script called for several setups, including an outdoor cafe scene (which was shot indoors), a living room scene, a bedroom scene, and a hallway scene. The challenge was to build all of these locations, including the outdoor cafe, within the confines of a sound stage that wasn't overwhelmingly big. The Art Director on the shoot somehow managed to pull it off by borrowing furniture and exotic decorations from several members of the crew, and other colorful set decorating goodies like satin covered pillows, multi-colored drapes, and fine paintings. When we finished editing, nobody believed us when we told them that it was all shot in one location. It's amazing how far a few well-placed props can go.

Wherever you're shooting, take a careful look around. If you don't mind doing some lifting, things can be arranged and rearranged to fit the needs of your production. You can easily turn indoors into outdoors by using patio furniture and appropriate set dressings and props like curtains, table cloths, dishes and utensils. You can even use an open indoor space like a large living room or a garage as a soundstage. This way, you can free yourself from the confines of trying to shoot in an actual room that is too small to maneuver your video gear.

From the simplest of home video productions to more complicated projects, a quick tour of the location in advance will make your life a lot easier come shoot day. And familiarity with your location will also make it easier for you to tackle those unforeseen pitfalls that are waiting for you around every corner. Be it too few outlets, or too many thunderstorms, you'll figure out a way to keep shooting!

The Least You Need to Know

- You can never have too much gear at a location. Always put some thought into your equipment needs well before the shoot.
- If you think you might need permission to shoot at your chosen location, you probably do. Forgetting or overlooking this puts your entire production in jeopardy.
- Weather conditions can also stop you in your tracks, but these days weather forecasting is becoming more of an exact science.
- Excessive sunlight and moisture can cause problems if you're not aware of them.
- Even the simplest prop or decoration can change the entire look of your video.

Chapter 9

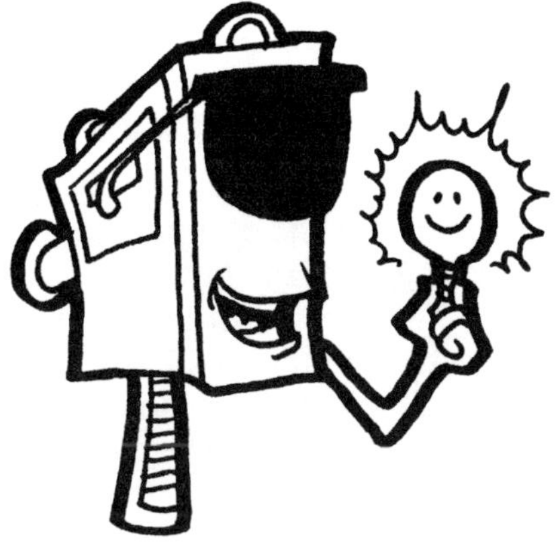

Cast Some Light on the Matter

In This Chapter

- The nature of light
- Three-point lighting
- Shooting in sunlight
- Hollywood lighting you can do at home

It doesn't matter if you're shooting with a $1,000 camera or a $50,000 camera, or if you're shooting on VHS-C or MiniDV. It doesn't matter if you've hired the Director of Photography from *Saving Private Ryan* to shoot your home video for you. If your lighting is crummy, your video is crummy. End of story. Lighting is the single most important factor in videography.

Combine a little lighting knowledge with your own creative vision and you will enhance the quality of your home videos by leaps and bounds. If you're willing to settle for ordinary looking home video footage, camcorders are incredibly versatile and designed to shoot in all kinds of light conditions. But if you want your videos to look more professional, it requires that you pay close attention to the amount of light hitting a scene, the angles in which it's hitting and the creative mixture of light and dark areas in your picture. And if you think you have to be a millionaire to afford all of the accessories needed to design with light, think again. Get ready to become a lighting professional with a few simple items you have lying around the house.

What Makes Light Tick?

You don't have to be a physicist to understand the nature of light and learn how to harness its power for your home videos. With a few basic principles under your belt, you'll be able to magically flick lightning rods from your fingertips. That's because light behaves in a very predictable way, and once you figure out its little quirks, your videos will look better than they ever have.

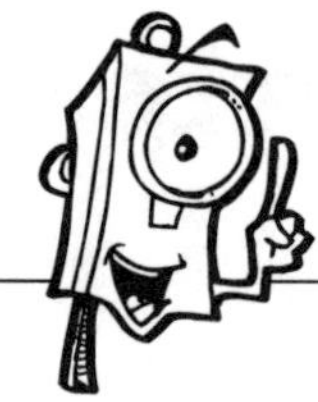

Candid Camera

Whenever you are designing a lighting scheme, indoors or outdoor, try monitoring your shot on a professional video monitor or any other TV set you can get your hands on. Viewfinders and pop-out LCD screens are notoriously inaccurate in portraying how lighting design is going to look on a real TV set.

One of the most interesting aspects of light behavior is perhaps its most puzzling. It's called the "Inverse Square Law," and it has a great effect on how close or far you place your subject away from the light source. It works like this: Since light travels in a circular pattern away from the source, the intensity is cut by a factor of 4 every time you double the distance from your subject. In other words, just because you've moved the light twice as far away, it doesn't mean you'll have half the light. You'll have much less, 25 percent to be exact. With this in mind, it makes it easier to adjust the lighting in your videos by adjusting your subject's distance from the light source. After experimenting and playing back your footage, you will develop a good feel for the effect that distance plays on lighting.

Another predictable aspect of light behavior is that it always travels in a straight line until it is absorbed or bounced in another direction. If you've ever aimed a flashlight at a mirror, you'd know what I'm talking about. Once you've figured out how to make light go where you need it, you can fill in shadows, soften bright lights and creatively tinker with your lighting design.

If you are using a lighting kit, most of the individual lights come with "barn doors" (see figure) which are side and top flaps that allow you to increase or decrease the amount of light hitting your subject. You can also aim the light more accurately while creating subtle shapes and shadows.

Color Temperature

If you are reading these words right now, it can be deduced that

- Somewhere nearby or overhead there's some kind of electrical lamp, fireplace or candlelight illuminating the room.
- You are outdoors or near a window and reading this by sunlight.
- It is night, and you are catching adequate rays from the full moon to read this book.

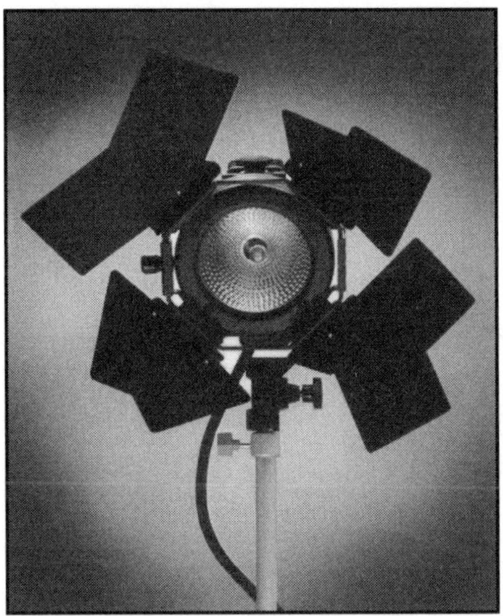

Video light with barn doors.
(Courtesy of Lowel-Light Manufacturing, Inc.)

No matter what kind of light source it is each emits a slightly different color. This is called *color temperature,* and it is measured in degrees on the Kelvin scale. This has a big impact on the overall color of your videos. Let's say you're wearing a white T-shirt. If you shot video of the shirt both indoors and outdoors and then compared the footage side by side, you would notice a difference in the shade of white. The human eye automatically and continuously corrects for different color temperatures. Unfortunately, your camcorder can't do this as effectively.

Light sources with higher color temperatures have a bluish quality, while lower ones tend to be more orange. While shooting, if you combine too many lights with different color temperatures, it can wreak havoc on your footage and throw your camcorder's auto-white balance into a funk. If you have a basic idea of the color temperature of the light sources that you're using, it's easy to learn how to mix and match.

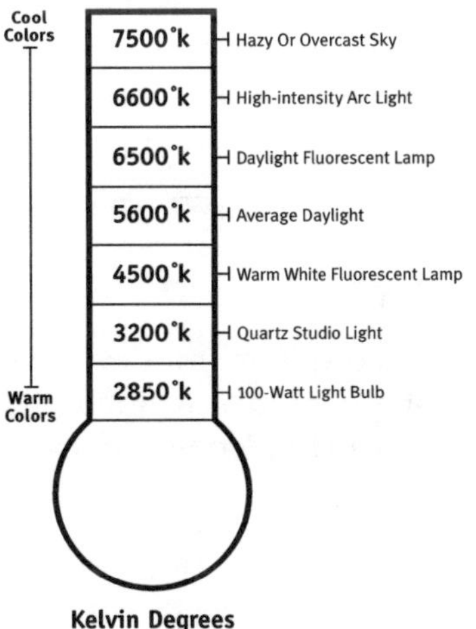

The color temperature scale.

Let's say you're using a lighting kit, and you decide to add a few standard household bulbs into the mix, along with some sunlight that's creeping in through a window. You'll notice that the household lights look yellow and the sunlight looks blue. Sometimes a mix of different color temperatures can be pleasing to the eye, but it takes a lot of practice to master the art. When you're starting out I'd recommend sticking with as few sources with different color temperatures as possible. If you're getting a blue tint in your video, figure out which light is causing it and shut it off and pull another light closer to the subject to make up for missing light.

Here are a few light sources that can easily sneak their way into your videos. They all vary in color temperature and, when mixed together, can have an ill effect on the overall color dimension of your video.

- Direct or indirect sunlight
- Overcast sky
- Car headlights
- Fireplaces
- Candles
- TV sets
- Fluorescent lamps

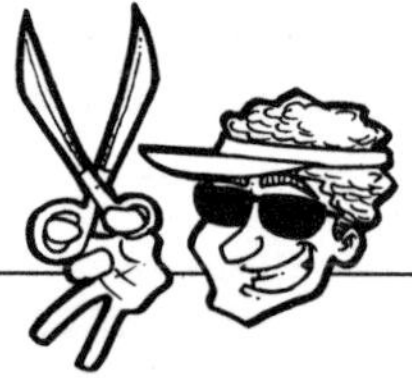

Director's Cut

Here's a professional solution that you can employ in your own videos. Whenever you're shooting in a room with windows, cover the entire window with a special film that prevents the color temperature of the sunlight to clash with the indoor lights. This film can be purchased for a few dollars at photo/video stores and looks a whole lot better than just closing the shades.

Just the Right Amount of Light

If you shoot with inadequate light, your video suffers from intense grain and unrecognizable colors. If you use too much light, your video will look washed out and harsh to the eyes. To shoot aesthetically pleasing video you must land somewhere in the middle.

My dad works at ABC in Manhattan as a video editor. When I was a kid, he used to take me to see *World News Tonight with Peter Jennings,* and I was amazed at how brightly lit the studio was. I even had the opportunity to sit in Jennings' chair once, and when my dad flipped on the studio lights, I felt like I was being abducted by a UFO! The intensity and heat was overwhelming and I remember wondering how Peter sits night after night without swimming away in sweat!

So when I started making my own home videos, my first instinct was to grab every light in the house and attack my subjects with a barrage of rays. But unlike the professional ABC studio cameras that thrive on bright light, my camcorder didn't react well to the high beams. The colors in my video were running, blotchy, and the picture was just plain overexposed.

In any home video project, too much light can leave lens flares, spots and bleeding. Thanks to your camcorder's ultra-sensitive CCD and iris, your video doesn't need a strong light source to record images. It can record in everyday light situations, but it records best in a predetermined range of light intensity that, depending on the camcorder, is geared toward consumer uses.

Outdoors, you can control the amount of light hitting the CCD by using a neutral-density filter. This cheap and easy-to-find filter goes a long way in salvaging video that would have otherwise been blown-out and unwatchable.

The best way to become familiar with the lighting scheme that works best with your camcorder is to experiment. Try grabbing some common household lamps and experiment using the three-point lighting method (see below: Basic Three-Point Lighting). Keeping in mind the Inverse Square Law, change the distance of your subject from the light source. Before you know it, you'll find the perfect balance and your video will be teeming with vibrant colors, and attractive contrast and shadows.

Too Much Light and Dark in One Place

Comparing the human eye to your camcorder's CCD, your camcorder can only handle one-eighth the contrast range that your eye can. It's a huge difference that's often to blame for one of the most common lighting mistakes: poor contrast. If something looks good to the naked eye, it doesn't mean that it's going to look good to your camcorder.

Once you can recognize the calling card of poor contrast, then you've made it past one of the biggest home video roadblocks. The easiest way to control contrast is to simply splash more light on dark areas of your picture, or take light away from bright areas. The goal of this is that you still want to be able to make out detail in both the dark and light areas of your video. But since lighting for video is more art than science, you must figure out how to create attractive light areas and interesting dark areas. Like most lighting techniques, the best way to become a master of contrast is practice.

Outdoors, the biggest contrast problem is the sun (see the "Director's Cut" sidebar below). Reducing harsh light/dark areas usually means moving the subject into shade, or diffusing the sunlight before it hits the subject. (Some easy techniques are discussed below under, "Let the Sun Shine in Your Videos.")

Indoors, you'll run into problems when the lighting scheme creates a lot of shadows in your shot. The best way to manage shadows is to fill them in with additional illumination (see "Basic Three-Point Lighting," below), or to filter out or redirect the light rays. Two common methods of doing this are using a colored filter over the light itself, or to use an umbrella to soften direct rays. You can buy either of these accessories at any photo/video store.

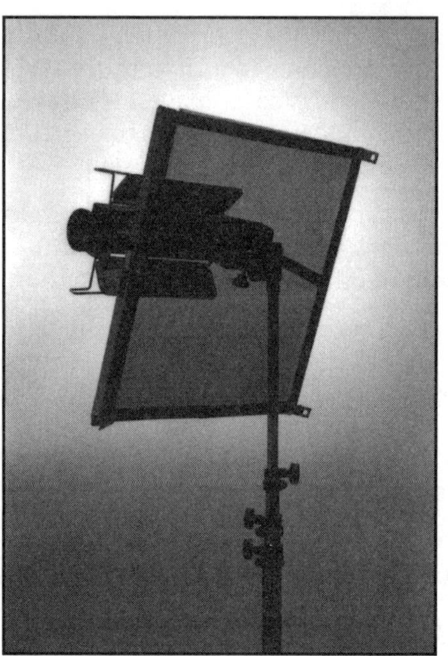

Lighting filter.

(Courtesy of Lowel-Light Manufacturing, Inc.)

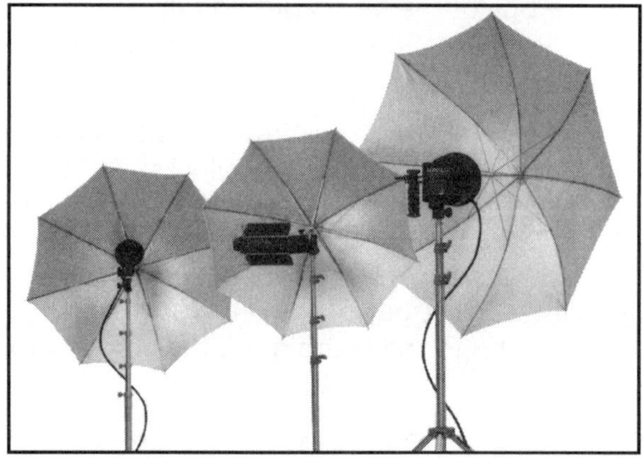

Umbrellas.

(Courtesy of Lowel-Light Manufacturing, Inc.)

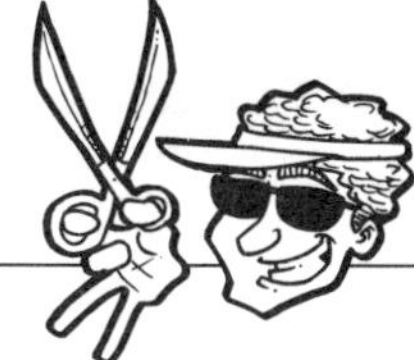

Director's Cut

"Whenever I'm planning an outdoor shoot and I suspect that it's going to be a bright, sunny day, I try to schedule shooting between 8:30 am and 11:30 am, and later in the day from 4:30 p.m. to about 6:30 or 7:00 p.m. When the sunlight is coming in from an angle, it's easier to avoid or use to your advantage than when it's directly overhead."
—Chris Ward, Senior Writer/Producer, Showtime Documentaries

Basic Three-Point Lighting

Whether it's too much or too little light, contrast or mixed color temperatures, there seem to be so many things that can go wrong with lighting. But once you've worked past making lighting mistakes that can ruin your videos, it's time to get really creative. There's a lighting design for every video that you shoot, and whether you've got a lighting kit, the sun at your back, or the nightlight in the hallway, you can make your own home videos look like real movies.

Whether your video is happy, sad, romantic, scary, or bursting with action, a combination of your newly found knowledge of light characteristics, and a simple technique called three-point lighting, will take you to the next level of home videography. Three-point lighting is a technique that is specially designed to help you choose the right lighting intensity, the right mix of lamps with different color temperatures, and to paint pictures with contrast. The three points are:

1. Key light
2. Fill light
3. Back light

Here's how three-point lighting works. All you need to know are the basics to get started and a little bit of practice to get really good.

The Key Light

The most direct and intense light in the three-point scheme, the key light casts most of the illumination that falls on your subject. Lighting professionals commonly use the comparison of a clock to illustrate how three-point lighting works. Think of your subject smack in the middle of the clock, (as viewed from above) and the camcorder is at 6:00. The key light is commonly found somewhere in-between 4:00 and 5:00 and elevated to an angle of 30 to 40 degrees over the subject, low enough to keep light from directly shining into the subject's eyes. This is usually referred to as the neutral position.

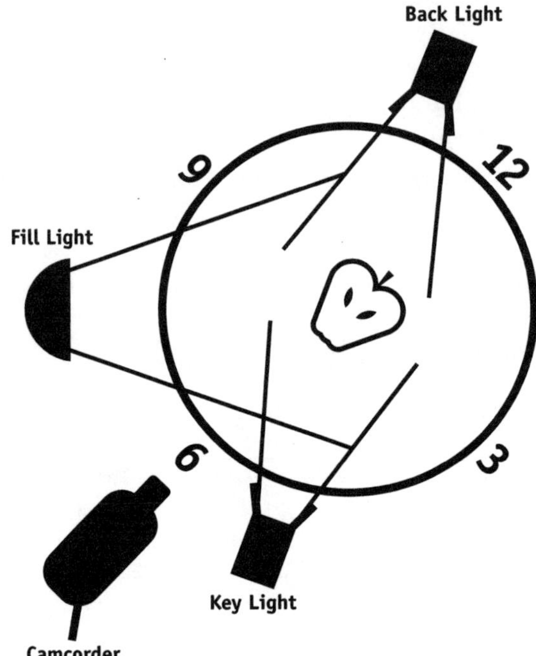

Basic three-point lighting.

With the key light in this position shadows are created, giving your picture a three-dimensional feel. When you vary the placement of the key light, you change the mood and feel of the shot. If you're looking to create a dramatic or romantic mood, you can move the key light toward the 3:00 position. This will create a dramatic half-shadow across the subject's face. By placing the key light behind the subject at the 12:00 position, a halo or ring forms around the subject, creating a weird or scary look. If you place the key light at the 6:00 position, you will create a flat, shadowless image. This is a common lighting design for newscasts and interviews.

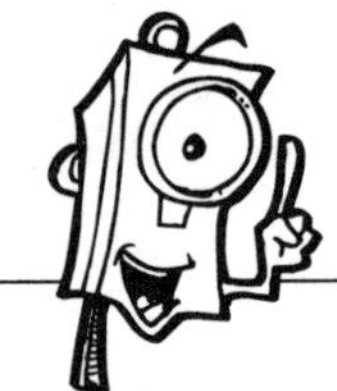

Candid Camera

When you are using the key light behind the subject, you can create silhouettes by aiming the light at the background and not the subject.

Key lights have two categories that they fall under, "hard" and "soft," and which one you choose has more of an impact than where you place these lights.

- *Hard light* intensifies the subject's outline, and makes even the slightest detail pop out of the screen. What's confusing is that "hard lights" are smaller, more distant sources like the sun.
- *Soft light,* on the other hand, reduces lines, especially on the face, and sets forth a much warmer, film-friendly look. "Soft lights" are usually larger and closer to the subject.

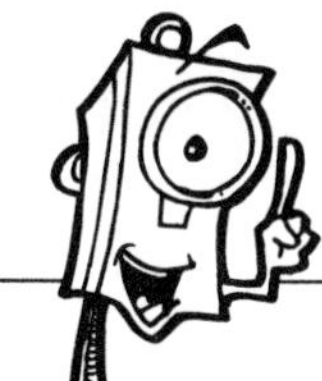

Candid Camera

If you are shooting indoors and there are no windows visible in the shot, the fill light tells the audience whether it is day or night outside. A higher intensity fill can help simulate daylight while a lower intensity fill suggests nighttime.

The Fill Light

The second light in the three-point mix, the fill light is usually larger and softer than the key light. Its primary function is to fill in shadows. Both indoors and outdoors, you can also use a reflector as a fill light. Some lighting experts argue that the fill light plays a more crucial role than the key light in the three-point lighting scheme because it is often used to help establish the time of day and the mood in a scene.

The neutral position for the fill light is across from the key light at the 8:00 position, elevated at an angle of 20 to 30 degrees above the subject's head. This position greatly reduces shadows cast by the key light. When you adjust the intensity of the fill light, the overall mood of the scene, which is greatly influenced by shadow, can change from straightforward to dramatic.

The Back Light

The third link in the three-point chain, the back light is called upon to separate the subject from the background. Similar to placing the key light behind the subject, the back light creates a halo around the subject's head and shoulders, creating a more three-dimensional image. The back light is usually placed somewhere around 11:00 and at a higher angle than the key or fill lights.

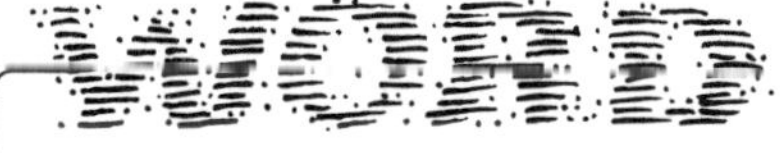

Blooper

If you're using a back light, make sure that it is not shining directly into the lens of the camcorder. This can cause ugly lens flares and it will often distract your camcorder's exposure system. Also, make sure that the light itself is not visible in the shot.

You can also choose to use a back light with a hard or soft quality. The brighter the back light in the scene, the more dramatic it looks. Pay close attention to the hair color of your subject. The lighter the hair, the less back light you should use.

In addition to using back lights, also consider using a background light to illuminate the background area in your shot. This creates a feeling of depth and helps to separate the different elements in your scene.

Let the Sun Shine in Your Videos?

Through the eyes of a lighting designer, that enormous ball of fiery gas at the center of our solar system is actually considered a small light source. It may give us life, dictate our seasons, and turn night into day, but it doesn't do much for your home videos except cast harsh shadows, increase areas of light and dark (contrast) and highlight surface flaws in people's skin and the environment. Any skillful lighting designer, however, can work around the limitations of shooting in direct sunlight.

Shooting on Borrowed Time

Unless you are shooting breaking news or a live sporting event, the easiest way to deal with sunlight is to avoid shooting in it at all. But if you have no choice but to shoot, the time of day will greatly affect the lighting condition.

Schedule your shooting time in the morning and late afternoon when the sun is at more of an angle in the sky, perfect for dramatic lighting design. Sometimes called "the Golden Hour," it's a time that videographers and moviemakers utilize to the fullest extent.

If you're stuck shooting midday in bright sunlight, keep one thing in mind: shade is your best friend. If you can shoot under an awning, the shady side of a tall building, or under a tree, your video is going to look much less washed out and overexposed.

Recently, I was shooting a documentary in Sydney, Australia, and with only a week to get all of our footage, we were on an extremely tight schedule. On the third day, the sun was shining bright and we were packed wall to wall with locations. In an emergency, we sent the production assistants to find a location for a two-hour long interview. They came up with a beautiful tree canopy that ran through the middle of Hyde Park. It was about a quarter of a mile long, but the canopy enabled us to do a walking and talking shot the entire length of the park in beautiful lighting conditions.

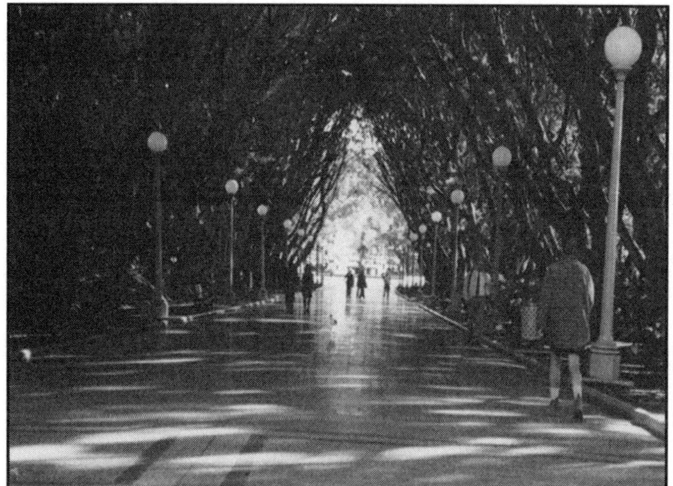

The perfect place to escape the blazing sun: A tree canopy in Hyde Park, Sydney, Australia.

Reflecting Sunlight

The sun emits enough light that you can use the sun's own rays to help eliminate the harsh shadows that the sun itself creates. Reflection is the name of the game and it is one of the most common methods that lighting designers use in direct sunlight. In fact, a reflector of any kind is one of the most valuable items you can keep in your lighting toolkit, and you don't have to be a millionaire to buy one.

Professional reflectors are reasonably cheap items at any photo-video store, but if you don't feel like shelling out the bucks, you can use just about anything that reflects light. White Oak tag (or foamcore) works well because one side is usually shiny and the other one is flat. The shiny side is great when you have really dark shadows that need to be filled. The flat side is perfect for softening harsh rays. You can also use aluminum foil, matte-board, or even large sheets of white paper.

Try experimenting with using reflectors in your shots. Place your reflecting mechanism of choice at different angles and different distances from the subject. With a little practice, you'll figure out the perfect mix of distance and angle to best fill shadows. Here's the only catch. You're probably going to need at least one other person either shooting or doing the reflecting, because reflecting light is something that you can't leave to its own devices. You need to constantly move and readjust the reflector as your subject moves. Or, you can purchase more professional reflectors that mount on stands. These can be easily redirected with the turn of a screw.

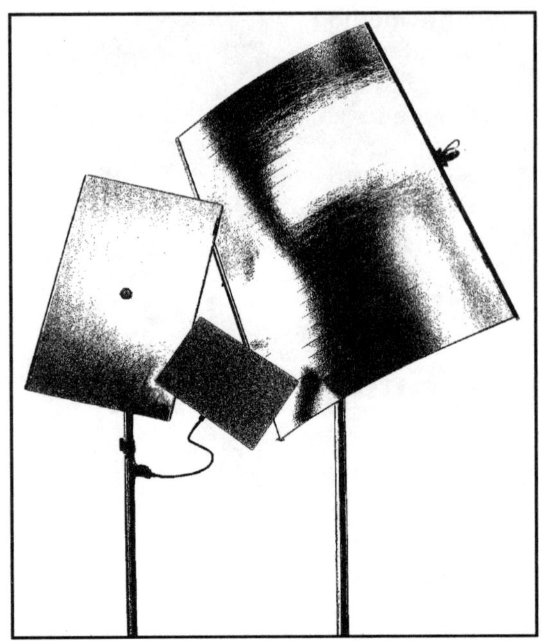

Professional reflectors.

Diffusing Sunlight

While reflection is great for eliminating harsh shadows in your video, diffusion is used by lighting experts to reduce the harsh contrast that sunlight creates. You can easily diffuse sunlight by actually placing an object between your subject and the sun. This can also be done using simple materials that you can find at home.

Since diffusion actually blocks the sun's rays and cuts down on the overall intensity of the light, it's a more comfortable method of sunlight control for your subject. If it's done properly, diffusion gives you most of the benefits of shooting outdoors on a cloudy day, including colors that are sharp and bright, and balanced lighting with little or no contrast or shadows.

I often use stark white bed sheets to diffuse light, but you can use anything that is thin enough to allow light to pass through. In gardening supply stores you can buy shade netting made to protect greenery from direct sunlight. Or, you can use drop cloths for painting that are commonly found in hardware or paint stores. Photo and video stores also sell inexpensive fabric diffusers that can be neatly folded up.

The next challenge is finding a way to prop your diffusion material above your subject and out of the video frame. I had my friend who enjoys carpentry as a hobby build me a frame made out of wood. It's light enough to hold over my head and large enough to diffuse whatever I'm shooting. If you want a lighter frame, you can build it out of PVC tubing.

Another sure-fire method of diffusing sunlight is the use of lens filters for your camcorder. Polarizing, neutral density, U/V (ultra-violet), or diffusing filters are invaluable tools in softening the harsh rays of the sun. This is especially true on humid days when the air is full of moisture, creating hazy sunlight conditions that can cause all sorts of problems with your footage.

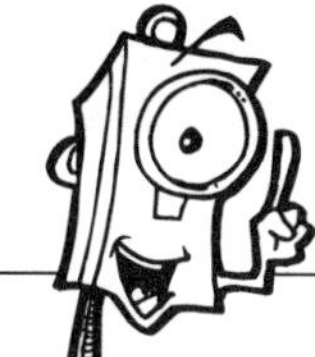

Candid Camera

No matter how sturdy or light of a frame you build for diffusion material, it's extremely hard to hold it steady. I often attach my diffusion frame to a painter's ladder with C-clamps. If you do mount your diffusion frame, watch out for the wind. It's no fun apologizing to an interview subject after the entire rig falls on her head after a strong breeze!

Hollywood Lighting on a Shoestring Budget

You don't need a van filled with expensive professional equipment to get close to the same results that Hollywood lighting professionals get in movies. In fact, most shoots can be pulled off without one piece of professional gear.

Any light that you have at home that can be unplugged and moved is a useful commodity for your production. If the light isn't providing enough illumination, slide it forward. Thanks to the inverse square law, most lamps that you can get your hands on will provide adequate illumination.

Here's a list of easy-to-find household items that are perfect for your lighting toolkit:

- **Quartz-halogen shop lights:** These low-cost lights usually cost anywhere from $10 to $20 and sometimes come with their own stands.
- **Car sunshades:** These come in different sizes, shapes, and colors and are great light reflectors. The best kind for video are the ones that have silver on one side for reflection and white on the other for soft reflection and diffusion.
- **Foamcore:** This cheap, lightweight board is great to have in your lighting bag of tricks. It can be shaped into any size that suits your production, and can be used as a reflector or diffuser.
- **Bed sheet:** Any thin, white sheet is perfect for diffusing harsh light.
- **Shade netting:** This is normally found in gardens to protect plant life from direct sunlight. Works just as well as professional video diffusion fabrics in blocking the light of the sun.

- **Aluminum Foil:** Taped to cardboard or any other flat surface, aluminum foil is one of the best reflective sources you can find. The shiny side is great for hard shadows, the dull side perfect for soft. If you crumble the foil and then unfold it, the light that bounces off the surface is nicely diffused, creating soft shadows.
- **Clothesline and clothespins:** Perfect for draping and suspending diffusion material like bed sheets and diffusion netting.

Whether you're a novice looking to experiment with how lighting can improve your home videos, or a more serious shooter with plans to make a major motion picture with your camcorder, a basic knowledge of lighting fundamentals will help you bring your videos to the next level. And as you can see, you don't need to spend thousands on lighting gear since most of what you need is already at your fingertips.

The Least You Need to Know

- Understanding the nature of light will help you control and direct it in your home videos.
- A basic three-point lighting scheme is the best way to achieve balanced, professional-looking footage.
- Shooting in direct sunlight isn't as easy as you may think.
- You don't have to be a millionaire to put together an arsenal of professional lighting gear.

Chapter 10

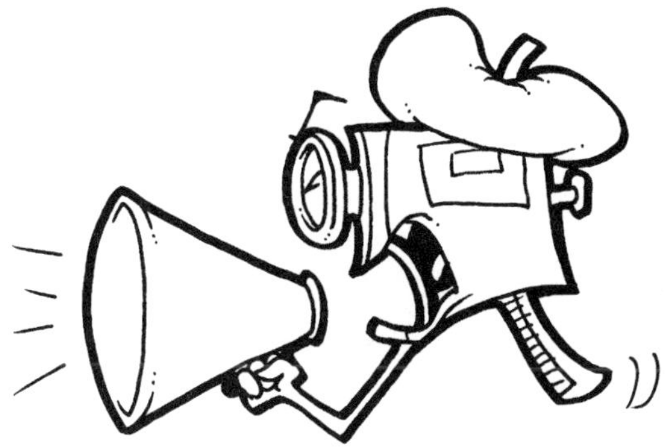

Quiet on the Set!

In This Chapter

- The truth about camcorder mics
- Inside microphones
- A quick tour of external mics
- Keeping things nice and quiet
- Using portable audio mixers

Home videos are synonymous with bad audio. When someone yells, "Quiet on the set!" while shooting a Hollywood feature film, people listen. When you're out shooting with your home video camera, if you were to yell, "Quiet on the set!" people would think that you had a few screws loose.

Since you can't control people sounds or any other type of external noise on your home video sets, it's time to employ semi-professional and professional audio-recording tactics. It sounds intimidating, but once you have a basic understanding of audio, it's not much more involved than buying a decent external microphone and mastering a few sound-saving strategies. Whether it's background noise, wind noise, crowd noise, appliance/machine noise, or traffic noise, after reading this chapter you'll know how to choose the right equipment and the best location for audio recording.

On-Board Camcorder Mics Don't Cut the Mustard

Last Wednesday at about 7:30 a.m. when my 10-month-old son Ben woke up, my wife was too exhausted to get out of bed. After several minutes of negotiations, I got up and took him to the living room to play while I did a few things around the apartment before work. Ben was chit-chatting away, so I sat down to watch him for a while. He was obviously happy to be hanging out with me so early in the morning. Then, all of a sudden, it happened. He looked up and with a crooked little grin on his face, he said the words I'd been waiting to hear for a long time: "Da da."

I launched from the couch and grabbed the first camcorder I could find and hit record. It turns out my boy is a natural actor. He stood up, came over to the camcorder, and had a lengthy face-to-face conversation with the lens. I got a few great soundbites. He said "Da da" again and "Ma ma," he even slipped in a "Pa pa" or two. I was elated because I knew that I could incorporate these clips into his one-year birthday party video that I had been planning.

It wasn't until later that I made a horrible discovery. The soundtrack of Ben's movie contained a lot more than just his voice. I had forgotten that I had turned on the dishwasher, and traffic on Fifth Avenue at that time of the morning was starting to heat up. Through the noise and car horns I could barely hear him speaking his first words. That's what I get for trusting my camcorder's built-in microphone.

Unless you're planning to shoot in a vacuum or on the set of a Hollywood film, in most cases your camcorder's mike isn't going to cut it—especially if you plan to watch your videos over and over or edit together a program for others to watch.

Close, But Not Close Enough

Which audio recording is going to sound better: a $1,000 microphone 20 feet away from the sound source or a $10 microphone two feet away? If you guessed the $10 mic, you're absolutely right. Rule #1 in recording audio for video: The closer you are to the sound source, the better your audio is going to sound.

This is a big problem for the average shooter who's concentrating on getting nice video shots because the distance that it takes to record quality video is usually too far away for recording sound. That's why camcorder mics are designed the way that they are, to pick up every sound possible. Camcorder manufacturers have good intentions in that they want audio recording to be idiot-proof, but they often forget about those of us who want our soundtracks to be noise-proof.

Luckily, manufacturers provide you with a way out of this mess ... the ability to add an external microphone to your video camera. But if you don't have access to one, there's something that you can do to get the most out of the on-board mic. First, you can forget about shooting video for a few minutes and move forward for an up close and personal audio recording of your subject by using your camcorder as a microphone only. After you're satisfied with the audio, then concentrate on shooting video. You can easily edit together your clean audio and good video later on.

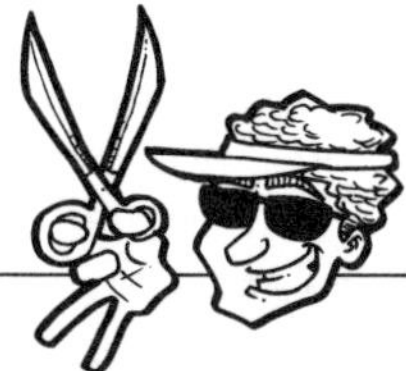

Director's Cut

In certain situations, you can use your camcorder in the place of a mini-tape recorder. You can even leave the lens cap on while recording to make it less distracting. This is perfect for classrooms, lectures, speeches, meetings, and so on. (See Chapter 25, "Getting Creative with Your Camcorder," for more interesting camcorder uses.)

When it comes to videotaping children, you'll find that your soundtrack is often compromised because much of the footage is shot from above or too far away. (See Chapter 11, "Setting Up Your Shots.") A good soundbite from your child is especially rare.

Little Camcorders Have Big Ears

Camcorder ears are big—too big, in fact. Camcorder mics are omni-directional, which means that they are designed to record sound from all directions, favoring ever so slightly the sound that is out in front. Let's say a red-tailed hawk decided to build a nest in your backyard. It would be great to hear the sound of the baby chicks chirping inside, but you'll have to get dangerously close to get a clean recording. Chances are you'll be shooting from a great distance away and your audio track will probably consist of the neighbor's lawnmower and the jumbo jet flying overhead.

Annoying external noises aside, your camcorder is going to have the biggest problem wrestling with wind-noise. Some camcorders have a wind-filter switch, but it usually doesn't work very well.

You can try turning your back to the wind so the mic is protected. This can be tricky, though, because trying to predict which direction the wind is going to blow next is like trying to anticipate in which direction a hovering dragonfly is going to dart. You can also seek shelter from the wind under big trees or behind houses and buildings. The best thing to do is to avoid wind altogether. If possible, shoot in the calm hours, clear weather, or indoors if it's too windy.

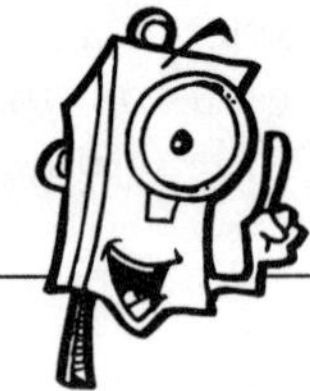

Candid Camera

One wind-breaking solution you can try is to carefully tape a cut-out piece of foam, cloth, bed sheet, blanket, or even a torn up T-shirt over your camcorder's microphone. You will definitely drown out some of the external garble, but it can leave your audio track sounding slightly muffled.

Additionally, most camcorder users also do battle with the system that controls the levels of on-board mics. The automatic gain control or AGC keeps audio input levels at an even keel by raising and lowering the volume as needed. When someone is speaking directly into the camera of if there is a loud noise nearby, the AGC will adjust the levels accordingly. If there is silence, the AGC will boost the record levels so even the slightest background noise sounds louder than a Pearl Jam concert.

The best way to get AGC under control is to turn it off altogether. If you're noticing excessive tape hiss or distortion from this feature, check to see if your camcorder has the ability to be switched into manual audio mode. If you carefully monitor your audio with headphones and make the necessary adjustments, your audio track will be much cleaner.

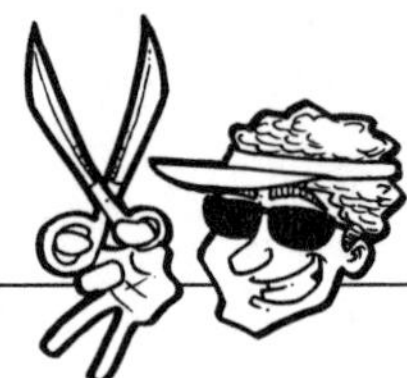

Director's Cut

Besides picking up all sorts of external noises, the AGC unfortunately picks up the sounds of the Zoom, Focus, and other camcorder buttons. The best thing to do if you're hearing these noises is to switch your camcorder into manual mode. Try to avoid zooming in and out since this feature is the biggest audio offender. As for button noise, only press them when it's absolutely necessary, or practice hitting the buttons gently to eliminate unwanted ambient noise.

Camcorder Zoom Microphone Myth

When you bought your camcorder, one major selling point may have been that it comes with a zoom microphone. But if you've ever tried it out you know that it sounds very weird when you zoom from wide angle to telephoto. That's because it's impossible for even the most expensive microphones to actually expand and contract the distance from the camcorder in which it records sound to perfectly match the camcorder's zoom. What's happening is the camcorder blends two different microphone signals together as the lens zooms in. One is a stereo microphone (both ears) that works well with the wide-angle setting; the other is a mono directional microphone (one ear), which matches the lens's telephoto position. This awkward transition from stereo to mono is unnatural and on many camcorders this feature can be overridden.

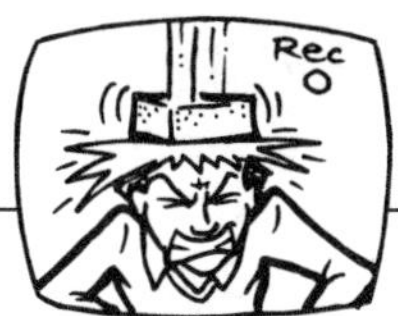

Blooper

Different types of microphones have different types of jacks. Since most consumer camcorders use stereo mini-plugs for microphone inputs, double-check with your salesperson that you have the right connectors for your camcorder.

Microphones Unplugged

So by now you probably get the picture. Camcorder mics play it by ear—a near-deaf ear, that is. If you want your home videos to be free and clear of the odious audio stigma it's time to think about adding an external microphone to the mix. Whether it's a lavalier, handheld, or shotgun mic, it'll make a world of difference in your audio track.

But before you rush out and spend hundreds on one, you should understand how each one works, and what they do in a given audio situation. Let's unplug a few of them and see how they work.

Pickups

Big, small, fat or skinny, all microphones perform the same task. They convert sound waves into electrical impulses that shape an audio track on tape. Each kind of microphone has its own pickup element that is responsible for converting raw sound into electricity. Most microphones have three different types of designs: dynamic, condenser and pressure zone (PZM).

Dynamic microphones are commonly found in consumer and semi-professional mic models. The pickup element is a moving coil that sparks a chain reaction between a diaphragm and a magnet creating electrical energy in the coil. These microphones are cheap, rugged, and, if you get close enough, provide decent quality audio.

A condenser pickup consists of a diaphragm that's attached to a condenser and a preamp that uses an external power source to increase the strength of the signal. It's much more delicate than dynamic pickups but the downside is they need a power supply, usually batteries.

Pressure zone pickups (PZM) have tiny elements suspended just millimeters above a solid surface inside the microphone. When these elements are disturbed they create sound waves that are then converted into electricity. PZM mics are high quality and are industry famous for their ability to reduce echo and background noise resulting in superior quality recordings.

Pickup Patterns

Microphones are also classified by their pickup patterns, omni-directional or uni-directional. The pattern in which the pickups are arranged will play a big part in how much of the outside world the microphone can hear.

We've already established that almost all on-board camcorder mics are omni-directional since they pickup sounds in a near-360 degree arc around the shooter. They're cheap, unselective in what they hear and record background and wind noise just as easily as they record a videographer narrating a scene.

Uni-directional mics, on the other hand, also known as "cardioid" because of their heart shaped pattern, pick up sound from one direction. A uni-directional mic is able to focus on the sound source you're pointing it at, reducing clutter, reverb, and other external noise from your sound track.

Uni-directional mics look much cooler than omni-directional mics and they cost more, but the difference in performance is worth the price of admission.

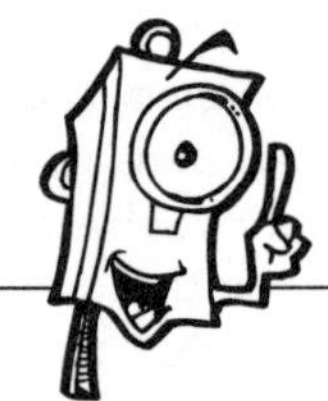

Candid Camera

The hypercardioid or superdirectional pickup pattern narrows the microphone's audio focus even further than a uni-directional microphone. It's like a mic on steroids, allowing you to shoot even further away and still record clean directional audio. These are the kinds of mics used during sporting events like football and basketball and are among the most expensive on the market.

External Mics in Action

In Chapter 3, "Cool Extras… Do You Need the Bells and Whistles?" we learned how much external mics cost and how they work. Now it's time to take a closer look at lavalier, handheld, and shotgun mics, and how and when to use them.

If you have a combination of a lavalier, handheld, and shotgun microphone in your audio bag, you've got what it takes to tackle any audio situation.

Lavalier

Sometimes referred to as "body" or "lapel" mics, lavaliers (lavs) are the most versatile microphones you can buy. When I first bought my camcorder, I bit the bullet and bought both a wired and wireless lavalier. It was one of the best video accessory purchases I ever made. The lavs are incredibly versatile and can be used in a wide array of audio situations. In emergencies I've been known to hold the lav tightly in between my thumb and forefinger and use it like a handheld mic for impromptu interviews.

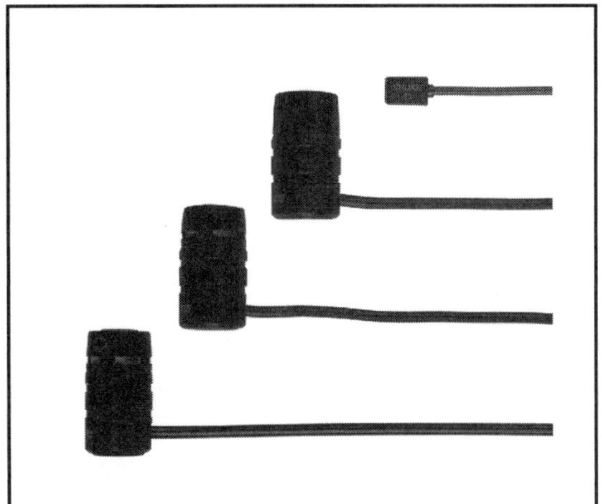

Lavalier (lav) microphones.

But when you clip it on, it's where you place it that's going to have the biggest impact on your sound. Most lavs are designed to be clipped somewhere on the source's chest in order to interact with the resonance or natural buzzing quality of a human voice. Usually clipped onto the seam of a button-down shirt, chest pocket, or any other invisible location, it takes a little time to position it for optimal audio. Aim for anywhere between 7 to 10 inches below your subject's chin. If you bury it too far underneath the chin, your audio is going to sound muffled. Too low, and your audience will be privy to the fact that your talent skipped breakfast since stomach rumbles are easily picked up.

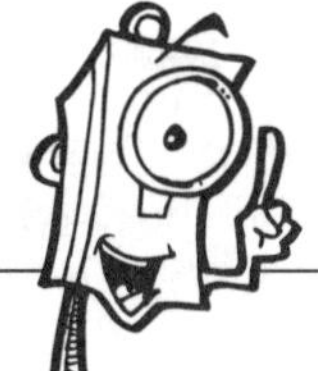

Candid Camera

When placing a lavalier mic, wear headphones and do several run-throughs of "Testing 1-2-3" to make sure you have healthy levels and a clean, balanced sound. In addition, headphones should always be worn (regardless of the type of mic you're using) while shooting to monitor audio.

If you're shooting outdoors or if you think that your subject might have a problem with popping P's, use a windscreen. (Most external mics come with a windscreen.) This may be a problem if you're trying to hide your mic but it's the best way to filter out unwanted noise. Don't forget about the lav once it's clipped in place. Keep checking to make sure that the head is pointing directly toward your talent's mouth. You can use a small piece of tape to help you keep it pointed in the right direction. Also, you should reposition or take off necklaces and other jewelry or clothing that may come into contact with the lav.

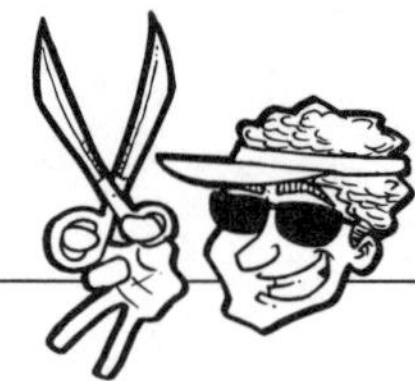

Director's Cut

The best place to run a lav cable is up through the shirt (jacket or coat) and out either through a button-down shirt, sweater, or out over the collar. You'll need to muster up the courage to politely ask your interview subject to snake the cable up for you. It makes for an embarrassing moment, but it's better than seeing an ugly cable running the length of your talent's body on camera.

Wireless Lav

You can place and position a wireless lav in the same manner as you would a wired lav, but there's a transmitter unit that you have to find a place to hide on the talent. Additionally, there's a potentially cumbersome receiving unit that you have to attach to yourself, or your camcorder. You can hide the transmitter in the talent's pocket or the back of a belt, but avoid the talent sitting on it. Since most cable noise originates at the point of connection, make sure all of the cables have plenty of slack in them.

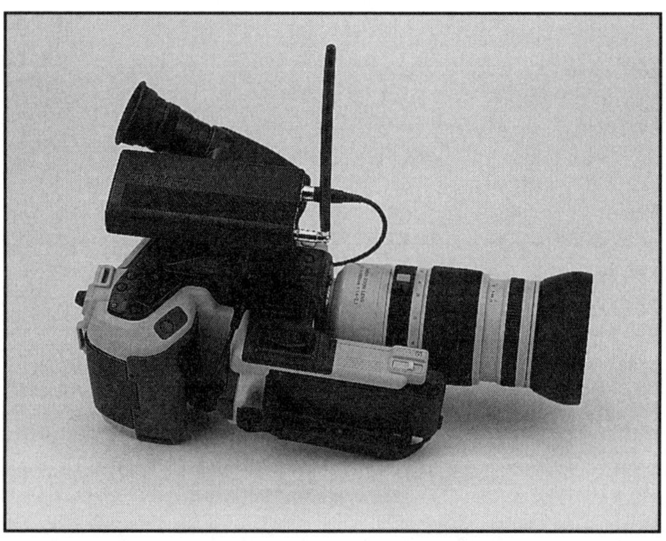

Camcorder equipped with wireless lavalier receiver.

The main pitfall with wireless microphones of any kind is that the batteries always seem to go dead at the wrong time. I have a cardinal rule when it comes to batteries. Whenever I'm starting a new shoot, I replace the batteries, regardless if the last shoot only lasted for 5 minutes. It may cost a little more money, but it's better than losing a nice chunk of audio because of a blackout.

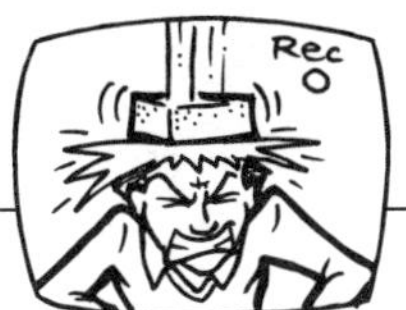

Blooper

Since wireless lavs come with long cables (between the mic and the transmitter), when hooking up talent avoid bunching the extra cable into a ball or loop. This can turn a mic cable into an antenna for unwanted radio signals, creating all sorts of funky noises on the soundtrack.

In the Palm of Your Hand

Handheld mics are staple items in any camcorder bag. They come in all different pickup types and patterns, competing with the lavalier microphone in versatility. The only drawback is that it's much harder to hide a handheld mic and they can distract the viewer's eye from the subject of your shot.

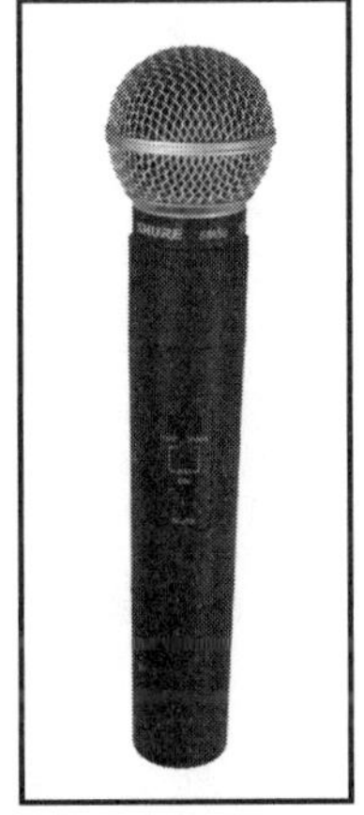

Handheld mic.

Many handheld mics also come lined with shock and noise eliminating material or foam that drastically cuts down on hand noise while holding and moving the mic around. Omni-directional handheld mics are the backbone of almost every major news organization on the planet because they can record human voices and ambient sound equally as well. Cardioid handheld mics cut down on external noise, making them perfect for interviews, music event and live recordings, but they aren't optimal for ambient sound.

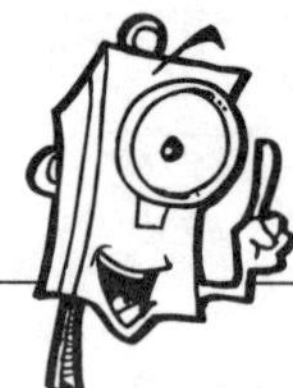

Candid Camera

Unlike a lavalier which requires a distance of 7 to 10 inches from the subject's mouth, handheld mics should be placed as close to the mouth as possible for clean sounding interviews.

Handheld mics can also be secured on mic stands in order to record audio great distances from the source. Wedding and event videographers often use a wireless version of the handheld mic that is great for interviews or leaving it next to a speaker to record the band while shooting the dance floor.

Have Gun, Will Travel

If you want to make your camcorder look as cool and professional as possible, outfit your unit with a directional shotgun mic.

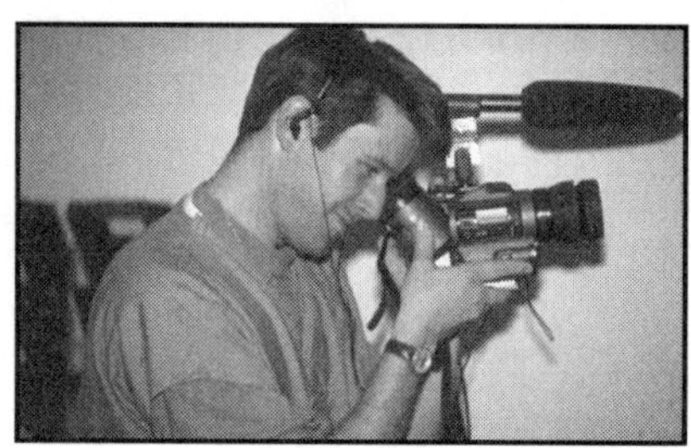

Panasonic AG-EZ1 equipped with a shotgun mic for the show Trauma: Life in the E.R. on The Learning Channel.

(Courtesy of N.Y.T. Television)

Cool looks aside, a shotgun mic on top of your camcorder can greatly improve upon the sound collecting abilities of the built-in mic. Shotgun mics are usually the most highly directional mics that you can buy. They reject sound from behind and a lot of external noise from the side and fixate on your subject.

If you find yourself in a situation where none of the previously mentioned external mics can be used or quickly accessed, mount a shotgun mic on a lightweight boom (you can buy one at any photo-video store) and place it directly over the scene just out of the camcorder field of view. This gives you a close audio proximity without any visual distractions in the shot. Hollywood features and on-location news crews commonly use the shotgun mic/boom combination for audio recording. You can also purchase those big, furry windscreens (Zeppelin) to eliminate noise if you're immersed in the elements. Recorded sound from boom mics rivals that of the most carefully placed lavalier.

Preserving the Peace and Quiet

The mic you choose isn't the only factor in quieting down your audio track. Location is equally important and goes a long way in determining how your video is going to sound.

Controlling or cutting down on reverb, especially indoors, can help sharpen your sound. Reverb occurs when sound bounces willy-nilly in a confined area, like the announcer's voice at a ball game or when you shout in a school gymnasium. Here are a few additional ways to cut down on unwanted noise:

- **Get Out of Sound's Way:** This is the simplest and most effective course of action. If you're shooting in a stadium, auditorium, or any other loud public place where you're experiencing uncontrollable crowd noise and reverb, try shooting out into the hallway or outside the stadium. You can always shoot your video shots and then record audio later when the place quiets down or empties out.
- **Relocate Within the Room:** If you're shooting in a noisy room with reverb bouncing all over the place, seek shelter in a corner, up higher, down lower, under the bed, in a closet, or on a step-ladder—any place within the room where the noise is less conspicuous.
- **Reduce Reverb:** There are objects that you can place on location with surfaces that are capable of absorbing or reflecting reverb, cutting down on the cacophony of sound. Carpet is a sure fire way to cut down on the echo, oversized furniture, drapes, blankets and echo-foam are also useful in cutting down on reverb.

On the Road with Portable Audio Mixers

Last but not least, you can add a mixer to the on-location audio mix. Most field mixers are small, battery powered, and very easy to use. The pros use them because they're perfect for controlling mic levels and are the best way to send clean, perfectly leveled audio signals into the camcorder.

It takes a little practice, but you must keep an eye on the mixer's and camcorder's VU meters to make sure that the audio signal is being recorded in a range that's optimal for the camcorder. You must also keep a close ear on the audio track with headphones. Mixers are designed so that any audio signal breakup can be easily detected. Levels on the field mixer can be adjusted on the fly using "faders," which are either sliders or knobs.

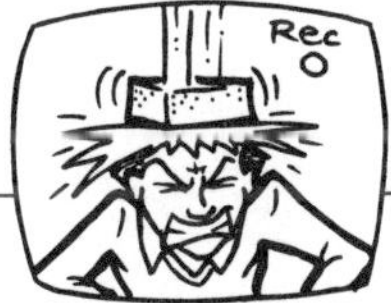

Blooper

Some field mixers come with special audio effects like EQ or echo/reverb. These can be useful in some situations but if they're overused, your projects will sound like an early '80s music video gone terribly wrong.

You can use field mixers on your own, but it's better if you employ the help of an additional crew member to operate it. If you're a one-person crew, place the field mixer on the ground at your feet or carry it over your shoulder with a shoulder strap. (Almost all portable mixers come with shoulder straps.)

It's pretty safe to say that on-board camcorder microphones don't do much for you if you're interested in great sounding videos. External mics can be the difference between clean sounding, professional-like audio and distracting soundtracks that are anything but a pleasant listening experience. And to be a better audio engineer, you don't have to sit through years of specialized training. Just shell out the bucks for a handheld, lavalier and/or shotgun mic, plug it in and start recording! All you need to finish the equation is a set of headphones and you're on your way to sound that will astound your audience.

The Least You Need to Know

- If sound is important to your production, bypass your camcorder's mic for an external mic.
- Understanding how mics work help you decide which one is best for any given situation.
- There are ways to escape reverb and other unwanted audio by moving your shoot within your chosen location.
- Portable audio mixers are the final step in recording professional-sounding audio.

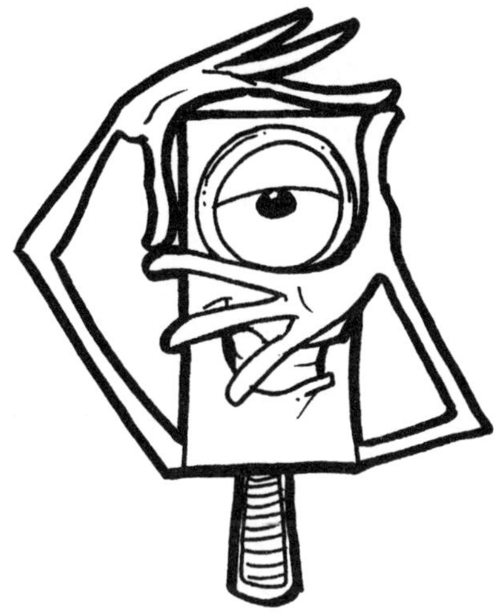

Chapter 11

Setting Up Your Shots

In This Chapter

- Why change angles?
- Types of angles
- Finding your own vantage point
- Keeping things balanced with visual composition

Sometimes we forget that the eye of the camcorder is in reality the eye of our audience. Even though home video is an extension of the way you see the world, sometimes it's important to free the camcorder and let it see things independently from your body. A variety of camera angles can inject life into your work. It provides a sense of visual variety and can add a new and welcome dimension to your programs. In this chapter you'll learn about different camera angles and how they can improve your videos. You'll also learn a few tricks of the trade that will give you a whole new perspective on setting up shots.

Why Mess with the Angle?

Not too long ago, a friend asked me to edit some footage together that he shot of his kids at their annual Halloween party. He had recently purchased the JVC DVM50, which is an ultra-compact MiniDV camcorder that is capable of delivering great looking images. (See Chapter 5, "Meandering the Maze of Manufacturers," for more info on the JVC DVM50.) He was more concerned with his camera work than image quality, so I assured him that after some clever editing, his video would look like something that could air on TV.

Boy was I surprised when I watched the tape. I really didn't think that it was going to be that bad! My stomach sank, and I knew that I had a big problem on my hands. Even though the images looked great, the content was extremely boring because my friend had made the mistake of shooting from a vantage point off to the side, preventing the audience from seeing his children's faces. To make matters worse, he was standing up the entire length of the raw footage. It looked more like security camera video than home video.

I tried to pull off a post-production miracle but was left with an unflattering, two-dimensional version of what really went on at his Halloween party. After watching what I had come up with, my friend was anxious for advice, so we spent some time watching video that I had shot of my son. I suggested that he should try to shoot from several different angles instead of just one. After seeing my footage, he was convinced.

A few weeks later he returned, excited to show me his latest Florida vacation video. It was like night and day. Just a few simple perspective changes had brought his video to life!

The moral of the story: Don't be afraid to experiment with different camera angles (even if they're wacky!). This will help you figure out what looks good, what works, and what doesn't. It's also a great primer for when you plan to try out some more serious video projects.

Unglue That Camcorder from Your Eye!

Shooting home videos can open up a world of unlimited creativity in your life. It isn't often that you get the unique opportunity for an audience to see the world through your eyes. But this fact shouldn't be taken too literally. The camcorder doesn't necessarily have to be an extension of your eye. In fact, hold it against your head as little as possible! You can place it anywhere that gives you the best view of your subject, or wherever you can find the most unique or creative angle to capture the action. It's completely your call.

But it's instinctive for beginners to lock the camcorder to their eye like my friend did. You see everybody else doing it, why shouldn't you? Because audiences far and wide are accustomed to watching network and cable TV shows and bore easily when exposed to lifeless home videos.

You can blame it on modern TV directors, producers, cameramen, and editors who employ a vast array of production techniques to make the programs more watchable. But I'll let you in on a little secret. Special effects and fake explosions aside, one of their biggest tricks for dynamic programs is to use a wide variety of camera angles to give viewers different perspectives on each scene.

The next time you find yourself shooting with your camcorder, do a little experiment. Hold the camera to your eye for a few minutes and shoot as you would normally. Then pull the camcorder away from your eye and shoot from any number of different angles, high, low, medium, moving, and so on. Upon playing back the footage you'll discover that some of the angles look artsy, some look goofy, but after a while you'll figure out the best mix that will spice up your production.

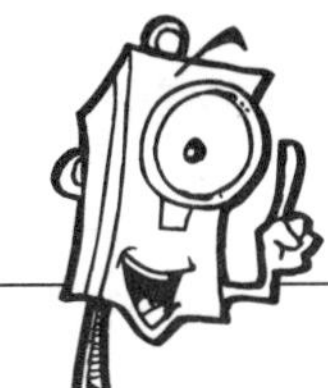

Candid Camera

Using a pop-out LCD viewfinder is a perfect way to break the camcorder-eye habit. You can hold the camcorder away from your body at arm's length, opening up new perspectives that would be extremely difficult to achieve using an eye-viewfinder.

You might be surprised to know that many major motion pictures are shot with only one camera. That means scenes are acted out again and again so there's adequate coverage for the editor to slice together a nice variety of angles. On TV, angles change so often because there's usually more than one camera on hand. But if you have the time and plan to edit your videos, you can pull off the same miracles as the professionals.

Shoot Three Dimensions with One Camcorder

Just because your TV screen is a flat surface, it doesn't mean that your home videos have to look two-dimensional. Think of blockbuster movies like *Star Wars, Titanic,* and *Jurassic Park,* for example. They might spend tens of millions on special effects, but the directors also call for a wealth of creative camera perspectives to help give their action a feeling of depth and a three-dimensional look. And if they can do it, so can you.

The best way to add a third dimension is to carefully scout the area before shooting. Choose a main angle to shoot from and then search for angles anywhere else keeping a three-dimensional framework in mind. Shoot from behind, above, below, off to the side or any other perspective that strikes your fancy. It's completely possible to drag your audience into the third dimension!

Recently, I went to a birthday party for my cousin's daughter Samantha at a play space for kids. My cousin was busy schmoozing with the guests and manning the still camera, so I grabbed his camcorder and started shooting. At that point, Samantha and one of the party planners were in the process of giving away party favors, so I quickly assessed the shooting situation and figured out all of the angles that I wanted to shoot from. First, I stepped all the way into the corner of the room to get a wide establishing shot of the scene. Then from the same angle I moved closer for some more detail. Next, I sunk low and began to move to where Samantha was actually sitting. I slowly inched forward on my knees while shooting to make the footage a little more dynamic. Once Samantha was in front of the camcorder, she smiled and made all kinds of funny faces while goofing around with the camera. I then panned down and took some close-up shots of the party favors, and followed her hand motion as she gave them out to the guests. The next shot was fun ... I took a look at the gift list and noticed that my niece Jesse was going to be called next. So I sat down behind her and shot the scene from her point of view. When her name was called, I crouched down, held the camcorder just behind her ear, and followed her all the way up. I wasn't looking through the viewfinder, but I was feeling confident that I was shooting great footage. After that, I just shot some low-reverse angles from behind them and one last wide-angle shot from a different corner.

This kind of multi-angle shooting offers viewers a multitude of different perspectives on the action. In this case, I knew that my cousin probably wasn't going to edit the video together so I started and stopped the camcorder without too much extra (boring) footage (see Chapter 18, "Editing on the Fly"). If, at a later date, he did decide to edit the footage together into a more interesting program, the edit would be a snap since the coverage is more than adequate and there's a boat load of interesting shots and angles to choose from.

The More the Merrier

It's unlikely that you will ever exceed the camera angle limit for home videos because there isn't one. Besides giving viewers a unique perspective and adding a third dimension to your pictures, visual variety is a common tactic to stimulate audiences.

Way back in high school, I remember spending days on a bicycle video that my father and I shot and edited together for film class. It didn't have much of a plot, just myself and a bunch of friends going up and down a "half pipe," a curved ramp that looks like a giant tube cut in half. My dad was unusually quiet during the editing process. When I finally showed the tape to my class, I discovered why.

The class's initial reaction was good: a few "Wow"s and "Oh my God"s, but after a minute or two the teacher said, "It's amazing how quickly this stuff gets boring." I dropped my head in shame.

Looking back, the video was a far cry from the exciting B.M.X. footage you'd see on ESPN with kids flipping and spinning 10 feet in the air. If my father and I had added just a few more perspectives to our limited shot repertoire, we might have been able to hold the class's attention for the length of the program.

Playing All the Angles

There are many more names for camera angles than actual camera angles. But whether it's a bird's-eye angle or a worm's-eye angle, don't worry so much about learning the lingo. All you need is a basic knowledge of the kinds of shots available to get your videos off the ground. What follows are more formal names for common camera angles that you can easily take advantage of in your home videos.

Simple High and Low Angles

Simple high and simple low angles are the most common types of shots in home video. Unfortunately, in the case of videotaping children, simple high angles are all too common and are notorious for robbing the audience out of precious moments that usually take place well below sea level. But overall, you'll find these kinds of angles very useful, and very hard to avoid.

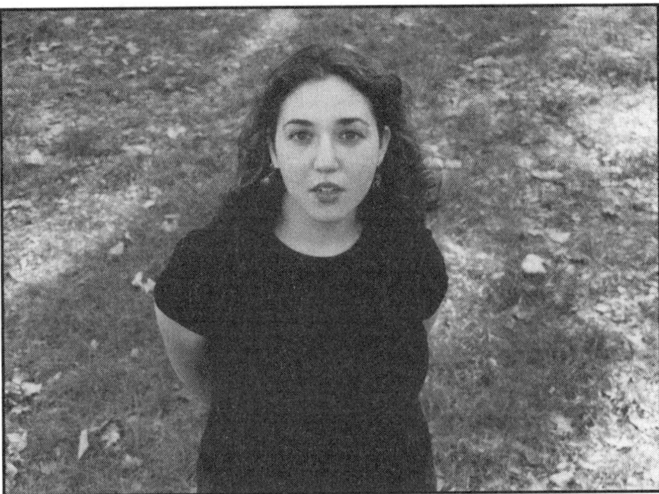

Simple high angle.

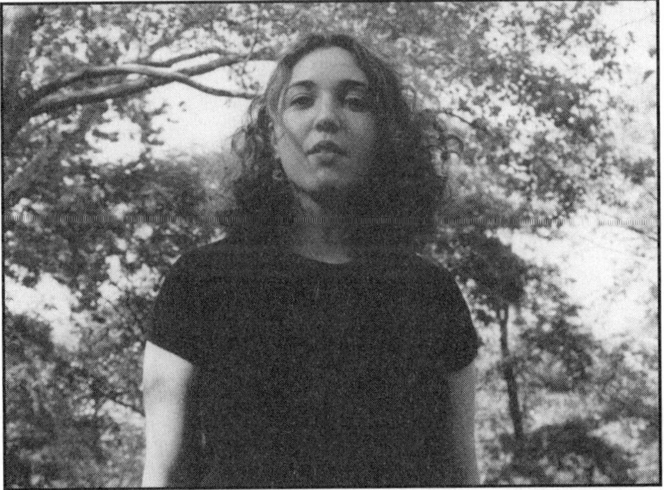

Simple low angle.

Simple high angles are also more common when you want to diminish your subject, making it look smaller or weaker in the scheme of things. This is a very common technique if you ever plan to shoot short fictional movies with your camcorder, or just to dramatize special events like weddings, graduations and birthday parties. I

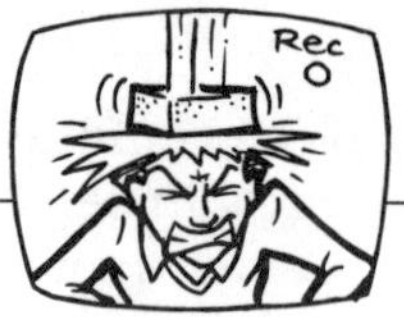

Blooper

One of the biggest home video infractions is overuse of the zoom. If you're looking to shoot a close-up shot, zoom in on your subject before you hit the record button.

often use this angle when I have my subject approaching something sizeable or formidable, like a person walking through a huge city for the first time. High angle shots can also be sprinkled throughout a program to give viewers an above-the-hairline picture of your subject.

Simple high angle shots are easy to pull off. In fact, if you're tall, just standing up straight with the camcorder is enough to be considered a simple high angle. Otherwise, you can step up on a stable chair, box, bed, and so on, to give you the ups that you need.

Simple low angles, on the other hand, can make the subject look powerful and dominating. And you don't have to be lying on the floor to get this type of shot, just lower yourself slightly and shoot upward on an angle. This works well when you're on vacation and you want to make the scenery or landscapes appear larger-than-life. It's also a great way to make children look more significant in size on the screen instead of seeing the tops of their heads.

Get a Little Closer

Close-up shots are common in movies, home videos, newscasts, and documentaries. In home video, you're bound to see a lot of close-ups because the camcorder user has discovered and fallen in love with the zoom feature. In Hollywood, documentaries, or any other dramatic form of programming, close-ups are used when the talent is about to say something important or receive vital information. They are also used simply to get a close identification shot of a talent (sometimes referred to as an "ID shot").

A typical close-up shot.

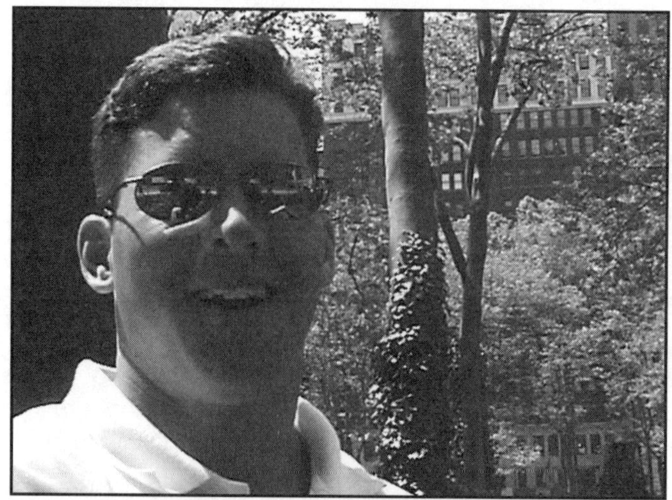

Depending on the purpose of your video, close-ups are invaluable. Not only do they work well for getting a close look at people's faces and their changing expressions. Close-ups can be used when your talent is performing a task or demonstrating something on camera. You can easily get a tight shot of the object and edit it in later.

I would recommend experimenting with a few different ways to shoot close-ups. Try moving very close to your subject with the camcorder zoomed all the way out. Then try shooting from further back by zooming in. The two shots will look very different and can aesthetically have a subtle impact on your production.

In addition, there are a few different types of close-up shots that you can use when videotaping people in your videos.

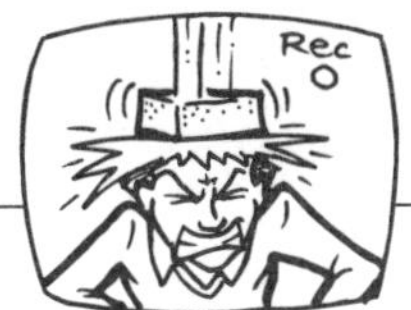

Blooper

Unless you're intending to shoot an extreme close-up (XCU), be careful not to chop off too much of a person's head or chin. If you have to make a choice when shooting close-ups, crop out the very top of the head just above the hair line. If your talent has a speaking part it looks awkward to chop off their chin or mouth.

- **Medium close-up (MCU):** A shot that crops from the top of the head to just above the belt line.
- **Head and shoulder close-up:** A close-up shot that crops from the top of the head to just below the shoulder line.
- **Extreme close-up (XCU):** This shot includes only a small part of the subject's face full frame. This usually includes the eyes or mouth for the most dramatic impact.
- **Low or high angle close-ups:** Simple variations from above or below. Generally used to add variety to a video.
- **Bird's eye or worm's eye close-up:** Takes the low or high angle close-up shots to an extreme and can be a lot of fun to watch, especially when videotaping children. These kinds of shots can be taken from directly over someone's head, or from directly under their chin on a slight angle.

One very common mistake that many new videographers make is to improperly frame a person in the shot by allowing too much headroom. This happens when the subject is centered smack in the middle of the picture. It is more pleasing to the eye to place the head closer to the top of the frame.

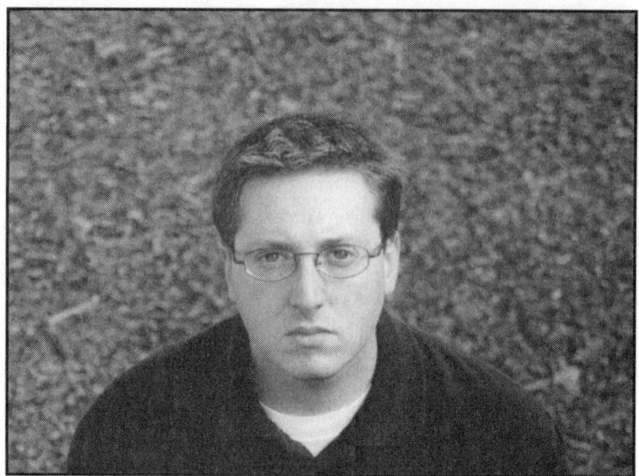
Too much headroom.

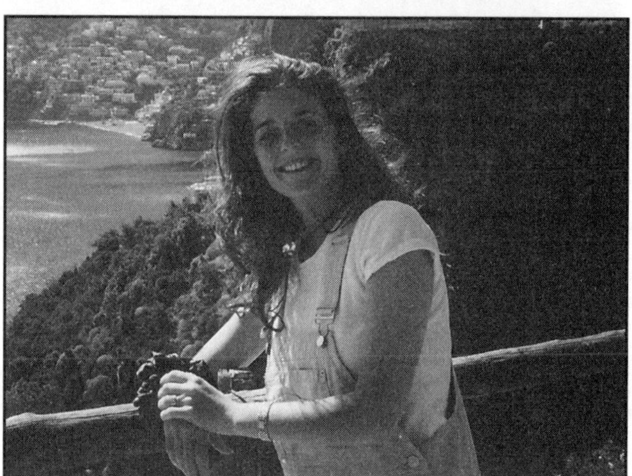
Well-framed shot.

Middle of the Road

Medium shots (MS) are often referred to as loose shots and, when shooting people, tend to fit half of their standing height in the frame. A medium shot offers less detail than close-up shots and is great for transitioning from wide-angle to close-up. At typical home video events like a birthday party, medium shots are common simply because the shooter is a comfortable distance from the action.

Shoot a Little Longer

Long shots are great for establishing location and giving viewers a sense of place. When shooting people, long shots are often referred to as full figure shots and as a general rule try to fit most, if not all of their standing height in the frame.

In home video, long shots are becoming more popular because resolution has improved by 50 percent over the last 10 years. Where a long shot on a VHS camcorder looks like little more than a blur, on MiniDV you can make out your subject as clear as day.

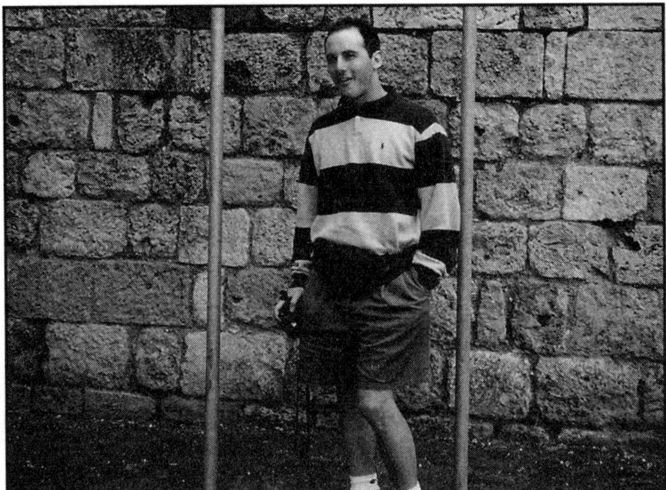

Long shot.

Telephoto

A telephoto shot differs from a close-up in that the camera is usually much further away from the subject. Professionals utilize telephoto angles to deplete their image of depth, giving it a flat, two-dimensional appearance. This is perfect for stylized shooting, to make a background pop out, or to paint pictures with abstract moving video images.

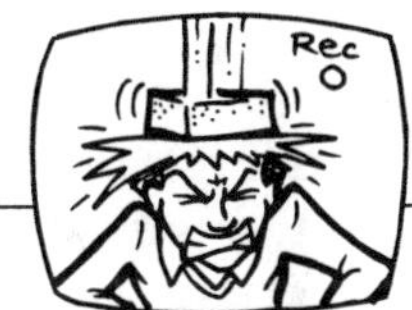

Blooper

When shooting in telephoto mode, every little movement is greatly exaggerated in the viewfinder. Use a tripod if possible.

In your home movies you can use telephoto angles to help exaggerate impending doom in a scene, such as a chase scene. Telephoto shots will visually place the chaser and the chased a lot closer together than they really are.

Telephoto shots have many other uses in home video. If you shoot wildlife or landscapes telephoto is a great way to get close to action without disturbing the scene or putting yourself in harm's way. On my honeymoon in Italy, I got a great zooming-out telephoto shot of my hotel from a tower across town in Florence that we used at the end our wedding video for the credit roll.

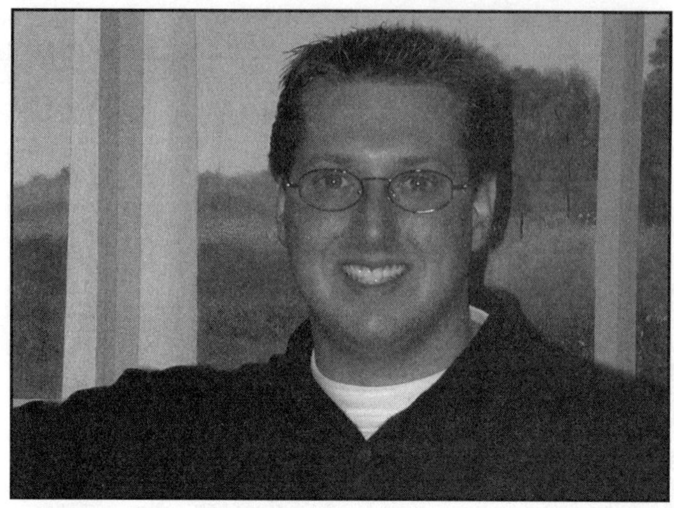

Telephoto shot.

Wide-Angle

When you have your camcorder's lens zoomed all the way back you're in partial wide-angle mode. Add an inexpensive wide-angle lens converter, and you've got what it takes to capture beautiful wide-angle shots.

Unlike telephoto lenses, a wide-angle adds depth to a scene. They can be used in just about any video shoot for establishing shots, action, sports, or city/landscapes. You see wide-angle shots on TV all the time, and as lens converters become more available to the camcorder community, wide-angles are making their way more and more into home videos. So the next time you find yourself on vacation or in a setting where you'd like to fit even more scenery into the viewfinder, snap to wide-angle. Wide-angle shots are visually attractive to look at and add depth to shots that normal camcorder lenses couldn't dream of.

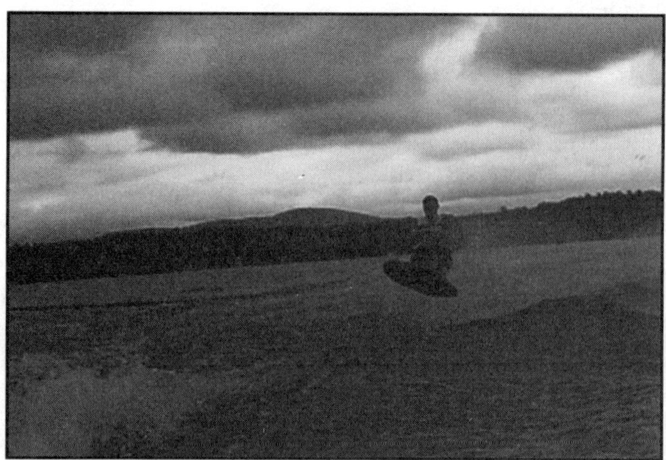

Wide-angle shot.

Bird's-Eye

Here's an angle that always adds a nice twist to your program. Unfortunately, it is the most underused shot in home video because, unless you have a crane at your disposal, in many cases a bird's-eye view is difficult to pull off.

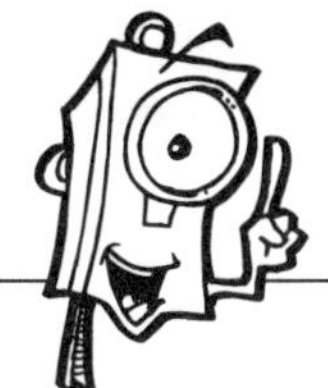

Candid Camera

An extreme bird's-eye view could mean shooting from a roof or from a window in a tall building. For a less dramatic effect, a bird's-eye view can be achieved by simply raising your tripod, or placing it on a chair or table.

But if you can figure out a way to elevate yourself above the scene for a shot or two, it's a great way to establish your location and to let your audience see the subject and setting in ways that would otherwise be impossible using a normal angle. This is especially true if you're using a wide-angle lens converter. With a little effort, you can really pack a lot of your scene into the frame.

I use bird's-eye angles when I'm looking to portray my subject as a small part of a much bigger picture such as someone walking down a city street or on a beach. It also works well when you want to give your audience the sense that they know something that your subject doesn't, like someone sneaking up on them from behind.

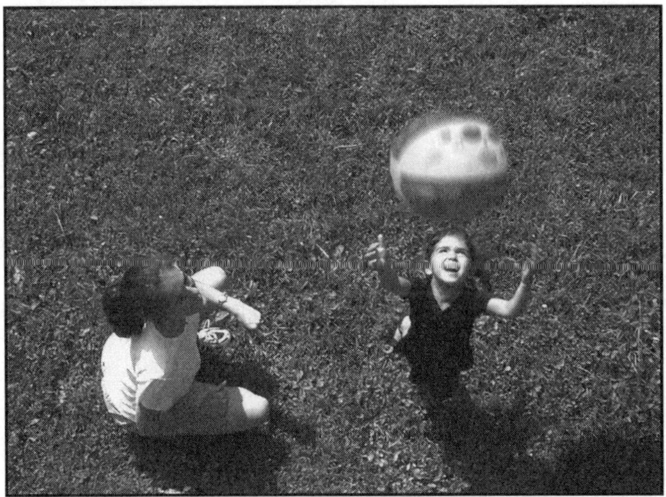

Bird's-eye shot.

How it was shot.

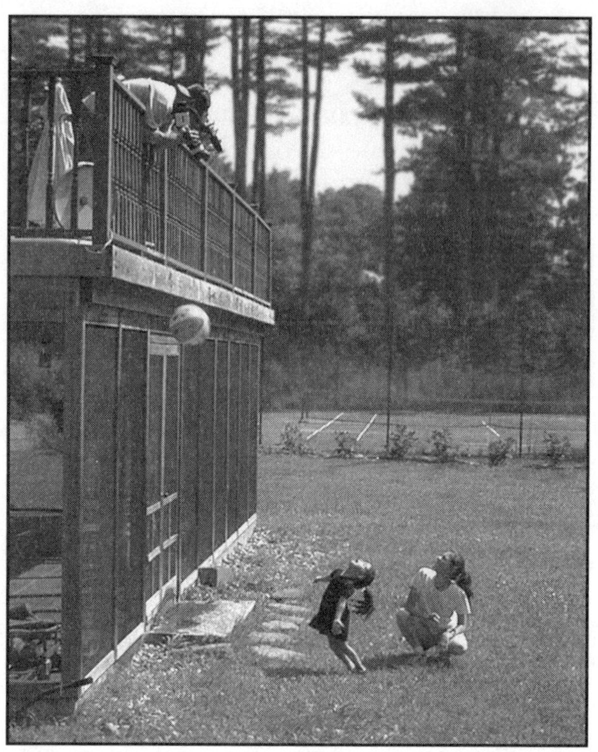

Worm's-Eye

This is one of my favorite camera angles, especially when the focus is on my son. Getting down low while shooting can be entertaining or dramatic. The applications of a worm's-eye angle are unlimited.

Even though my Canon XL-1 doesn't have a pop-out LCD viewfinder, it's easy to get a worm's eye shot because it has a well-placed handle that can be used while bending down to navigate near the floor. As my son zips around while dismantling our apartment, I capture the action from his viewpoint with the XL-1. Everything looks big and imposing down there, and all of the shelves, covered outlets and chairs look so enticing.

What's Your Angle?

With a basic knowledge of the kinds of shots available to you as a home videographer, all it takes is a little experimentation to get really good at giving your audience different perspectives. You can also learn a lot by checking out the variety in camera angles on TV. Decide which shots you think look cool and try to implement them in your own productions.

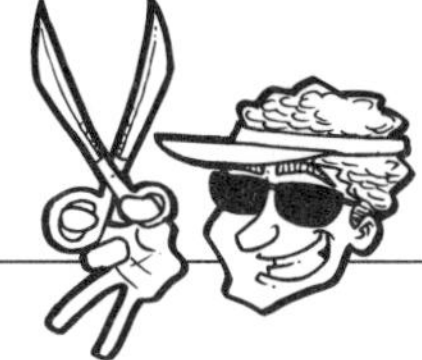

Director's Cut

Getting a worm's-eye view doesn't necessarily mean you have to sprawl yourself on the ground. With a little practice, you can frame a subject down low quite nicely without even glancing in the viewfinder.

Before my son was born, I didn't have much experience at all videotaping children. As we started to watch more and more children's programming, I found myself taking pointers from PBS on the best way to capture my son in action.

There's one show in particular that has caught my eye morning after morning. It's called *Zaboomafoo,* and it airs weekday mornings on PBS (check your local schedule). You can learn a lot about production from these kinds of shows, especially techniques to keep a captive audience. Content aside, children's programming is pure bubble-gum TV aimed at an audience cluster that has the shortest attention span on the face of the planet. But morning after morning, children across the land sit transfixed by the visual experience of *Zaboomafoo* and other fine programs.

There's also something else at work here that goes a long way in attracting children and parents. It's called imaginative camera angles, and if you can figure out how to implement them in your home videos, audiences far and wide will flock to your TV set. Cameramen for these shows obviously don't hesitate to get their clothes dirty. They crawl on the floor, climb trees, and hang from ropes if they have to. Whatever it takes to get an interesting angle.

Here are a few suggestions that you can try at home:

- **Wheelchair:** If you have access to one, a wheelchair can help you with smooth motion, low angles, and POV shots.
- **Bicycle:** If you can ride one-handed, a bicycle shot may work for you. These shots look similar to wheelchair shots, but a bicycle is faster and more maneuverable.
- **Roller Blades/Skateboard:** This is an ultra-smooth way to capture action. With both hands free, you've got more of an opportunity to hold the camcorder steady. It's also helpful to have someone pushing and guiding you from behind, freeing you up to fully concentrate on your camera work.

- **Car:** This is an obvious one, but only shoot out of a car window if you have someone else driving. If you hold the camera steady against the frame of an open window, you can get reasonably smooth tracking shots if the road isn't bumpy. Never hang your body or sit outside of the window.
- **Boat:** If you can employ a boat to cruise the shoreline while you're shooting, you're going to come away with some nice looking footage. Since a boat ride can be significantly bumpier than a car, it may help to lock your camcorder down with a small tripod or hold it at arm's length to reduce rocking.
- **Roof:** If you have access to a non-slanted roof, by all means, take a few shots from there. We're not talking the top of the Empire State Building, however. Make sure the roof is low enough for you to make out the action below. Telephoto lenses work well in this situation.

Setting the Stage with Visual Composition

Another factor to keep in mind while choosing a camera angle is the art of visual arrangement within your video frame. Think of your TV as a painter's palette, a blank slate to fill with whatever you see fit. It could be an element in the foreground or background that helps convey a message or a clever prop or any visual image that complements the action of your scene. Composing your images on the screen takes a little bit of thought, a good sense of visual balance, and a lot of practice.

Keep an Eye on the Foreground and Background

Simply put, the background is the area behind your subject and the foreground is the space between your subject and the camcorder. Choosing the right background is a key element in visual composition, yet it can be tricky business. Generally, you don't want to shoot against a bland background like a white or gray wall. Aim for a visual background, either moving or still, which helps your subject pop out on the screen and not blend into it. If your subject is wearing a white shirt and you're shooting up against a white wall, the only thing you'll see is a floating head and a walking pair of blue jeans.

Working with visual elements in the foreground can be even trickier because they are often in motion. This problem is amplified whenever you set the camcorder in motion. Sometimes you don't know what's going to pop into the frame at any given moment. The only way around this is to practice your shot a few times before rolling tape. This way you'll be more prepared for the unexpected snafus that pop up from time to time.

Balance Is Key

I spent the first few years of my career typing on-air graphics for the local news and I picked up something there that I've put to use not only in my career as a TV producer and editor, but in producing my home videos. It's the simple rule of balance, or achieving an on-screen symmetry in the elements that comprise your picture. Sometimes referred to as the rule of thirds, you chop up the screen into three parts vertically and horizontally, and balance your visual elements in the cross-lines of those sections. If your subject is sitting on a park bench and there's a tree in the foreground hanging into the frame, adjust the camcorder so that the tree is all the way in the right or left third, and place your subject all the way to the other side.

Visual balance is an advanced concept. A sense of visual composition is innate (and hard to learn if you didn't inherit it). The best way to get a handle on a concept like the rule of thirds is to practice.

Ostracize Unwanted Images

Sometimes the elements that you choose to keep out of your video frame are more important than what you choose to leave in. A misplaced element on camera could mean the difference between professional looking footage, and footage that was shot in your childhood bedroom.

How often have you watched video where there's a chair in the way, a car or some other moving obstruction, or someone busy doing something else in the background? Controlling what ends up on screen goes a long way in reducing overall audience distraction.

Here are some elements you may want to keep out of your pictures:

- Too much furniture
- Moving cars in the foreground
- TV sets that are on while you're shooting
- Walls—indoor and outdoor
- Fences
- Shooting through windows or screen doors
- Excessive greenery like tree branches or leaves leaking into your picture

What they do on TV, you can do at home. TV producers, directors, and camera operators are constantly dipping into a vast array of camera angles and positions to keep viewers interested. In the NBA, there's a "jam-cam" mounted on the very top of the backboard aiming directly down at the rim. This bird's-eye angle offers sports fans a perspective they would never see in the real world. Similarly, the "catcher-cam" gives baseball fans a view of the game directly behind home plate. People look forward to these kinds of shots. Interesting angles are visually relieving, especially if they are used to add variety to any program.

Coming up with different angles isn't rocket science. If you're videotaping your children, there's nothing they can do that you can't. Get in the tub with them, climb a tree with them, even hop on the back of a tricycle if you have to. All you need is a camcorder and the gumption to go out there and get the shot!

The Least You Need to Know

- Different camera angles add depth, visual variety, and different perspectives to your home videos.
- Learning all of the camera angles means that there's a good chance you'll use them in your next project.
- There are all sorts of techniques to get different perspectives while shooting.
- Strong visual composition of your video frame makes for balanced, dynamic-looking footage.

Part 3

Lights, Camera, Action!

You've heard the phrase a million times: "Lights, camera, action!" But now you're about to find out exactly what it really means to be at the helm of your home video productions.

As director, you might have to choose actors and actresses to star in your videos, conduct interviews, or maybe even manage a small budget. And since most home video budgets are miniscule at best, it probably means that you'll also be shooting your projects yourself while directing the action. It can be a daunting task.

What you really need is to plow through Part 3 of this book to learn how to become a jack-of-all-trades. Maybe one day you'll find yourself convincing your nervous aunt to relax on camera, coaxing your kids to smile after blowing out the candles at their birthday parties, or even coaching Leonardo DiCaprio in a kissing scene in a major Hollywood feature film. Whatever the production, if you master some basic directing skills, your home videos will end up looking like a million bucks.

On the other end of the home video spectrum, you'll want to get as many people involved as possible—especially if it's a special occasion or once-in-a-lifetime event that you're shooting. Children are always willing participants, or maybe you can recruit your significant other to shoot a little. Whatever the case, you don't want to let life's special moments pass you by in the viewfinder of a camcorder.

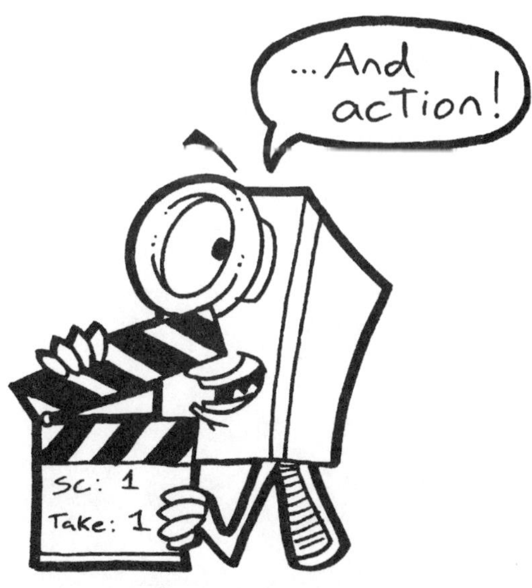

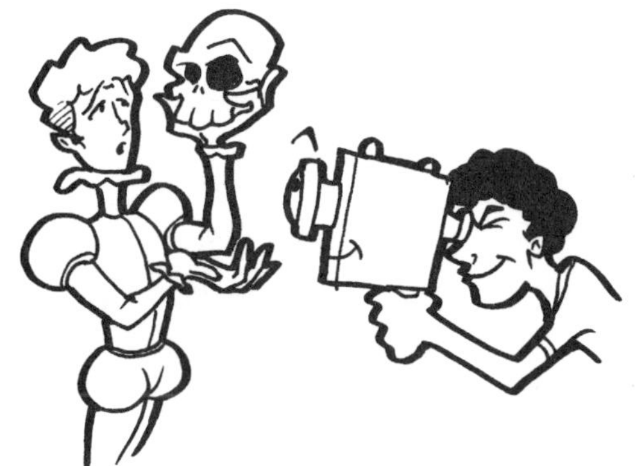

Chapter 12

Your Supporting Cast

In this Chapter

- ➤ Rounding up the best "talent" for your production
- ➤ Getting your kids into the act
- ➤ Prompting your cast
- ➤ A little narration never hurt anybody

As the director of your home video mini-movies, documentaries, or whatever else your imagination can conjure up, it's time to take the final step before actually rolling tape. You have to assemble a cast and crew to help make your vision come to life on the screen. Whether you need actors and actresses, crewmembers, or voice over artists, you can draw from your friends, family, and even children for help. Or, if you've got the bucks, you can hire professionals. Whatever the case is, you've got a home movie to make, and the show must go on!

Swimming in the Talent Pool

According to the Merriam-Webster's WWWebster Dictionary (www.m-w.com), the definition of the word *talent* is

> 1) *archaic:* a characteristic feature, aptitude, or disposition of a person or animal; 2) the natural endowments of a person; 3a) a special often creative or artistic aptitude; 3b) general intelligence or mental power: ability; 4) a person of talent or a group of persons of talent in a field or activity.

In TV production, the word *talent* refers to anyone who physically appears on screen, or whose voice can be heard in your production. It doesn't matter if it's the star of your video or an extra who's barely visible far off in the background. And it doesn't matter if the talent has any talent. Talent is talent. End of story.

Assessing the Needs of Your Production

Let's say you're planning to shoot this short video drama that you wrote:

"Don't Jump!"

FADE IN:

INT. N.Y.U. LIBRARY – DAY

COLE BAUER walks into the library at New York University and takes the elevator to his favorite study area on the 10th floor. The middle of the library is wide open, and Cole glances down at the lobby as he walks by. Everyone in the library seems to be cramming for finals. Cole sits down and works for no longer than a minute before one of the students sitting nearby suddenly speaks out.

STUDENT

Great! Just what we need. Another person. Like it's not crowded enough in here!

Cole looks up to see that the student is referring to him.

COLE

What did I do?

The student doesn't answer but continues to ramble. Cole is trying to concentrate but finds it impossible.

STUDENT

(Loudly)

How in the world am I ever going to pass this exam with all these people around?

The student is really beginning to loose it. He looks around with a wild look on his face as other students in the library stare at him in disbelief.

STUDENT 2

Listen dude .... We're all dealing with the same stuff! Get out of here if you can't take the pressure!

COLE

(Annoyed)

Can you guys keep it down please?

The student suddenly tosses his books against a wall and rushes past Cole's desk to the railing. Cole stares after him, dumbfounded.

STUDENT

I hate this place. I hate this place. I HATE THIS PLACE!!!!

He runs over to the railing and hops over it, holding on with one hand as he tries to muster the courage to leap. Cole can't move. Another student hops up and screams into an emergency phone. Within seconds the library faculty, hundreds of feet below the student's feet, scramble toward the staircases and elevators. A librarian on the 10th floor slowly approaches the student.

LIBRARIAN

Hey, why don't you step back over the railing and talk about it for a minute ....

STUDENT

Get away from me!

Extremely agitated, the student stumbles but manages to regain his position. Cole slowly approaches the scene.

COLE

Hey, I'm sorry for whatever I did. Please .... I'll leave. You can have this whole place to yourself.

STUDENT

Don't play games with me. I'm serious! I'm gonna do it. I'm gonna do it right now!

The student breathes deeply in and out several times, psyching himself up for the plunge. Cole dives forward and grabs the student by the jacket just as he leaps from the balcony ....

I don't want to spoil the ending, but let's just say that it's unlikely that anybody dies because Cole does a lot of weightlifting in his spare time!

Whether you have a script like this one, a working outline, a simple shot list, or even an idea in your head, you need to go through it page by page to figure out exactly what elements are needed. And when it comes to making home movies, most of the time you'll find that you need to scale things back a bit to match the resources you have available. Depending on the kind of project you're working on, this may include

- Actors
- Extras
- Crewmembers
- Specialty crew (makeup and wardrobe)
- Props and set decorations

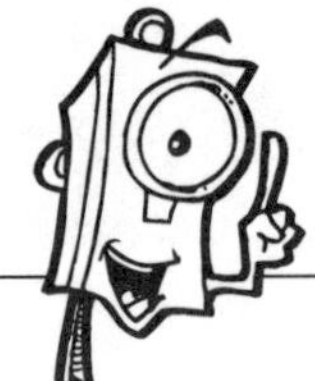

Candid Camera

When a Hollywood feature script is broken down, the list gets into much greater detail, which can include stunts, special effects, animals/animal handlers/trainers, and sound effects.

So in the case of "Don't Jump!," you've got a lot of legwork to do. First and foremost you need to get permission to shoot in the library, but that's a whole other discussion. (See Chapter 8, "Scouting Out Your Location.") If you do get permission, then you need to find someone to play Cole, the crazy student, the other angry student, the librarian, other students sitting in the library getting annoyed, additional extras as gaping onlookers and the scrambling faculty/staff below.

Additionally, if you're going to be shooting and directing, it would be great to have production assistants to do crowd control, and several others to help with lighting and audio, and possibly even makeup and wardrobe.

Giving the script a once-over for resource availability is an invaluable part of the process because after going through your script shot by shot and scene by scene, you may discover that you need to rewrite certain parts of the story where the resources stretch the limit of possibility. If I were shooting "Don't Jump!," I might think about rewriting the part where dozens of faculty and staff below the scene scramble to get to the troubled student. The reality of the situation is that it would be extremely hard to secure and coordinate enough people to pull it off visually.

I'd also be figuring out ways to stage the part where Cole grabs the student by the jacket as he's about to jump. Will I need a professional stuntman? Probably not. The N.Y.U. library would never let me dangle one of my actors from the 10th floor balcony anyway (and I would never take that kind of safety risk). So I'd probably find a stairwell or overhang with the same shaped balcony and act the scene out there, relying on slick editing to create seamless action. If you shoot the 10th floor balcony from the lobby floor, you can safely hang the student's arm or a little bit of his upper torso over the railing without causing too much concern, or you can drop a pen or anything else from above and edit it in later. This is a great way to create the necessary dramatic tension without putting anything or anyone at risk.

Good Talent Is Easy to Find

Hollywood movies spend a lot of money on having professional casting agencies choose talent for the roles. Talent scouts and casting agents generally have great intuition and they are very skilled at what they do since they spend most of their time doing it.

But for 99.9 percent of your home video projects, the casting responsibilities will fall directly into your lap. Let's say you've done a script breakdown for "Don't Jump!" and you have a really good idea of how many people you're going to need. Where do you turn next?

First on your list, you need two convincing stars to play Cole and the role of the troubled student. Since the camcorder's eye will be on them for a good part of your production, the audience should never question whether or not they are both college students. They also should be well spoken and capable of pulling off dramatic performances. This doesn't necessarily mean that they need a minimum of 10 years of theatre experience to get the part. For a project like this it's hard to find actors and actresses of that caliber.

The best place to start looking is your own circle of friends, family, and associates. There's always a natural performer or a ham in any group who would be willing to perform for the sheer fun of it. If I were casting this movie I'd ask my friend Ken to play the troubled student. He has done some theatre and is always willing to join one of my goofy productions for kicks. My brother-in-law Glenn, on the other hand, has no acting experience but is a natural performer and would be able to pull off the role of Cole without a second thought. In casting your home movies, don't hesitate to grant friends and family their first on-camera opportunity. You never know when the next Leonardo DiCaprio will come out of the woodwork.

Once you have the starring front-line out of the way, you need to find a whole lot of extras. After recruiting the rest of your friends and family to fill the roles, the most obvious place to find more is the N.Y.U. Library itself. Go there in your free time and pick out a few librarians and students who you think might fit the part and ask them if they would be willing to participate in a short video project. If they can't do it, ask them if they know anybody who would. It can't hurt to go right to the source for extra bodies.

In a pinch, you can contact local theatre companies, or place an ad in local newspapers or on the Internet. You can also find a local community center, school, or wherever acting classes are held, and post an ad on a bulletin board. If you were shooting at a college, you could also try contacting their theatre department to ask if they can recommend anyone who would be willing to star in a short film. You'd be surprised at how many people would jump at the opportunity to act and for something cool to put on their resumes.

There's also a publication called *The Ross Reports* (1-800-817-3273) that lists talent agencies and casting directors who can help you find actors and actresses for your project.

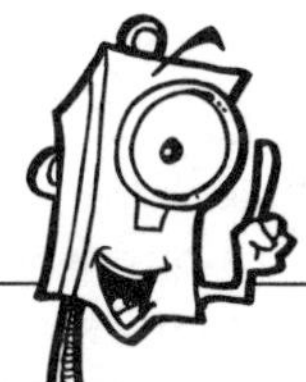

Candid Camera

If you get enough outsiders who are interested, you can hold a "cattle call" audition where everyone has a chance to show their stuff. If you do this, make sure you get everyone's information and their availability.

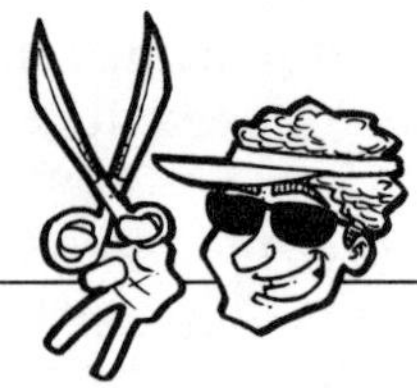

Director's Cut

You can also search the same channels for members of your video crew. Friends and family are always willing to pitch in, but it's a lot more fun to be on camera than behind it!

Santa's Little Helpers

No matter how many people you have helping on your video crew, you can bet that you'll always need more. Children are always willing participants in any adult activity, and there are many positives in getting children off to an early start in videography. In fact, one of my son's first toys was the Fisher Price camcorder.

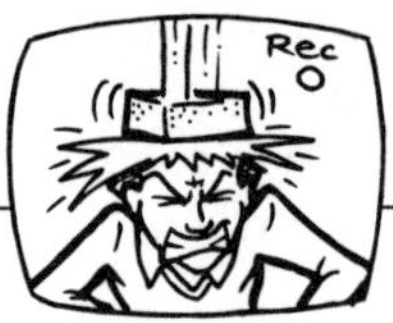

Blooper

If you are working on a very important project, the only downside that I can think of in having children on the set would be a poorly timed temper tantrum or any kind of noise-making during a scene or interview. As wonderful as children are, sometimes it's hard to foresee when something like this will happen. Just as movie star tantrums cause delays and cost overruns on movies, kiddie tantrums may have the same effect on your set.

It's amazing what takes place in a child's mind. They see the world with a sense of awe and wonder. I often try to capture this energy, especially when I take on a new project at work. The first thing that I do is ask myself how a child would solve the problem at hand. It's a great way to get a completely untainted and innocent viewpoint. Creativity in children has no boundaries. In adults, boundaries are often created by years of attitudes and experiences and can often block the raw creative energy that flows through everyone. Having children around any kind of creative activity is beneficial for everyone involved.

Exposing children to an activity like videography can be invaluable in their own creative development. It can also help to increase their self-confidence and give them a sense of responsibility. A while back my sister-in-law Joy asked me to help her practice for an audition she got for a TV show. I came over with my camcorder and rounded up my niece Jesse to help me with the cue cards. Even though she couldn't read at the time, she was able to change cue cards when I signaled to her. Whether it's an on-camera appearance or production assistance on shoot day, kids will cherish the experience.

If you plan on getting other people's children in your productions, you might find yourself squaring off with "stage" moms and dads. It can be difficult enough dealing with friends (who you suddenly discover have inflated egos), but handling an overzealous parent can stretch the limits of accommodation and patience.

Helping Talent with Their Lines

If you're able to secure experienced actors and actresses for the roles in your video, chances are they'll have the ability to memorize large amounts of the script. But if you're working with an inexperienced cast, or someone who isn't totally comfortable in front of the camera, remembering dialog can quickly become a problem.

One of the oldest tricks in the book for helping talent with their lines is the use of cue cards. You see Letterman, Leno, and many other talk-show hosts using them. Cue cards can be made out of any large sheet of paper such as oak tag and should be written in heavy black, felt tipped marker. Set up your cue card "operator" as close to your talent as possible so the cue card operator doesn't interfere with the camera, lighting, or audio equipment.

You can also hide pieces of paper or cardboard with your talent's lines somewhere just off camera. This is a common technique used in soap operas where dialog can be re-written up to the last minute. In your production, it will be less obvious that your talent is looking down or off to the side for prompting. You can hide the paper in a dinner menu, you can tape it to a wall, or place it flat down on a table.

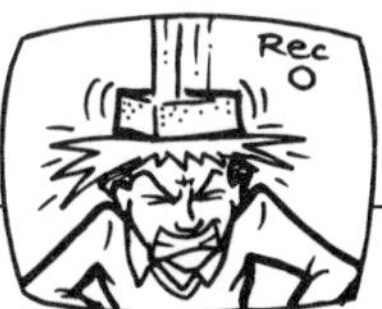

Blooper

Since there's only so much you can cram on a cue card, if you have a long script, you'll probably have to change cards while the talent is performing. The best way to do this is to change them as silently as possible, or drop them softly on the ground in a pile. Do a practice run and ask your audio engineer if the sound is audible in the headphones.

The other method of feeding talent their lines is the use of a teleprompter. The really good ones fit over the lens of the camera and the reflection of the moving text is mirrored directly in front of the lens so the talent doesn't appear to be reading. A good prompter setup can cost several thousand dollars.

While these high-end prompters are out of the question for home productions, there are several low-cost alternatives. You can make a homemade prompter yourself with a PC or Mac loaded with the latest prompting software, or you can use everyday word processing software. Most of the software is inexpensive and very easy to use.

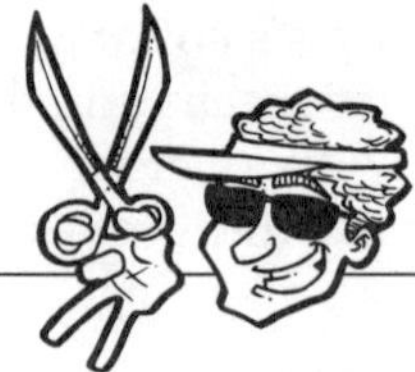

Director's Cut

You can use your personal computer just off-camera to display your script on the screen. Make your document full screen and use a large font. Ask a friend or a member of your crew to slowly scroll as your talent reads.

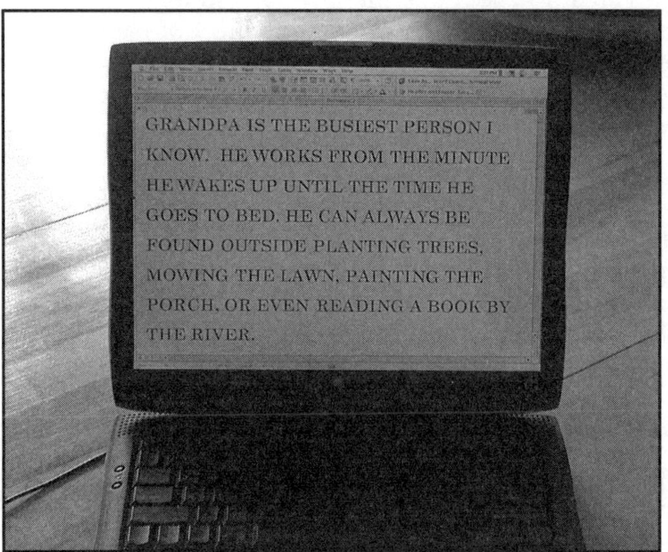

A teleprompter on a Mac computer.

You can find a list of companies that make prompting software in Appendix C, "Camcorder and Accessory Manufacturers." In most cases, you can jump in for less than $100 and the software is simple to install and use on your computer. While this method of teleprompting isn't always ideal for outdoor shoots, indoors, you can place your PC close to your set for inconspicuous viewing.

Voicing Your Videos

If you decide to use narration or voiceover (VO) in your production (to be done while shooting or during the editing process), finding the right talent could potentially be the trickiest part of staffing your production. Voiceover work is one of the most specialized skills in the television industry. If you think that all you need is a pleasant sounding and authoritative voice to narrate, think again. The VO artist has to be a master-manipulator of the spoken word. In addition, a deep understanding of inflection, diction, and tone are vital to any narrative read.

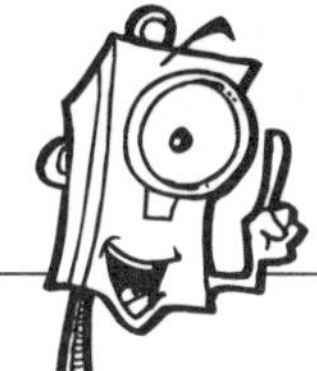

Candid Camera

You can easily add narration to your videos after you've shot. This can be done with simple editing gear, or by using the "audio dub" feature on many VCRs. (See Chapter 19, "Putting That Old VCR to Work: Linear Editing.")

Both in my professional career and in my home video projects, VO is just as important of an element as video quality, music and shot selection. If your talent is truly talented, even the most poorly produced home video is given a sense of importance and legitimacy.

VO artists come in all sorts of shapes and sizes. You've probably heard your favorite actor or actress on a TV commercial or narrating a documentary. Gene Hackman, Martin Sheen, Richard Dreyfuss, Michael Douglas, John Lithgow, Kathleen Turner, and Christine Lahti all do VO work in their spare time. Other VO professionals do specialized voices for animated programs and commercials, or narration for documentaries, promotions, CD-ROMs, and training tapes. In the digital age the opportunity for voice work is constantly growing.

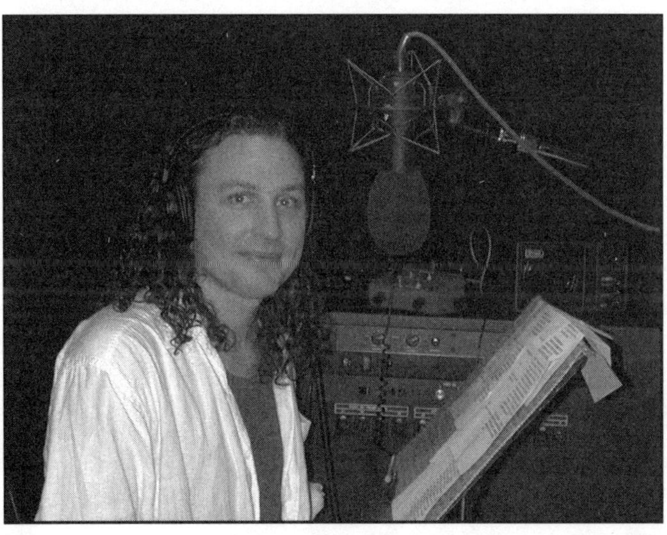

Professional VO artist recording at Broadway Sound in N.Y.C.

Professional voice-over artists are extremely well paid for their skill. I can spend 30 minutes with talent for projects at HBO and sign checks for thousands of dollars.

Since most home video productions don't have the bucks to lure a voice-over professional, it's time again to search your personal circle of contacts for someone who has a strong voice and that, with a little coaching, could pull off a nice narration. Or why depend on someone else if you can do it yourself? If you're interested in laying down the voice tracks in your home videos, consider taking a public speaking or acting course to train yourself to speak better. (See "Training Your Own Vocal Chords," below.)

If you're auditioning others, record your prospective narrators on tape (you can do this with your camcorder). Listening to the recording is the best way to determine which voice will work best. If you're at a loss for finding someone in your own circle, consider looking in your own community for potential narrators: college Speech (or Communications Arts), Theatre, or Radio/TV/Broadcasting departments, community or regional theatre groups, or local (especially small town or college) radio or TV stations.

But since 99.9 percent of our readers won't have the budget, what should they do? I would suggest they audition friends, friends of friends, acquaintances, and so on, by recording voices they think might be appropriate and listening to how they sound.

Training Your Vocal Chords

If you listen to TV and radio, you know that people whose voices are broadcast on a daily basis know how to breathe life into the spoken word. Whether they're reading a script or ad-libbing dialog, they know how to inflect and pause tastefully, and convince listeners that they're an authority on the subject. Or they can effortlessly finesse a "stylized" script.

If you've got a strong voice, you're one step ahead of the game. But you don't have to sound like James Earl Jones to deliver good narration. In fact, a recent trend in TV is to use people who have an "everyday" sound and not the omnipresent voice of God or overexcited radio D.J. or game show host. If you have the chance, check out the promos that air between movies on Cinemax or American Movie Classics. They write their scripts like the announcer is having a casual conversation with the audience.

The best thing you can do to improve your voice is practice. You can tape commercials and programs off the air and imitate the existing announcer, or you can write some copy and just read it over and over again until you get it right. You can also tape your voice with your camcorder. Listen back and figure out what sounds good, and try to focus in on that.

Recording Your Narration

You can record yourself or your talent in numerous ways, including, as mentioned earlier, reading directly into the microphone of your camcorder. But if you're looking for a perfectly clean and rich sound, putting your talent in an isolation booth or any other area that is devoid of all sound is the best bet for a perfect recording.

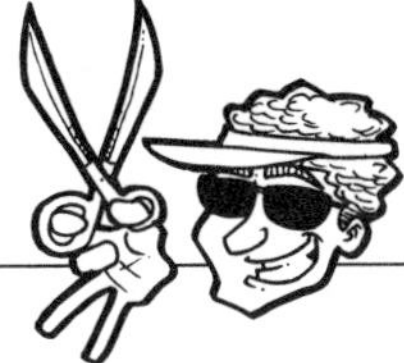

Director's Cut

"The most important advice for anyone trying to do voiceover is to be natural and don't overact. Sometimes it can be intimidating to hear your voice on tape and people tend to talk differently when using a microphone. It works much better to relax and be yourself." —Jeff Bottoms, voice-over talent, MTV, ESPN, CBS, and The Movie Channel

Whenever I walk into the sound booth at HBO Studio Productions, it is so perfectly quiet that I can hear my hair growing. Isolation not only cuts out external noise, but it also gives the microphone the best opportunity to record your voice.

In most studios there's a high quality microphone mounted on a boom stand that is aimed at the talent's mouth. A windscreen, similar to the one you would use for a lavalier microphone, stops the popping P's, B's and slurring S's.

You can record in a makeshift isolation booth like a closet, bathroom, or even a shower. The less background noise the mic picks up, the better your recording is going sound. Suppose you choose a hallway closet as your narration location. Begin by removing everything from the closet, find a spare scrap of carpet and place it on the floor. Next, tack some thick blankets to the walls and you've got an instant isolation booth.

If your production has a little money to throw around, you may decide to spend it on the narration. If so, you'll want to find a cheap studio to record in. Check out your local paper, the Web, or take a look at your local record or musical store. There are usually ads posted that may include inexpensive studio time. I've seen prices range anywhere from $20 to $200 per hour. Aim for the lower end of that scale!

Directing Your Talent

Just like any other actor on your set, the VO artist should be treated with respect and consideration. Make sure you've had a detailed conversation on what you expect before the talent enters the booth.

Also, during the recording session, always give your announcer feedback after each take. There's nothing worse for talent than to work with a director or producer where they have to wonder for the entire session how they're doing. A positive word when your talent does something well goes a long way.

If you're lucky, the talent will get into the groove within a couple of takes. When they finally nail it, always have them read it again for safety. Also, have them read the same lines at different speeds if possible. You never know when you need to save or add time to your overall program length. Before they enter the booth you can also help them mark their scripts and make notes as to where you would like them to inflect and emphasize. During the recording, make sure your talent "slates" each take with a verbal cue before they start reading. This way, it will be easier for you to take notes and to locate the lines you want when you edit.

When you first get yourself involved in home video production, you should never hesitate to bring along your friends and family. This way, you'll have a lot of fun and nobody will fault you for making beginner mistakes. Plus, situations and circumstances that arise from a home video production usually generate funny stories can last a lifetime. Whether it's your children, brothers, sisters, parents, and so on, get ready to have fun, and make home movie history!

The Least You Need to Know

- For your cast and crew, use as many people as you can get from your circle of friends, family, and associates.
- Involving children in your production can benefit you as well as them.
- Memorizing lines is harder than you think. Try using cue cards or a teleprompter.
- VO is an art and skill that can drastically improve the production value of your videos.

Chapter 13

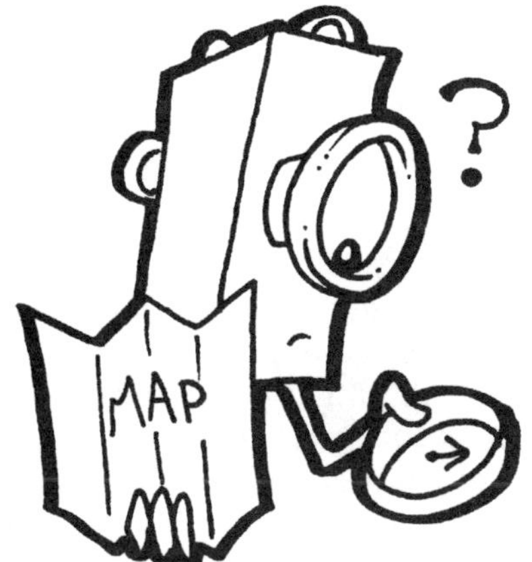

A Step in the Right Direction

In This Chapter

- Taking charge of your home videos
- Actor vs. director
- Getting your cast comfortable with the camcorder
- Interviewing the easy way
- Directing yourself out of a jam

Welcome to the director's chair! The job is yours whether you like it or not! You've got an idea or even a script, you've done all the pre-production preparation, you've secured your talent and crew, and you've just bought a brand new Mini-DV camcorder to shoot your mini-movies. Even if you plan to just shoot footage without ever editing a frame of video, it's a good idea to brush up on your directing skills. That's because your footage will probably feature a lot more people than inanimate objects like trees and concrete buildings. People bring your videos to life, and learning how to coach and relax them for the camera will significantly improve your footage.

So now that you're the captain of the ship, get ready to steer your home video productions in the right direction. At first, it will be simple projects where you'll need to become skilled at helping your cast of characters to be comfortable on camera. Later, when your projects become more advanced, not only do you have to be the master of the schedule and budget; you've also got to wrench a good performance out of your cast and crew. And to do that, you need to prepare yourself for the potential snake pit you're about to jump into!

You're the C.E.O of Your Video

Most Hollywood directors probably aren't financial geniuses or experts in time management. When it comes to making movies, the major studios hire executive producers, producers, and a team of production managers to handle all the money matters. They want the director's focus to be on creative matters and not the monotonous financial and schedule details.

In the world of home video, however, all the responsibility falls directly into your lap. When it's just you and your camcorder, you'll find yourself shelling out cash and generally jumping through hoops to keep things moving forward. If you've got a bigger production planned, one minute you'll find yourself guiding the cast and crew, the other you're handling cash and tinkering with the shooting schedule. And you've always got to be on guard for unforeseen situations and emergencies that strike any video production from time to time. Even if you're just shooting a birthday party or a wedding, you need to be on your toes at all times.

Battling the Budget

Whether you're working on a project for a client where you're given a budget or digging into your own pocket to fund your own home video, you've got to keep close track of the bottom line. Since cash can disappear quickly when you've got people to pay and equipment to rent, you want to scan your resource pool before shelling out the big bucks. If you're in a jam and you need to rent lighting or audio equipment, try to scale your needs down to the bare minimum. If cash is extremely tight, explore the possibilities on what expenses can be cut from the production. Borrowing gear from friends or family is always a plus, but do you want to be responsible if something breaks? (And there's always at least one thing that breaks on a video shoot.)

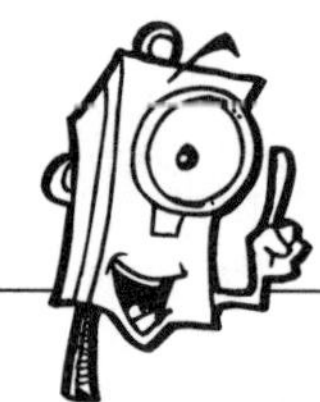

Candid Camera

One of the best ways to save money is to avoid renting any lighting equipment. There's an abundance of household materials, lights included, that can be used in the place of professional equipment. (See Chapter 9, "Cast Some Light on the Matter.")

The other option is to try and get others to support your project and lend you the equipment. If your video can be seen as promoting your town, business or an institution in any way, you have more than ample reason to approach them for support. If I were planning a shoot at the N.Y.U. Library, for instance, I'd go right to the film department and ask them for support. Depending on the purpose of your project, people may be very interested in helping you out because it results in free publicity for them. And there's a good chance that they would be in a much better position than yourself to soak up a loss if something breaks out in the field.

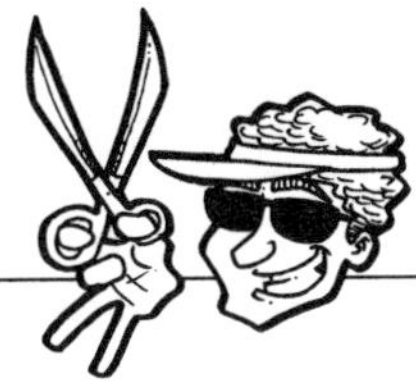

Director's Cut

"When I'm directing a shoot and I don't have a Production Manager keeping things on time for me, I absolutely panic. There's nothing worse than trying to manage a shooting schedule at the same time. It always takes my mind off of directing the talent."
—Alberto Ferreras, Senior Writer/Producer, HBO/Cinemax

Scrambling to Keep on Schedule

Your second big challenge takes place while you're directing your video. You've got to make sure that your shooting schedule (if you have one) goes according to plan. If something gets held up, you have to be prepared to think fast on your feet in order to come up with smart, realistic solutions to make up for lost time. Like most things in video production, practice makes perfect, but there are a few things that anyone can do, regardless of experience, to keep the shoot flowing smoothly.

First and foremost, always have your schedule written out (preferably a computer printout) as early as possible. If you are employing the help of friends and family or even a real video crew, try to have a first draft several days before you plan shoot. This way, you can open a dialog with everyone involved to get input. It's always a great idea to give your staff the opportunity to be involved in the planning of the schedule. They'll appreciate it much more than if you were to toss a schedule at them without asking for feedback.

The other thing you can do is have a list prepared of "plan B's" that you can go to if things go wrong. Break down the entire day in order of importance and mark the shots that are not critical to cover. Always concentrate on scenes with heavy dialog and acting. You can always come back to pick up establishing and other location shots at a later date. Many Hollywood features shoot with only one camera, and they hardly ever shoot the entire movie in sequential order. This is a precedent that all home videographers should follow. Especially if you're planning to edit your footage later, or even if you're covering a special event like a wedding or a birthday party, shooting things in sequence isn't necessary.

Don't Forget to Ask Permission!

One detail that is often overlooked by videographers is to ask the talent's permission to include them in your home video. If you don't expect your project to go further than an audience that you've assembled in your living room, it may not make any difference. But if someone takes interest in your project and for whatever the reason wants to put it on the air someplace, if you don't have written permission from your talent, you risk a lawsuit. It's more of a common tale than you think because home video content has more of a home than ever on broadcast and cable TV.

Also, if you're shooting a corporate video or anything else that can be used to promote an institution or business, getting releases is a must! The friends who happily agreed to help you with your project could suddenly start to question the whole deal when they see themselves doing something funny but stupid on TV.

Actor vs. Director

Actor vs. director. It's one of the most infamous rivalries in the entertainment industry. No matter what the scale of your video, whether you're producing a training tape for your business or a short film for your friends and family, you're guaranteed to have the unique opportunity to partake in the actor/director battle on some level.

It is understandable, however, why some actors display less than exemplary behavior during a shoot. In my experience, I've found that the biggest complaint that actors and actresses have is they never feel like they're fully a part of the production. When you have a large crew that spends a lot of time fiddling with getting the shot right, sometimes the talent is left feeling like an outsider. And this is true whether they have acting experience or are just your cousins who agreed to help you.

It's also tough for talent because every word that they speak, every expression they make, and their every move, however slight, is directly under a microscope. And whenever any kind of video lighting is involved, it's a very hot spotlight that can make for some seriously cranky moments.

It's your job as director to ease this tension as much as possible in order to achieve a positive environment for the creative process to flow.

One of the most effective ways to ease tensions is to confront them before they happen on the set. A short rehearsal before the scene, or preferably days before the shoot, can go a long way in relieving some of the nerves that can naturally build up on location. It is also a great forum for you to communicate exactly what you want from the talent, and in turn, they can give you realistic feedback.

Another key factor on your part is confidence, or lack of it. If your talent senses that you're not in control 100 percent of the time, they can lose patience very quickly. If something goes wrong, don't panic. Deal with it as calmly as possible, like you knew that it was going to happen all along, and now that it has, no worries, mate. If you sense that your talent is questioning a decision of yours, take the time to explain exactly why you're doing what you're doing. As difficult as it may be, if the talent has feedback, listen to it, and if it makes sense, take their advice. Don't let yourself get bullied around, but leave yourself open for creative collaboration. Film and videomaking of any kind is a team sport. It's almost impossible to do everything yourself and have all the right answers 100 percent of the time.

I recently got stuck doing audio for a documentary shoot. After one particularly long morning of shooting, I heard the talent, who forgot he was wearing a wireless microphone, angrily voice some concerns about the project. He was upset that we were working with a skeleton crew (Director, Producer [me] and D.P.). I quietly pulled the director aside and explained what I had heard. Not long after the director announced that we were taking a two-hour lunch and would be shooting very lightly for the rest of the afternoon. We had the rest of the week to shoot, so it was worthwhile for us to alter our schedule. The talent was in a much better mood after that, which made for more comfortable shooting conditions.

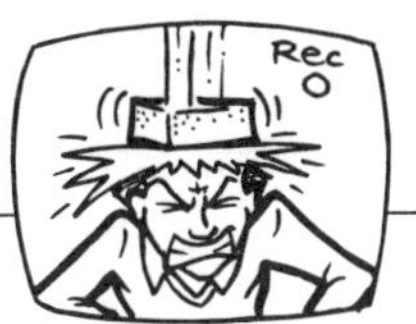

Blooper

If the actor/actress is not performing the way you expect, never publicly criticize him or her in front of the rest of the cast and crew. That's a bad management tactic to adopt. Take the actor aside or have a brief conversation between camera setups. The talent will appreciate your diplomacy.

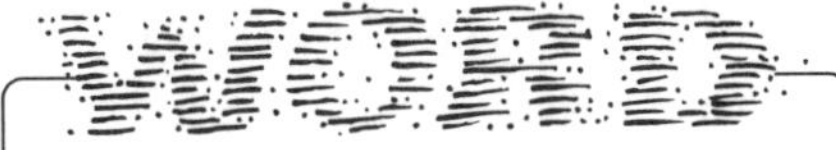

Blurred Word

D.P. stands for **Director of Photography.** It's a neat way of saying cameraman or the person responsible for shooting a video project. The D.P. works very closely with the Lighting Director to get the best picture quality.

Actors (even amateurs, and especially children) can sense when you are at sea. Directors should always exude confidence, even when things go awry. Nothing makes actors more nervous than a fumbling director!

Don't Be Nervous; It's Just a Camcorder!

As I mentioned, a large part of your cast may end up being family members and friends, a group of people who probably don't speak in public for a living, or perform on-camera for that matter. Some people hate camcorders. As soon as the red recording light goes on, they run for the hills.

This goes out to my wife, Debra, who has declared war on my camcorder, movie camera, and every other various recording device I use to capture the moment. (Even though she looks absolutely breathtaking and is perfectly well spoken on screen.) One day I'll put together a funny clip reel of her pushing the camcorder away spanning from our honeymoon to our 50th wedding anniversary. But for now, whenever she asks me to turn off the camera, I do.

As a director, there's nothing worse than forcing someone you know and love to talk on camera if they're noticeably uncomfortable. When you're looking for intelligent

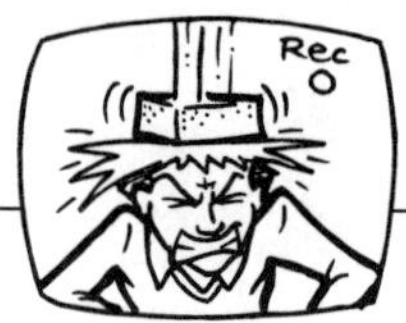

Blooper

Just as some people don't like to have their picture taken, you need to be extremely sensitive to the fact that some people don't like to be on camera. Although you might not be able to tell, some people find themselves extremely uncomfortable, even fearful of the camera lens. In fact, it can be worse than the fear of a still camera, because photos only take a fraction of second to happen. Videotaping can go on and on ...

and comfortable on-camera communication, it's very challenging when someone is nervously twitching and shifting in their chair. And you never really know who's going to perform and who's going to fold until you turn the camcorder on. If you're working with a group of people, you can resort to a technique that is often used in theatre. Have your cast go through a simple series of physical exercises before filming. You can also do "teamwork" drills like passing a phantom "air-ball" back and forth. This helps to keeps everyone relaxed, yet sharp and on their toes.

On the other hand, you might encounter jokesters or people who tend to overact and get corny when the camcorder turns their way. You can either avoid them altogether, or give them their moment in the spotlight and record them for a little while (you can always edit them out later). Or you can pretend that you're recording when you're really not. If you find yourself missing key moments, you can politely ask them to step aside.

When filming a video for my friend's birthday party last year, I wrote some speaking parts for my friend Rick, and our other friends, Larry, and Chris. I expected that Larry and Rick, who are the world's biggest hams on camera, would give great interviews and Chris, who's a bit shyer when the camcorder turns his way, would be much harder to direct. To my surprise, it turned out to be completely the opposite. While Rick and Larry are natural ad-libbers, when they were placed in a more formal, sit-down interview setting, they stiffened up and read their lines, devoid of their usual flair. Chris, on the other hand, took my direction extremely well and ended up giving a convincing and relaxed performance. So it would make sense, when shooting special events and occasions, to allow for ad-libbing and not try to stick too closely to a prepared script. You'll avoid trying to force a suddenly voiceless participant to do your bidding and you'll get unexpected performances out of others.

If you find that your talent is agitated by the camcorder, take a quick break and ask everyone else in the room to walk out for a few minutes. Then calmly reassure your talent that because it's video, the shoot can operate on auto-pilot and nobody else has to be in the room. If fear of public speaking is the problem, your talent will perform more comfortably in an empty room. After a while, you can start inviting the crew back, one by one, to check audio levels, camera shots and lighting. Before you know it, everyone's eased back into the room and your talent couldn't care less.

You can also divert your talent's attention to an off-camera object or person. This is a common method for calming down talent since it forces them to focus their conversation elsewhere so they're not thinking about the rolling camera.

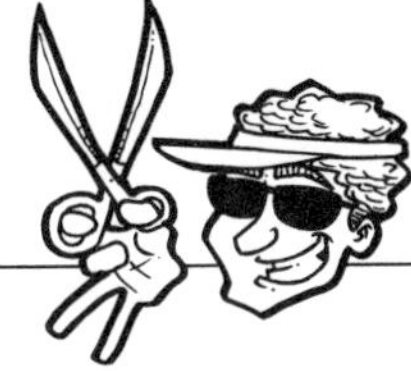

Director's Cut

If the blinking red recording light is distracting to your talent, it can be shut off on some camcorder models. If not, place a piece of tape over it.

Interview Basics

The interview is one of the most effective techniques for capturing the spoken word on tape. But in everyday situations, getting most people to talk to the camcorder can be a chore. When someone agrees to a formal interview on camera, however, they have accepted the fact that they have no choice but to talk, which gives them more time to prepare and think about what they are going to say beforehand.

Interviews also help set home video apart from still photography as a powerful and interactive medium. Interviews document the way people think, the way they speak, and the way they feel about a certain subject at a given time.

About a year before my grandmother passed away, I spent some time videotaping her and asking questions about everything from her views on religion to our family history. While it's not a tape that I pop into the VCR on a daily basis, I'm very glad that I took the time to interview her because now I realize that it's a family treasure. Down the road, I will be able to show my children exactly what their great grandmother looked like, what she sounded like, and her insights into our family history and life in general. Thanks to home video, for the first time in human history a unique line of communication has built a bridge between distant generations.

From a directing standpoint, interviews can be challenging to pull off, and there are only two options for setting them up. You can either appear on-screen with the talent, or you can fire questions at them from a location off-screen.

Candid Camera

A documentary aired on cable TV called *Bubbeh Lee and Me* that demonstrates the archival power of home video. It's about a grandson who videotapes and interviews his grandmother while visiting her in Florida. The program plays like a video-tribute to the grandmother, who, as we discover, is quite an amazing person. It was after watching this program that I decided to interview my grandmother.

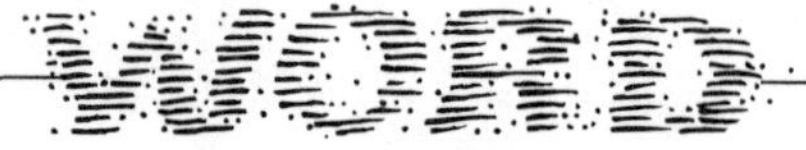

Blurred Word

B-roll is an old editor's term that refers to a two-tape video editing system (A tape and B tape) where the A-roll is the main footage and the B-roll is supporting footage and cover shots. You can have the audio from the A-roll shot continue to play underneath B-roll shots.

The two-person interview seems to look better on camera and opens the door for creative editing by cutting away to reaction shots and "B-roll" while cutting out bad audio moments. I rarely use the two-person setup, however, because I think that the director's presence on-screen can be a distraction to the program. (Unless, of course, you're Rob Reiner in *Spinal Tap*.)

The off-camera interview, on the other hand, is much easier to pull off from a directing standpoint. This is the most common type of interview where the director or anyone else asking the questions, sits across from the interviewee, just out of the video frame. If your subject is nervous or uneasy about the camcorder, this forces their attention out of the line of fire. You will see off-camera interviews in documentaries, movies, news programs and so on.

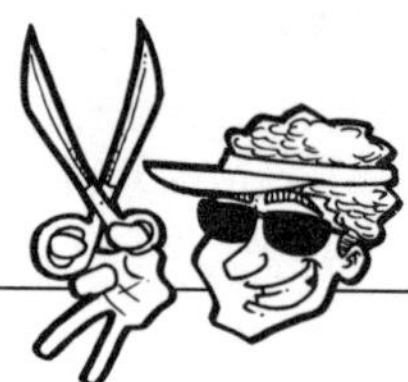

Director's Cut

If you're having a particularly tough interview always try to engage a difficult or uncooperative interviewee with questions about something they are passionate about. It's better to hear Uncle Buck wax enthusiastically about his chicken farm or Aunt Sally's eyes light up when talking about her knitting business than to hear short, uninteresting answers to questions you had planned to ask.

Directing Your Way Out of a Jam

In the world of shooting video, the unexpected can crop up at any minute and it's the director's job to put out any fire. At any given moment, be prepared to become an emergency equipment technician, firefighter, psychologist, coach, mediator, paramedic, even a police officer. Usually it's something as simple as broken equipment. In rare cases it can be as serious as someone getting injured on your set. Whatever the case, if you don't act quickly a situation like this can quickly escalate and destroy your shoot.

On a lighter note, there's a legendary directing-disaster story that came out of WRGB-TV in Albany, where I began my broadcasting career. One of the news anchors, while chatting with the sports anchor between stories, began to giggle somewhat out of control. When it came time for her to read the next story, she saw the words "bubonic plague" in her script, and she completely lost it. I always wondered what the director of the newscast was thinking at that point. Do you stay with an out-of-control anchor who's supposed to be reading a serious story, or do you fade to black and go to a commercial? The director of a local news program is under a lot more pressure than home videographers, because everything is happening live and there's no way to correct a mistake with creative editing. It's a situation that I don't envy.

On your set, there are hundreds of other variables that can sneak out of the woodwork and eat your production for lunch. Here's a list of potential shoot pitfalls and some quick solutions:

- **Equipment failure.** This is the silent killer of home video shoots across the land. You never know when cameras, microphones or lighting equipment will decide to quit. The best thing to do is tote along as much spare equipment as possible, or find a place in advance where you can obtain or rent gear in a pinch. (See Chapter 8, "Scouting Out Your Location.")
- **Unruly actor.** This doesn't happen very often, but if it does, be prepared. Do whatever you can to resolve the actor's gripe—if it's a direction issue, shoot it both their way and yours. If the actor is just completely out of control, don't hesitate to boot him or her from the set and fill the role with an innocent bystander. You'd be amazed at how quickly you'll get an apology when they're sufficiently cooled off.
- **Injury.** If someone gets injured on your set, always have a basic first aid kit with bandages, aspirin, and so on. Depending on the scale and purpose of your production, you can very well be responsible for any mishaps.
- **General cast and crew discomfort.** This can crop up at unexpected times. Your talent may need a refresh on the makeup, or your crew will get hungry, thirsty, and potentially cranky. Bring along some aspirin, makeup, food for breakfast, lunch and/or dinner, drinks, and other healthy snacks to nosh on, a razor and shaving cream, an electric shaver, comb, blankets, folding chairs, and even a mirror.
- **Sound or video glitches.** This can be one of the worst feelings: shooting an entire day to discover that the video or sound is faulty. This can be a creased tape, a head clog, or a buzzing in the audio track. The best thing to do is take a few minutes after each shot to watch and listen to the footage to make sure nothing's wrong with it. That's the beauty of shooting on videotape. It's a lot better to discover a problem on the set when you can do something about it than in the edit room.

- **Bad weather.** Unfortunately, no matter how carefully you try to forecast the weather, there are times when Mother Nature unleashes her fury on your production. The only thing to do in this situation is to search for an indoor location to finish your shoot. If this isn't possible, you can either reschedule, or outfit your camcorder, equipment and crew with rain gear and continue shooting. Sometimes rain can add a nice dramatic effect in a video.

The Least You Need to Know

- Directing your home videos can be as challenging as running a small business.
- Prepare yourself for some minor squabbles with your cast.
- If someone is uncomfortable on camera, do whatever you can to make that person feel more comfortable. Never force the issue, however.
- Interviewing is a skill that can be perfected with a little practice.
- Always be prepared to handle any crises, from simple equipment failure to injury on the set.

Chapter 14

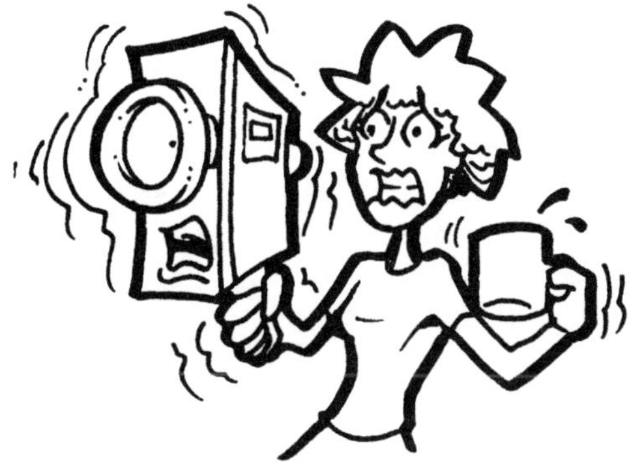

Taking the Jerk Out of Your Camera Work

In This Chapter

- Eliminating unnecessary camcorder motion
- Using your own body to achieve steady shots
- Smooth camera moves
- Taming the overzealous zoomer

Most home videos can be spotted a mile away. You can see them shake and wiggle on shows like *America's Funniest Home Videos* or *The World's Most Amazing Videos* on NBC. It's the jerky camera motion that sets home video apart and can take even the best quality MiniDV footage and make it look like it was shot on a trampoline. So if you can figure out how to terminate the twitch, your home videos can look as good as anything you'd see on TV.

But this isn't an easy thing to do since camcorders are smaller than ever and almost impossible to keep in one place. A tripod is always your best weapon against the wobbles, but a sturdy tripod is cumbersome and can be a real drag to tote around in everyday shooting situations. So you must rely on equipment that you have at your disposal, your own body being the best alternative, to help you keep your video on an even keel. And once you master some simple handheld techniques, you can easily pull off professional looking camera moves that will impress viewers and keep them away from the Dramamine.

Poetry in Motion

"Never mistake motion for action."
—Ernest Hemingway

I recently lent my camcorder to a friend to take with him on vacation. When he got back, he talked me into watching some of his footage. The tape was cued to a shot of his daughter on a beach building a sandcastle with a shovel and a pail. He was standing about 15 feet away from her, and for a full five minutes (which in TV terms is an eternity), repeatedly zoomed in and out without moving himself or the camcorder an inch. To top it off, the zooms weren't very smooth. His daughter's image danced from the top of the screen to the bottom every time he changed the camcorder's focal length. My friend had committed one of home video's biggest sins: trying to replace real action with motion, in this case unnecessary camera motion.

Misdirected motion, however, is one of the most common mistakes and a tough concept to get a handle on. If your video is perfectly still, you audience will be bored to tears. Too much and they will lose interest even quicker. The challenge for videographers is to strike the perfect balance somewhere in between.

The reason motion can become such a problem is that there's an inherent difference between your TV set and your own image processing system. Your eyes and your brain are one of the most advanced image stabilization systems on the planet. Try staring at an object hanging on a wall and begin to shake your head really fast. It's easy to keep the object perfectly centered in your field of vision. Even if you get up and jog in place, the object stays reasonably still.

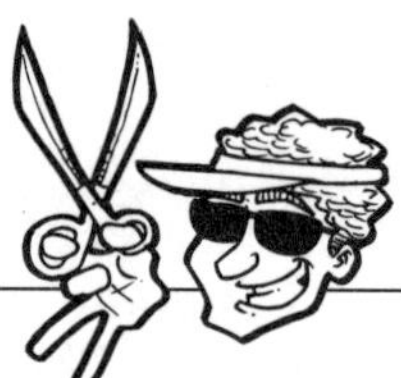

Director's Cut

The independent film *The Blair Witch Project* is shot in documentary style and features extensive handheld camerawork shot on a Hi8 camcorder. Even though the film did astonishingly well at the box office, scores of people were reported to have suffered from motion sickness while watching the film.

On a TV screen, it's difficult to conceal movement because the actual screen, which represents a tiny fraction of your field of vision, is a non-moveable object. This means that every little jump or shake within that screen is amplified because there's nothing to counterbalance it. In reality, when you walk from place to place, the images that you see are bouncing around just as much as the images in your home videos. But your vision is not confined to a 27-inch still frame, so the motion can hardly be seen.

But remember, it's the shake, rattle, and roll that you're looking to eliminate. Camera moves, if done right, can look perfectly smooth and can easily add visual variety to your videos.

Steady Shots Without Gettin' Jiggy Wit It!

As I've mentioned, a tripod can be the most valuable weapon you have in the battle of the bounce, but tripods may not be convenient to carry around. So, in the absence of true support, with a little practice, you can teach your body to act like a tripod. It's a technique that's easy to learn and once you've got it mastered, you can begin to pull off some smooth camera moves with your newly discovered steadiness.

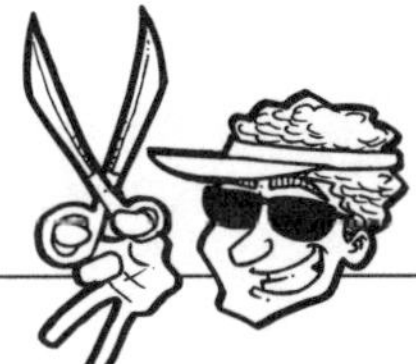

Director's Cut

"One of the most common mistakes I see when I watch someone's home video is too many quick camera movements. When moving the camcorder, slow it down and keep the motion as smooth as possible to better allow the viewer to follow the action."
—Anthony Salerno, Director of Photography, *Entertainment Tonight,* The Discovery Channel, *Good Morning, America*

Becoming a Human Shock Absorber

In our quest for steadier shots, we should take advice not from soldiers, but athletes. If you think that sturdy camera work means that you'll have to stand as stiff as the Terminator with your sneakers bolted to the ground, you're in for a pleasant surprise.

I compare the shooting posture that I'm about to teach you with the defensive stance that athletes use in basketball, tennis, or even wrestling. With your legs spread a little bit farther than shoulder-width apart, bend your knees slightly and put your arms out in front of you for balance. It gives you the low center of gravity that you need for stability and to absorb shock. Plus, it's subtle enough to take the spring out of your step without leaving you looking totally foolish.

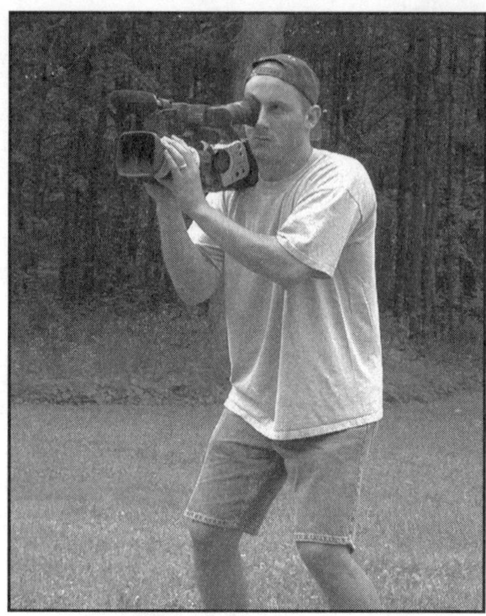

Ideal shooting stance.

When playing sports, you need to be ready to quickly move in any direction while remaining light on your feet. If you use this stance as a videographer, you're more prepared to deal with the occasional bump in the road or wind gust that may come your way.

In the Palms of Your Hands

No matter how good your stance is, if you don't know what to do with your hands, you're not going to get the steady shot you're looking for. The best way to stabilize your camera is by holding it with two hands. Whether you're using a tiny MiniDV or a full size VHS camcorder, both hands will help you lock down your shots and will cause your upper torso and arms to absorb much of the shock.

Whenever possible, dig your elbows into your sides or abdomen for added stability. Also, take advantage of anything you can to remove the strain from your arms, especially when you're holding the camcorder out in front of you, away from your face. No matter how light camcorders are, after a while of holding it front and center, it starts to feel like a lead weight.

Try the Knee-Pod on for Size

Wherever possible, seek the assistance of any surface or object that can help you steady your camcorder. It could be a table, doorknob, wall, banister, a friend's shoulder, or even the top of his or her head. Once you position the camcorder, you can either bend down to get a glimpse through the eyepiece, or you can use your trusty pop-out LCD viewfinder. You can also use furniture, floors, or moldings to get high or low shots for variety.

After my son was born, I found myself searching for a better way to get steady shots down on his level near the floor. It's pretty challenging and tough on the back to constantly bend down while looking through the viewfinder. Sometimes I would attempt holding the camera at my feet while trying to frame the shot without looking, but the results were nominal at best. And when you're trying to shoot children, pets, or anything else that takes place at ground-level, good video moments are rare and in order to capture them, you need to be in the right place at the right time.

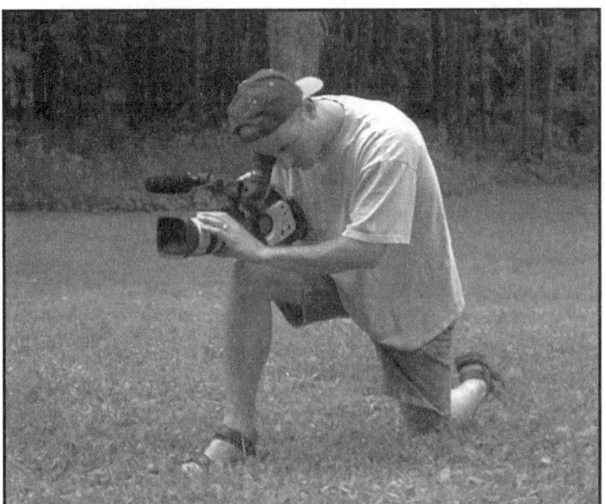

"Knee-pod" shot.

So, in order to increase my odds of being there when something incredible happened, I came up with the "knee-pod" shot. It's as simple as dropping as close to the floor as possible with one knee forward and as high as possible while putting the other leg behind you for stability. (See preceding figure.) Place the camcorder on you knee and voila! You've got a knee-pod! Your knee acts as a little platform that works very much like a tripod. You can smoothly pan from side to side, and tilt up and down.

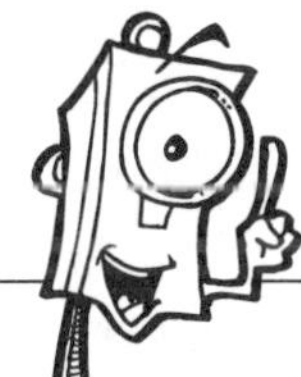

Candid Camera

Just as you would for any other athletic event, it helps to stretch before you suddenly drop to the floor. Not that videography is a huge workout, but when chasing children or pets around, you never know!

Here are a few other tips to help you achieve steady shots:

- Use an external or pop-out LCD screen as much as possible while holding the camcorder away from your body.

- Try keeping both eyes open when you shoot. It takes a little practice, and is especially hard when you're manually focusing. But it helps you keep track of the bigger picture and that ultimately results in smoother shots.
- Try to avoid holding the rubber part of your camcorder's eyepiece directly against your eye. Even if you're holding it an inch away, your camcorder won't be affected by sudden head movements.
- Breathe slowly and deliberately. Camcorders are so sensitive that they can pick up slight movements in your chest and other parts of the body.
- In potentially bumpy situations, use the widest lens angle that the situation will allow. Wide-angle lenses are much less sensitive to movement than telephoto.

Getting Funky with Camera Moves

Now that you've got the stance mastered, you're ready to put that camcorder to work. Even the most professional-looking camera moves are completely doable without any additional equipment. It's videomaking the natural way!

Camera moves are appropriate when the action of your subject calls for it. This is totally open to interpretation and a whole lot of creativity. Let's go back to the video of my friend's daughter playing in the sand for a minute. While her entire body isn't moving very much, her hands are certainly busy enough. So instead of hanging out 15 feet away playing with the camcorder's zoom, my friend could have left the lens in wide-angle and slowly walked over to his daughter and panned down to get a close-up shot of her hands. While walking forward, the viewer gets a good feel for the scenery of the shot and before boredom sets in, the shot changes to reveal what the little girl is doing.

There are all kinds of camera moves that you can use to help make your videos more visually impressive. Once you learn the following techniques, you can easily try them out in the field to find out which ones work best for you.

Panning and Tilting

Panning and tilting are by far the most basic and commonly used camera moves. A pan is simply a side-to-side move, and a tilt is up and down. While there's relatively little camera movement involved besides rotating the camcorder on an axis, pans and tilts are very tricky to execute without a tripod. But with a little body-finessing your pans and tilts will look super-smooth.

Before you attempt a panning shot, take a careful look around to make sure that you have a clear frame. Let's say you want to get a shot of someone riding by on a bike. Plant your feet firmly on the ground and assume shooter's posture. In this case, you shouldn't move your feet at all; you can use the natural flexibility in your hips to help you rotate with the action.

There's actually one other method that I use to stabilize the camera that works especially well when panning without a tripod. Hold the camcorder close to your eye with your right (or left) hand. Now take the other arm and cross forearms. Then grab the triceps muscle of your shooting arm (that's the one along the back of your upper arm). You'll look like a genie about to grant a wish, but the camcorder wont move an inch. This position also works very well when tilting the camera up and down.

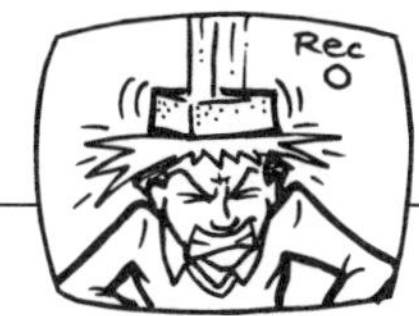

Blooper

Whenever I plan to do a lot of panning with my camcorder, I usually turn off the image stabilization system. Sometimes image stabilization can misinterpret the beginning of a pan and try to counterbalance the motion, ruining the beginning of the shot.

Keeping Your Video on Track

Tracking shots bring panning and tilting to the next level. Unlike a pan or tilt, the camcorder and the shooter both are physically moving with the action. Either back and forth, side to side, or up and down, if you can figure out a way to pull it off, your videos are going to look very cool. And all you really need to make it happen is a set of wheels.

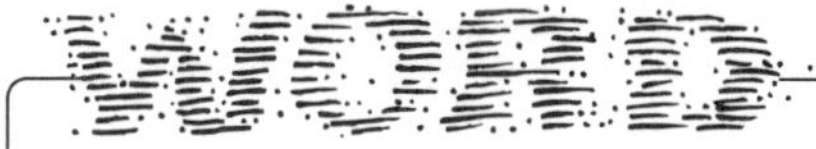

Blurred Word

A **dolly shot** is when the camcorder moves toward or away from the subject in a straight line. A **dolly** is a camera mount (tripod) with wheels.

Back and Forth

When you move the camcorder toward or away from your subject, it is considered to be a "dolly" shot. These are great for point-of-view shots or just to give your audience a unique perspective on the subject and scene. Professionals pull off this shot with highly functional tripods that can be rolled smoothly along most surfaces. But you don't need a million-dollar piece of equipment. A dolly can be done with stuff you can easily get your hands on at home.

In low-budget filmmaking, the wheelchair is one of the most commonly used dolly devices. With large rear wheels and front wheels that soak up a lot of shock, you can get pretty smooth dolly shots with one. And you can rent one if you anticipate doing a number of dolly shots.

In case you can't get your hands on a wheelchair, the next best thing is an office chair with wheels. The one benefit that an office chair offers is that it usually allows you not only to navigate in any direction, but you can also swivel in the seat offering a high-tech pan, and with some chairs you can even tilt up and down.

If you can't pin down an office or wheelchair, you can dolly with almost anything that has wheels. A car is always great for dollying. In fact, many big-budget productions use cars and other motor vehicles for this kind of shot. Not only can you control the speed with great accuracy, a car also has its own built in shock absorber system. A bicycle is also a great dolly tool, but it is a little more dangerous to navigate. If you're using a bicycle, never hold the camcorder directly to your eye. Use either a pop-out LCD viewfinder or blindly frame the shot as best you can. You should also wear a helmet.

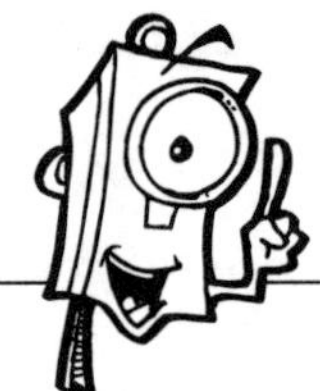

Candid Camera

When using a wheelchair or a rolling office chair to execute a dolly shot, it's best to have someone navigate for you. And if you have the opportunity, rehearse the shot before recording.

Another more obvious method is simply walking with the camcorder. Unfortunately the easiest way to do something isn't always the most effective. Unlike a car or wheelchair, it's extremely hard to keep the camcorder perfectly still while bouncing up and down while walking. But if it's the only choice you have, implement the fundamentals of smooth handheld shooting, and your shots will look fine. Try bending your knees a little bit more than you normally would. You might look like a gorilla strolling along, but sometimes you have to stretch the limits of vanity in order to get good shots.

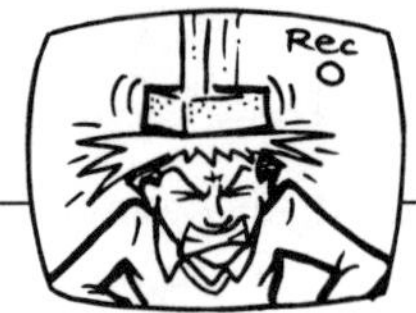

Blooper

Safety should always be a big consideration when trying to figure out the best dollying method. Never try to dolly and drive a car at the same time. You should always have someone else driving the car for you.

Personally, I love to use in-line skates for dolly shots. It's safer than bicycles and easier to film with one eye while gliding along. You also have more flexibility in that you can maneuver and quickly change direction without much effort. If you plan on taking the in-line skate approach, again, remember to wear a helmet!

Dolly shots are considered to be more advanced types of shots, so they warrant a little practice beforehand. If possible, take the camcorder out of automatic mode. Excessive movement in any kind of shot can throw the focus or exposure off. Do a dry run of your shots two or three times or until you get it right.

Side to Side

Unlike panning from side to side, a "truck" shot is a more dramatic move from side to side, also in which the camcorder and the shooter are moving. Truck shots are usually performed in a perfectly straight line. An "arc" shot is actually a combination of a dolly and truck shot where the camcorder moves around the subject in an arc.

Truck shots are harder to swing because they're harder to navigate and shoot while motoring from side to side. I've actually taken some nice truck shots while standing sideways on a skateboard. An assistant holds me tightly in place from behind and slowly moves me where the shot calls for me to go. With additional support, the skateboard doesn't fly out from underneath my feet. Thanks to the swivel motion of an office chair, you can get nice looking truck shots, but a wheelchair is out of the question because it's very hard to twist completely sideways while trying to shoot.

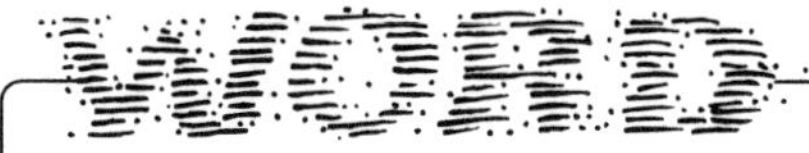

Blurred Word

Truck shot is the physical movement of shooter and camcorder from side to side in a straight line. An **arc shot** is a combination of a truck shot and a dolly shot.

Up and Down

Ever see a movie where the camera seems to effortlessly move up and down, over cars, bushes and fences like they weren't even there? What you're not seeing is the million-dollar crane on wheels supporting a platform for the camera. It's actually a classic Hollywood image ... to have a director perched high atop the scene on a crane looking through the camera with a bullhorn in hand.

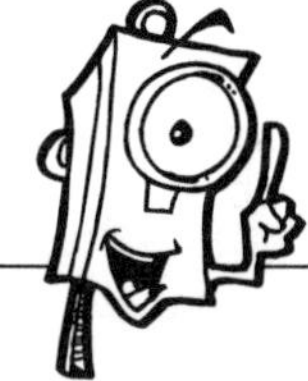

Candid Camera

Arc shots are actually smoother to do when walking. Simply move around your subject in full shooter's posture while taking short, deliberate steps.

This type of shot is called a "pedestal" or "crane" shot and I can honestly say that Hollywood professionals have a clear advantage over home videographers in this case. If you want to physically move your camcorder up and down from a high vantage point to a low one, or vice versa, one step short of renting a crane, it's very difficult to do. Other non-ground based equipment like helicopters, hang-gliders, small planes, even tightropes are all hard to come by, expensive to rent, and potentially dangerous.

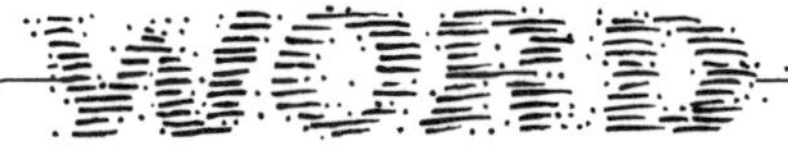

Blurred Word

A **pedestal shot** or **crane shot** is the physical motion of the camcorder and shooter from a high vantage shot to a low one, or the other way around.

If you want to try a pedestal shot, you'll probably have to rely on your own body to get a good shot. So far, our own bodies have served us well when it comes to camera movement. The same is so when moving from high to low or from low to high. The hard part is actually squatting down or standing up without hitting a rough spot. You can also stand on a sturdy table, or slowly step down a ladder or even a staircase to achieve the effect of a crane shot. This will give you more depth than relying on your standing height alone. The key here is do whatever you're going to do very sloooooowly. Especially if you practice a couple of times, you'll find that you can easily change your vertical position without bumping around.

To Zoom or Not to Zoom

This is a tough one to avoid, because chances are the zoom is your favorite feature on the camcorder. But it's definitely worth mentioning when talking about smooth camera motion because a zoomed-in lens is the easiest way to put all of your anti-jerk efforts to waste.

I have a general rule when it comes to using telephoto lens angles. I only zoom all the way in when I am too far from the action and have no way of getting any closer, or when I've taken my tripod along. As I've said before, when you're zoomed all the way in, it's almost impossible to keep a steady image while holding the camcorder.

It's also important to remember that using the telephoto setting changes some fundamental qualities of your video by compressing images and masking distance. In some cases this can be an esthetically pleasing technique. But if you want your viewer to get the feel of the scene, telephoto just isn't going to cut the mustard.

By using wider angle settings, you're guaranteeing much steadier shots and you have the additional benefit of recording clear audio when you're closer to the subject. Even though zooming is fun, resist the temptation. Your home video viewers will thank you for it!

The Least You Need to Know

- Too much camcorder movement is extremely distracting to your viewers and diverts attention from the real action in your scene.
- You can use your own body to stabilize the camcorder.
- Using your body and other simple items you have lying around, you can pull off Hollywood style camera moves.
- Zoom only when absolutely necessary. Telephoto angles are much less stable than wide-angle shots.

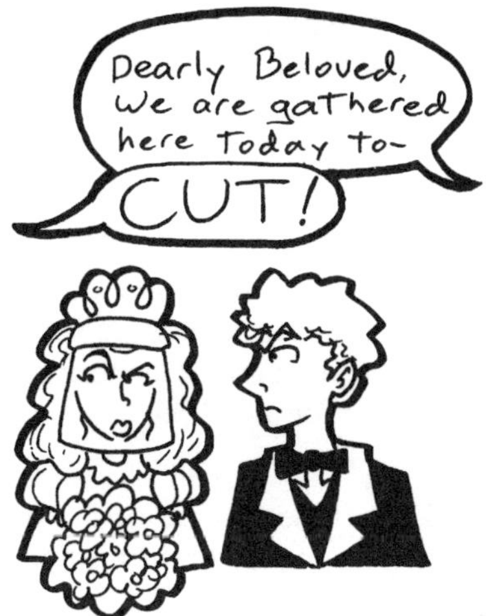

Chapter 15

The Basics for All Occasions: What to Do When …

In This Chapter

- The adventure of the wedding video
- Vacation and video go well together
- Pack your camcorder, it's a birthday party!
- Camcorder Olympics
- Celebrate the holidays with home video
- Capturing your graduate on video
- BabyCam 101

Why do we buy camcorders? To record and preserve the most important events in our lives as they unfold. Be it a wedding, holiday, birthday party, graduation, or even the arrival of your new baby, camcorders are capable of preserving these events long after your memories have receded into the halls of history.

Ten years ago, great-looking event videos weren't accessible to the average consumer because high-end camcorders and equipment cost a ton of money. But then technology came along and placed these tiny, highly functioning, yet inexpensive digital camcorders into the palms of our hands. Not only do they blow away the video images of old, but they also require a fraction of the equipment needed to supplement light and audio.

So start shooting and shoot often! Because life can be like crossing a rocky-river, skipping from one special moment to the next. Now is the time to fill your library with well-shot and creative videos that everyone will want to see again and again.

Untying the Wedding Video Knot

A good place to kick this off is the most videotaped event in human history: the wedding. Even though some wedding videos can be a blast to watch and provide some funny outtakes, they can be prohibitively expensive to have professionally shot and edited. It can cost anywhere from $500 to as much as $3,000 for a full package of shooting and editing.

Unfortunately on the long list of wedding-day expenses, the video is one of the first items on the chopping block. Most people either appoint a friend or family member for camcorder duties, or don't bother shooting anything at all. It's a shame because a wedding is a once-in-a-lifetime event, and it shouldn't have to go undocumented on video. With the help of some low-priced yet high-quality consumer equipment and a few tricks and techniques, you can create a wedding video just as well as any "professional" crew.

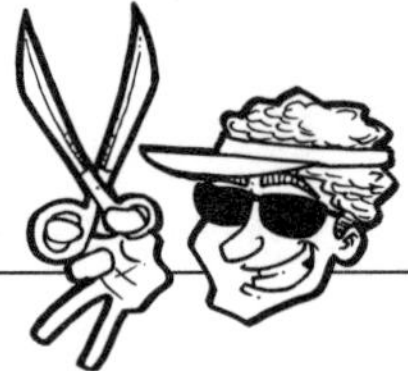

Director's Cut

I strongly recommend that if it is your own wedding, never make the mistake of taking on all the video responsibilities. It can put a damper on the day. The same is true for friends and family. Try to hire an acquaintance or someone else whom you trust with a camcorder, and who won't be insulted by not making the first round of invites. If you must rely on friends and family, make sure they split the responsibility equally so one person doesn't get stuck shooting for the entire affair.

As we've learned, one of the most important steps in video production is careful planning, or at least to give it a token forethought as to what's in store when it comes to shooting conditions. When Cousin Mitchell asks for help in videotaping his wedding, rest assured that you have some serious planning to do. Since location scouting is usually difficult or inconvenient, try to find out as much as you can about the lighting and audio conditions.

Weddings are an exact science in that they usually closely follow a pre-set schedule. This offers you the unique opportunity to be in the right place at the right time for key moments. You can also figure out when there are going to be "down times" that you can collect interviews with guests and shoot establishing and beauty shots of the location. You can always ask the bride to help you make a schedule because in most cases she has the tightest grip on the overall plan.

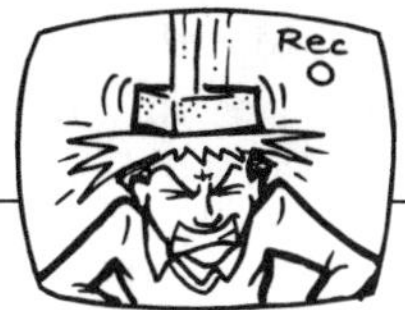

Blooper

Always check with the wedding coordinator to make sure that you're allowed to videotape (and use clip-on lights) during the ceremony. Depending on the kind of wedding it is, very often camcorders are banned to the back of the room until the ceremony is over. If this is the case, bring along your tripod for shooting in telephoto mode.

As for equipment requirements, a strong on-camera light is completely portable and the best bet for indoor weddings because they are usually lit down for effect. On the audio end of things, a handheld mic is a must for interviewing family and friends. If you want to get really fancy, grab a wireless handheld mic and when the band is playing, set it next to a speaker for a clean music recording.

Here's a quick list of things you'll want to bring along on a wedding-day shoot:

- List from bride and groom of people they want interviewed.
- List of things the bride and groom would like you to shoot. This includes exterior shots of the building and signage, the invitation, centerpieces, tables, floral arrangements and so on.
- Schedule (including specific times) of events.
- As many spare tapes and batteries that you can carry.
- Telephoto and wide-angle lens converters.
- Clip-on lights (battery powered).
- Handheld and/or wireless or wired lavalier microphone.
- Shotgun microphone if you'll be shooting from far away during the ceremony.
- Bad weather gear for yourself and your camcorder.
- Extension cords and other A/V cables and connectors.

We'll get more into editing and post-production in Part 4, but I can say now that it's good to collect pictures, invitations, or any other party-paraphernalia that you can get your hands on. You can put them under a camera at a later time and edit them into the final program.

While we're on the topic of editing, I can tell you that most professional wedding videographers will offer you program "packages" with lengths of an hour or more. This is how wedding videos got their bad reputation. I am a strong believer in keeping the wedding video short—no more than 40 minutes to an hour, tops. This is the perfect length to keep an audience interested without driving them to drink. (An hour is pushing it!) You can always look back on the raw footage if you want to watch the affair in its entirety.

Vacation Preservation

Anyone who has ever been on vacation knows that tourist spots are breeding grounds for camcorders ... and camcorder envy! From Iceland to Ireland, fathers far and wide walk with the finest Sony's and Canon's hanging from their necks. It's a silent competition where nobody ever emerges victorious since there's always something new on the horizon.

Now the trick is to actually shoot footage that other people will want to watch. And that's not as easy as it sounds because most people head for the hills when they hear the dreaded two words: "vacation video."

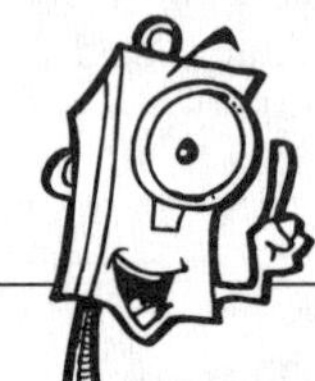

Candid Camera

When vacationing, pack all of your equipment and accessories before leaving. Never rely on finding what you need once you're there. This includes extra tapes, tripods, on-camera lights, external microphones, extra batteries, lens filters and a sturdy and spacious camcorder bag to fit everything into.

Good vacation videos have their roots in good vacation planning. Some people prefer to travel without a set plan, others have it scheduled down to the minute. If you want to have an idea of what equipment you'll need, it's always helpful to write out an outline of the highlights and the hot-spots included in your travel itinerary. Let's say you're headed for Italy's Amalfi Coast. You'd know that you're going to need a telephoto lens converter (see Chapter 3, "Cool Extras ... Do You Need the Bells and Whistles?") and, if you're willing to tote it along, a tripod for capturing the depth and beauty of the towering cliffs. You'd also know that on one of the days you're going to sail to the island of Capri. In this case it would be great to have polarizing and neutral density lens filters for toning down shadows and controlling the sun's rays reflecting off the sea.

Here's a chart of vacation situations you may encounter and the equipment solution for any conditions.

Situation	Equipment Solution
Beach, sand, water	Camcorder protection (plastic bag, or camcorder protective housing), U/V, polarizing, neutral density filters, lens cleaning tissue and solution

Situation	Equipment Solution
Snow, ice	Camcorder bag for protection from elements, lens filters, spare batteries
Outdoor tourist attractions	Telephoto and wide-angle lens converters, a tripod (if possible), lens filters, light reflectors
Indoor tourist attractions	Clip on camcorder light, spare batteries, shotgun microphone, headphones
Outdoor sports or events	Tripod, lens converters, lens filters, shotgun microphone

Once you get where you're going with the appropriate equipment on your person, your video will greatly benefit if you invent a unifying theme for your video. It could be as simple as focusing on one of your travel mates as they reveal the adventures of the journey to the camera. If you were in a large European city for example, you can do a bit on mopeds as a form of modern travel. In the Cayman Islands, you can hone in on scuba diving as an entertaining and beauty-filled diversion. If you're on a cruise or staying in a nice hotel, since there's always an exotic looking meal right around the corner, you can focus on food to help tie your video together. The possibilities are endless and anything that you incorporate will tie your videos together and prevent you from shooting all that excess footage that inevitably bogs a program down.

Once you have a few themes hammered out, it's time to think about shooting. I find that vacation is a great time to practice shooting and experimenting with different camera angles, depth of field, lighting, framing, focusing, and especially interviewing. As a general rule, take the camcorder out of auto-mode whenever possible. Auto focus and auto-exposure can often misfire, making your videos look amateurish. Excessive zooming is always a no-no. Not only does it drain your battery, but it's also very distracting for viewers to watch.

Here are a few other things you should be aware of while vacationing:

➤ Take some time to shoot establishing and beauty shots. If you're not going to do this on vacation, when will you ever do it? This could be a wide shot of the ocean and palm trees, or a close up of a rock with waves slowly running over it. Anything that you see, figure out a creative angle for your viewers to see the same thing.

Blooper

Check with your travel agent to see if the tourist attractions you plan to visit allow camcorders at all. If you walk into a Vegas casino or the Sistine Chapel with a camcorder in hand, you'll be stopped in your tracks before you can even take off the lens cap!

- Gather as many collectibles as you can from your vacation locale. You can shoot beach towels, key chains, postcards, maps, T-shirts, and anything else you can get your hands on and edit the footage into your program later.
- Don't forget about sound! If you're hearing something that tickles your eardrum, sit perfectly still with the camcorder and record for a few minutes. You can also edit this raw audio into your program.
- Try to interview people who live where you are vacationing. It goes a long way in giving your program a "local" feel.
- Protect your camcorder from the elements. Vacation spots can often spring extreme conditions in your camcorder's direction. It could be as simple as raingear or even a plastic bag to protect your camcorder from humidity and moisture. Also, always use an ultraviolet (U/V) lens filter as a clear lens cap.

One final note on vacation videography. It's always a good idea to exercise good manners when shooting. Be considerate of others around you and remember that you're not the only one enjoying the locale. Don't hog a good vantage point if others are waiting to shoot, don't push people out of the way, don't use distracting lights when others are around, and so on. Further, be mindful that some of the local folk may not want to be videotaped. Simple courtesy will keep everyone happy and may lead to invitations to shoot people or places that you otherwise might not have.

Birthday Bash

Not a year goes by where most people don't have at least a few birthday parties to attend. And if you have kids who are of party age, you'll find yourself at one almost every weekend!

But whether it's a birthday party for your 3-year-old niece, or for your dad's 60th, you can bet that if you're in the right place at the right time, you can count on at least a few classic camcorder moments.

Most birthday parties, like weddings, are similar in that there's often a large amount of people jam packed into a small space. Whether it's a backyard, living room or restaurant, you're going to have to fight for elbowroom.

When you arrive at the party, track down the person in charge for the lowdown on the day's festivities. If it's indoors, you can pretty much count on a low-light situation, and with a lot of people present, the audio track has the potential of becoming a bit muddy. If you have access to a clip-on light for your camcorder, bring it along. If you're shooting outdoors, bring the usually array of lens filters.

Again, do your homework in advance. Will the party be indoors or outdoors? Will it be in a basement, playspace, backyard, deck, or patio? If it's for kids, what kind of entertainment is being offered? Parents can rent lost of cool stuff like ice cream trucks, portable petting zoos, clowns, and gymnastic equipment. Also, find out the set up for the cake and the inevitable singing of "Happy Birthday." With this knowledge you'll have a better chance of being in the right place at the right time. And if it's a party that you're hosting, delegate the video responsibilities to anybody willing to shoot.

I've had amazing results at parties by clipping a wireless microphone on the birthday girl or boy. It's a great way to catch those candid moments from a distance and it helps to focus your video on the person of the day. It's also good sometimes to shoot from a distance in these situations because you never know who's got camcorder queasiness.

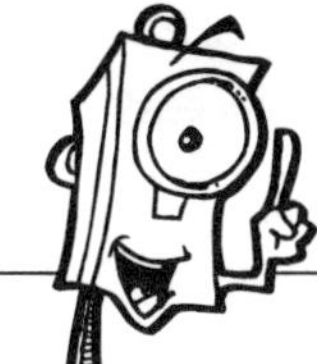

Candid Camera

One of the best birthday party accessories you can pack is a wide-angle lens converter. Because space is limited, you can cram more of the action into the frame without being too far from the subject.

Camcorder Athletics

If you've ever tried to videotape a sporting event, you'd know that it's more challenging than playing in the actual games that you're shooting.

Why is it then that sports look so good on TV? Whether it's football, golf, basketball, baseball, auto racing, or downhill skiing, professional sports producers throw an unsightly amount of cash into the production. Take a Monday night football game on ABC for instance. They've got a mobile unit of huge production trucks on location where the games are produced. Inside there's a control room and edit rooms where a team of producers, directors, technical and associate directors, editors, and audio engineers put the broadcast together. Additionally, they've also got a team of graphic designers and statisticians to put the icing on the cake.

It would be next to impossible to shoot anything that looks even close to what you'd see on ESPN, SportsChannel, or any of the major broadcast and cable networks. That's mainly because they've got a massive network of cameras to help them cover the event. At any given moment they can have as many as five cameras covering a single play. But with a little planning and practice, you can make your sports videos a lot more visually exciting and interesting to watch.

Whether you're shooting from way back in the bleachers, or up close and personal from the sidelines, finding the action in the viewfinder can be like searching for a needle in a haystack. If you want your videos to look presentable, you need to use a tripod. Take it a step further and hook up a telephoto lens converter for smooth tight shots on fast moving action that almost always takes place far away from the camcorder.

Other sports like tennis, golf, and swimming present a different equipment scenario since you can usually set up your camcorder very close to the action. While a tripod is still an invaluable tool, try screwing on a wide-angle lens converter to help compress more of the action into the frame.

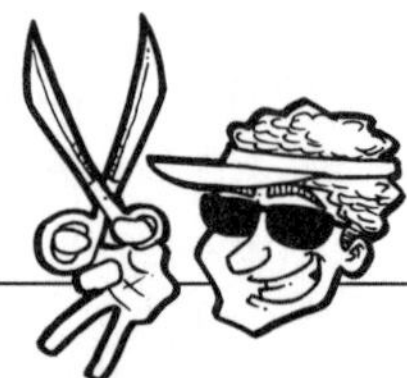

Director's Cut

If sports are going to play a big part in your overall home video game plan, go for the best quality Mini-DV camcorder your budget will allow. The superior video quality will help compensate for distance from the action.

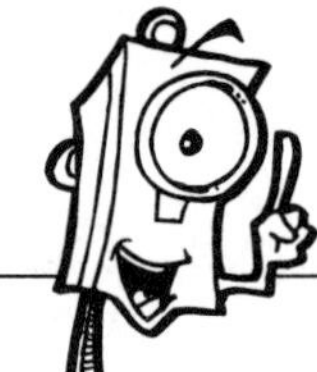

Candid Camera

If you shoot a lot of sports footage, another neat idea is to edit together a year-ender highlight tape. Try to incorporate other people's footage with your own to give your program multiple vantage points.

One of the best ways to defeat the monotony of sports videos is to utilize the work of other videographers at the scene. Whenever I videotape a sports event I'll strike up a conversation with anyone else shooting and ask if they'd be interested in swapping dubs of footage. In my experience, it turns out that 7 out of 10 people are willing to do it. It won't cost you more than the price of the videotape and the time it takes to strike a dub. It's mutually beneficial because any additional footage that you include in your final program means that you have multiple camera angles, which greatly improves visual variety. You could even plan ahead for this for, Little League or to Pee Wee Hockey games, as you might be friendly with some of the other moms and dads. After the first game, you could even work out a shooting schedule with them to relieve some of the responsibility.

Home Video for the Holidays

Holiday videos are always enjoyable to to make and to watch because they are usually happy, fun-filled events that can be colorful and bright to look at. If you put your videographer's hat on, your Thanksgiving, Christmas, Hanukkah, Halloween, and any other holiday under the sun will be more enjoyable than ever.

A theme for your holiday video may seem like a contradiction in terms because the theme is really the holiday itself. But there are creative approaches that you can come up with that can really enhance and tie together your video.

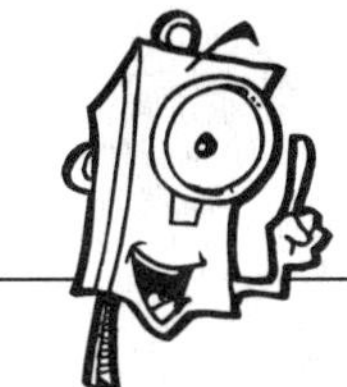

Candid Camera

Since much of the holiday videotaping takes place indoors, an on-camera light or a simple lighting kit is invaluable in supplementing low indoor lighting.

If a Halloween party is on the agenda, you can organize all of the guests together for an on-camera costume contest. You can also get them to give an on-camera description of their costume. During the Christmas holiday season you can hone in on houses that overdo the decorations. In some towns, these houses can attract quite a crowd. Think about interviewing the homeowner and the visitors alike for some interesting holiday banter.

Last year for the holidays we created eight short segments focusing on each present that was given to the kids each night of the holiday. We revealed what the gifts were in advance and then asked the children what they were wishing for. It was pretty funny when six out of eight of the gifts matched up to the wishes.

Several years ago my father cut together a funny Thanksgiving day video that I think is worth mentioning. It's a tradition in our house to cook the turkey in the outdoor grill instead of an oven. It comes out really good, but it takes about eight hours to slow cook. So my father documented the day, from purchasing the bird at the butcher to cooking updates and chefs tips. He then videotaped the carving and everyone enjoying his meal during dinner. He was able to squeeze a lot of other footage in of children and the guests, but the whole turkey theme helped to tie everything together.

A Video Diploma

Graduations pose many of the same production challenges as shooting sports videos. However, graduations, like weddings, are once-in-a-lifetime events and you have a lot less leeway for experimentation and settling for distant and obscure looking footage. You only have one shot at capturing what you came to record.

Graduations can take place either indoors or outdoors, typically in late spring. You won't have much control over seating since there are usually assigned seats, so make sure you bring along the trusty tripod and telephoto lens converter. If not, stabilize the camcorder as best you can by using a chair in front of you or even your knee.

After the ceremony, use other students with their parents as a backdrop and grab some quick interview questions with the graduate. Here are a few that might spark some interesting answers:

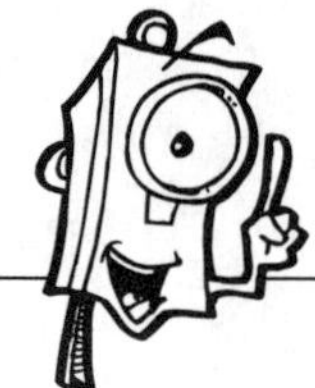

Candid Camera

When your soon-to-be former student is ready to pick up the diploma, ask permission to move forward to get a closer shot. Sometimes the ushers don't take their jobs too seriously and will let you sneak by. Again, a little courtesy towards the other parents and guests is in order.

- What are you going to miss most about school?
- What was your favorite subject? Your least favorite subject?
- What do you really love doing, and do you plan on making a career of it?
- Where do you see yourself in 5 years? 10 years? 20 years?

You want to ask any question whose answer will help paint a picture of what life was like at the time of graduation. Interviews are hard to come by and somewhat of a hassle to pull off, especially on such an exciting day when graduates have a million other things on their minds besides your video. But squeezing in a quick interview session won't take much time, and it will add a new dimension to your video, and another treasure to your video archive.

New Arrival/Baby Delivery

This is one occasion where you must check with your doctor in advance on the policy on camcorders in the delivery room. Ever since the recent explosion in camcorders, doctors in general have become much more lenient about allowing them.

My wife and I got lucky because our doctor was very easy going and allowed us to tape the entire event (from a nonrevealing vantage point, mind you). This is a scary thought, but the first time that I ever laid eyes upon my son was through the viewfinder of my Canon.

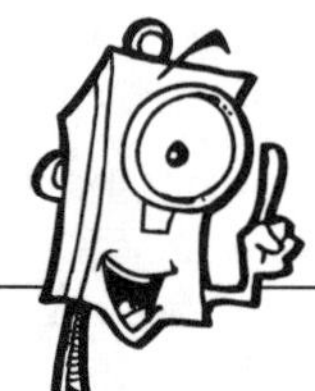

Candid Camera

Due to legal restrictions, most doctors will not allow you to record the actual birth of your baby. You can roll almost immediately up to the actual birth, and then can resume when the doctor gives the O.K.

On the technical end of this kind of shoot, the lighting is superb because the hospitals set up what resembles a three-point lighting scheme that is perfect for video, or even film shooting. I relied on the camcorder's on-board microphone because there were so many different sounds that I thought would be vital to the soundtrack and didn't want to risk cutting anything out with a directional microphone.

I was also lucky because I had the honor of sharing the experience with my mother-in-law, who happened to walk into the room just at the right moment! After the doctor had swaddled Benjamin in a towel and handed him to my wife, my mother-in-law grabbed the camcorder and captured our first moments together as a new family. We're talking some priceless video here.

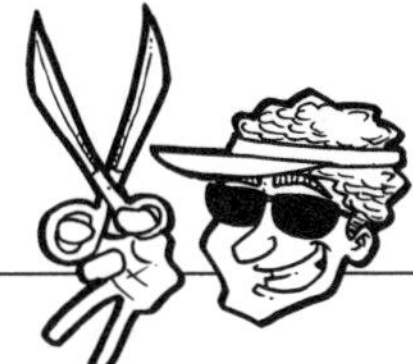

Director's Cut

Delivery videos can be considered family treasures and as such, should be treated with extra special care. After you're done recording, take the tape out without rewinding it, click the record-inhibit switch, and put it in a safe place. When you get home, make a couple of dubs for protection. Store the original in a cool, dark place. (For more on tape preservation, see Chapter 27, "Preserving Your Home Videos.")

The Least You Need to Know

- Good wedding videos rely on careful planning in order to be in the right place at the right time.
- Look for a unifying theme to tie your vacation video together. Avoid shooting hours and hours of useless footage.
- Prepare yourself to be packed in tight when shooting birthday videos. Pack a clip-on light and a wide-angle lens converter.
- Tripods are essential to take the shake out of your sports videos since you often have to rely on telephoto lens settings.
- Get as close as you can to the soon-to-be ex-student on graduation day.

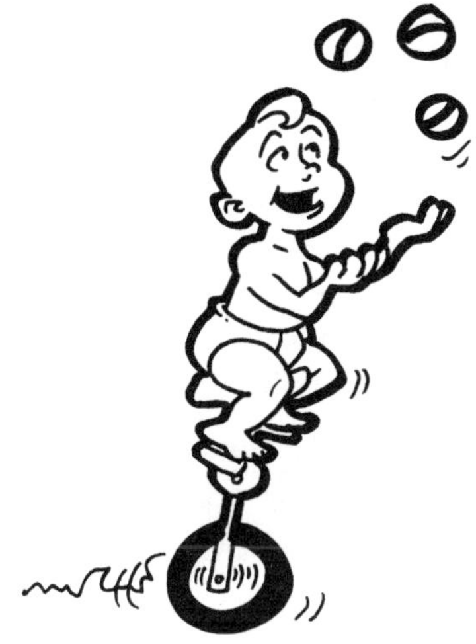

Chapter 16

Getting Your Kids to Perform

In This Chapter

- "BabyCam" (0 to 3 months)
- "Infant-vision" (3 to 24 months)
- "Toddler TV" (2 to 4 years)
- Videotaping your teens and young adults
- Some simple show ideas

Kids and camcorders make a very nice mix. In fact, many people buy camcorders for one reason: to document their children's lives as they grow up. Camcorders are practically a requirement in hospital maternity wards, and at birthday parties, holidays, and family gatherings far and wide. Never before in human history have we been able to record and document with such accuracy the most important events in our lives.

Videotaping your children is always an adventure, because you never know exactly what's in store for you at each of their stages of development. If you have a basic idea of what to expect, you'll be more prepared to capture those magical camcorder moments as they present themselves!

BabyCam (Approx. 0 to 3 Months)

Babies grow up so fast that sometimes it's hard to foresee what might be coming next. That's why you should take the newborn stage (0 to 3 months) for all it's worth because videotaping your children will never be this easy again! At first, the sight of the camcorder, like anything else, will be foreign and in need of exploration. But after your baby has been exposed to the camcorder for a little while, it will become as familiar a sight as the Cookie Monster or the TeleTubbies.

But don't expect your baby to hop right up and look deeply into the lens of your camcorder. In the newborn stage, your child is not capable of self-locomotion, and is completely dependent upon you for moving from one place to another. This opens up a world of close-up video opportunities, and as unfair as it may seem, videotape the little rascal until you run out of tape! It might appear as though you're taping the same thing over and over again, but when you begin to watch your footage back, you'll be astonished at how quickly your child progresses. And thanks to your camcorder, you're able to document and pass on this miraculous story of growth and development.

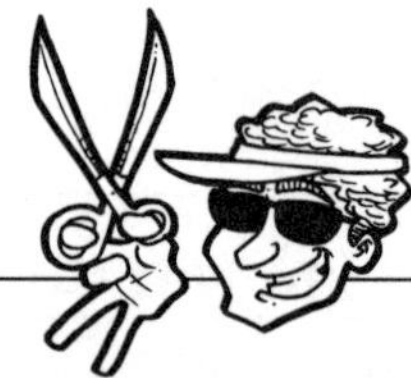

Director's Cut

All children develop and reach milestones at different paces. The developmental milestones mentioned here are generalizations that are based on national averages. For more detailed information, check out the following books:

Babyhood : Stage by Stage, from Birth to Age Two; How Your Baby Develops Physically, Emotionally, Mentally. Leach, Penelope. Knopf.

The Complete Idiot's Guide to Parenting a Preschooler and Toddler, Too. Boyd, Keith, MD; Osborn, Kevin. Macmillan.

What to Expect—The First Year. Eisenberg, Arlene; Murkoff, Heide E.; Hathaway, Sandee E. Workman Publishing Company, Inc.

What to Expect—The Toddler Years. Eisenberg, Arlene; Murkoff, Heide E.; Hathaway, Sandee E. Workman Publishing Company, Inc.

With a little practice, you'll quickly become child-savvy with your camcorder. This means you'll be more alert for the perfect video moments that would otherwise fall through the cracks. The newborn stage is a great time for you to sharpen your skills since your baby won't be able to escape the loving eye of your camcorder. It's a time of discovery for your children who are just starting to realize that they have hands that are attached and can be moved by simply willing it to happen. And there's nothing more comforting for your baby than to shove those fingers right in the mouth! If captured correctly, all of these moments make for precious home video.

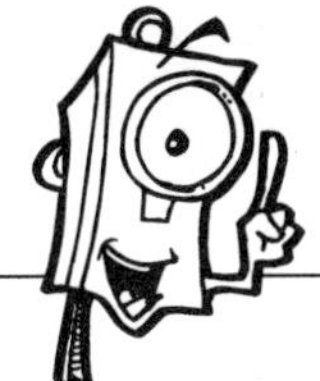

Candid Camera

Another benefit of the newborn stage is that you can get extremely close to your baby's face without her reaching out to try to eat the camcorder. These extreme close ups offer the best representation of what your baby really looks and sounds like. Try not to use lens converters in this type of situation because they tend to soften the picture and remove precious details in the face.

There are two major problems that you're going to encounter when shooting indoors: lighting and lack of camera angles. Since much of the action takes place in dimly lit bedrooms and in cribs, you'll have to beg, borrow and steal for any bit of light that comes your way. One thing you can do to improve your shots is to keep a lamp near the crib or in the bedroom that can be easily accessed and turned on, but far enough away from your child's reach so as not to cause problems. As I mentioned earlier, even the cheapest lamps can be used in place of professional lighting gear. When you have only a few seconds to flip on your camcorder in order to capture a magical moment, you don't have time to be picky about your lights. Anything will do. In addition, you can bounce any available light off of the ceiling to soften and diffuse harsh shadows that are common in household lamps. As a general rule, the more light the better. Your camcorder will record images in low light, but it often uses an electronic gain feature that can add grain to your video.

The other problem that has marred "BabyCams" across the land is lack of variety of camera angles. I've conquered this problem by repositioning my boy instead of the camcorder. Whether I use a pillow, blanket, or even a towel to prop him up, I always make sure that the hand of an adult is not too far out of the frame, since newborns are unstable and can suddenly fall sideways at the drop of a hat. We also had great success with a "bouncy seat" or even a nursing (boppy) pillow to hold him safely in place. The "bouncy seat" was especially good because it kept him lying back on an angle that was perfect to capture natural light coming from a ceiling or through a window. He could stay put for an hour or longer, perfectly comfortable, freeing him up to explore his immediate surroundings and to chitchat with the camcorder about his findings.

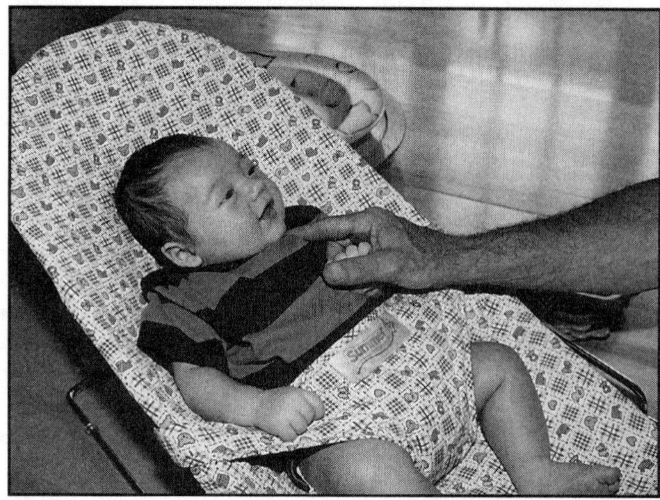

Bouncy seat video.

Another great "BabyCam" location is a car seat. Since you're outdoors, depending on the weather, the lighting is usually even and bright. In the newborn stage, and for several months afterward, we had our son facing toward the back window which made shooting even easier. My wife would duck down into the hatchback of our Jeep and slowly rise over the seat catching Ben in all his glory.

Here are a few other milestones in the newborn stage that you'll want to keep a close eye out for:

- Baby's first bath
- Baby's first ride in the car
- Smiling/laughing
- Trip home from the hospital
- Parent/child classes like "Mommy and Me"
- Bris, baptism, or christening
- First diaper changing (if you can bear it!)

"Infant-Vision" (Approx. 3 to 24 Months)

This is where the real fun starts to kick in. Your child's personality begins to emerge, and some major milestones are reached. From this point on, each and every day you'll come across a unique camcorder moment that you haven't seen before. The only problem ... your child's activity level has most likely increased tenfold, making it much more difficult to keep the camcorder focused on them. And close-up shots are pretty much out of the question because most babies see foreign objects in front of their faces as something they want to snack on. My camcorder has fallen victim more than once to the prying jaws of my son.

When I set out on my journey to shoot the best "infant-vision" possible, I made a deal with myself (and my wife) that whenever it looked like things were going to get messy, I'd use only my Hi8 camcorder and not my MiniDV. This would allow me to immerse myself in the action without constantly worrying about the camcorder. This includes footage from the beach, pool, bathtub, playground, sandbox, and those high-chair shots in which I often find myself and my camcorder in the path of flying food.

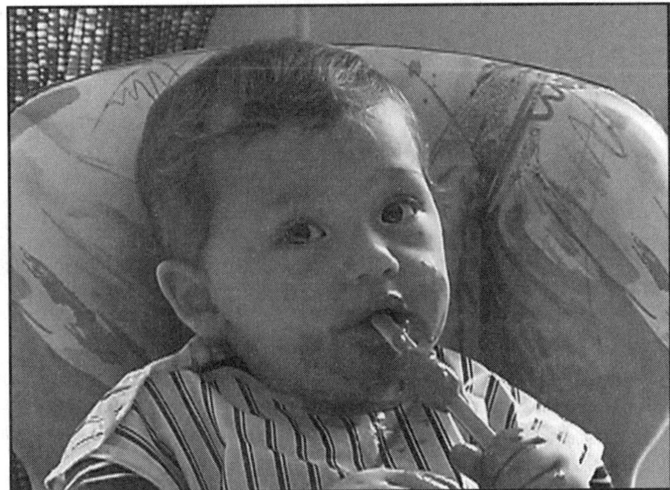

Benjamin Beal at mealtime.

Anywhere after 11 weeks or so, something magical happens that will forever change the way you shoot video. Your child will start to smile and laugh. Once this happens, capturing it on video becomes an obsession, and at times it's not as easy pull off as it sounds. In fact, getting a laugh or giggle is far from an exact science, and if your child isn't in the right mood, you're going to feel silly in the attempt. And forget about the humble little chuckle or giggle. You want to record that deep belly laugh that rises from the tips of your child's toes like a misplaced hiccup. And you never know what the catalyst is going to be. Be it a sudden move, funny face, or strange sound that sets them off, you've got to have your camcorder already rolling or else you're going to lose the moment forever.

My favorite method for getting a great video-laugh is to hold the camcorder with both hands at my chest with the lens zoomed all the way out to wide-angle. I call for my son's attention, and when he looks, I start spinning with the camcorder slowly at first, then picking up speed. Every now and then I suddenly stop with him cracking up perfectly centered in the frame. The faster I spin, the harder he laughs.

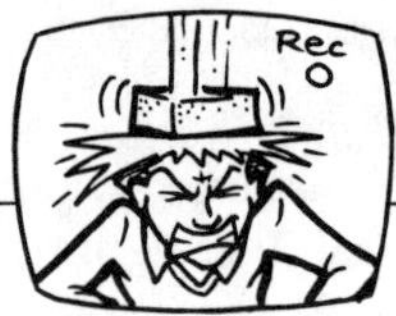

Blooper

Whenever you are videotaping a toddler, prep your camcorder as if you were about to head out into bad weather. You can buy protective gear, or you can cut a lens-sized hole in a plastic sandwich bag, and wrap it around your camcorder. This gives you waterproof protection while allowing you full access to the controls. Also, always use a clear ultraviolet (U/V) lens filter for ultimate lens protection.

Any silly adult behavior will do. The simplest way to make a baby laugh with a camcorder is to quickly move as close as you can, and then pull away really fast at the last minute. It's guaranteed to work for the first few times, but your baby may get frustrated with this after a while!

Here are a few methods for quick-camcorder laughs:

- Play peekaboo with the camcorder lens.
- Hide the camcorder behind your back, cover your baby's eyes, and then move in for a sudden tight shot. The sudden appearance of a foreign object is enough to get a giggle!
- Put a coat, towel, or sheet over your head with the camcorder's lens sticking out.
- While playing hide-and-seek, go into a closet or bathroom door and peek out just enough to get a shot with the camcorder. Call your child's name until she finds you.
- A little tickling never hurt anyone!

Besides laughing, you'll also want to catch other major milestones on camera. Beginning at 3 to 4 months, most babies begin to make rapid progress. It begins with rolling over and sitting up, and before you know it, they'll be crawling, pulling themselves up to stand, cruising along furniture, taking their first unaided steps, and beginning to learn their first words, most importantly "Mama" and "Dada." Here are a few other milestones that make great "Infant-Vision":

- Eating first solid food
- First birthday party
- Dressing up in favorite clothing
- Any park activity like swings and slides
- Chitchatting in gibberish
- Turning the pages of a book
- Scribbling with crayons
- Drawing shapes and circles
- Cutting with safety scissors
- Throwing and kicking a ball

Sounds like a lot, huh? It's easy to get overwhelmed, but just prepare yourself to be ready to strike when the moment arrives. Just like anything else in videography, a little practice goes a long way. And the better you know your subject, the better you can ascertain how they are going to react and respond to certain situations. Kid video is no different than other forms of videography, and a good grasp on the fundamentals of shooting will take you where you need to go.

To recap, always pay close attention to the lighting since dim conditions can degrade video quality quicker than anything else. Audio is another biggie, especially since your children will never sound like this again, so getting a clean recording is essential. Also, force yourself to switch the camcorder out of automatic mode whenever you feel it's appropriate. If nothing else, turn off the auto focus because a lot of your shots take place at close range and nothing is more distracting than watching your camcorder randomly search for the right focus.

Another fundamental that should never be ignored, especially when shooting "Infant-Vision" is variety of camera angles. This is especially true if you don't plan on editing your footage after the fact. (And let's face it, most of us don't edit our "Infant-Vision" footage.) Get as low as you can whenever you can, letting your audience see the world through the eyes of a child. When you're standing up and shooting down toward your children, the harsh angle distorts the picture and action of the shot, and takes away precious detail from your children's faces. Straight-on shooting always works best.

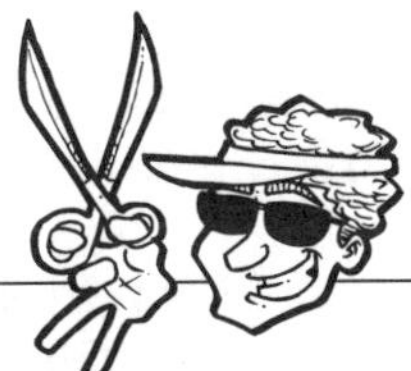

Director's Cut

When my nephew first became comfortable with the process of walking, I would hold the camcorder down at his level and slowly backpedal. He would follow me all over the house, reaching out and laughing as he walked. This made for some hilarious video.

"Toddler TV" (Approx. 2 to 4 Years)

Welcome to the joys of toddlerhood! This is perhaps the most enjoyable, yet challenging stage for capturing your toddler on TV. By the time children reach two, not only are they zipping all over the place, but they often reach twice their birth height by the time they're two, display vast improvement in coordination and balance, and vocabulary really begins to blossom, maxing out at about 1,500 words or more! What's more, most are able to compose simple sentences and have a better comprehension of time and place. In general, they begin to realize that the world doesn't revolve around them, and they have only one thing in mind: to explore every nook and cranny of whatever environment they're in.

"Toddler TV" might require a shift back into your camcorder's automatic mode, because your little one is never in one place for too long, making it almost impossible to pull off manual adjustments. Just hit the auto switch and hope for the best! Whenever possible, try to shoot outdoors during periods of even lighting since low-angle indoor shooting can be a lighting nightmare.

Additionally, by this age you'll start to get an idea of how comfortable your child is with a camera turned their way. If they've been exposed to a camcorder for their entire lives, by now it's a familiar sight and probably won't cause any anxiety. But many other children hate the sight of a video camera, and very much like camera-shy adults, run in the other direction as quickly as possible. If this is the case, try to invent subtle ways to introduce your child to the camcorder without it causing too much of a disruption in the given activity.

One sure way to ease their tensions is to hand the camcorder over to them and let them try it on for size. You might be thinking that I'm crazy for even suggesting letting your little ones mess with such an expensive piece of equipment. And maybe you're right. But I've found that when you hand over your camcorder under very close supervision, children tend to treat it like the tool that it is, and not a toy.

I've always thought that the benefits that children receive from early exposure to a camcorder far outweigh the small risk of them damaging it in some way. Not only does it offer them a new outlet for fun and creativity, but also you may discover that your child has a gift for speaking in public, a knack for acting, singing, or even performing. Or, at the controls of the camcorder, you might discover that your child has strong visual skills. Additionally, when you watch the videos back in front of a small crowd, it offers the children a unique opportunity to experience how people react to their work or presence on screen without the immediate pressure of being in front of a crowd.

There are also a few camcorder activities that you can participate in with your toddler to help spark their interest and get them to feel more comfortable around the camcorder. My favorite is the video-letter to grandparents, aunts and uncles, or other family members and friends. Simply work out a little message or skit to perform and roll on it.

If your child is uptight about appearing alone on camera, set your camcorder on a tripod and join them on screen. It can be as simple or elaborate as you choose. If you've got the combination of children and camcorders on the receiving end of your video letter, suggest that they create a response on the same tape and send it back your way. This is a fun method of communication, especially when there's distance separating the two parties. After the tape has gone back and forth a few times you've got a self-edited program that is fun to watch.

Another video gimmick you can easily create is a video invitation to a party, family gathering, or any other event that you have in mind. It can be as simple as a skit, short poem, mini-play, or you can even write and perform a song. It is a unique way to get your message across and only takes a little bit of time to create. Just make sure that your invitation list isn't too large because after a few dubs onto VHS, it can get a bit costly.

Televising Teens and Young Adults

As children grow into young adults, video opportunities still present themselves, but chances are they happen less frequently and are sometimes difficult to predict. Adolescence and teenage years can be marked not only by an increased sense of self-consciousness, but enthusiastic parents who chase them with camcorders can often repel your teen. This is especially true in public situations.

Again, you can ease some of the tension by handing over the camcorder and letting them have the freedom to experiment with it. This has many benefits, including the fact that it helps to prepare them for a future filled with video and other information-delivering media both at home and in the classroom. Video is emerging as a powerful educational tool where documentaries, movies, and other video programs are often substituted for a curriculum of 100 percent textbooks. Additionally, remote-classrooms have emerged as an educational medium of the future. Students can now attend class via the Internet or satellites from the other side of the globe.

A camcorder can also help your teens discover who they are, and who they want to become. If you let them, videography can be a creative endeavor that teens and young adults are free to explore on their own. In doing so, they may discover hidden talents that they can use creatively no matter what career paths they choose. Nowadays, anyone can make a video, but not just anyone can make a *good* video. A talent for videography can prove useful in everything from working on promotional videos for your business or company to recording events at your school or church.

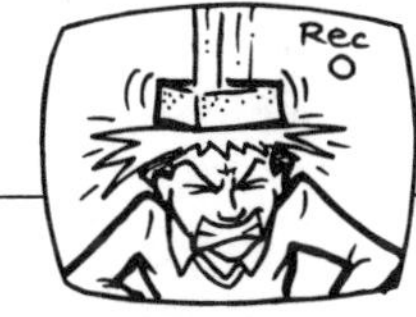

Blooper

I've learned from experience that if someone vehemently doesn't want to be videotaped, forget about it and move on. By the time most children reach their teenage years, you'll have a really good idea whether or not they want to be on camera. Forcing the issue can be counter-productive.

In addition, if your teen is showing an interest in video, you have the perfect opportunity to make it a family activity. With video arising as a popular medium in classrooms, you can often help them turn an imaginative assignment into a video project for the entire class to enjoy. From mock commercials, mini-movies with a message, plays, a documentary, or newscasts, the creative possibilities are endless.

Simple Show Ideas

Children of all ages love to perform and put on shows. And why not put on shows for the camcorder? What follows are a few show ideas that you can easily re-create. Like any creative video application, the possibilities are infinite. You can use these ideas as a jumping-off point to create your own fun shows.

Aside from being a whole lotta fun to make, video shows can help your child become more comfortable in front of the camera and will ignite their natural creative abilities. It can also improve their overall communication skills by helping them become better speakers and performers.

One important point to keep in mind ... don't be a control freak when filming kid shows. Give your children the opportunity to realize their own concepts as well. More importantly, let them see the consequences of their ideas, good or bad. That way they'll learn how to judge what will work and what won't. Above all, this should be a fun activity and not just a ride for your children on an overzealous parent's ego trip.

Clothing and a Camcorder: More Than Just a Fashion Statement

There's nothing that your child enjoys more than getting outfitted in mommy and daddy's clothing. Whatever your child fancies as far as apparel is concerned, let him or her give it a whirl, and then start rolling. It's funny stuff and great bribery material for later on in life!

For girls, it could be jewelry, makeup, and other assorted grownup garments. For boys, maybe it's daddy's hat or athletic equipment. Or they can easily be dressed up like superheroes, cowboys and Indians, even ghosts and monsters.

Whatever the attire, shoot in a well-lit area without anything too distracting in the background since your goal is to have your child as the center of attention. You could package it as a "runway" show with neat music, or you can follow them around the house, even out in the street with their costumes on and videotape people's reaction to them. This is even more of a possibility on Halloween where everyone is dressed up and it's like one big fashion show.

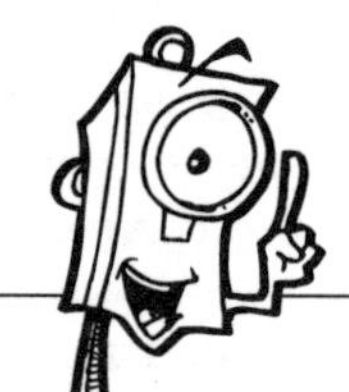

Candid Camera

A humorous video-fashion show will also work if you swap your children for pets.

Videotaped Mini-Play

Here's a good one since it doesn't take a lot of effort to transfer a mini-play from the stage to the screen. And subject matter isn't hard to find since plays are an integral part of many a scholastic curriculum. You can also check your local bookstore for abridged versions of popular plays that are easy to perform and fun for children.

Mini-plays can be constructed from fairy tales and favorite stories such as Willie Wonka and the Chocolate Factory, Mary Poppins, Snow White and the Seven Dwarfs, Cinderella, and many others—and the abridged versions can be as entertaining as the originals, especially when it's your children doing the acting.

Mini plays look best on videotape when you construct a simple set with a light background behind the actors and actresses. This could be a solid colored wall, or you can tape or tack a sheet or blanket to a wall. Create spotlights and back lighting for effect using lamps that you have lying around the house.

Talk Shows

If your kids like to talk, you might as well put their talents to good use by producing a simple talk show. Create a mini set in your dining room, living room, or any place in the house that has a formal look. If possible, create a three-point lighting scheme for the set using household lamps or a cheap lighting kit. The camcorder mic will do, but if you have access to a shotgun mic mounted on a boom, or a couple of lavalier mics, even better.

The topic of your show can be about anything under the sun including food, sports and family matters, or you can model your talk show's topic after an interesting topic on TV. Assign one of them as the host, and make the other ones guests. It'll open up an interesting, often hilarious forum for dialogue.

Camcorder Commercials

This is one of my favorites. You can do a commercial for real products, but it's more fun when you make something up! I've made commercials for products like the "Earthquake Shake" and "Rare Gordon" sneakers. The "Earthquake Shake" commercial was the most outrageous because it involved a blender that went haywire and spit its contents all over my actor!

The "Rare Gordon" spot was a lot of fun because we used a mini basketball and hoop to simulate the high-end Michael Jordan commercials from Nike. We taped Achilles-like wings to a regular pair of sneakers and taped the actor jumping from a table and flying through the air before dunking the mini-ball. A combination of slow motion and a low camera angle made it look like a good simulation of any "Generation-X" commercial on TV today.

Talent Shows

This is a fun approach and a great way to get everybody in on the action. Talent shows are easy to record and can be pulled off in any kind of lighting and audio condition. Appoint someone announcer duties to introduce each act and their given talents. Take it a step further and pin a wireless microphone on each of the performers before they hit the stage. Your camcorder mic will do the job, but you'll pick up a lot of extra noises from the sidelines.

The Least You Need to Know

- In your baby's first couple of months, take advantage of all the camcorder opportunities. Your baby will never be this agreeable again!
- In between the first couple of months and about two years, your child is going to be on the go, and there are a ton of milestones to capture with your camcorder.
- When videotaping your toddler, you might as well flip the camcorder back into automatic mode, because they'll never be in one place for too long.
- Camcorders can be not only a creative outlet for teens and young adults, they can also help them find their place in the world.
- Convince your children to create shows with your camcorder. It will help ignite their already blossoming sense of creativity.

Chapter 17

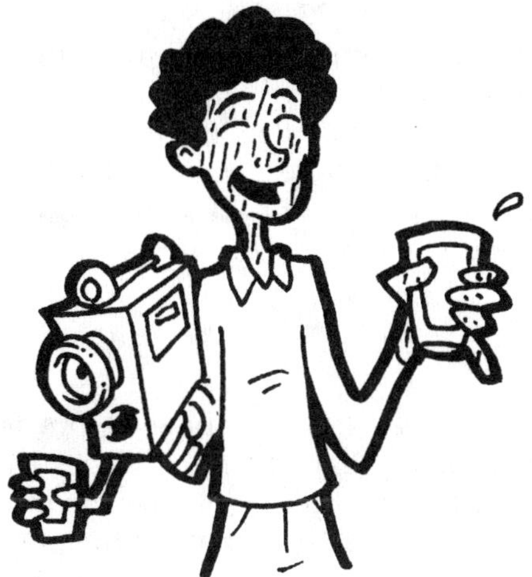

Getting Out from Behind the Camcorder: Learning to Enjoy the Event

In This Chapter

- Living vicariously through your camcorder
- Passing along your video responsibilities
- Teaching your loved ones how to shoot
- Nifty camcorder tricks to get yourself on TV

One rainy Sunday afternoon we had nothing to do, so my father-in-law popped in some home video footage that he had shot over the past couple of years. He owns this really cool JVC camcorder that was one of the first to employ the pop-out LCD viewfinder, and he had spent a lot of time shooting with it. After watching for about a half hour, I started to get the feeling that something vital was missing from his footage, but I couldn't quite put my finger on it. Then, all of a sudden, it hit me. My father-in-law was nowhere to be found in his own videos! Not once in over four hours of footage does even an elbow or finger of his show up on camera.

Yeah, the videos looked great, and there was a ton of footage of all of the kids, friends, and family, but it occurred to me that the videographer's absence on screen left the viewer with an empty feeling. Additionally, when my father-in-law revisits the footage years down the road, he's robbed himself of the precious experience of seeing exactly how he looked and sounded in the late 1990s. Anyone who gives up their own time and effort to shoot video deserves some camcorder time themselves. Even Hitchcock never failed to give himself a cameo appearance in his own flicks.

But videographers across the land find themselves in a Catch-22. If they want to appear in front of the camera instead of behind it, who's going to do the shooting? And if nobody's qualified or willing to give you some relief, you're forced to witness some of life's greatest moments through the lens of your camcorder. In this chapter you'll learn how to get yourself on TV and give yourself a well-deserved break from shooting. Whether you do it yourself, get someone else to do it, or leave the camcorder to its own devices, get ready to share the spotlight in your own home videos.

Is It Live, or Is It Memorex?

Videography is certainly fun, but when you're the only one shooting and everyone is relying on you to provide them with footage, it gets to be a drag in a hurry! Especially when you're experiencing one of life's special moments, sometimes it's better to witness something with your own two eyes rather than with a camcorder glued to your head. But the big question is, would you rather experience a once-in-a-lifetime event first hand at the expense of not documenting it for future viewing? You may not have to answer this question if you figure out how to spread the video wealth.

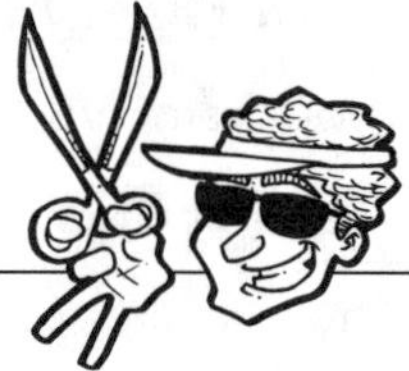

Director's Cut

"If I had the choice, I'd rather record the event on tape than not have captured it at all. I might get a better look without my camera, but it's a small price to pay. Even though I'm in the film industry and work with video equipment all day long, I still have a deep desire to document events for future generations to see."
—Diane Houslin, Writer/Producer/Filmmaker

The first time I ever really thought about the impact of being overly burdened by the camcorder was when I was in the delivery room when my son Benjamin was born. I had the opportunity to videotape the event and when the doctor lifted my newborn son into the air for the first time, it was a moment I'll never forget. My heart was pounding in my chest like a bass drum in a funk band, and my eye was squeezed so tight that I could feel blood vessels bursting in my forehead … . Wait a minute, I suddenly realized that … I have one eye shut! That could only mean one thing. I'm watching this whole thing through the viewfinder of my Canon! The fact that I almost forgot that I was taping startled me. Had I gotten so used to such a narrow reality that I couldn't tell the difference anymore? I just couldn't escape the thought that the first time I ever laid eyes upon my son was through the lens of a camcorder!

And it didn't end there. I watched his first steps, his first real meal of solid food, his first clap-hands, and many other key moments of his childhood through a viewfinder.

It might not sound like a big deal, but I think this situation is indicative of a much larger problem that I found myself swimming in as my son began to grow older. I was spending way too much time behind the camcorder and not enough time out in front of it!

Delegating the Video Chores

When it comes down to it, there are really only a couple of ways to avoid getting stuck videotaping your life away. Be extremely generous with your camcorder! By now there's a good chance that you're probably well on your way to becoming a good shooter, why not spread the wealth a little? You have to remember that, regardless of being a very expensive item to buy and repair, camcorders are pretty durable and can hold up to a lot more mistreatment than you might think. Besides, it's nobody's intention to purposefully break your sensitive piece of electronics. Sometimes you have to take a chance if you ever want to get out from behind the controls.

I've always been a big believer that children should be offered positions on your camcorder relief staff. Not only are they perfectly capable of taking on the task of videography, with a little bit of instruction and trust on your part, they can become pretty darn good at it. Besides, what child wouldn't be gung-ho about taking on an adult responsibility? It's mutually beneficial since you get a breather, and they get to experiment with a new way to have fun and be creative.

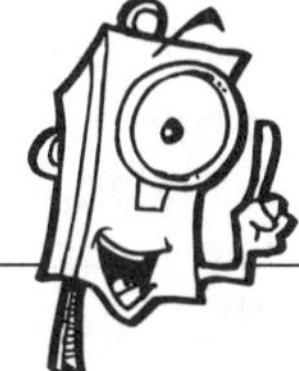

Candid Camera

Typically, what's a good age to let your child start experimenting with the camcorder? You can begin anywhere from 4 to 5, or as early as you think your child can discern the difference between a toy and a serious adult appliance that should be treated with care. If my 10-month-old ever got hold of one, you'd have camcorder soup on your hands!

A few things you should keep an eye on when letting your kids take the helm—too much camera movement and overuse of any and all camcorder controls. Children, much more than adults, tend to be completely spellbound by the fact that they can control TV and not the other way around. Give them a simple run-through of the basics of shooting smooth home videos, and they should get the picture. That's not to say that you shouldn't let them have fun with the camcorder. You'd be surprised at how great videos can look when shot from a kid's-eye view.

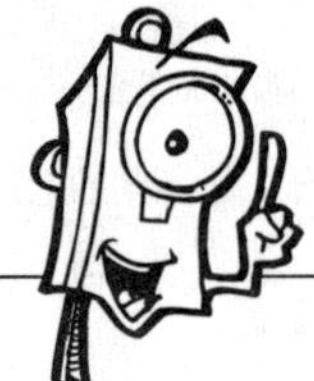

Candid Camera

During our honeymoon I often gave my camcorder to strangers. I learned that the best idiot-proof way to avoid confusion is to set the camera's lens to wide-angle and hit the record button before handing over the camcorder. Then it's really just a point and shoot operation.

The other choice that you have involves taking a bit of a leap of faith, but usually is worth the initial anxiety. Fellow tourists, party-goers, or any other assorted stranger can easily help you become a part of a video moment. This is one sure way to put your camcorder's automatic features to work for you. Usually, the first thing out of someone's mouth when you hand them a camera or camcorder is, "How do I work this thing?" Simply reassure him it's as easy as taking a still-shot. Just hit the red button, and point and shoot. Sometimes, however, people will cringe at the sight of a camcorder and the possibility that they could get stuck taping people they don't even know for a half-hour. Be sure to let them know that you only want a minute or so of footage. Any footage that they shoot, no matter how short, is footage where you appear on camera.

My motto is, if you can trust a stranger with your still camera, why not trust them with your camcorder?

Teaching Your Significant Other to Shoot

Whether you're married, or are in any kind of relationship, the best break that you can get from your camcorder is to pass it along to your significant other. It's very rare to find a relationship where both parties are avid camcorder enthusiasts. That's why it pays to pass along some video knowledge to take some weight off of your shoulders.

There's one thing that I quickly realized when I broke into the TV industry. Many people seem to associate camcorders and video gear with men. If you've ever taken a look at who's toting the camcorders at any tourist location in the world, you'd know what I'm talking about. And in the television industry, a lot of the women who I work with often complain that broadcasting is a male-dominated industry and it's sometimes hard for them to compete.

While discussing this with my wife, she brought up the point that women don't get into videography as much as men do because growing up, she felt as though she was often steered away from using electronic gadgets. I guess she may have a point. Take a look at any advertising campaigns for major-brand camcorders. They're all pretty heavily targeted toward the male market segment.

My wife, in fact, usually doesn't want to have anything to do with electronics, and it took a lot of nudging on my part to get her behind the video camera. I recently bought her a cellular phone that, among its many high-tech features, had voice-mail capabilities. After a solid week of leaving her messages with no response, I asked her if she realized that the phone had voice mail. Even though I had told her about it when I first gave her the phone, she really had no interest in figuring it out. But after forcing her to listen to me explain how it worked, she was an instant voicemail pro, and now, she couldn't live without the feature. It was the same thing with the camcorder. Once she started shooting, she actually began to enjoy it and we both discovered that her footage, on a good day, was just as good, if not better, than mine.

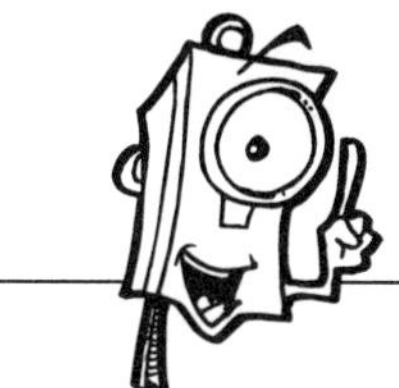

Candid Camera

National sales figures suggest that men are responsible for 75 percent of all camcorder sales.

The key to teaching your significant other about something he or she doesn't seem to have even the slightest interest in can be summed up in three words. Keep it simple. And that's pretty easy to do, because camcorders can be very simple to use if you don't get carried away. The only features you really have to worry about teaching are start, stop, and zoom. But take it easy on the zooming lessons! Those three things can take even the most inexperienced novices where they need to go. The other thing that you'll want to drill in is to keep the camera as steady as possible. As I've said before, shaky video is the trademark of the video-novice and can go a long way in distracting viewers.

Free Yourself from Camcorder Jail

If you can't get anyone else to shoot for you, it's time to resort to plan B. And plan B is all about the funky things you can do to get yourself out from behind the camcorder. In some cases it may mean you lose control of the way your video is shot including camera angles, camera moves, zooming and focus, but if you want to take a breather, this is just what the doctor ordered.

Tripods

Here I go again, talking up those tripods. Yes, I admit, they're invaluable in keeping your video from having the shakes, but they can also be utilized to free yourself from the clutches of your camcorder. And you don't need to shell out hundreds for a tripod you plan to use with this purpose in mind. Just about anything with three legs and a camcorder slot on top will do. (See Chapter 3, "Cool Extras ... Do You Need the Bells and Whistles?")

Let's say you're assigned the task of videotaping Uncle Arthur's 50th birthday party, but you're not in the mood to spend the entire time walking around with the camcorder. Spend the first 15 minutes or so walking around and shooting establishing

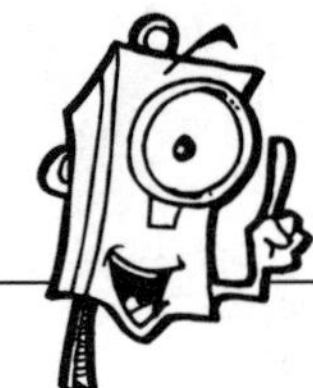

Candid Camera

Since most camcorders come with remote controls, every now and then you can operate the zoom from far off in the crowd. This can be useful if something interesting is going on center-stage. If your camcorder has a large focal range, you'll be able to get very close to the action.

shots, close up shots of the guests, and interviews with Uncle Arthur and other interested parties. Then when you're ready to mingle, pick out a good location that offers a decent bird's-eye view of the party, mount your camcorder on a tripod, and let 'er rip. Raise the tripod as high as necessary to get all the appropriate portions of the scene into frame. You could put it on a sturdy table or anything else that has a flat, wide surface like a sun-deck. (Just make sure you secure your rig.) If you haven't placed the camera too high, check your shot. Hit record, and let the camcorder go to work.

Tripods are also useful for getting low angle shots of children as they play close to the ground. From the corner of a room, you can leave the camera unattended and recording for hours, without the children ever catching wind of your video-activities. As long as you don't mind wasting some tape (one of the cheaper priced items in video-land), you can walk away with some great candid moments. It also opens up new opportunities for you to step into the scene and get yourself on camera.

Look Ma, No Hands!

If you don't have a tripod at your disposal, find any flat, stable surface and prop your camcorder there. It could be a table, chair, box, or anything else you can think of. Just be sure to check your shot, and if possible, stabilize your camcorder with a light-adhesive tape like masking tape.

I've seen a few zany applications of the "no hands" principle put to good use. One worth mentioning, a friend of mine once attached his camcorder to a rope and suspended it from a fixture in a room where he was having a graduation party. Literally hundreds of people showed up and each and every one of them, at one point in the night, grabbed the camcorder and spoke a few words of wisdom. The rest of the time it spun slowly around, getting some amazing and interestingly angled shots of the event at hand. And it was an absolutely perfect place with lighting in mind because the light directly overhead lit the scene brightly and evenly. When we watched the footage back, we realized that my friend had come up with a really unique way of recording an event.

"TreeCam" Anyone?

Trees can work very well as remote propping locations for your camcorder. This is definitely a last resort, but the "TreeCam" has been known to bail me out of a few video impositions. To attach your camcorder to a tree takes some athletic ability, but once you've got it up there, it's mounted for good and you'll be happy with the unique vantage point a tree can offer.

Instead of attaching your camcorder with rope or tape, try using a bungee cord instead. (You can pick one up at your local hardware store.) Bungee cords are very elastic and won't scratch your camcorder or leave glue marks. Simply wrap the cord around your camcorder's handle a few times, wrap it around the tree, and hook the ends together. Make sure the branch you choose is thick enough so that your camcorder won't slip and slide. You can also wrap a towel around the branch or camcorder to increase stability and prevent scratches. If the camcorder is too high for you to check the shot, aim it as best you can by eye and hope for the best. A little experimentation never hurt anyone.

You Can Chew Gum, Walk, and Shoot Video at the Same Time!

Let's say you're doing some shooting while walking on the beach with your family. You desperately want to get yourself in the shot, but there's nobody available who can relive you of camcorder duty. There are a few slick camera techniques that you can pull off that will not only get you in the shot, but also give you unique camera angles that will impress your audience.

Single-Handed, Slick Shooting

This may sound like a no-brainer, but the best way to get yourself on camera while still participating in the action is to set the lens into wide-angle mode and with one hand, hold the camcorder as far away from you body as you can, aiming it at yourself. It sounds almost too sophomoric to even work, but after a little practice, you can get some amazing footage with yourself in the center of the action. I have used this method often to acquire footage, some of it I've even used in documentaries and promos. I always use this method to film my son and me together on camera. It's perfect for low angle shots. You can stabilize the camera by resting your hand on the floor, aiming upward toward the action.

I also used this method for my brother-in-law Dan's bachelor party video. When my other brothers-in-law and I were planning the video, we decided that it would be better to try to capture some candid moments with Dan instead of shooting a straight interview. So one day while walking with the family, I held the camcorder low and began to fire one question after another at Dan, which he proceeded to answer without even considering the possible consequences. He told us his favorite guitar player, his top 20 stock picks, and why he prefers the Macintosh computer to the IBM PC compatible. We even recorded his pin number when he took cash out from an ATM! But even better than that, my brother-in-law Glenn convinced Dan to sing the theme to *Mr. Roger's Neighborhood,* in which he delivered a beautiful rendition, and which I

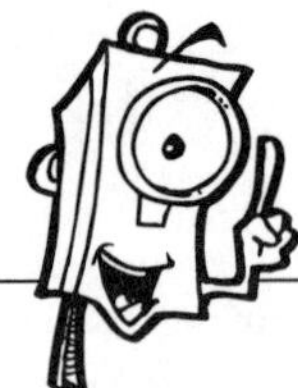

Candid Camera

When shooting with one hand while holding it away from your body, make sure that you have the image stabilization feature activated. While it can't take away every shake, it can help take the edge off of the major jitters.

recorded note for note! The resulting show that we put together from this candid footage was the highlight of Dan's bachelor party and provided us with a few moments we will never forget.

Getting the Most Out of Your Pop-Out LCD Viewfinder

Next to image stabilization, I've always thought that the pop-out LCD viewfinder is one of the most useful features ever to hit the world of camcorders. Not only is a great tool in helping you to stabilize images by enabling you to hold the camcorder away from your head, but it's great for monitoring the action while including yourself in the shot. Most pop-outs reverse the video image when you flip it around 180 degrees facing the front of the camcorder. This is perfect for those slick, single-handed shots.

Mirror, Mirror on the Wall

When all else fails, you can resort to a mirror to capture yourself in action. This can work with a small mirror that you have hanging on the wall, or even better if you have an entire wall in your house that's mirrored. We have a wall like that in our dining room and I have recorded some fine family moments using our reflected image. It really works well and can also be used to manipulate some neat camera angles.

The Least You Need to Know

- Watching your life pass by through the lens of a camcorder can make you feel very unfulfilled and removed from the events.
- Pass your camcorder along to anyone who's willing to shoot, be it your spouse, children, or a perfect stranger.
- You can let the camcorder do its work on its own by mounting it on a tripod, wall, table, or even a tree!
- If you get stuck shooting, you can get yourself on camera by aiming the camcorder at yourself or shooting in a mirror.

Part 4

Video Perfection—Rescued in the Edit

Every single thing that you watch on TV these days has been edited in some way, shape, or form. And the beauty of editing is that it's so subtle, you don't even realize that the programs you're watching have been chopped down at all.

But take away the editing, and an audience instantly cringes. Even the most professionally shot unedited footage is enough to drive viewers batty.

This is exactly why your friends and family are terrified of the possibility of having to sit through your home movies. They're accustomed to being forced to watch long-winded footage where they have to wait and wait and wait for any juicy tidbit. I admit, you've got quite a battle on your hands when trying to win an audience over.

Video editing is the only way you're going make your home movies more watchable. And you don't have to put up the house in order to afford a powerful editing system of your own. In fact, you can easily get away with simple editing using your camcorder and an extra consumer VCR.

And thanks to great advances in technology and ever-falling computer and hard-drive prices, you can take a step into the future of editing with nonlinear editing software. Now computers can process your video footage in the very same way they process words: cut and paste. Now you can have the power of a multi-million dollar TV studio right at your fingertips!

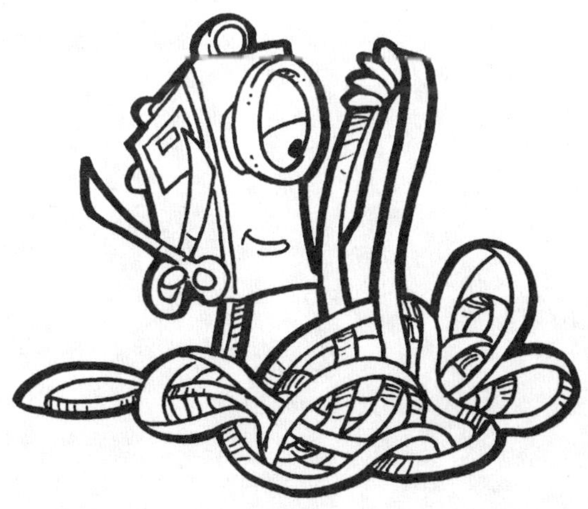

Chapter 18

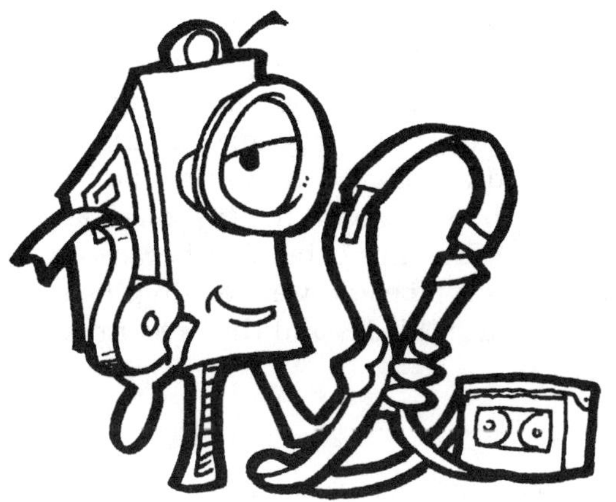

Editing on the Fly

In This Chapter

- Video editing: a brief history
- The essence of editing
- Editing your videos while you shoot!
- Shooting to edit later

With very few exceptions, every TV program, commercial, documentary, and movie has, in one way or another, been through the process of editing. National newscasts and other high-end productions like the Superbowl, the Academy Awards, and the Olympics are usually edited live while the event is taking place by a director and a team of technicians in a control room. Big-budget films, TV shows, and other forms of programming undergo a more rigorous post-production process that can take weeks, even months, to complete. Without editing, footage from even the most professional camera operators would drive most avid TV watchers insane!

Editing is no longer just for professionals. You, too, can edit your videos. But you can do it at your own pace and according to your own budget. As you'll learn in this chapter, all you really need is your camcorder and a little creativity to make interesting and entertaining videos. At first, editing is an unnatural procedure, but it makes your programs feel more natural to watch. And with a few of the basics and a lot of practice, editing can be a snap. So get ready to do some cutting and pasting!

So, What Is Editing, Anyway?

Simply put, editing is the process of eliminating unwanted footage and the sculpting and organizing of the good footage into a coherent program package that is more viewer-friendly than the raw footage in its entirety. Video editing is a fine art and a craft that has been in the making for at least 40 years. However, video editing got off to a rocky start. Up until the mid 1950s, the broadcast television industry shot their programs on film. Then Ampex Corporation hit the scene with the first black and white video recorder that used 2-inch-wide tape. When my father first began editing at ABC in the late 1960s, they were still using 2-inch tape and were editing their footage by physically cutting the videotape with razor blades and then reconnecting the desired footage with thin, adhesive tape.

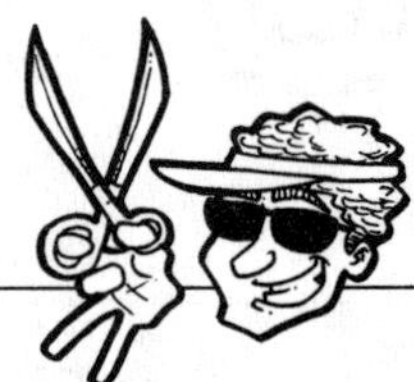

Director's Cut

"When I first started to edit using 2-inch tape, I was terrified to make a mistake. We had to douse the actual videotape with a special solvent so we could see where to slice it with the razorblade. If you made a mistake, you were out of luck! There was no second chance."
—Harvey Beal, Senior Editor, ABC

As video technology emerged, more advanced electronic editing systems took over, virtually eliminating the need for splicing tape by hand. In 1967 a new system called timecode made editing even more precise by assigning each video frame a number based on a 24-hour clock. Now, editors could pinpoint a frame, enabling them to edit more precisely than ever before. Soon after, SMPTE (Society of Motion Picture and Television Engineers) developed a standardized system called SMPTE Timecode that is still in use today.

As edit control systems got more advanced, videotape technology started to bolt ahead and the physical tape size got smaller and smaller. Suddenly, a higher-quality 1-inch tape replaced the 2-inch tape. Then 1-inch became ¾ inch and then ½ inch and now there are tapes that are no thicker than 8mm or ¼ inch. Consumer grade VHS (Video Home System) tapes are ½-inch wide, as are many of the higher-end professional tape formats like DigiBeta and BetaCamSP. As the tapes shrunk, so did the equipment, making editing even more accessible on a non-professional level.

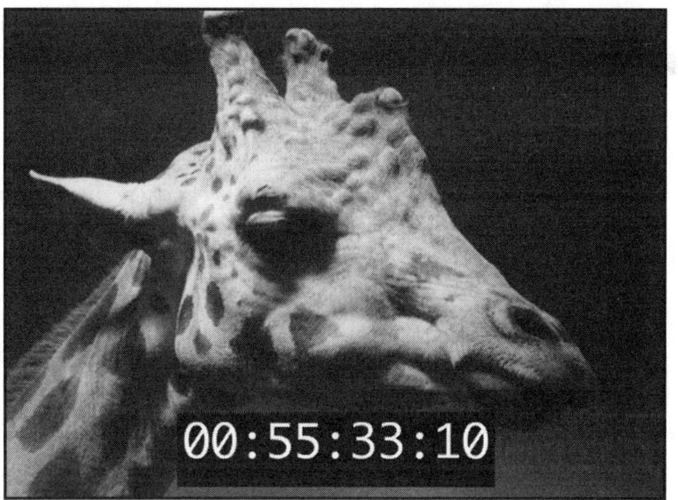

Home video with time-code superimposed.

Linear vs. NonLinear Editing

Today, as a consumer, you can choose between linear edit control systems where one tape is edited onto another, or nonlinear editing systems where the actual footage is transferred and edited on a computer. Many industry folks believe that linear editing is going to be totally replaced by nonlinear editing and in 10 years or less will be a distant memory.

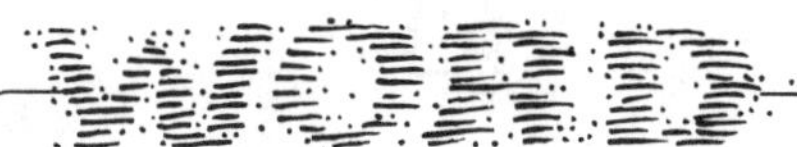

Blurred Word

SMPTE Timecode is a system of assigning each frame of video a number that's based on a 24-hour clock. Some camcorders have timecode that you can see in the viewfinder and possibly use for editing later on.

Linear editing is the process of assembling clips from a "source" tape or tapes and compiling them onto a "master" tape. Depending on your edit system, multiple video sources can be blended together in a video mixer to create effects like dissolves, wipes, and picture-in-picture. The main drawback with linear editing is that once you've compiled a bunch of clips together into a program, it's difficult to fix mistakes and change things. It usually requires dubbing off an entire segment and reassembling onto a new master. If your tape isn't digital, this could mean that you're loosing another video generation, which negatively affects video quality.

Nonlinear editing, on the other hand, takes place entirely in the digital domain and is the most advanced editing technology to date. Video clips are "captured" or downloaded onto a hard drive where they are visually represented as clips in nonlinear editing software such as Adobe Premiere. The clips can then be manipulated in any way you see fit, from simple cuts and dissolves to more advanced motion and special

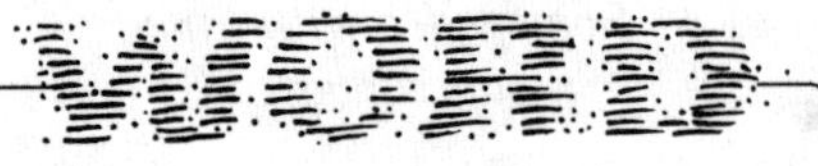

Blurred Word

A **source** tape is the tape where all the raw footage you plan to edit with exists. A **master** tape is the tape on which all the video clips are compiled in the order you choose.

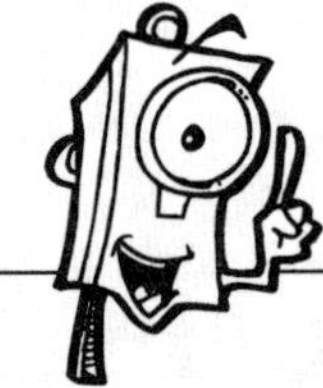

Candid Camera

Many nonlinear editing software packages utilize a "timeline" or "sequence" where your video clips are assembled. This can be considered a virtual "master" tape where clips can be cut, pasted, or moved anywhere on the timeline.

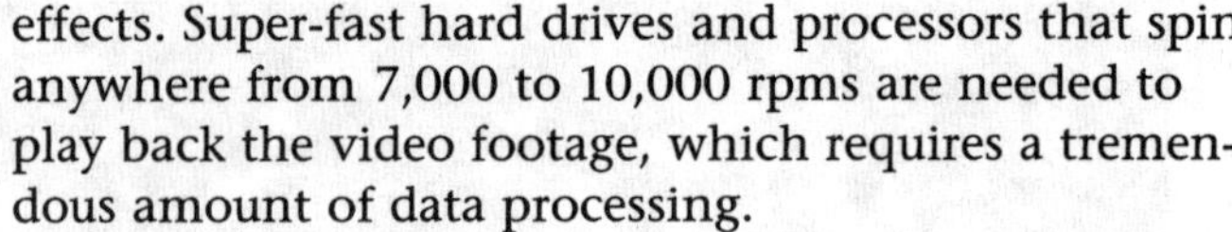

effects. Super-fast hard drives and processors that spin anywhere from 7,000 to 10,000 rpms are needed to play back the video footage, which requires a tremendous amount of data processing.

With even the simplest nonlinear editing program, you can cut and paste video images as easily as you can manipulate words with word processing software. Just a few years ago, you had to shell out tens of thousands of dollars just to get in at ground level. (Unfortunately, that's when I got in.) But now you can have nonlinear capabilities for not much more than the price of a new computer.

What Editing Can Do for You

Since both linear and nonlinear editing systems are available to consumers at ever-decreasing prices, editing can easily become a natural and integral part of the home video experience. Once you understand the basics of editing, your videos will never look the same again, even if you're simply performing basic edits with your camcorder alone. Editing opens up a brand new world of creativity, and allows you to manipulate images to convey any message that you want. This can be a powerful tool, and a new way to entertain, amuse, and inform. Now, the only difference between you and professional editors is what your imagination is capable of creating!

In Chapters 19 through 21, we'll discuss the actual editing systems and how to use them. But before we do, it's a good idea to think about editing before you shoot and how you can shoot with editing in mind.

The Art of Continuity and Combining Shots

We experience smooth continuity on TV every day. In fact, it's so subtle that we don't even think about it. But on rare occasions when continuity breaks down, it sticks out like a sore thumb. The typical home video, for instance, can be plagued with disruptive continuity. Video instructors often compare shaky, zoom-riddled home video shots with little or no continuity to long, run-on sentences without any commas or periods.

That's not to say that poor continuity doesn't occur on the professional level. It's just that professionals are adept at covering their tracks. Most movies have at least one or two continuity issues, some are chock-full of errors and it can be challenging and a lot of fun to catch one. The last one I caught was in a big-budget Hollywood movie that will remain nameless. The actor, a very famous actor mind you, was wearing a tie for the first half of the scene. Then suddenly, when the camera cut back to him, the tie was gone. Oops! There's also a famous scene in *Gone with the Wind* where Scarlet enters Ashley's birthday party. The next shot is of Melanie. In the following shot of Scarlet, she has an obviously different hair style.

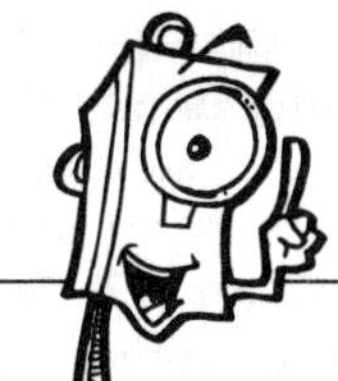

Candid Camera

Most movie crews have at least one person whose job is to maintain on-screen continuity. This can be anything from tracking wardrobe, to keeping track of the time of day in each scene.

Combining a Variety of Shots and Angles

A well-shot and edited home video utilizes a comfortable blend of wide-angle, medium, and close-up shots. In addition to varying distance, a hearty mix of camera angles can also be used to increase visual variety that ignites viewer interest.

Let's say you want to put together a funny little video sequence of a man who has been doing battle with a little mosquito that's been terrorizing his house. Right now the man is lying peacefully on the couch reading a newspaper.

1. You could begin your mini-movie with a wide-angle shot establishing the room and the man on the couch.
2. Next, you can cut to a medium shot from a different angle to get a closer look at the man's face, and the fact that he's very interested in what he's reading. All of a sudden, we *hear* a slight buzzing sound.
3. Cut to a close-up of the man's face as he looks around curiously.
4. Cut to a close-up shot of a tiny mosquito that's landed on the wall near the man's legs.
5. Cut to a medium low-angle shot of the man inching up slowly as he rolls the newspaper into a thin tube.
6. Cut to an extreme close-up of his hands as they roll the newspaper.
7. Cut back to a medium shot of the man as he slams the paper full force into the wall. We hear buzzing as the mosquito escapes the attack and zips by the man's head.
8. Cut to wide-angle shot of the man bowing his head in frustration as he drops back into reading position.

In this example, you can see how a variety of angles and scale changes helps to tell the story in an interesting manner on screen. Based on this outline you could put together a storyboard that will give you an even better idea of what angles you need to shoot. After you're done editing, the action will flow continuously and flawlessly. The viewer will never have a clue that the action didn't take place in real time and that the camera stopped to set up for each shot. In fact, it will look like there were two or more cameras shooting the action.

Moving in the Right Direction

Another major factor that contributes to the continuity in your home videos is screen direction. Again, it's something that you might not recognize until you see someone botch it up (or you botch up it yourself). It's a simple concept that requires you to keep the action happening in the same direction on-screen. But sometimes it's not as easy as it sounds, especially when you're editing with just your camcorder or when you have more than one camera on location.

Let's say you're taping your brother as he jogs through a neighborhood. You begin the sequence by waiting for him at the end of the block. As he approaches and passes the camera, you are on his right side. This would make him appear to be coming from the left of your screen. If in the next shot you reverse the side that you're shooting, your brother would be going from right to left. The resulting sequence from the two shots would make the runner appear as if he'd reversed directions somewhere along his path and began running the other way. In other words, your brother has "crossed the imaginary line" with the camera since his screen direction exceeded 180 degrees.

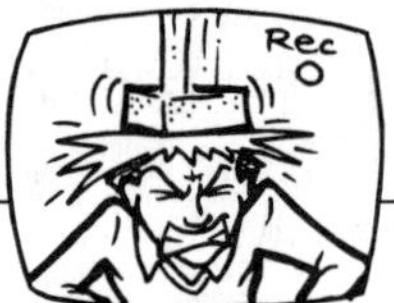

Blooper

Though varying the scale and camera angles can help keep your videos interesting while casting the illusion that they take place in real time, too many scale changes and cuts to extreme angles create confusion and can be distracting to your viewers.

Screen direction can become a major hassle during live sporting events where there are multiple cameras for the director to choose from at any given moment. This also happens in wedding videos very often where there are two cameras. If there is one camera in front of the bride and groom during the ceremony, and another in the audience, it would appear as though they were switching positions every time there was a camera change.

Another neat trick that you should be aware of that's related to screen direction is the timing of entering and exiting the video frame. This is especially important if you're going to be doing in-camera editing. It means that you have to pay close attention to your subject as it enters and exits the camcorder's field of vision. For example, in one scene of a video that I produced there's a shot of my mother as she goes to turn on a television. As she bends down to turn it on, I cut to a close-up of the TV before her hand enters the frame, and cut away after she's pulled her hand away. If I were to cut to the next shot before her hand left the frame, the continuity of the action would be disrupted. This is considered to be one form of a "jump cut."

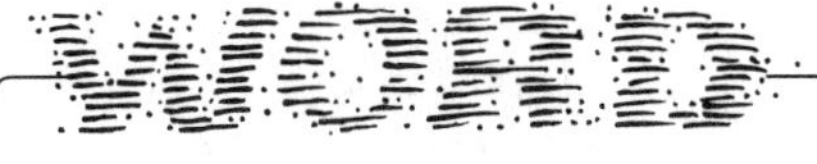

Blurred Word

A **jump cut** is an inappropriate and disruptive edit that results in an eye-catching breakdown in continuity. Jump cuts are often used intentionally in music and sports programming where smooth action is secondary to moving the action forward.

You can also use entrances and exits to pass time in your video. The one rule you must keep in mind, however, is that there needs to be at least one clean entrance or exit to make the transition appear seamless.

A man leaves his house on a bicycle and is going to the supermarket to pick up some milk. You don't want to have to tape his entire journey, so you shoot him leaving the house, and arriving at the store. Upon leaving, you need to have a clean exit. If the man doesn't leave frame before you go to the next shot, then you need to allow for a clean entrance on the other end instead of cutting to him as he's arriving at the store to make up for passage of time.

Squeezing Wasted Time Out of Your Videos

So we agree that instead of recording every single action as they occur in real time, we need to take shortcuts in order to crunch out the boring stuff and leave in the stuff that people are going to want to watch. In order to do that, at the very beginning it's important to determine what scenes are necessary, then figure out how to create transitions to allow the video to flow seamlessly. Besides allowing for clean entrances and exits in order to compress time, you can also use dissolves from one shot to another, or fades to black as transitional devices. A dissolve is a nice transition where one video picture slowly melts away as another picture replaces it. Dissolves are mainly used to signal to the viewer that there has been a passage of time.

Until very recently dissolves were only available in high-end production facilities. Now, many new camcorders come with a digital version of the transition built in. A fade-to-black transition is also available on most camcorders. Similar to a dissolve, a fade is more final of a transition usually signaling the beginning or end of a program or segment.

Another method to compress time that works really well is to pick out action that repeats itself from scene to scene and focus in on it. Back to the jogging video, if you slowly zoom in on your brother's feet as he's running, you can quickly cut to another close-up of his feet after he's gotten to where he's going. Then simply zoom out to reveal his new location.

Similarly, swish pans can also be used to move the action along in your videos. A swish pan is a rapid pan with the camcorder's lens zoomed in as far as possible. This works best when you have your camcorder mounted on a tripod and creates a lot of fast motion in your video. It's as easy as swishing into or away from the action. But remember the law of screen direction. If you swish pan in two different directions the transition won't make sense to the viewer.

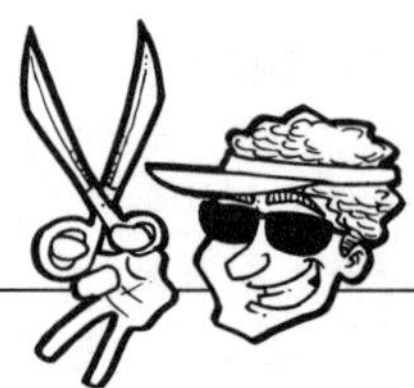

Director's Cut

If I can't dissolve or fade to black, another great way to signal the passage of time is to zoom all the way in on your subject until the auto-focus blurs out. Then I start the next shot all the way zoomed in and blurry and pull out to reveal the subsequent scene.

The most common method for crunching time in any TV or film production is using "cutaway" shots. These shots can be any angle or any scale, from wide to close-up, to low or high and are related to the main action of the scene, but offer the viewer a different vantage-point by revealing more or less detail. Cutaways are commonly used as a transition, or to cover up just about any imperfection in video, from jump cuts or a flubbed line of dialogue to poor focus or collapsed continuity. Cutaways can also show more or less detail that can help the flow and the dramatic impact of a program. Cutaways can also create the illusion that several shots blend together perfectly in real time when in actuality the shots were taken at different times. And, cutaways are totally consumer-friendly and easy to do directly in your camcorder, or with simple post-production equipment. Without cutaways, editing video would be one of the most difficult professions on the planet.

Shooting While You Edit

Editing video on the fly with your camcorder is a great way to jump in on the ground level of post-production and to sharpen your visual and creative skills if you ever plan to edit with real equipment. In-camera editing requires that you carefully select your shots (either in advance or on the spot) and stop and start the camcorder at preselected moments, thereby telling a story while keeping your footage precise and visually interesting.

This technique was widely attempted in the days of 8mm and super 8mm film cameras. Instead of shooting hours upon hours of footage like we do with our home video cameras, film shooters would shoot more sparingly, waiting for key moments before pulling the trigger. This was basically because film stock was more expensive than videotape is today, and they had the additional cost of developing. Unfortunately, their footage still looked comparably as bad as home video with jump cuts, crazy zooms, and pans. A basic knowledge of simple editing concepts like angle and scale changes, screen directions, and transitioning time would have taken film shooters a long way. For them, it's a little too late. For us, we can still do something about it!

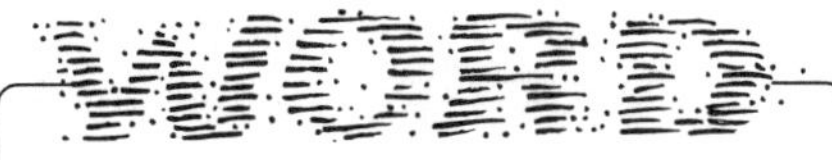

Blurred Word

Postproduction is the process of putting together and adding other finishing touches to a program after it is shot. This can include editing, special effects and audio mixing.

Additionally, the benefits of in-camera editing far outweigh the negatives. First and foremost, the tape that you yank from your camcorder when you're finished shooting is the final product. No long hours of editing to worry about. It's all done! And there's always the added benefit that the footage is first generation, first quality. That means that the picture is clean and pristine, exactly the way camcorder manufacturers intended the video to be viewed. Most other forms of linear editing require that you edit from one tape to another, taking your final program down at least one whole generation.

The only major drawback to editing on the fly is that you have limited creative control over what your final program looks like. A lot of the time your shots don't look exactly as you might have envisioned them and once they're down on tape, there's not really much you can do about it. This is another situation where practice will make all the difference.

The Art of Starting and Stopping

When editing on the fly, you need to have precise control over the starting and stopping of your camcorder in order for your shots to begin and end exactly when you want them to. Before camcorder technology became so advanced, in-camera editing was extremely difficult because the camcorder wouldn't start and stop accurately. Additionally, every edit point would contain an ugly glitch that would disrupt the sync and continuity of the program for as long as 2 to 3 seconds, completely defeating the purpose of editing in the first place.

Almost all camcorders on the market today come with flying erase heads that let you stop and start the camera without causing any glitches along the edit line. You'll notice that flying erase heads work by rolling the tape back slightly, perfectly aligning the frame and tracking of the tape, creating a seamless edit that picks up exactly where you left off.

I'd suggest not to pause the camcorder too closely to a key moment, like when the bride and groom have just finished giving their vows at a wedding. Give the moment a few seconds of breathing room before stopping to prevent the possibility of the camcorder rolling back and recording over the footage.

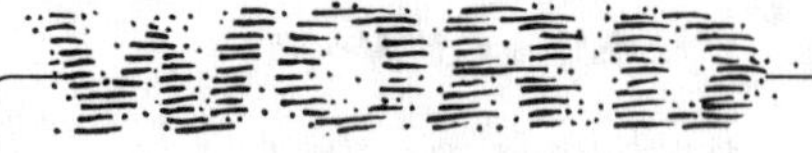

Blurred Word

Flying erase heads allow you to start and stop the camcorder without creating any distracting glitches across edit points. You can start recording again exactly where you left off, leaving a clean edit point no matter how much time passes in between shots and how many times the camcorder has been turned on and off.

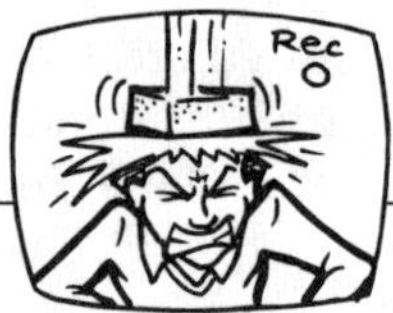

Blooper

No matter how advanced the camcorder, sometimes it's very hard to time exactly when the camcorder will start and stop rolling. It may sound like it stopped at the right moment, but upon playback you might discover that you chopped off a key moment. Once you practice this method, however, your camera's internal timing becomes second nature and you'll be able to start and stop on a dime.

Oops ... Can We Do That One Again?

If you're editing a video on the fly in your camcorder, you will inevitably record a shot that you want to shoot over. On some camcorders there is an edit search or review feature that allows you to get close to the unwanted portion of your shot and record over it.

Since this method isn't frame accurate, the best way to do a re-shoot is to change the angle or scale of the replacement shot. This can help you cover your mistake by simulating an intended edit.

Can I Add a Shot or Two?

In most cases you'll want to avoid attempting this. Whenever you try to record new footage over already existing footage, you usually get a clean edit on the in-point, but the out-point is almost always marred by that ugly glitch problem we talked about earlier.

The only work-around here is to either dub off the shots that you want onto another tape and re-shoot the bad scenes, or you can simply start from scratch. The second option is usually the least desirable, especially when you're pleased with the footage or performances that you've already captured.

If you plan to do a lot of editing on the fly with your camcorder, (and I think that this is a good option for everyone to consider from time to time) make sure the camcorder you buy has all the appropriate features to accommodate this. This includes:

- Flying erase heads
- Fade to black button
- Digital transitions like wipes and dissolves

Shooting to Edit

Shooting to edit is a completely different gig than editing in your camcorder, and is a common method of shooting for both amateurs and professionals alike. It allows you to shoot a scene as many times as you want, changing the angle, performance, scale, and so on, giving you the most creative choice. It also helps you create the illusion that there are several cameras recording the event and that you're effortlessly cutting from one to the other. This is definitely an advanced way of shooting meant for people who plan to edit their final footage. Most movies, documentaries, music videos and most other programs that you can think of are shot in this style. Not only does it expand creativity, but also it eliminates the horrible pressure of having to nail something on the first take.

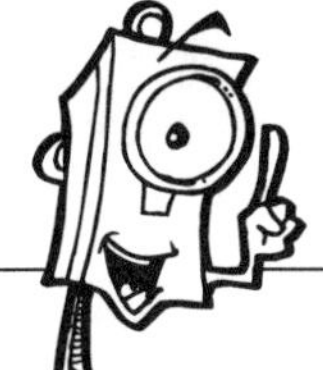

Candid Camera

Whenever I shoot to edit later, I always have a plan of action. This could be a script, storyboard, or simply a shot list. If you don't have direction, you'll probably spend countless hours shooting, giving yourself more footage to screen through and making key moments more difficult to pinpoint.

The Least You Need to Know

- Video editing has taken 40 years or so to emerge into the advanced craft of today.
- Editing is easy and effective when you have a wide variety of different shots to choose from.
- Passing time in your videos can be done with a few simple editing techniques.
- You can edit full-length programs effectively directly in your camcorder without ever popping the tape out.
- When you plan to edit your video at a later time, you have more creative freedom and room for experimentation while shooting.

Chapter 19

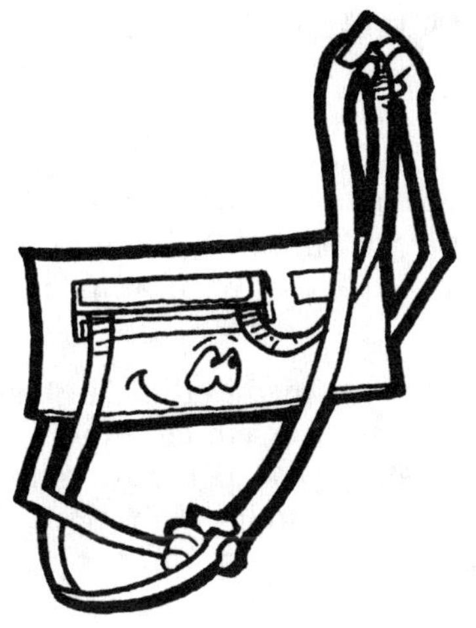

Putting That Old VCR to Work: Linear Editing

In This Chapter

- Editing video with a camcorder and a VCR
- Wiring basics
- Preparing to edit
- Minimizing generation loss
- How to assemble edit

It doesn't take a million-dollar studio to become a crack video editor. In fact, it's a proven fact that with a firm grasp of a few basic editing concepts, all you really need is a camcorder to edit together programs that people will want to watch again and again.

But wouldn't you like to gain even more creative control over your programs without spending another dime on new equipment? Well, if you've got an extra VCR lying around, get ready to take the art of editing to new heights.

You might not have realized that you could create a fully function editing system with simple consumer equipment, but it's completely doable. And if you're dreading the potential cabling and connector nightmare to wire up your home system, fear not. After reading this chapter, you'll not only be the best home video editor on your block, you'll also be an expert at cabling up your camcorder to a VCR.

Simple Editing Setups Using Equipment You Already Have at Home

In the United States, approximately two out of every three homes have at least one VCR. That's a pretty staggering number considering that there are over 600 million people who live in the United States. From this statistic, we can safely deduce that a large majority of camcorder owners also have access to a VCR. For what we plan to do in this chapter, this is a very good thing.

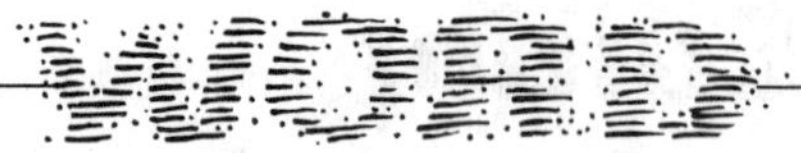

Blurred Word

Assemble editing is the process of selectively recording video and audio clips to another videotape. The edits are laid down on the "record master" in a linear fashion, from start to finish.

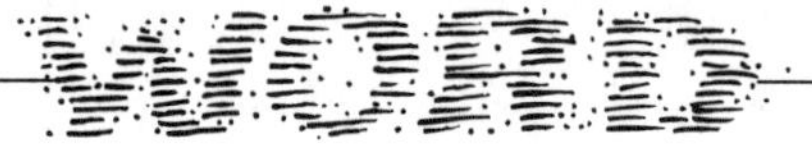

Blurred Word

A **source deck** (your camcorder in this case) plays back the footage you have acquired in the field. A **record deck** (your VCR) is connected to the source deck and is used to compile the final program.

In its rawest form, *editing* is defined as the act of eliminating unwanted footage and reassembling the highlights in an order that makes sense, perhaps even telling a story. It's not a very complex definition; and trust me when I tell you, in its rawest form, editing is not a complex thing to do. This is especially true when you're utilizing your own camcorder and VCR to do simple assemble editing. Later on, if you decide to break out the big bucks and buy some nifty post-production equipment, you can guarantee that the act of editing will be easier. You'll also have more handy tools at your disposal. But no machine can replace the creativity that you have in your mind. Anyone who has the will to edit can learn to live with the limitations of the available equipment. Here are a few simple ways to configure your equipment.

Camcorder to VCR

Under this arrangement, you're using your camcorder as the "source" deck and your VCR as the "record" deck. This means that the camcorder sends the pictures and sound over to the VCR where they are collected and reassembled in any order you choose. It may sound simple to do, but if you don't know precisely which buttons to push, it can get confusing in a hurry.

A major plus of using the setup is that your camcorder and VCR don't have to be the same tape format in order to be able to assemble edit. In other words, if your camcorder is a Hi8 and the VCR is full size VHS, (the most commonly available VCR) you will end up with an edit master that is on VHS. Similarly, if you purchase a MiniDV VCR, you can edit your Hi8 footage over to MiniDV. This setup offers the most versatility because universal cabling schemes make it entirely compatible between different formats.

It is the actual wiring of the two together, however, that scares a lot of people away. But as long as you have the right cables and converters, wiring is a snap.

Let's say you've chosen to go with the camcorder-to-VCR setup. The only things you'll really need to get started are three RCA cables (they usually come with your camcorder or VCR, and are often connected together), one for each of your right and left audio channels, and one for video. Make sure your VCR has RCA inputs for audio and video. If not, consult your owner's manual or ask an audio/video professional for help at your local electronics store.

One of the best things about cabling consumer gear together is that the colors are the same for audio and video RCA cables and jacks. Stereo right is red, stereo left is white and video is yellow. From this point on, it's basically connecting the colors.

1. Find the yellow video *out* jack on your camcorder and plug in one end of the yellow RCA cable.
2. Then find the yellow video *in* jack on the VCR and plug in the other end.
3. Do the same with the red audio right RCA cable and the white audio left RCA cable, plugging them into the corresponding red and white *out* jacks in your camcorder and the *in* jacks in your VCR.
4. Depending on the model VCR you have, there might be a button to select a video input. Flick this switch to the appropriate setting. You'll know that you've got it right when you can see a picture on your TV from the camcorder.
5. If there's only one audio jack on either the VCR or camcorder, I suggest you use a "Y" connector. This adapter can convert between

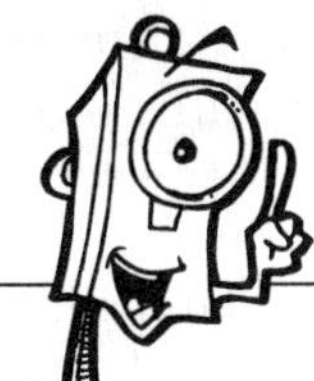

Candid Camera

If you decide to use your camcorder as a source deck for editing, be aware that editing puts extra wear and tear on your camcorder. This means you'll have to clean the recording heads more often, and the overall life span of your camcorder can be shortened. If you get really good at the camcorder-to-VCR setup, I'd recommend upgrading to the VCR-to-VCR approach. (See "Give Your Equipment a Break!" later in this chapter.)

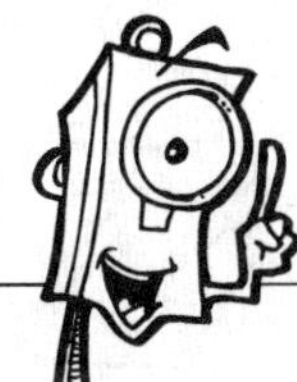

Candid Camera

If you're using a Hi8, SVHS, or MiniDV camcorder chances are you'll also have the option of using a Y/C (S-Video) cable for video. If your VCR has a Y/C input for video, I highly recommend using it over the yellow RCA (composite) jack because the picture quality is noticeably better.

mono and stereo jacks. This way, you eliminate the chances of having sound coming out of only one speaker. These adapters are available at Radio Shack or other electronics stores for only a few dollars.

Just a note here. Make sure you patch the "out" jacks on the camcorder (source deck) into the "in" jacks on the VCR (record deck). (See the following figure.) The labels on the jacks can be hard to read. Once you've got all the wires in place, you're ready to roll.

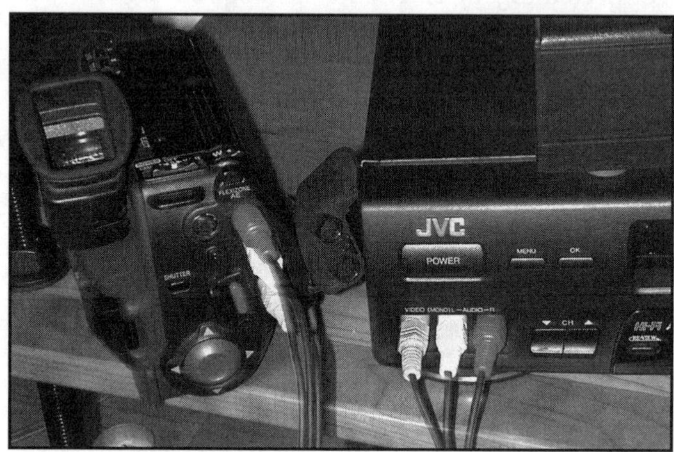

Common camcorder-to-VCR hookup.

VCR to VCR

With the VCR statistics in mind, it's probably safe to say that if you've got one VCR, chances are you may have access to another one. If this is the case, and you have the time and motivation to disconnect one of them, then you can hook one VCR up to the other one and perform the same kind of assemble editing that you can with your camcorder hooked up to the VCR.

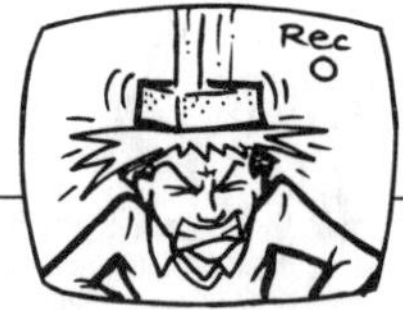

Blooper

Whenever using your camcorder as a source deck for assemble editing always use the a/c adapter for plugging into a wall outlet. If you rely on the camcorder's battery while editing, chances are it'll go dead before you're done!

Cabling the two VCRs together is the same as cabling a camcorder to a VCR:

1. Plug one end of your video cable into the yellow video *out* jack on your source VCR.
2. Plug the other end of your video cable into the yellow video *in* jack on the record VCR. Make sure you've got the proper video input selected on the record VCR.

3. Plug the red audio right cable and the white audio left cable into the corresponding red and white *out* jacks on your source VCR and the *in* jacks on your record VCR.

Again, be sure that all the cables connect to the *out* jacks on your source VCR and to the *in* jacks on your record VCR.

The key benefit to using this method is to steer some of the wear and tear away from your camcorder. VCRs are also easier and less cumbersome to edit with than camcorders. The buttons are bigger and more push-friendly than the tiny buttons on your camcorder.

There are also some strong disadvantages, however, to the VCR-to-VCR hookup. First and foremost, if your VCR isn't the same format as the tape that you use in your camcorder, then you'll have to make a dub of your raw footage onto VHS, or whatever format your VCR requires. This takes your raw footage down an entire generation, so by the time you've edited your program together, you're already down two full video generations. This can soften the picture's quality considerably, especially if you plan to make copies of your program for others to enjoy.

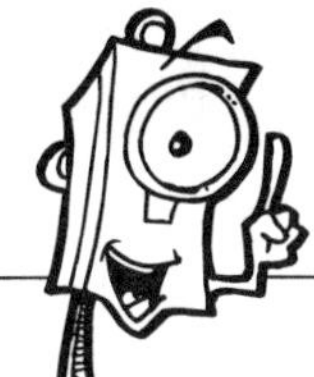

Candid Camera

The best way to get around most of the major problems of the VCR-to-VCR setup is to buy at least one VCR that is native to the format you're using. If you're working with SVHS, Hi8, Digital8 or MiniDV, you might want to consider biting the bullet and buying two. This way, you'd always be working with high-band video. Hi8 and SVHS have approximately 400 lines of resolution while Digital8 and MiniDV have as many as 500. Regular VHS only has 250.

Another annoying problem stems from not using a VCR with flying erase heads. Sometimes your edit points will be marred with rainbow-colored glitches that make the picture hop and skip and that can last for as long as two seconds. The chances are good, however, that your VCR and/or camcorder has flying erase heads because they have been an industry-standard for a while. If you're stuck without flying erase heads, you may want to consider scrapping the editing gig until you upgrade VCRs.

Adding a Monitor to Your Editing Outfit

In order to see what you're doing, you're going to need to hook up a monitor. Regardless of what you may have heard, you only need one monitor to see both the record and playback decks as you edit. By hooking up the monitor to the output of the record deck, you're creating a loop that allows you to see the playback of the source deck when the record deck is stopped, or you hit record with or without hitting pause. By hitting stop and then play on the record deck, you can always check your edits at any point during production.

If you've got a newer TV, the connections and colors will be exactly the same as they are on your camcorder and VCR. It's the same drill all over again.

1. Run your video cable from the yellow composite video (or Y/C) *out* jack on the record deck and cable it to the yellow composite video (or Y/C) *in* jack on the TV.
2. Connect the red and white audio cables to the corresponding red and white audio *out* jacks on the record deck and the red and white audio *in* jacks on the TV.

On some of the older TV sets, you may notice that there is only one input jack. This is for a coaxial cable connection that carries both audio and video. Most VCRs will also have a coaxial output. If you hook them up this way, you only need to make the one connection between the record VCR and your TV. Again, if you can't figure out your connections, consult your manual or seek advice at your local electronics store.

Wired for Sound and Picture

Wiring is the most important link in the home video editing chain. Good wiring techniques are an absolute must to get the best possible picture and sound quality. And once your system is wired up, it's hard to find the culprit cable that could be injecting distracting video or audio noise into your system. That's why it's essential to nail this kind of problem before it happens.

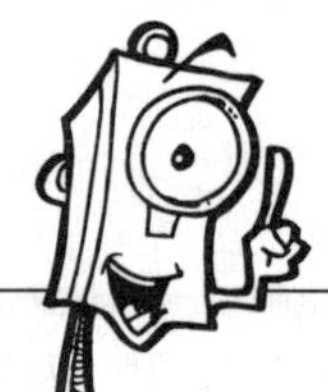

Candid Camera

A great place to mail order cables and just about anything else related to home video is

Markertek Video Supply
4 High St., Box 397
Saugerties, NY 12477
1-800-522-2025
www.markertek.com

Using Quality Cables

Surprisingly, a lot of people shrug off the fact that quality cables are essential in any audio/video setup. And you may be wondering why I'm babbling on about this. A cable is a cable is a cable, right?

Not quite. All kinds of external factors can cause interference in the wire's signal flow, like electrical appliances, magnetic sources, and the ever-present broadcast and radio frequencies. Unless your cables have the proper protection (sometimes called shielding) any or all of these factors can diminish the quality of your work.

The best way to figure out the quality of your cables is to look at the price tag. It's a very simple equation, the more you pay, the better the cable. And this isn't the area to skimp. In fact, you should purchase the best cables that you can. If you're not sure which ones to choose, you can always ask a salesperson. He'll have no problem steering you to the most expensive cables!

Keeping It Neat!

Generally, when I shop for cables, I look not only at the price tag, but I also pay close attention to thickness and the condition of the connectors. A few times I've even gone for wiring that has gold plating at the point of connection for better conducting of electricity.

Try to keep the length of your cables under six feet. Any longer, and they become more susceptible to outside interference and signal loss. As a general rule, keep your cables as short as possible.

Also, keep your wires untangled and whenever possible, group them together with wire-ties, string or rubber bands. Wires that are tangled together into a spaghetti mess are also more susceptible to unwanted noise.

The Lowdown on Adapters

Unless it's absolutely necessary, avoid adapters like the plague. Be very wary of ones that don't quite seem to be tight enough; the slightest tension and the signal can suddenly cut out completely. Use adapters sparingly and if possible, replace adapters with the proper cables.

A Little Preparation Goes a Long Way

Preparation is 90 percent of the post-production battle. If you have all of your ducks in a row before you sit down in your new home studio, editing can be a truly enjoyable process where your creative juices flow unhindered. The last thing you want to do once you begin is to find yourself sorting through miles of videotape and paperwork.

Take Note of It

Taking notes while screening your footage is the least stimulating leg of your journey. Logging tapes is work—hard work. But it's time very well spent. The last thing you want to do when you're on the brink of performing that perfect edit is to waste precious minutes searching for the shot.

Logging is the simple act of matching tape time with your selected shots. If you have a VCR or camcorder that keeps track of hours, minutes and seconds, then you're notes are going to be very accurate. If your VCR only has a simple tape counter, rewind your tape all the way to the beginning and reset the counter. This way, your notes will always have a reference point after you eject the tape. Also try to use a page that's formatted with separate columns for the timecode, comments/shot name and approximate running time. This will make searching for shots in your edit a snap.

For me, note taking is a great way to watch all of my footage back in a more objective environment where I'm less distracted than I am out in the field. This enables me to

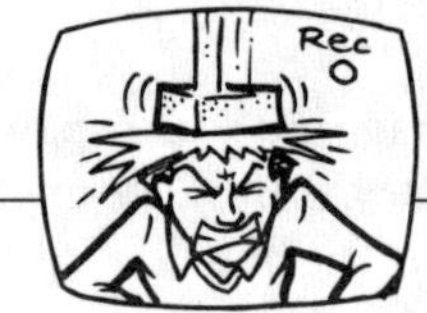

Blooper

Make sure you zero your VCR's tape counter before taking notes.

begin conceptualizing about the possible executions I can take with my footage. I always keep a separate note pad handy when I'm logging tapes so I can quickly write down any ideas that come to mind.

Prepping Your Edit Master Tape

It is a common practice in the video industry to edit programs onto a tape that has been recorded with a black signal from start to finish. I think this is also a good habit to get into if you plan to edit your home video.

The main reason for this is that a tape that hasn't been blacked plays back with white snow in your VCR. (Put a brand new tape in your VCR and hit play. You'll see what I mean.) Sometimes, if you're performing tight edits, you can get flashes of this white snow in your program, distracting viewers.

To record a black signal, simply record on your camcorder with your lens cap on or on your VCR with no incoming signal (turn your TV off). If you're using your camcorder, do this in a quiet room so as not to record any unwanted noise that could distract you later during editing. You can also plug a microphone (with the on/off switch off or powered down) into the microphone jack on the camcorder.

Write-Protecting Your Source Tapes

This should be a no-brainer, but I can't tell you how many times I've ruined portions of my source tapes by not write-protecting them after shooting. All videocassettes have a mechanism usually located along the spine that allows you to switch the write-protect feature on and off. On VHS tapes, there's a little tab that you can actually snap off after shooting. Then, if you ever want to re-record over the tape, you can cover the hole with a little piece of adhesive tape.

Cutting Generation Loss Off at the Path

Let's face the facts. Unless you're editing with MiniDV or other high-band formats, you're beginning the editing process with footage that's already not the best quality. Editing can only make matters worse since you are taking your footage down a full generation right from the get-go. As generation loss becomes more of an issue, lower-band footage like VHS and 8mm can quickly decompose. And it's the video track that suffers most, leaving you with fuzzy, blurry-looking footage with colors that bleed into one another.

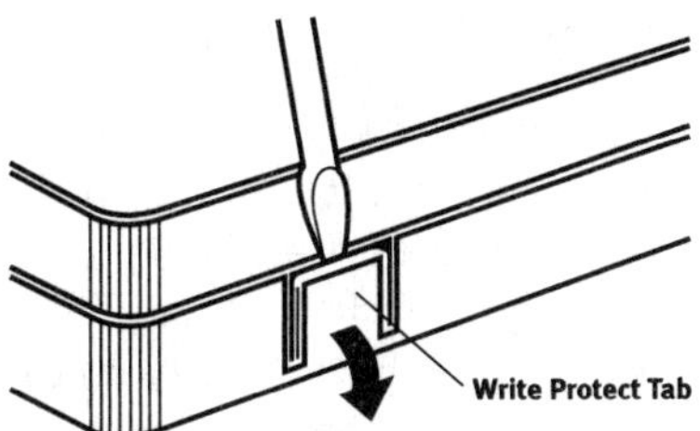

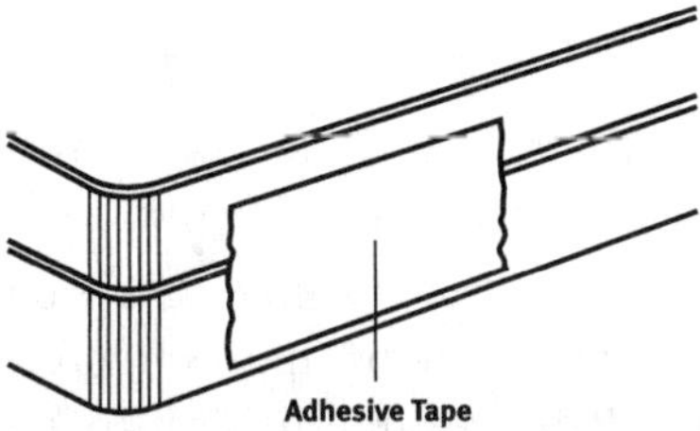

Write-protecting a VHS tape.

Choosing the Right Tape for the Job

The tape that you choose both for shooting in the field and for your edit master has a great effect on what your final product will look like. Most manufacturers like Maxell, Sony, and TDK offer several qualities of tape including low band, medium band and high band. This is another scenario where the most expensive is definitely the way to go.

High-quality tapes have a higher concentration of magnetic particles that help store and playback your images at the best possible quality. Pay close attention to packaging when planning a purchase. The tapes that have hard plastic cases are usually best for your home videos.

Give Your Equipment a Break!

There's one very important point that you should keep in mind when planning your home video setup. Camcorders are not designed for use as source machines for editing. Editing is a machine-intensive process that involves constantly shuttling the tape back and forth. This puts a lot of wear and tear on your precious machinery, which in turn can affect the quality of your videos.

The other thing you can do to protect your equipment is to clean the record heads every now and then. You can buy head-cleaning kits that contain a cartridge that you insert into your camcorder or VCR and run a short cleaning cycle. If you don't mind spending a few bucks, you can also bring your equipment in to an electronics store or dealer and have the heads cleaned. Leaving this to a professional is also good because they usually give your machine a thorough once-over.

Adjusting the Tracking

Most VCRs have a little tracking knob that even the slightest turn can have a big effect on the way your picture looks. When you turn it, you are tinkering with the actual alignment of the videotape inside the unit. Before I begin to edit, I always adjust the tracking just to make sure that everything is perfectly lined up. There's nothing more frustrating than editing a program together only to discover that the tracking is way off.

Assemble Editing for Idiots

Finally, you're ready to edit!

1. Slip your new edit master tape into the record deck, rewind it to the beginning, switch it to SP (standard play) and zero the VCR's counter.
2. Then hit play and let about five minutes of black go by before you lay down your first edit. This way you'll have room to edit in an open-credits sequence later on if you choose. Also, most videotape imperfections occur at the head of the tape because it's tightly wound around the spool.
3. Next, load up your source tape and rewind it to the beginning, resetting the counter.

Assemble editing is sometimes referred to as "pause" editing and is very much like the process of editing on the fly with your camcorder.

1. After you've located your first shot on the source tape, roll back approximately 10 seconds and then hit pause. If you have carefully logged your tapes, finding the shot should be a snap.
2. Next, hit the pause button on the record deck.
3. Then hit record, or record and play at the same time. (Check your VCR's manual if you're not sure which buttons to push.)

You are about to make your first edit. You should be able to see your source shot cued up and ready to roll in the monitor. Here goes.

1. Hit play on the source deck.
2. Have your finger ready to un-pause the record deck when the shot gets to where you want to come in.
3. When it gets there, hit the pause button, and you're editing!

4. After you have visually spotted your intended out-point, let the source machine roll for at least seven seconds to allow for some leeway in the edit point.
5. Hit pause again on the record deck to halt the edit.

The only tricky part now is to cue the record deck back up to exactly where you want to start the next edit.

1. Hit the pause button.
2. Then hit the record/play buttons again, and you're in the editing groove.
3. Repeat this process again and again until your program is complete.

If you use the fundamentals you've learned in the previous chapters on shooting to edit and using a variety of camera angles, scale and motion, your viewers are going to dig your videos!

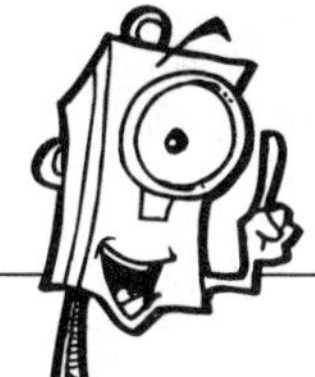

Candid Camera

One thing that you need to be aware of while assemble editing is the timing of both your source and record decks. Just because you hit record on one deck and pause on the other doesn't mean it's going to happen right then. It may take a few seconds to get rolling. Once you've figured out this timing, you can get pretty close with your edits.

The Least You Need to Know

➤ You can edit your own programs with just a camcorder and a VCR.

➤ Wiring up your home video equipment is easy. Just match the colors!

➤ A little preparation can cut your post-production time in half.

➤ Generation loss is the killer of home videos. But there are a few things you can do to minimize it.

➤ Simple assemble editing is as easy as hitting play on the "source" deck and record on the "record" deck.

Chapter 20

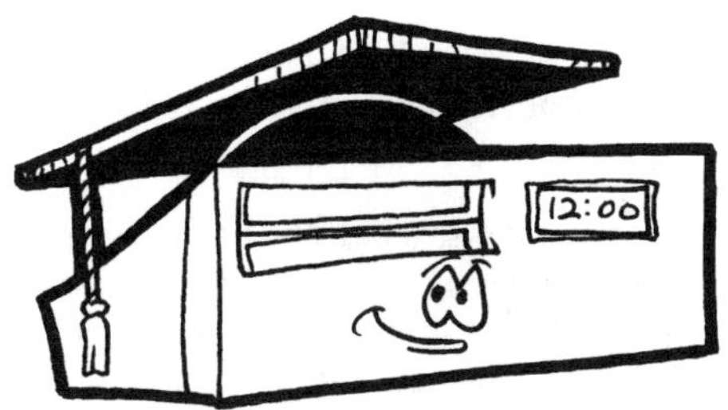

Linear Editing: The Next Step

In This Chapter

- All about editing VCRs
- Taking charge of your programs with an edit controller
- Idiot-proof insert editing
- Video mixers
- Editing extras

O.K. You've got simple assemble editing under your belt. How would you like to max out your creative possibilities with more advanced editing tools and techniques? It's going to take a bit more cash to break into higher-end editing, but prices are dropping by leaps and bounds every day, and you may find that it's a worthwhile investment.

Depending on how far you want to take it, there are all sorts of editing tools at your disposal. Whether you opt for a high-end editing VCR, edit controller, or even a special effects generator, you're going to attain a production value that will astonish you. And with higher-end editing tools, the act of editing itself becomes much more of a natural process than the clunky pause and play editing method.

Editing VCRs

Even though you can get the job done with "pause editing" on consumer VCRs, you can really make miracles happen with VCRs that have been specifically designed for editing. Editing VCRs are definitely a step up in price, sometimes costing as much as $1,200 for a prosumer or professional deck with all the bells and whistles. But if you're looking to make one of these high-end VCRs the centerpiece of your home-editing setup, get ready for control and accuracy right down to the frame.

Besides offering you flying erase heads which are key to crystal clear edits and high-band formats like Hi8, SVHS, and MiniDV, editing VCRs offer a wide array of professional features that make editing a snap. Additionally, they are extremely durable and designed to withstand the rigors of constant use. Linear editing is a machine-intensive activity that requires you to constantly wind videotapes back and forth. Consumer decks are easily overwhelmed by overuse and abuse while editing decks are ready to roll through thousands of hours of thrashing.

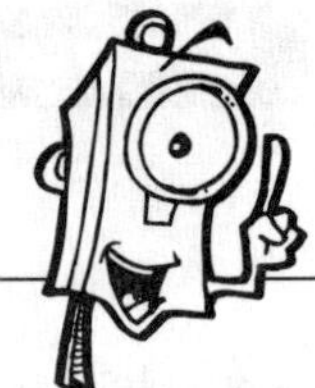

Candid Camera

Most editing VCRs also allow you to do "insert editing" in addition to "assemble editing." With insert editing, you can selectively replace audio or video into any portion of your program at whatever length you choose. (See "The Art of Insert Editing" later in this chapter.)

Take a Jog to the Shuttle

No, it's not a quick visit to NASA. I'm talking about one of the most useful features that can be found on an editing VCR, the jog/shuttle wheel. One of the biggest frustrations when you edit with a consumer VCR is locating the exact point (or close to it) in your video that you want to pinpoint. The jog/shuttle wheel takes video-accuracy to the next level.

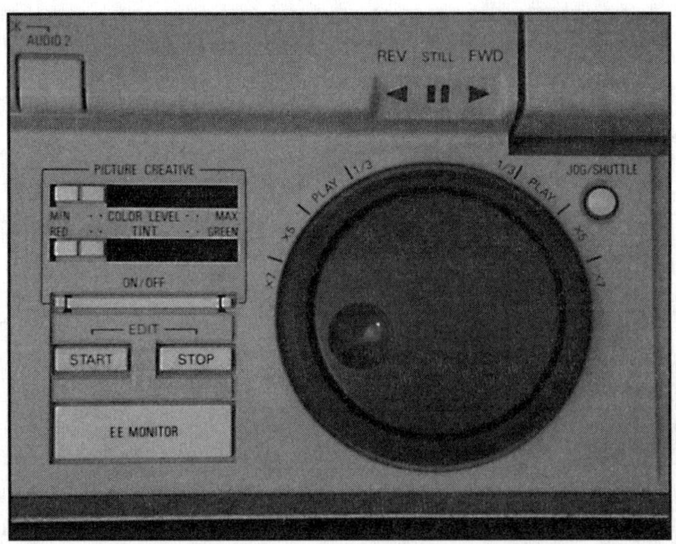

Jog/shuttle wheel.

Borrowed from high-end professional video equipment, the jog/shuttle wheel is a large dial located on the face of the VCR. The outer ring, called the shuttle control, lets you scroll through your video at variable speeds, enabling you to stop on a dime. The jog control, located inside the shuttle dial, can be manipulated with your fingertip and lets you fine-tune your location on the tape by moving the video forward or backward frame by frame. Once you've worked with jog/shuttle controls, it's extremely difficult to go back to the old pause editing method.

> **Blurred Word**
>
> **Time base corrector (TBC)** is an external box or internal circuitry inside your editing VCR that corrects the timing of analog video sources.

All in Good Time

The next nifty feature built-in to most editing VCRs is something called a time base corrector. A time base corrector (TBC) corrects subtle timing problems inherent in analogue video sources. This helps to get rid of jerky, unstable video and makes your final edit master look sharp and clean.

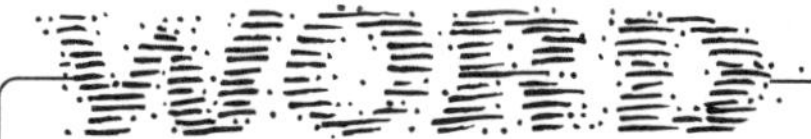

> **Blurred Word**
>
> A **processing amplifier** is similar to a TBC in that you are affecting the video images with digital circuitry. This allows you to adjust the color and other subtle video properties on the fly.

The more advanced your setup, the more a TBC becomes a necessity. In fact, a lot of prosumer and professional gear require that you run video signals through some sort of time base corrector. Some video purists argue that TBCs slightly degrade the picture because the footage is actually processed by electronic circuitry. I've found that TBCs only make my product look better and help me keep all of my video sources perfectly in sync.

Color Correction

Most VCRs that come with an internal time base corrector also have another digital adjustment called a processing amplifier (PROCAMP). This allows you to make subtle adjustments to the picture quality of your source footage. This is useful if you want to correct the overall color of your video, or if you shot without adjusting the white balance.

It's About Timecode!

This is my favorite editing feature and will forever replace your VCR's clock counter. Editing VCRs that have timecode support mark each frame of video with a unique address that doesn't get erased when you power down or eject the tape. In fact, the address is recorded into the videotape itself.

Timecode display.

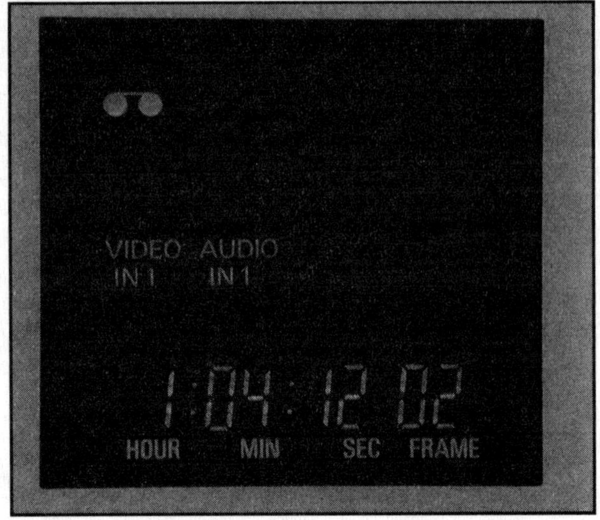

The only problem with this feature is that it's difficult to nail down a universal format. MiniDV decks have their own numbering system in which each frame of video is marked, while Hi8 decks use a special rewriteable time code. Professional decks use SMPTE timecode which numbers frames according to a 24-hour clock. If you're considering putting together an editing system based on timecode, do some research on the Web, in magazines and at your retailer to make sure all of your gear is compatible. Once you steer around some of the roadblocks and misinformation that usually accompanies any purchase of a timecoded deck, you will ease very nicely into using timecode as a powerful editing tool that helps you keep your shots in order and drastically improves your editing accuracy.

Take Charge with an Edit Controller

Now we're getting into some serious gear here! Not only do edit controllers look really cool, they streamline the cockpit of your editing setup making it an uncomplicated and relaxing place to do work while giving you unprecedented control over the equipment.

An edit controller acts as a home base where you can control all of your essential video gear. On lower-end models, you can loop the actual video input and output from your source and record deck through the edit controller, similar to the way you would wire two VCRs together (see Chapter 19, "Putting That Old VCR to Work: Linear Editing"). This isn't the best method, however, because the video signal can degrade slightly as it passes through the controller.

High-end VCRs also have inputs and outputs for editing protocols such as LANC/Control-L and Control-S that allow the VCRs to talk to each other and perfectly synchronize the edits. Protocols control many of the major deck controls like play, record, rewind and fast forward, as well as the timing of the deck during editing. (See the section in Chapter 2, "Taking Control with LANC/Control-L Connections.") When you loop an editing protocol through the controller from the source and record VCRs, you're giving the controller the responsibility to synchronize editing. But as you'll see, edit controllers take it a few steps further than a stand-alone VCR editing system.

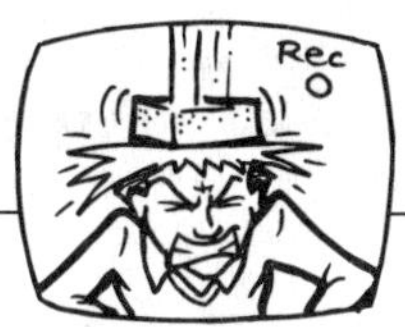

Blooper

Beware of trying to hook up two VCRs that have different editing protocols. The best thing to do before buying a system is to double check to make sure that the VCRs are not only compatible with each other, but with the edit controller as well.

When choosing an edit protocol, ask your retailer which one is compatible with your system. If you're building a system from scratch, or if you're simply adding more gear to your existing setup, make sure that the specific edit controller or deck is compatible with your protocol. You'll most likely find LANC/Control-L since it's become standard on many consumer and prosumer camcorders. Most of the other protocols like Control-S, Control-M and Control-P, however, work pretty much the same.

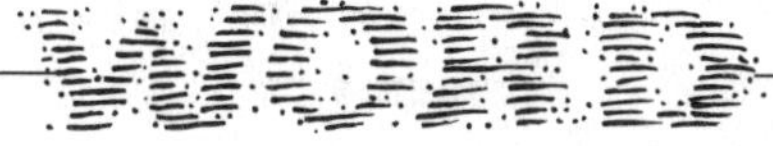

Blurred Word

Pre-roll is the part of the program that takes place before the intended edit point. Whenever you mark your edits and hit the preview button on your edit controller, the system gives you several seconds of pre-roll so you can see how the edit works in context. It also gives the decks time to get up to speed before actually performing the edit.

Just a quick side note, if you've decided to go the MiniDV route, you'll never have to worry about buying equipment with different editing protocols. Almost all MiniDV camcorders and decks have FireWire ports which transfer digital (CD Quality) audio, first generation video, timecode, and deck control. (See the section in Chapter 4 titled, "IEEE 1394 (FireWire/i.LINK) Port.")

Not only can you mark in and out edit points on both the source and record VCRs, but you can also preview the edit before actually recording it to tape. In other words, you get to see what the edit will look like before you actually do it. If you don't like the way it works, you can clear the edit points and start from scratch, or you can adjust the in and out points by as little as $\frac{1}{30}$ of a second (one frame of moving video) using little plus or minus buttons.

What makes the preview feature even more powerful is the fact that you can view several seconds of "pre-roll" before the edit takes place, giving you insight as to how the edit works in the context of the program. This makes a world of difference over the instant starting and stopping of your edits as with the pause method. The edit controller does this by automatically backing both machines up and playing them at the same time in perfect sync according to your edit marks. It's a great feature that gives you a feel for the overall timing of your piece. I got into the habit very early on of previewing every edit before I lay it down. This has also helped me catch video glitches that can be easily eliminated with a simple trim of the plus or minus button.

The Art of Insert Editing

This is the feature that can change your life! I've told you all about assemble editing with consumer VCRs, and I still stick to the statement that if your program is well thought out in advance, you can work around the limitations of assemble-only editing. But insert editing opens a new door to creative freedom and lets you work somewhat out of sequence if you so desire. You can lay down an audio track first and cut video over it to the beat. Or, you can cut the video and add your music later. Even if you want to change one shot, you can pinpoint the unwanted shot with great accuracy (depending on the editing setup) and paste over it with the new shot. Here are the advantages of insert editing:

1. Unlike assemble editing where the audio, video and control track (see below) are all recorded at once, insert editing lets you edit with audio and video as separate elements.
2. It allows you to insert a video shot into your program without any glitches on the edit points.
3. Depending on your equipment, insert editing can give you accuracy right down to the frame.

Insert editing can be used in all kinds of programs. From music videos to wedding videos, insert editing makes postproduction a truly enjoyable activity.

Control Track

Before learning how to do an insert edit, it's important to have a basic idea of what's going on technically. When you hit the record button on a VCR, besides the audio and video signals, the machine lays down something called a control track which, upon playback, tells the VCR that the tape has been recorded on. A brand new tape without a control track typically plays back white snow on your TV.

The control track also tells your VCR what speed to play the tape back (standard play or extended play). When you're recording in your camcorder, a brand new control track is recorded onto the tape every time you hit the start and stop button.

Here's how insert editing works: your editing VCR allows you to record either audio or video without recording over the control track. This is totally different than assemble editing, which lays down a new control track every time you make an edit. Since the control track isn't being touched, it enables you to make perfectly clean edits on the tape—both at the in point and the out point. You might remember that when assemble editing, if you try to insert a shot you might get a clean in point, but you will definitely have an ugly two- or three-second glitch at the out point.

You Wanna Insert Edit? Here's How

Even though most edit controllers are designed to make insert editing a snap, you can do it on many editing VCRs without an edit controller attached. A lot of the fundamentals of simple pause editing come into effect here, but there are a few unique twists.

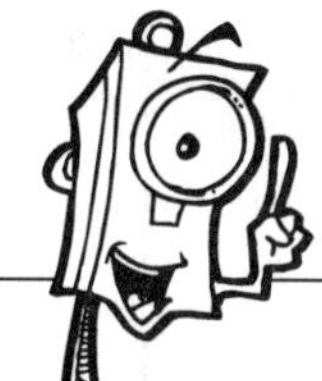

Candid Camera

Whenever you plan to do any kind of insert editing, it is essential to use a tape that has been "blacked" in advance. When you record black onto a tape (recording on your camcorder with the lens cap on or on your VCR with no incoming signal), you are creating a new control track. (See "Prepping Your Edit Master Tape" in Chapter 19.)

Again, insert editing requires that your record tape has an existing control track all the way through. If you have both of your tapes in the VCRs and have an idea where you want to perform an insert edit, follow these simple instructions. This is one of the most common ways to insert edit from VCR to VCR but you'll definitely want to double check your VCR's specific controls in the user manual.

1. On your record tape, locate the out point where you want your audio or video insert edit to end, press the pause button and reset your VCR's counter to zero.

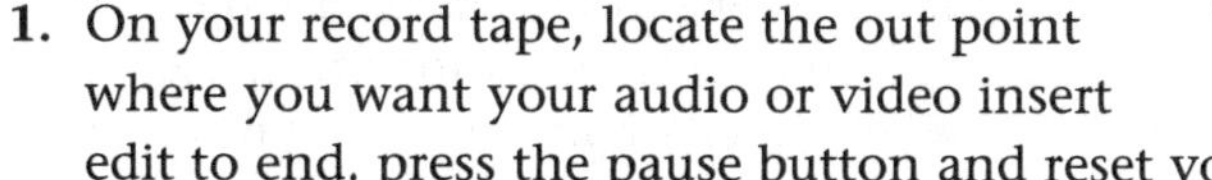

2. Locate the in-point where you want your insert edit to begin on your record tape, and press the pause button.

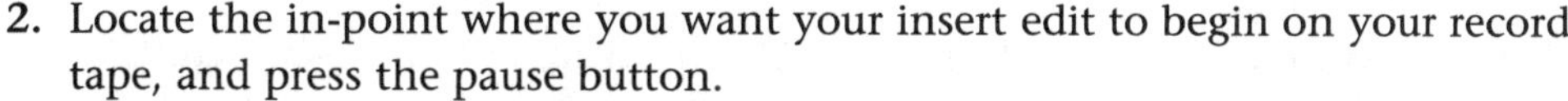

3. Press Play and the Audio/Video dub (insert) buttons at the same time.
4. Hit the memory button.
5. Hit play on the source VCR to start the video or audio that you want to lay down on the record tape.
6. When you get to the intended in-point, hit pause, and your insert edit will begin. Since you've hit the memory button, the insert edit will automatically stop exactly where you planned.

If all has gone well, you will have a perfectly clean edit on both ends of the cut points on the record tape.

Getting Insert Editing Under Control

With an edit controller, you can take insert editing a step further. Let's say you're putting together some footage that you shot for your 20-year high school reunion party. In an interview one of your old pals reads everyone's name in the yearbook into the camera. You decide that it would be appropriate to use cutaway shots of photos from the yearbook that you also shot with your camcorder. The first name that you want to paste a shot over is Scott Adams. Here's how to insert edit with an edit controller.

1. On the record tape, right before the speaker says the word "Scott," you would hit "Mark In."
2. On the source deck, you would find the beginning of a section of Scott's picture that you want to cut in, and hit "Mark In" on that side.
3. Then go back to the record side and after the speaker says "Adams," hit "Mark Out." You don't have to hit "Mark Out" on the source side because you have initiated what's known as a "three-point edit." (You only need three points marked in order to perform an edit of any kind.)
4. Somewhere on the edit controller, there will be a row of buttons that allow you to choose your audio and video tracks. In this case, you will hit only the "video" button since you want to leave your audio intact.

And that's all there is to it. Hit preview to check your edit, and then lay it down!

Video Mixers

A video mixer is the perfect companion to a good edit controller. In a nutshell, a video mixer, or switcher, lets you combine two or more sources of video onto your record master tape. It can also provide special effects like color correction, strobe, painting, and superimposing (keying) images over a background or moving video. (See "Editing Extras" later in this chapter for more on special effects.)

While linear multi-source editing, or A/B roll editing, is a high-end editing technique, it is worth discussing here for two reasons. The first is that the equipment necessary to pull off A/B roll editing is becoming cheaper by the minute. Additionally, a solid grasp of the A/B roll editing concept provides a good background for the next chapter on nonlinear editing where A/B roll editing can be done as effortlessly as tying your shoe.

A/B roll editing can help you to create effects like wipes, dissolves, flips, and page peels where one video source gives way to another. It takes a little time and previewing to get everything lined up just right. But once you do, just press a few buttons on the edit controller and video mixer, and the edit-effect happens right in front of your eyes. You can also use a video mixer to superimpose titles over moving video, or to create other neat effects like picture-in-picture.

Besides A/B roll editing you can also treat one, two, or more of the video sources with an effect like color correction, paint, mosaic, and even freeze frames. Even though some video mixers also have a full-featured bank of special effects, if you plan to use a lot of effects, you may want to consider a stand-alone special effects generator. (See "Editing Extras" later in this chapter.)

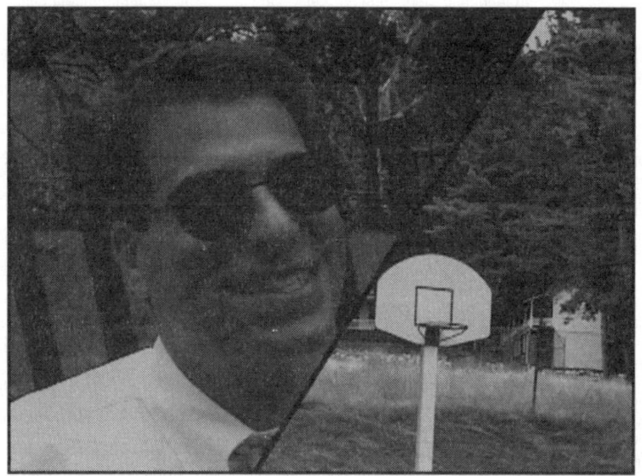

Video source A wiping into video source B.

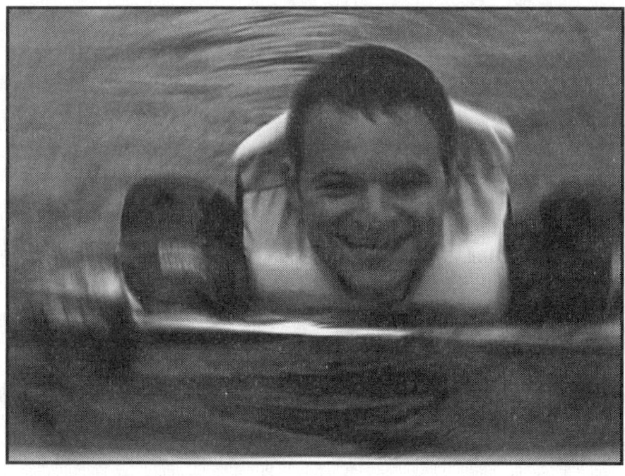

Video treated with a radial blur effect.

Editing Extras

Special effects generators (SEGs) go hand and hand with video mixers. In some cases, if you have one, you might not need the other, but if you're looking to max out your editing studio, having one of each couldn't hurt.

SEGs take special effects to the next level. Especially if you're interested in doing more than A/B roll editing, SEGs can make your videos look close to broadcast TV, especially if you choose your effects tastefully and don't overuse them.

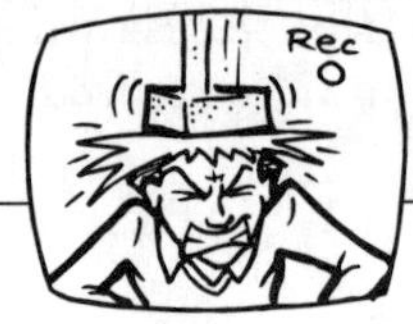

Blooper

Overusing special effects is a problem that often comes up in wedding video production. Sometimes there are so many swirls, blurs, whooshes, and blasts that you can't even tell who's getting married. Just because you have these high-end tools at your disposal doesn't mean that you have to use them every other shot.

If you are operating with an edit controller, special effects generator, and a video mixer, chances are you'll want to look into purchasing a good titling tool. Sometimes called "character generators," these tools are used to create and superimpose titles in your video productions. A nice, clean, possibly animated title can add a lot to your video and provide you with a clever transition from one point to another.

You can purchase either a stand-alone titling box, or run one on your home computer. All you have to do is patch it into your video mixer, and you're ready to title. Both options are good and offer a ton of different fonts and animation templates to choose from. More advanced titlers allow you to fade your titles in and out, add colored backgrounds, or even perform credit "rolls" or "crawls."

Besides adding production value to your home videos, character generators are fun to use and are a great way to communicate vital information to your viewers.

The Least You Need to Know

- ➤ Editing VCRs have many high-end functions that give you unprecedented control and ease of use.
- ➤ Editing controllers streamline the entire process by allowing you to control the source and record VCRs, and most other equipment you have hooked up.
- ➤ Insert editing allows you to edit in either video or audio clips any place in the video without breaking the control track. This means if you lay in a video clip, the existing audio will remain untouched and vice versa.
- ➤ Video mixers can blend two pieces of source footage together. This is useful for creating dissolves, and other neat effects like picture-in-picture.

Chapter 21

Nonlinear Editing: Your Computer Can Process a Lot More Than Words

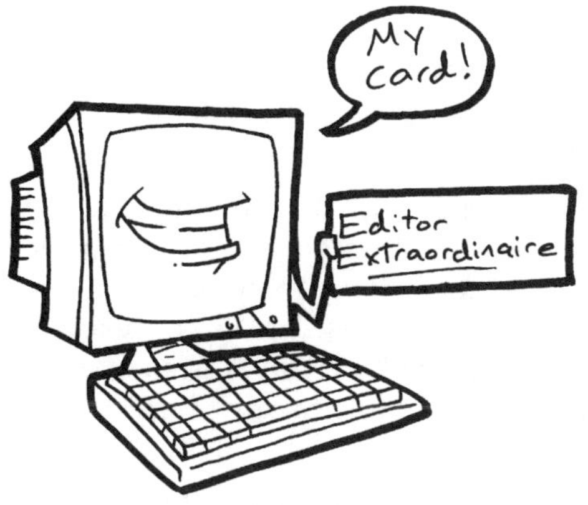

In This Chapter

- Nonlinear editing in a nutshell
- The Future is all digital
- Nonlinear hardware
- Nonlinear software
- Tips and tricks

"Nothing in this life is to be feared, it is only to be understood."
—Marie Curie

The term *nonlinear editing* is enough to strike fear in the hearts of millions of home videographers across the land. But if more people understood the fundamentals of nonlinear editing, they'd realize that it's not only an easy and fun way to make great home videos, it opens up an entire universe of creative possibilities.

And with the falling prices and blazing fast speeds of today's computers and peripherals, it's relatively inexpensive to hop in on the ground floor. In fact, most modern home computers, if outfitted with the essentials, can be configured and optimized for nonlinear editing without much effort. This incredibly versatile tool that was once nothing more than an editor's fantasy, is now in the hands of the everyday consumer.

Nonlinear Editing: The Inside Scoop

In a nutshell, nonlinear editing is the process of transferring your home video to the hard drive of a computer where you can manipulate, edit, rearrange, and organize the images in just about any way under the sun. When you're done doing your digital magic, you can then send the final product back to videotape, or distribute it on the Internet, CD-ROM, or even by e-mail.

Digital nonlinear editing became available to consumers in the early to mid-1990s. The intentions were good, but computers at the time were simply too slow to handle the tremendous amount of number-crunching it takes to digitally manipulate full screen video images. Today, processing power is no longer a problem. Not only are computers pushing the blazing fast 500–600 MHz mark, the hard drives needed to store and play back digital video are increasing in capacity while rapidly decreasing in price.

Today, if I priced the nonlinear editing system that bought 2½ years ago I'd get really depressed. It probably would cost me less than half of what I originally paid. The 200 MHz Power Macintosh computer that is the brain of my system is a turtle in today's terms. In fact, the 400 MHz Macintosh PowerBook G3 that I'm writing this manuscript on is not only faster than my desktop computer, with a video capture board that I bought for less than $200, it doubles as my portable nonlinear editing system. This is ultra convenient when I'm away from my home studio or on a shoot when I need to quickly see how scenes are going to cut together.

The Digital Domain

Digital video looks so much better than analog video because it is highly resistant to noise that can disrupt picture quality. To record an analog signal onto videotape, it takes a continuos signal to keep the image looking crisp. Unfortunately, noise signals are also continuos, and can often come into conflict with the analog signals.

Digital video, on the other hand, translates the analog video signal into a series of pulses, (or ones and zeroes) that are much more resistant to noise. It is also these zeroes and ones that end up on your hard drive for editing. This is why you can make perfect copies of digital videotapes, or from your hard drive to digital tape. Overall, digital video is superior because right now, it's the only format available to consumers that eliminates generation loss.

The Journey from Videotape to Hard Drive

The path that video takes from videotape to your computer is less complicated than you may think. The simplest nonlinear setup consists of:

- A fast computer and hard drive.
- A video capture card and/or a FireWire port.
- A VCR and/or camcorder.
- A TV.

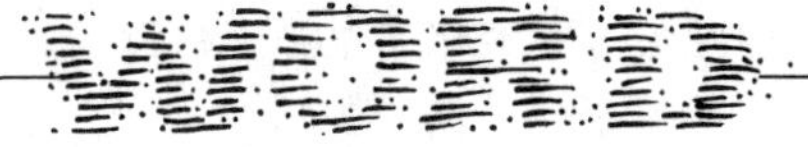

Blurred Word

A **video capture card** is an electronic board that attaches to the motherboard of your computer. Its advanced circuitry is able to read an analog video signal in real time and transform it into digital information (0s and 1s) that is stored on your hard drive. After the video has been "digitized" by the video capture card, it is ready to edited with nonlinear editing software.

The video capture card serves as the heart of the operation by "digitizing" the analog video stream passed along by the VCR and turning it into digital information that can be stored and played back on a hard drive.

As video is being digitized it can typically take up 4.5 megabytes per second which adds up in a hurry. In order for the computer to keep up and be able to process the tremendous file sizes of digitized video, the computer uses a "CODEC" (compression/decompression) scheme in which the video is crunched as small as possible when it's captured and then expanded upon playback. You might have heard of a few of the CODECs: MJPEG, MPEG, MPEG-2, and so on. Most video-capture cards also capture audio at the same time as video. Once the video is stored on the hard drive it's ready for editing.

Hooking your VCR or camcorder up to the video capture card is a snap:

1. Locate the *video in* jack (composite-yellow jack or Y/C) on the video capture card and plug in one end of an RCA cable or S-Video (Y/C) cable.
2. Plug the other end into the *video out* jack (composite or Y/C) on your camcorder or VCR.
3. Locate the left and right *audio in* jacks on the video capture card and plug in both RCA cables (red for right, white for left).
4. Plug the other ends into the corresponding *audio out* on your camcorder or VCR.

If you have opted for a DV nonlinear editing system, the process is a little different. In fact, there's no digitizing that takes place at all because your video is already in a digital format. ("Digitizing" took place in the camcorder at the time of shooting.) Instead of a video-capture card you'll need a FireWire card or a computer with a FireWire port built in to directly transfer digital video information from your MiniDV or Digital8 camcorder to your computer hard drive. Technically, it's the same thing as copying files from one disk to another.

And Now the Fun Begins!

Computers are amazing devices. Combine them with video editing and you've got a miracle on your hands!

Since computers have instant access to the data on hard drives, shots and scenes can be located and recalled at any time, completely eliminating winding back and forth with a slow VCR. Any limitations that you experienced with linear editing setups are virtually eliminated. Now you're free to concentrate on creative editing instead of tinkering with equipment.

The typical nonlinear software interface is often compared to word-processing software. You can cut, paste, delete, move, and rearrange video clips, and if you don't like something, you can always hit the undo button.

And that's only the beginning. With the click of a mouse you can also transition between shots, use filters, special effects, and layer more video and audio sources than you'll ever need in your lifetime. Video editing is done on a "timeline" or "sequence" that is a virtual representation of a record-master videotape.

Nonlinear editing software interface.

(Courtesy of Avid Technology.)

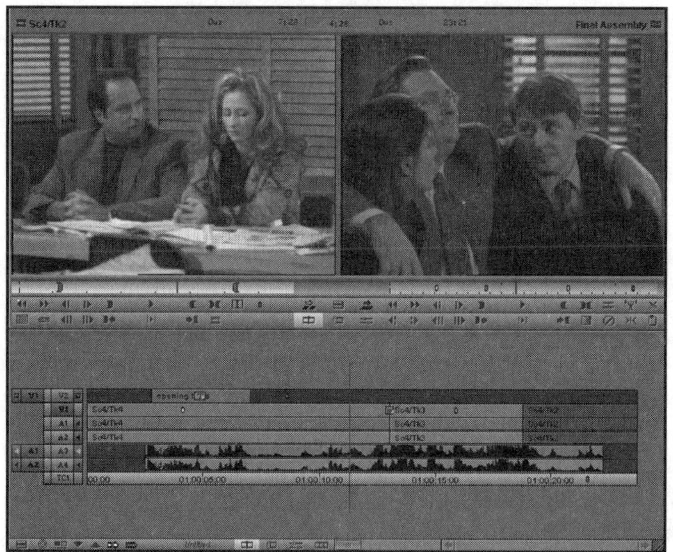

Here's a great feature that leaves linear editors drooling. Not only are you able to cut and paste just single shots, you can also shift entire segments of your program around. Let's say you want to insert a quick interview with a guest in the middle of your wedding video to break up the monotony or to transition between segments. No problem. Simply highlight the segment you want to move and drag it over. You can do the same with music, titles, photos … or anything else that you can dream up.

Your Digital Future

Nonlinear editing has not only taken the home video market by storm, it has already romanced the professional film and video market. Long ago, editors and video engineers across the globe recognized the potential and power of nonlinear, and it is their vision that has paved the way for the nifty consumer products that are hitting the market full-force.

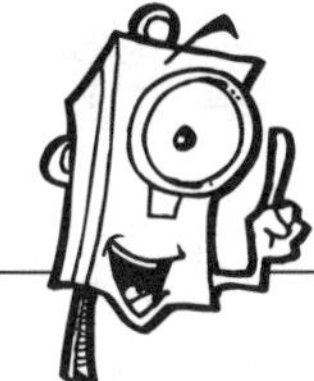

Candid Camera

A lot of the nonlinear editing software has adopted the traditional "film style" or linear editing interface with the source footage on the left and the record master on the right.

Think about the movies, programs, commercials, and other forms of video and film programming that very well may represent the biggest source of relaxation and entertainment worldwide. You can bet that most of the films, shows, and promotions have been edited on high-end nonlinear systems like the AVID Media Composer or Media 100, to name a couple.

I've always thought that film editors benefit the most from nonlinear. I've worked on films where we've had up to 30 hours of raw footage digitized at one time! Having instant access to all that footage makes a huge difference to editors who, in the past, had to manually scroll through rolls and rolls of film while editing with a razor blade.

I'd be willing to go as far as to say that nonlinear editing has greatly improved the quality of movies and TV shows that you see today. This is mainly due to the fact that the creative people who are responsible for making these forms of programming now have the unlimited opportunity to experiment. I've found that experimentation plays a huge part in the creative process because sometimes you stumble across something amazing by accident that you otherwise wouldn't have discovered. Just imagine the cool stuff you'll stumble across in creating your home videos!

Hardware Is an Easy Nut to Crack

Your nonlinear beginner's kit starts with choosing the right hardware, and it's not an easy choice because there are many solid entry-level products to choose from. The first decision you'll have to make is whether you're going to buy a new computer or use one that you already own. You'll want to utilize the fastest computer that you can get your hands on with a large capacity hard drive. This will not only speed up the act of editing it will also increase the amount of high resolution video that you can store, and cut down on processing time (known as rendering) when you apply transitions and special effects to your video.

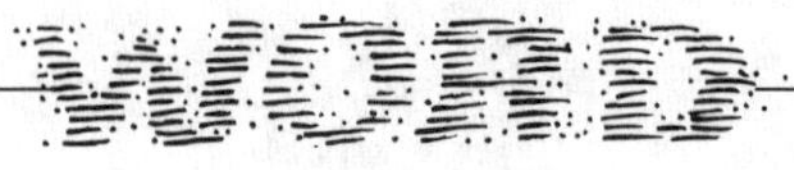

Blurred Word

Rendering refers to the frame-by-frame process of re-creating video that has been altered by a transition, filter, or effect. Most nonlinear systems actually create brand new frames of video that eventually make up a new, altered video clip.

Platform Wars: Mac vs. PC

Here's an argument for the ages: Mac or PC? Just when you think one computing platform is outwitting the other, the other one catches back up.

I have been editing video on a Macintosh since nonlinear editing software and hardware hit the scene. If you asked me in college, however, if I could ever imagine myself using a Mac, the answer would have been an emphatic no. But I've passed along my Windows-based PC to my parents and have become a full-fledged Mac person. I used to think that PCs were great for productivity applications like word processing, spreadsheet, and online communications and that Macs were far superior with anything involving graphics or full motion video. In recent years, however, these stereotypes have been totally smashed. In the land of video editing where Macs used to rule with a sovereign hand, PCs have quickly invaded and caught up. If you've ever browsed the digital video magazines, you'd see that a lot of the new nonlinear software and hardware releases are based on the Windows NT or Windows 98 operating systems. Whichever platform you choose, you're going to be able to edit video, and do it well. It's basically a matter of preference.

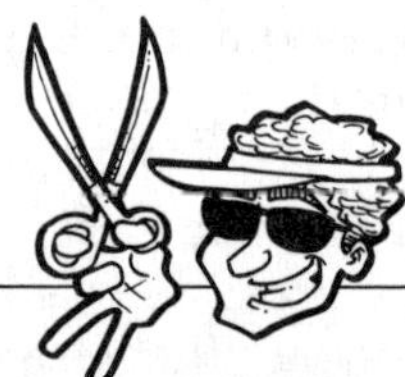

Director's Cut

It's hard to say which platform to go with—Mac or Windows-based PC—because both of them are pretty close to being equal in performance. The only way to really choose is to decide which operating system you're most comfortable using and stick with it. The last thing you want to do while learning brand new nonlinear editing software is to re-learn an operating system.

Video Capture Cards on a Budget

One of the nice things about buying an entry-level video capture card is that they usually come bundled with nonlinear editing software. In a lot of cases if you purchased the software alone, it would cost you more than the board itself.

Package deals are also highly recommended because they tend to reduce incompatibility issues between hardware and software. You can bet that if they're bundled together, the manufacturers have gone through great pains testing that the two work well together, and can always answer questions after a purchase.

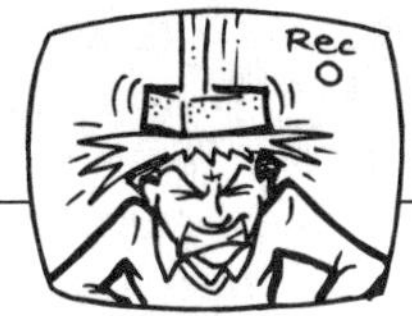

Blooper

If you're interested in a certain video capture board or a specific piece of software, make sure that they are both compatible. There's nothing worse than making a purchase and discovering that there's a conflict.

Video capture cards come in all different shapes and sizes, and there are plenty to choose from in the entry-level category. Here are a few companies that manufacture inexpensive video capture cards:

- Pinnacle
- Truevision
- Media 100
- Matrox
- Fast

Also refer to the nonlinear editing software list below.

The Falling Prices of Hard Drives

Out of any hardware purchases that I've ever made, hard drives are always the most frustrating because the prices always seem to plummet significantly immediately after I make the purchase! The external 4 gigabyte hard drive that I bought 2½ years ago with my system for $3,500 can be picked up today for around $700.

For most consumer nonlinear applications, you'll definitely want to add at least one A/V (audio/video) ready hard drive to your system configuration. You can install this either internally into your computer, or even better, you can buy one that comes with its own external case. (I'd strongly recommend this for nonlinear beginners.) You'll also need a special card for the A/V hard drive that hooks up to your computer's motherboard in an expansion slot. This kind of an installation is relatively simple once you get past the initial shock of having to open up your computer's case. The safest bet is to have everything done at your retailer or electronics store. Any way you hook them up, A/V drives are much faster than regular hard drives that come with computers and are built tougher in order to handle the constant transfer of large amounts of data.

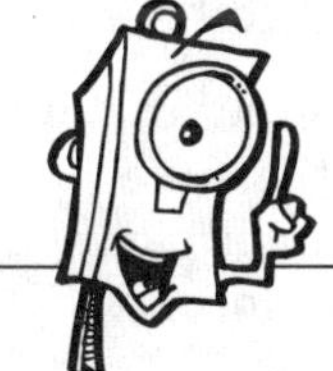

Candid Camera

A/V drives spin extremely fast, from 7,200 rpms (rotations per minute) to as much as 10,000 rpms.

The best thing you can do is to add a "disk array" to your system. Also known as a R.A.I.D., it may sound like a brigade of flying saucers, but it's actually two hard drives that are wired together to act as one big hard drive, capable of handling much higher data rates which are necessary for full-frame video at 30 frames per second. It's the perfect configuration for digital video. You also need special software that "stripes" the two drives together, forcing your system to view them as one.

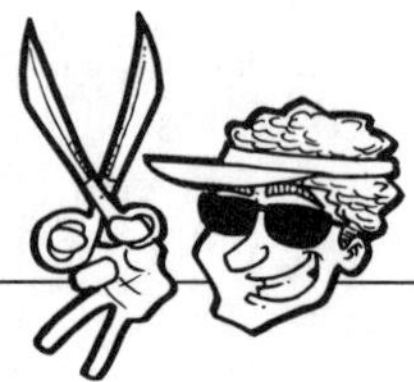

Director's Cut

While you're adding high speed/capacity hard drives to your system, you might want to consider adding as much RAM as you can afford to your computer. Nonlinear editing systems work best when they're not hindered by too little RAM.

How Does It Look on TV? Choosing a Video Monitor

Even though a lot of nonlinear editing software programs allow you to see your video as you edit directly on your computer screen, you're going to want to hook up a real TV set to the "video out" port on the video capture card. This will give you the best reference as to what your final product is going to look like.

I'd recommend grabbing a small TV that you might have lying around the house before spending any money on a monitor. You can hook up pretty much any TV set as long as you have the right cables to make a connection. (See "Adding a Monitor to Your Editing Outfit" in Chapter 19. Connect the computer to the TV as you would a record VCR to the TV.) Otherwise, you can pick up a cheap color TV set for under a hundred bucks.

The other option is to purchase a professional monitor. They are a lot more expensive but they offer the best possible color reproduction and have other high-end features like multiple inputs and underscan/overscan which allows you to check the edges of your video.

The Right Nonlinear Software Isn't Hard to Find

Like I mentioned, there are a bunch of great entry-level nonlinear editing software packages on the market. Even the higher end products have decreased enough in price to make them attractive to even the most novice nonlinear editor. Here are a few highlights from some software packages that have caught my eye:

- **Avid Cinema:** (Mac/PC) This is the ideal nonlinear software package for beginners. Avid is an industry leader in high-end editing systems for movies, broadcast and cable, making Cinema a solid choice. Movies like *Titanic* and TV shows like *Seinfeld* are all edited on Avid systems. This software is priced at just over $100 and was specially designed for people who are not technically savvy and have little to no experience editing video. You're not going to get all of the bells and whistles of a fully featured nonlinear editing package like Adobe Premiere (see below), but the software will actually walk you though the home movie-making process. From storyboarding to video capture to editing to sending the movie back out, this program makes it a snap. You can also add a custom soundtrack to your movie and add effects and transitions. When you're through, you can export it for use in presentations, or send it out over the Web, via e-mail or in various other forms of multimedia.

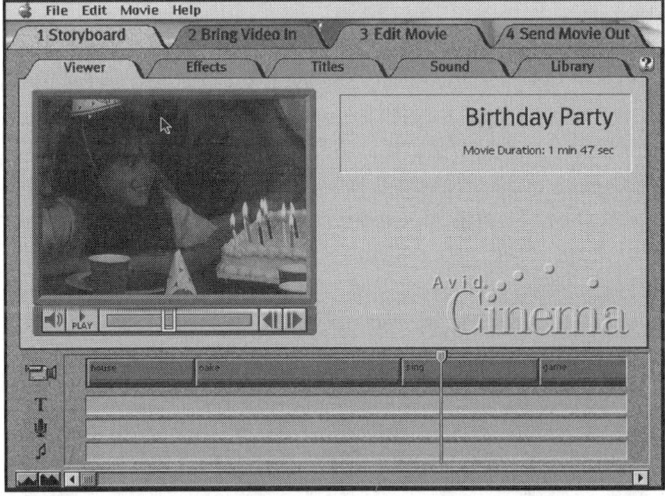

Avid Cinema.

(Courtesy of Avid Technology)

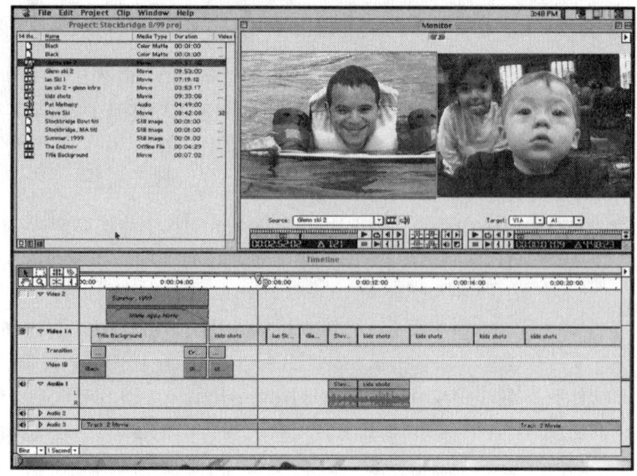

Adobe Premiere.

(Courtesy of Adobe Systems, Inc.)

- **Adobe Premiere:** (Mac/PC) One of the first nonlinear editing packages to be made available to consumers, Adobe Premiere is the granddaddy of desktop video-editing software. Premiere is loaded with high-end features for the advanced editor, yet is simple enough for novices to start cutting. The program offers a mature interface and support for frame-accurate editing, machine control, hundreds of effects, video filters, and transitions. It also features three-point editing, titling, audio editing and processing, and multiple tracks of video and audio. Premiere is often used for multimedia, Web video, and even broadcast television. One of the best things about the software is that it is compatible with many video capture cards (and FireWire) and is commonly included for free when you purchase these cards. I learned how to edit on the computer using Adobe Premiere, and it is my top recommendation for nonlinear software for consumers, prosumers, and even professionals.

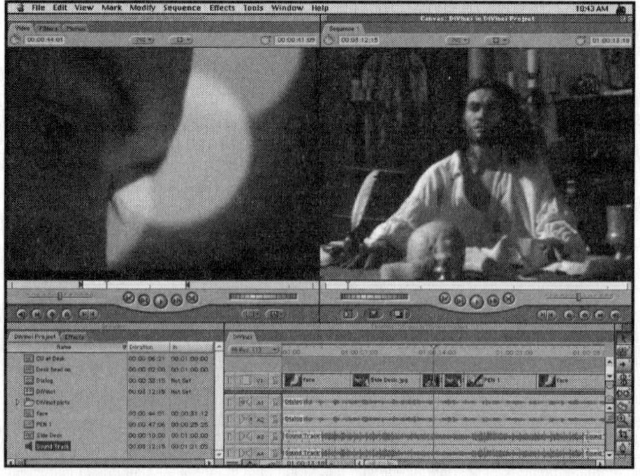

Apple Final Cut Pro.

(Courtesy of Apple Computer, Inc.)

- **Apple Final Cut Pro:** (Mac) Apple's recent contribution to the world of nonlinear editing, Final Cut Pro is a powerhouse of a program. Sporting a cool-looking interface and very advanced feature set, Final Cut Pro has attracted a strong following in the editing community. Using Apple's Quicktime technology, the software is compatible with either DV or analog footage. It also has many of the same features that both amateurs and professionals are after, like transitions, special effects, titling, and multiple tracks of audio and video. Final Cut Pro is a great choice for hobbyists who are serious about editing and getting their MiniDV or Digital8 footage to look its best. I've used the program quite a bit, and I'd also recommend it to beginners since I found that the interface is user-friendly and the program is simple to install and hook up to a camcorder.

There are literally dozens of nonlinear editors, and many of them are very similar—like buying a car, it comes down to personal preference and compatibility. This is one area that's constantly changing for the better. Be sure to check out the latest video magazines, the Web, and your local reseller for the latest and greatest programs. You can also check out the following programs:

- In:Sync Speed Razor
- Digital Origin Edit DV
- Ulead's Media Studio Pro
- Video 1, 2, 3 by WebKapture

Nonlinear Tricks and Tips

Since video editing is a daunting task to your computer, sometimes you have to make the best out of the limited resources that you have available. Here are a few tips and tricks to help keep your system running smoothly and your video looking great.

1. Don't overuse the hundreds of filters, transitions, and effects that come standard with most nonlinear editing systems. Besides annoying your audience, special effects usually take some time to render and the resulting media files waste precious disk space.
2. If at all possible, dedicate your computer to video editing. Try to do your word processing, Internet surfing, or number crunching on a different computer if possible. Using the same computer for everything, can cause a conflict down the line that could potentially crash your system, or even worse, erase precious data by causing hardware failure. It's also taxing on your system to have multiple programs running at the same time.
3. Store all of the media files onto the dedicated high performance hard drives. Bins, sequences, libraries, or any other nonlinear project-related file should be

kept on your computer's internal hard drive. Additionally, try to keep all of your files neat and in directories or folders where you can easily locate them. Also, it's usually best for the nonlinear software to reside on a different drive, if possible, than the media files you create.

4. Always protect your computer with a surge protector. You never know when a power surge or bolt of lightning is going to strike. If possible, purchase a surge protector that also protects your modem telephone line. A few years ago my modem got nuked in a thunderstorm even though I had the main power supply protected.
5. Always provide your computer system and peripherals with adequate ventilation. Your equipment needs to breathe in order not to overheat. Overheating is one of the leading causes of consumer equipment failure.
6. Always back up your important project and media files onto some kind of removable storage. The digitized footage in most cases will be too large to realistically back up, but if you happen to be working with timecode, you can always redigitize the media if you have saved the project files. (Redigitizing is a common feature of many nonlinear editing programs.)
7. Since nonlinear programs push your computer to the max of its computing ability, consider running diagnostic and disk optimization software on a regular basis to keep your machine running smoothly. One of the most popular programs of this kind is Norton Utilities.

The Least You Need to Know

- Nonlinear is the most versatile type of editing. Thanks to the instant access abilities of a computer, you can cut, paste, move, and affect video in infinite ways.
- Nonlinear editing has invaded the home video market. Almost every TV show and movie has been edited on digital systems.
- Most home computers have at least some capacity to edit video. The faster the computer and the larger the hard drive, the bigger and better your final picture quality.

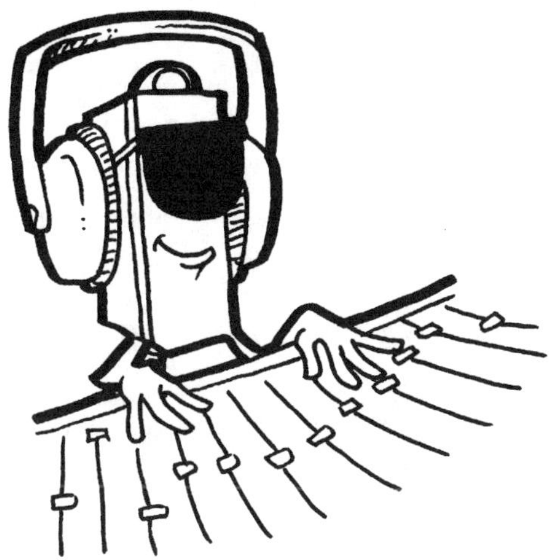

Chapter 22

Mastering the Mix

In This Chapter

- What music means to your videos
- Sound effects send your projects to the next level of cool!
- Perfecting sound processing
- Natural sounds tie things together
- Fixed in the mix

Guess what? You can manipulate your soundtrack just as easily as you can edit moving images. Sound editing has a great impact on your home videos and goes a long way in supporting and enhancing the picture. Now, with some simple linear or nonlinear editing gear, you can take control over a vital piece of the home video puzzle.

Becoming a sound magician requires a basic understanding of the elements and how to utilize them in your video projects. Whether it's music, sound effects, narration, dialog, or ambient sounds, these factors can all have a big impact. And even more important than placing the elements in your soundtrack is to figure out how to mix them together smoothly. A powerful, yet tasteful audio mix can add to the overall impact and continuity of your videos.

Sound Effects on a Shoestring

There's no better way to bring your video to life and round out your audio track than adding some sound effects. Besides being a powerful dramatic or comedic tool, sound effects are a load of fun to insert into your program. The trick is finding the right one.

Can you imagine a Bruce Lee movie without all of the bone-shattering kabams! and crashes? It's a pretty dull thought. Not that your videos are going to contain large-scale explosions, brawls, or car crashes that you're going to need to beef up, but subtle sound effects when tastefully used can go a long way in making your work more realistic.

Sound effects libraries are also available in the same way that music CDs are available for licensing. You can locate any sound that you can possibly imagine on CD, from the flapping of a bird's wings, to the flushing of a toilet. And sound effects CDs come in all different shapes and sizes, anywhere from a single disk to 200-disk sets. I've found that sound effects disks can be as inexpensive as music CDs.

You can also have a lot of fun capturing sound effects on your own. You've already got a great tool for recording high-quality stereo sounds: your camcorder. Why not put it to work?

Sound effects are taking place all around you. All you have to do is listen, and then point your camcorder in the right direction. If you're planning to ride on a train, take a few minutes to record the whistle blowing or the sound of the metal wheels rolling on the tracks. If you're on a boat, grab some sounds of the water slapping against the side, or the sounds of Seagulls chirping overhead. Concentrate on getting the microphone as close to the sound source as possible. Similarly, if you're going to be at a tennis match or basketball game, record some sounds. Sports sound effects are always hard to come by and are very useful in many home video projects.

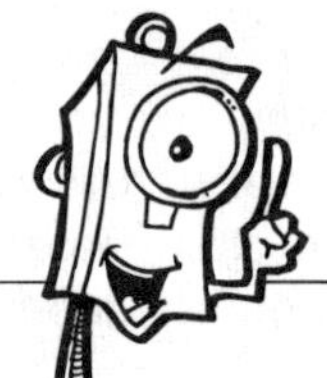

Candid Camera

In your camcorder bag, you can keep a separate "sound effects" tape that you use just for that purpose instead of burying recorded sound on other tapes.

The Power of the Tune

When my father and I took on the task of editing my sister-in-law Pam's wedding video, we were able to save a vital piece of the program thanks to some slick music editing. Before the actual ceremony took place, there was an extremely long segment that was shot in real time where the families walked down the aisle and found their seats. There was a piano in the background playing your typical walking-down-the-aisle music. The whole segment went on for about 10 minutes, which, as my father and I found out, is an absolute audience killer. When my father and I tried to cut down the footage to eliminate the monotony, we discovered that the piano music in the background was being abruptly cut off resulting in choppy, unnatural sounding edits. After hours of trying to finesse the edits to no avail, we shuttled the source tape ahead and discovered that the genius wedding videographer had recorded about five minutes of clean piano music with the crowd in the background. All we had to do was edit in the clean music over the section we had edited, and all of a sudden we had a smooth section on our hands.

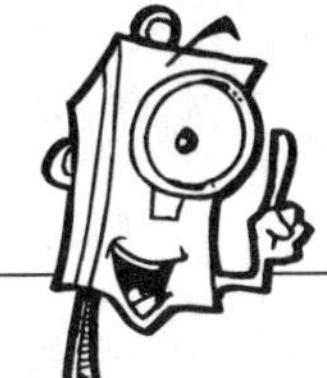

Candid Camera

At the time of this writing digital quality music is available to download via the Internet. The music can then be played back on a multimedia computer. The music is saved in digital form in a file format known as "MP-3," using just enough compression to enable files to travel well across the Internet.

Images aside, music is the most powerful element that you can introduce in your home videos. A song is capable of inspiring viewers by invoking feelings and emotions. Or, music can be used as a background element that has a quiet, yet dramatic influence on the audience. Think of the way big budget Hollywood filmmakers utilize music in their movies. In some scenes you can hardly hear the music bed that is softly tying everything together, and in others, a theme song marks the movie's pinnacle and instantly becomes a top 10 FM radio hit.

On many levels you can conduct the same kind of energy into your home videos. You can also use music to help dictate or even manipulate the mood of your piece. For example, let's say you're producing a commemorative video to celebrate the life of your 95-year-old grandmother. You decide to use dramatic orchestral music in several places to help paint a serious picture. Now, suppose you were to use the same orchestral music over footage of children playing on the beach. It would instantly capture the attention of your audience (whether they're aware of it or not). Subconsciously, the seemingly out of place music can spark expectations of maybe a kidnapping or shark attack.

The best part about adding music to your videos is that it's relatively easy to do. As you've learned in previous chapters, all you really need is a simple editing setup with a record VCR that is capable of audio dubbing. Even better, a simple nonlinear editing setup can give you unprecedented control over every part of your soundtrack, from audio levels to special audio effects. Many makes and models of VCRs and camcorders have the audio dub feature.

A Musical Dilemma

O.K., by now you're probably amped up about giving your video the musical edge. All of the tunes you hear on the radio, MTV, VH1, and from just about every other music outlet under the sun can easily be found at the record store or via the Internet, and usually in CD digital quality. CD's sound far superior to audio cassettes and records.

But if you decide to use music from your personal CD collection, you could be asking for trouble. Most music that is published today is protected by copyrights that prohibit anyone but the music's artist to profit from its use. The law views copyright infringement in the same way as any other kind of theft. In fact, even if you're using music written by a long-dead composer that's in the public domain, the *performance* may be copyrighted.

You may be thinking that if you're only showcasing your video to family and friends and not profiting a dime from it, how in the world can you ever get caught? I'd say that you are probably 99.9 percent right. But is that one-tenth of a percent worth the risk of getting caught and sued for copyright infringement?

A good habit to get in is to determine whether or not your production will ever have any type of public performance like a classroom, church or public access TV, or if you're planning to distribute it (for free or for profit). If so, you should get permission to use the tunes before you edit them into your program. It may not be as expensive as you think. The cost (and need) to license musical works has a lot to do with the number of people who the video is going to be distributed to, or the potential audience if it is going to air on TV or somewhere else. Getting permission after you've finished your program can be a huge hassle. And if permission isn't granted you can guarantee you'll find yourself at the controls re-editing your piece. I cut a short film a few years back and included tunes from Billy Joel, Ben Folds Five, Steely Dan and a few other artists. Just recently, I decided to send it to film festivals, but I was told that unless I had permission to use the popular music, I had to cut it out of the program. I ended up re-cutting the entire piece with cheap stock music that I got permission to use.

Another option you have available to you is to search for a song that is in the public domain. Simply put, this is music that is no longer protected by copyright laws and can be used by anyone for the purpose of performing, arranging, reproducing, recording, publishing, or even using in your videos. As a general rule, music or lyrics written and published in the United States before 1922 is considered to be in the public domain. In some cases, composers pass their work along to the public by choice. Tunes like "Home on the Range" and "Farmer in the Dell" are in the pubic domain, but a popular song like "Happy Birthday" is still protected by copyright law.

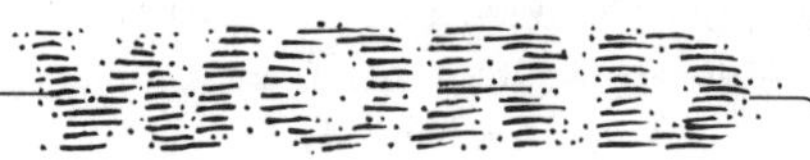

Blurred Word

A **copyright** is ownership of a work or piece of music that is registered with the Library of Congress Copyright Office. This grants the creator or artist the exclusive right to profit from that work. Anyone else who wants to use the work must license it from the copyright holder.

Use of public domain music is not an exact science, however. You should do the proper research and make sure the song is indeed in the public domain before incorporating it into your video. There's a Web site that has a list of safe songs and links to other public domain resources on the Internet: www.pdinfo.com.

Royalty-Free Music CD Libraries

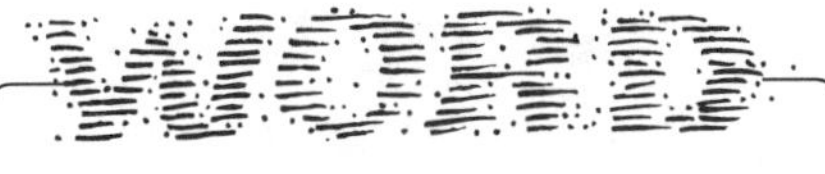

Blurred Word

Needledrop licenses allow you to use the copyrighted work on a per-use basis.

The other viable option for videographers on a skeleton budget is to buy a royalty-free music library on CD. Advertisements for these can be found in the back of many video magazines, and the CDs are usually sold at reasonable prices. When you purchase a music library on CD, in most cases you are also getting a "buyout" license that gives you the legal right to use the music for all of your video needs. Or, you can obtain the music library for almost nothing, and license the tunes as you need them. This is called "needledrop" licensing. Over the long haul music libraries can make a lot of financial sense.

These music libraries contain every type of music available on the planet. Jazz, Rock, Blues, New Age, you name it. Just listen to a few television commercials, shows, or promotion. Chances are that 95 percent of the music you hear is from a music library. You can buy comprehensive sets that offer a wide variety of many different types of music, or you can buy one that specializes in just one area.

Make Beautiful Music Yourself

The last and often least desired musical option is to write original tunes yourself and use them in your videos. The key word here is "original." If you simply create a new rendition of a copyrighted work, you're venturing into infringement territory. Here's where public domain comes into play again. A church organist playing a Bach tune is fine, but playing an Elton John tune is not.

With technology seeping into the musical instrument market, music is a lot easier to make these days. With a tiny bit of talent and a whole lot of gumption, you can compose some serious, full-sounding music on synthesizers or keyboards that allow you to program chord progressions and drum beats. Or you can buy electronic drum kits that allow you to add instrumentation to your own rhythms. You can also take the computer route; there are literally hundreds of software packages that make composing a snap, and often you don't even need an instrument hooked up to your computer at all. The nice thing about these high-tech composing and instrument options is that there's usually a high-quality jack for clean sounding recordings. Or, you can save your work as a digital file that can then be imported into your nonlinear editing project. Most of these programs use compatible audio file formats like Quicktime and AIFF.

Processing Sound

Creative video effects have become a permanent part of postproduction. You can make your picture purple, flip it around, slow it down, or speed it up. The possibilities are endless.

A lot of people aren't aware that there's a wealth of effects that can be applied to the soundtrack of videos. It's done with effects processors that are either embedded in nonlinear editing software, or that come as stand-alone units and can easily loop into your linear editing setup. You've probably heard of the most common ones and the most easy and fun to use in your movies ... reverb, EQ (equalization) and compression. And in the jungle of professional editing tools that you can buy, the analog and digital effect processors it takes to pull off these cool audio effects are among the most affordable items. What follows are the most basic sound processing effects available that will help pump of your home videos.

Reverb

O.K., O.K., O.K., ... you've probably heard of this one. It's one of the most entertaining audio effects and is commonly used in conjunction with microphones at live events and concerts. It is also a powerful audio postproduction tool.

Reverb units simulate the natural decay or bouncing effect that happens when sound is echoed in an enclosed area or in open space like a canyon or mountain. If I were actually to speak the word "O.K.," you would hear it first at full volume, then lower repetitions of the word would ring out. Reverb effects are perfect for creating surreal, spooky or just plain weird sound design.

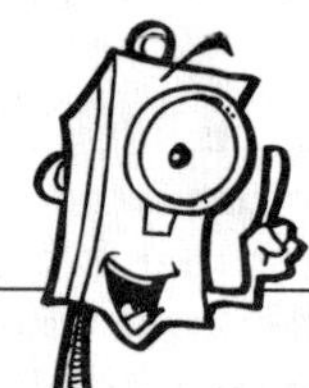

Candid Camera

Reverb is most often used to create the feel of an environment. If you're working with the audio track of someone speaking in a small bedroom and you want to create the feel of a larger room or even a hall, you can add a little bit of reverb to recreate the natural audible feel of a more spacious surrounding.

The reverb effect is also great for sports videos. If you're shooting basketball or volleyball in a gymnasium and you decide to add narration during editing, with a little reverb, you can make your narrator sound exactly like he/she is in the gymnasium reporting live at the event. You can also add scary sounding reverb to your Halloween videos. Children's voices are always extra-spooky sounding when injected with a little reverb. Similarly, you can add a "chorus" effect for an even ghostlier sound. "Flange" effects can even make a human voice sound like a robot. Chances are, if your digital sound processor has a reverb effect, it will also probably have chorus and flange, among others.

Sound processing effects are all fun to experiment with and can add a new dimension to your projects. Just as anything else in home video, you should be careful not to overuse these effects as your audience can easily grow tired of hearing the same thing over and over again.

EQ (Equalization)

Ever wish you could make that muddy audio track sound a little bit crisper? What about the interview that you recorded where the speaker was practically chomping on the microphone? Or that birthday party where the screaming kids in the background drowned out just about every other sound on the video? Wouldn't it be great to bury some of the disruptive bass and make it sound more balanced?

Here's where an equalizer, commonly known as an EQ comes in. Since every sound that you hear is made up of a spectrum of frequencies, an EQ can be used to manipulate a range of frequencies. This means that you can take a little bit of high end away from a soundtrack to make it sound less like it was recorded through a tinfoil filter. Similarly, if you want to yank the disruptive sounding bass from a bad interview soundtrack, it can easily be done. EQs are a great way to balance a soundtrack and make it sound like it was professionally recorded. Just like reverb/delay effects, EQ comes as either a stand-alone processor, or built into nonlinear editing software.

Besides making your audio track more ear-friendly, you can also treat specific sections of your audio with EQ in the editing process to achieve different sounding effects. There's a neat EQ trick that Hollywood filmmakers use all the time that you can easily do in your own project. If there's someone talking on the phone or listening to a radio, you can simulate the voice on the other end by stripping it down with EQ. All you have to do is record your voice separately with your camcorder, run it through a heavy dose of EQ, and edit it into your program. If you are using a nonlinear system, (Adobe Premiere, Final Cut) it's as easy as selecting a clip in your timeline and applying an EQ filter to it.

Overall, EQ and your home videos are a good match. Since a lot of your recording is done with the omni-directional on-board camcorder microphone, you're always going to have a lot of extraneous noise to deal with. Whether it's people talking in the background, crowd noise, or even an airplane flying overhead, EQ can help you take the edge off of the harsh sounds.

Compressors

Compressor effects take you one step closer to the professional level, but the equipment is still well within reach of the average videographer. Unlike EQ which effects certain aspects of the frequency range for a certain sound, compressors adjust the overall volume (level) of a sound signal. It does this by reducing the harshness of louder sounds and bringing up softer sounds. Compressors (like EQs) result in a more even, professional sounding audio-track. In fact, most of the sound in commercials that you hear on TV are heavily compressed to make them sound louder than the programs they are sandwiched between.

I actually use a compressor (and an EQ) in my editing setup and hardly ever have to make any adjustments to the settings. Ever since I got it I've noticed that both my professional projects and home video have more of an audible impact and the overall sound quality is crisp, clean and pumped-up. Compressors are especially useful when applied to your narration track. It helps the voice cut through music, sound effects, or any other sound you may have in your program.

If you buy a compressor or have access to one, give your video a listen with it both on and off. You're guaranteed to notice a big difference.

Beefing Up Your Soundtrack with Ambience

Very similar to the collection of sound effects while you shoot, recording ambient sound is the craft of capturing the unique "audio personality" of each location in which you're shooting. Ambient sounds comprise the combination of specific location noises and reverberations that subconsciously tell you, or your viewers, where you are. When you edit ambient sounds into your audio track, not only do you clue viewers in to the location, you can also help to maintain continuity by virtually erasing disruptive gaps in the soundtrack.

Recording ambient sound takes a few minutes and a little bit of peace and quiet. (No talking!) Upon arrival or departure at your given location, seek out a quiet spot where you can set the camcorder down and record the natural ("nat") sounds. Make sure the microphone is pointed in the direction of any one sound source that you might find useful later like a babbling brook, chirping birds, or the sound of waves crashing against the shore. If you're shooting in a busy city, hold the camcorder right outside the window and record the screeching tires of taxicabs and the wail of a distant police siren. The goal here is to get the camcorder as close to your sound source as possible.

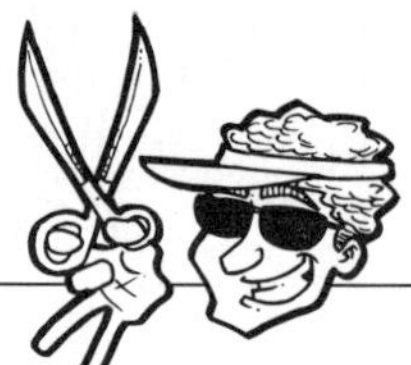

Director's Cut

"Whenever I'm shooting with my video camera, I always make sure to record at least a few minutes of ambient sound just in case. It has saved me on more than one occasion in covering up rough spots in my programs."
—David Preisman, Enhanced Television Producer, Showtime Networks, Inc.

With simple post production techniques like audio dubbing and nonlinear editing (see Chapters 19 through 21), you can paint your videos with ambient sound. Don't worry about maintaining perfect sync from shot to shot, sometimes a little "bleeding" over the edges of your video edits goes a long way in creating a smooth feel.

Once you've collected them, try pasting different ambient sounds into different sections of your video. Just for kicks, cut in some pre-recorded crowd noise over a sporting event that you've shot. Or turn some video you shot while hiking into an urban adventure by cutting in some city street noise. Ambient sounds are also available in CD libraries and can be a ton of fun to play with. Sometimes your ears tell you as much about your videos as your eyes.

Becoming a Mix-Master

You've rounded up your music, dialog, narration, sound effects, and possibly even ambient sounds. That's just about everything you're going to need to create a dynamic soundtrack for your project. Now, the last thing on your list is to mix all the sounds together so that they blend naturally and help the overall flow of the video.

There's nothing more distracting than trying to watch a program where the announcer seems to be screaming at you while you're struggling to hear the dialog or music. It's safe to say that most of the members of your audience have never even heard the term "audio mixing," especially where video editing is concerned, and are easily distracted and even annoyed by a bad mix. The point is, if mixing is done right, your audience won't notice it. On the other hand, if mixing is done incorrectly, it can draw attention to itself and away from the intended focus of the video.

Mixing can be a very challenging step, especially if you're working with a linear editing setup. With a little practice, however, you'll develop a real feel for tweaking the levels of each and every sound in your video. All you need to become a mix-master is a simple audio mixer or a record VCR that allows you to control and monitor the incoming volume. The good thing about mixers is that they're cheap, and the better ones usually come with EQ and possibly even reverb effects already built in.

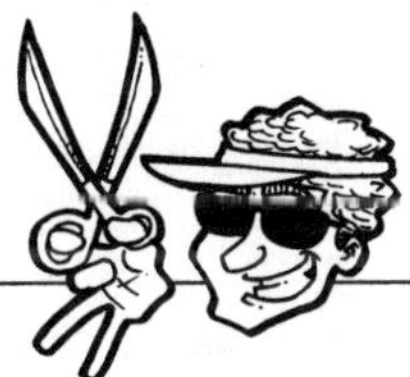

Director's Cut

I've seen simple audio mixers that allow you to adjust the levels of multiple inputs being sold at electronics stores like Radio Shack for under $50.

In the world of nonlinear editing, on the other hand, audio mixing is almost as easy as tying your shoelaces. Once the media is digitized onto your hard drive, adjusting the levels is as simple as sliding a level meter up and down with a click of your mouse. In some programs you can even ride these levels up and down using "rubber band" level controls. On most nonlinear editing software packages, an audio rubber band is actually a line that runs through the middle of your audio clip. By sliding this line up and down, you raise or lower the audio level. You can also ride the levels up and down by setting "nodes" on the rubber bands. This is perfect when you need to lower music when narration begins. You can slowly ramp down the volume just before the narration begins and then ramp it back up when the narration ends. Or, you can instantly raise the level of the sound of a car as it passes by onscreen. With rubber bands, you have 100 percent control over every aspect of your soundtrack.

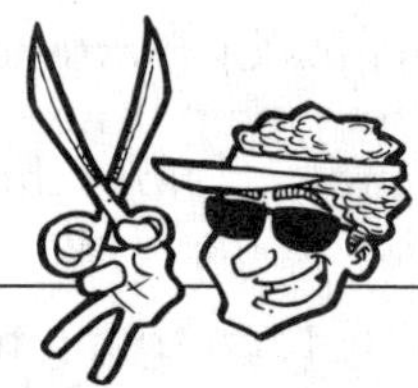

Director's Cut

"I write and mix music for film and television for a living. When I first tried the audio rubber band feature when it hit the scene a few years ago, it changed my life in a big way. I couldn't imagine ever going back to the old way of mixing."
—Glenn Schloss, Sound Designer, G&E Music

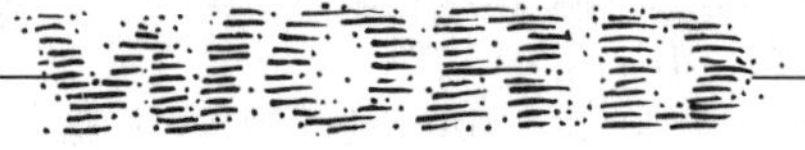

Blurred Word

A **cross fade** or **sound dissolve** in the audio track is when you bring down one audio source while simultaneously raising up another audio source. A cross fade in the audio is almost identical to a video "dissolve."

With your computer you can also add all kinds of audio effects to the soundtrack like reverb/delay, compression and EQ to name a few. And, if you're producing a music video for the Chipmunks, you can speed the audio up or slow it down. Or for a wild sounding effect you can play the audio track in reverse.

Another nice feature of nonlinear editing with your audio track is that you can create custom "cross-fades" in the audio that make two different audio clips sound like they're blending together. This is similar to a video "dissolve" where one video source melts away into an incoming video source.

The actual process of mixing will vary greatly depending on what tools or software you have available, but the fundamentals of good mixing are pretty much the same. Here are a few things to keep an ear out for when audio mixing:

- **Always keep an eye on your recording levels.** You can monitor this on the record VCR if you are linear editing, or, if you're working with nonlinear editing software, you can usually open up an audio mix window that measures incoming audio levels. If you find that the VU meters are constantly in the red, your audio is going to sound distorted and over-modulated. If this is the case, you can adjust the incoming levels either in the computer or on the record VCR until the meters are out of the red.
- **Keep all of the speaking parts audible.** Nothing can ruin your video quicker than leaving your audience struggling to hear what's going on. Music, sound effects, and ambient sounds are fun to include but if you don't keep a close ear on their levels, you can easily drown out a human voice.
- **Don't overuse any of your sound elements.** Let's say you're using a corny sound effect during a fight scene in your video. If you were to introduce that same sound effect later on in a completely different scene, your viewers will remember and give you the evil eye. Also, it's not necessary to pack your video wall to wall with music or ambient sound. Sometimes the content of a given shot or scene will work better without any sound support. With a little trial and error you will quickly learn how to tastefully utilize your audio elements.

The Least You Need to Know

- Music adds a whole new dimension to your videos and helps you control viewer mood and emotion.
- Sound effects are a perfect compliment to your audio track and are cheap to buy or easy to collect on your own with a camcorder.
- Sound processors let you fine-tune your audio track to get things sounding just right.
- Natural (ambient) audio helps to smooth out the overall soundtrack of your production and can help communicate a sense of place.
- Mixing everything together can be challenging and thrilling once you get the hang of it.

Part 5

Round Up the Gang ... It's Showtime!

So you're almost at the end of a very long road. You've bought a camcorder, you've planned your program, you've directed it, and you've edited it together. Now the only thing left is to show it off to your friends and family.

Believe it or not, holding a screening for your home movie isn't as easy as it sounds. Not only do you have to worry about catching everyone together all at once, but you also have to help to make your audience as comfortable as possible so their attention is undisturbed during your presentation.

If being the center of attention is not your thing, don't worry. Screenings are not the only way for your work to be seen. In the pages that remain you'll learn how to distribute your videos via multimedia (CD-ROM and the Internet).

There's also a growing demand for your home movies in the public eye. From breaking news to network TV shows like America's Funniest Home Videos, *there's a good chance that if you're lucky enough to capture the right moment on tape, it could very well end up being played to a national audience.*

You get all this plus some final words on additional camcorder uses, and the best way to store and preserve your videocassettes so they'll continue to provide you with a lifetime of fond memories.

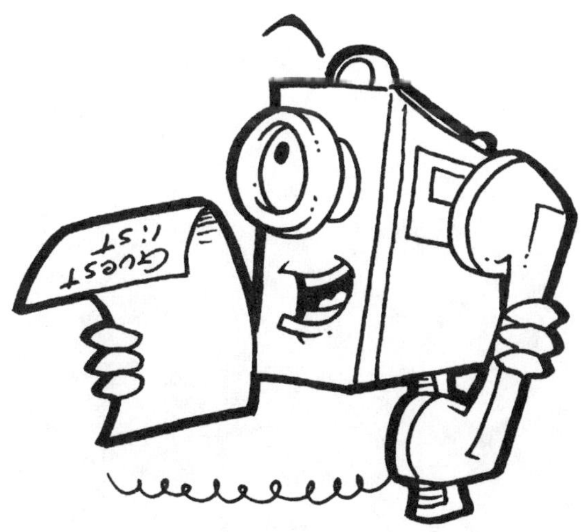

Chapter 23

Time to Show Off Your Video Masterpiece

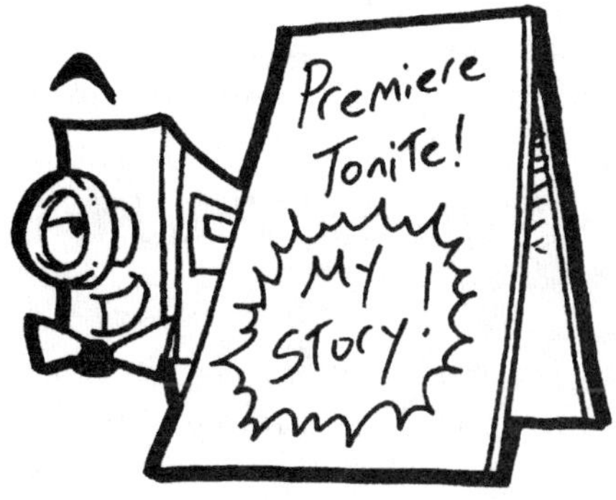

In This Chapter

- Your home videos in the spotlight
- Audience appreciation
- Meaningful screenings
- Equipped for success
- Tuning up your TV

Just like the millions of photographs taken each year that are dropped into closet-cluttering shoeboxes, there are countless hours of entertaining home videos worldwide that sit dormant on shelves, without any hope of ever seeing the light of day. It's hard to believe that so many people spend so much time and effort making home videos yet never take the time to share their work with others. If only you owned your own TV network then you could invent a show that featured your work. Unfortunately, there are only a small handful of Ted Turners and Rupert Murdochs in the world, so you're stuck figuring out a different way to put your videos on display.

So get ready to enter into the potentially scary yet pleasurable world of video screenings. And the ability to captivate an audience is hard work. Not only do you have to understand their needs and desires as viewers, but you also have to make them as comfortable as possible during the screening and to make it a cinematic experience in order to keep them coming back for more. A violation in any of these areas is the best way to get yourself a permanent place on the home video screening blacklist.

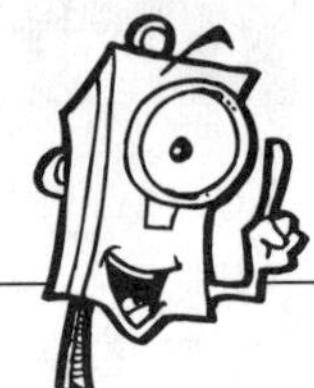

Candid Camera

By editing your home videos and creating interesting programs that your viewers will want to watch, you will forever break the molds and stereotypes which have historically deterred people from watching home video.

So instead of subjecting your crowd to the typical disorganized video with jolting pans, zooms, and horrendous audio, surprise them with a well thought-out and nicely edited program with music, a variety of camera angles, and most importantly, smooth and steady shots. Break out a tempting platter of food and drinks, and your audience is going to love you for it.

Your Home Videos: The Main Attraction

The first time I ever asked my family to watch one of my videos, I really had to talk them into it. Growing up, they would see me playing around with video and film cameras, but they never really made the connection. I think they were expecting to be bored stiff (just as we all had been watching dad's amateur efforts!), and I got the feeling that my sister was eyeing the door. But once they buckled in, they were instantly drawn into my mini-movie, and they actually sat, seemingly captivated, through all 10 minutes of it. After that, they looked forward to my features and were always more than willing to watch.

Similarly, you might find others reluctant to watch your videos. That's why many people shoot a ton of video, and then hoard their work away in a plastic bucket under the bed, refusing to share them with anyone. I look at it this way. By definition, *video* was made to seen, not stored. And you can guarantee that if you present them correctly, people will come up to you again and again, asking to see more of your videos.

Home video is such an attractive medium because for most people, it is sharper than even their own memories and more capable of playing back moments in time exactly as they happened. And let's face it, life goes by quickly and we have very few methods available to relive the special moments and events that make life worth living.

At this point, however, it is only fair to warn you that there is a growing population of frustrated home video viewers who have been conditioned over the years to bolt as soon as you hit the play button. You have to earn back their trust. Prove to them that your work is more entertaining than just boring raw footage. Let's do something to get this audience segment back before we lose them forever.

In general, it takes a lot of guts to share any creative piece of work with other people. This can be especially true when your friends and family are members of the audience. Maybe it's the fear of rejection, or maybe it's that deep-rooted grade school fear of being the classroom laughing stock. The truth of the matter is, when you create something and share it with others, you feel exposed and wide open to personal criticism and critique. Whatever the case, the only thing that's going to make it easier is to do it, and do it as often as you can.

Looking back at the first time I played a video that I had written, shot, and edited to my family and friends, it was a terrifying yet exhilarating experience. As soon as the video began, time seemed to slow down to a near standstill. I was left squirming in my seat because since I had seen the video a hundred times, I knew exactly what was coming next. I hung on every word, every reaction, and was invigorated by even the slightest laugh.

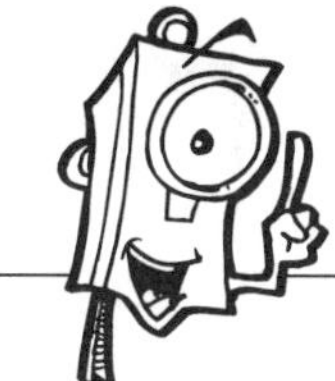

Candid Camera

After the first few times people see your work in your presence, you begin to relax and learn how to sit back and enjoy the experience. And you'll be surprised at how quickly your viewers will gain confidence in your abilities as a videographer and creative artist.

When it was all over, I almost passed out when everyone actually applauded the program. After the euphoria wore off, we had a little discussion that gave me an insight on the things they really liked and would remember most about the program. The next time I made a video for the family, I concentrated more on the things I knew they liked.

Appreciate Your Audience, and They'll Appreciate You

There's one thing that you should remind yourself of over and over again at every stage of making your home movies, from the planning, writing, and shooting, right down to the editing of the final product. If you don't appreciate your audience, they certainly won't appreciate you!

This may sound a bit harsh, but in order to develop a good rapport with the crowd, you need to have a basic understanding of the fundamental relationship between your audience and yourself as someone introducing them with creative material.

One of the major building blocks of any relationship, whether it's your sister, mother, or even your spouse, is consideration. The same is true for the relationship between the videographer and viewers. Here are a few simple questions that you can ask yourself in order to help prepare yourself for a fruitful relationship with your audience. They can also help you make decisions that will ultimately make your videos fun to watch.

- Will the audience be interested in watching your video?
- If they do begin to watch it, how long can you hold their attention?
- Is there a point at all to your video?

Don't Keep the Crowd Incarcerated

Audiences in general have famously short attention spans. This is especially true for viewers of home videos and as you've learned in previous chapters, you have to do everything in your power to keep them tuned in.

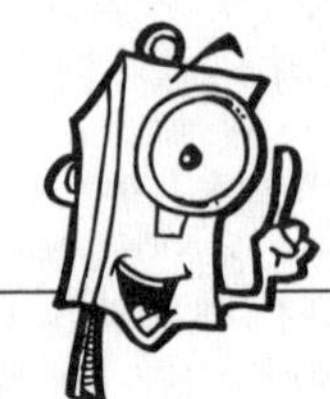

Candid Camera

As a general guideline, once you get past the 10-minute mark in your home videos, the attention span of your audience rapidly fades. Even the most slickly produced home movies can't captivate the crowd for unlimited amounts of time. A home video longer than 20 minutes can get you into trouble. If it's over 30 minutes, make sure to provide blankets and pillows!

Most Hollywood moviemakers have the art of crowd captivation down to a science. Whether it's huge explosions, high tech special effects, or compositing and computer animation, big bucks are being spent to keep movies interesting.

Home videographers, on the other hand, have very few high tech tools to work with. So you must rely largely on the raw power of storytelling to get your point across. And a big part of storytelling involves not wasting the audience's time with extraneous details. Why spend 20 minutes on people dancing at a wedding when you can get at least one shot of everyone's face in less than five minutes?

I usually aim for home video/program lengths of five to seven minutes. Just like a song. Short, and to the point. In fact, a lot of the programs that I've put together have actually been music video-like montages and sound-bite clip segments that are edited to one piece of music. This way my videos have a clear beginning, middle, and end. And the length is long enough for people to thoroughly enjoy the content without getting drowsy.

What's the Point?

If your video doesn't have a point, chances are you're going to have trouble holding the audience's attention for very long. Even if your video has no real intention, you can usually find a unifying theme to help tie things together and make the experience more interesting for people to watch. It could be as simple as a narrator telling a story, or to focus on a reoccurring event, theme or visual landmark.

Recently, I took on the task of producing a 65th birthday party tape for a friend's dad. He came over with tons of photos and old Super8 film footage of his dad and the family. Even though we were inundated with potential material for use in the final program, we struggled with a unifying concept. Finally, we came up with a simple theme: "A Brooklyn Boy's Journey Through Life." Everything in the video somehow related back to his Brooklyn roots and how all of the major decisions in his life were based on the fact that he was afraid to leave. From the meeting with his future wife at Brooklyn College, to his decision to go to Brooklyn Law School, we had chosen a main road to travel which all the side streets of the video connected with.

Will They Really Want to Watch?

This is a good question. Generally, viewers are rarely rude and have no intention of hurting your feelings. But the real question is, what are they really thinking? You don't want someone to be smiling on the surface while digging their fingernails into their palms. You must choose your audience wisely. Better yet, choose the subjects and movies that you're interested in working on, and then scout out the ideal crowd.

Let's say you've put together a quick video on amateur auto racing. You might have better luck showing it to your brother than to your sister. Similarly, if your wife forces your buddies to watch your wedding video on poker night, you can guarantee that the following week they won't be back for more!

Setting Up a Screening

Sharing your work with others isn't always as easy as it sounds. You can always make copies of your tape and send them to your intended audience, or over time you can play your videos to people one at a time as the opportunities present themselves. But you'd be missing out on the unique experience of a larger-scale audience reacting to your work.

I've found that the best way to put your video on display is to arrange a screening. I'm not talking about renting out Madison Square Garden, but you can certainly jam pack a lot of people into the TV room of your house without too much trouble. And the more people that you round up, the more enjoyable the experience is going to be for you.

You can treat a screening as an event in itself just like you would a birthday party or graduation. Or, you can attach it to another scheduled event. Either way, you'll want to make your screening a cinematic experience by combining viewer comfort with the highest possible audio and video quality.

When the Moment Is Right ...

Choosing the moment is key in planning a screening. The goal is really to round up as many people as possible at one time. If your screening is the only thing you have on tap for the evening, you might want to plan other events before or after since your video probably won't take up much more than a half hour of time. You can easily make a night out of it by screening your video and then heading out to a ball game and/or dinner.

If you decide to attach a screening to a bigger event, you've got an already-assembled audience that's just waiting to be captivated. Birthday parties are an obvious choice

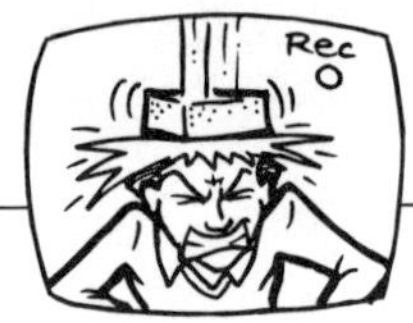

Blooper

For your own peace of mind, it may be a good idea to keep the head count lower the first time you hold a screening. Trust me, it'll keep your stress level to a minimum and is a lot easier on the nerves.

because there can be as many as 50 to 60 people in attendance. I've been in movie theaters with smaller crowds.

Besides being the highlight of your event, it's also a thoughtful and unique gift to give the person of the day. Here are some other events that you can easily attach a screening to:

- Anniversaries
- Wedding after-parties
- Wedding showers
- Bachelor parties
- Holiday parties
- Reunions
- Graduation parties

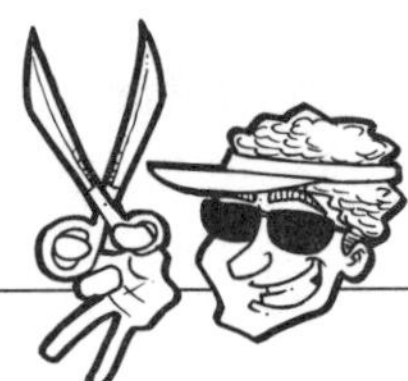

Director's Cut

This may sound a little grim at first, but video is a very powerful tool in commemorating people who have recently passed away. After the initial shock has worn off, a video tribute is a good way to bring back the good memories and to help ease the pain of losing a loved one. It can also help yourself work out your grief in a way that's loving and will be appreciated by others who knew the person.

Kicking Back with the Crowd

Before holding your screening, consider the amount of people you are planning to invite. If you're going to use your living room or den as the screening area, it may get a bit tight depending on the amount of people present. Also, you must take into account that people like to be comfortably seated, maybe not as comfortable as they would in stadium-style movie theater seats, but at the very least they shouldn't be standing up.

If you're working with a small space, make sure there are enough chairs and couches for everyone. Bridge chairs work well, or you can steal seats from the kitchen or dining room. If you must resort to having people sit on the floor, you might want to lay out a blanket, pillows, or cushions to make them more comfortable.

If your home can't handle the volume of people, you might want to consider booking your screening someplace else. Many neighborhood bars and restaurants welcome screening crowds and usually have the appropriate audio/video support.

When I was planning my best friend's birthday party we made the audio/video support a priority and chose a place that had a projection TV screen that took up an entire wall. The place also had amazing sound and comfy round-the-room seating.

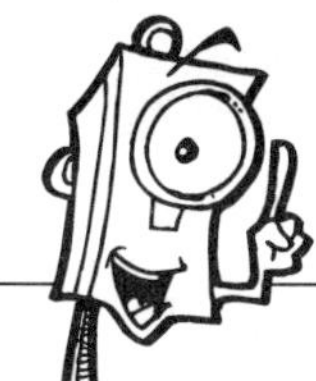

Candid Camera

A comfortable crowd is an attentive crowd. Ever watch a movie in a theater where the seats felt like they were made out of cement? It's extremely distracting to constantly readjust your position to get comfortable.

The Easiest Way to Your Audience's Heart Is Through Their Stomachs

A tasty snack is a great way to enhance your screenings and to help give your audience every opportunity to enjoy the show. According to my sister-in-law Joy Bauer, MS, R.D., who's a world-famous nutritionist (and coincidentally the author of *The Complete Idiot's Guide to Total Nutrition*), "healthy" is important so that your audience will be around longer to enjoy more of your videos. "Creamy" will work for those mushy, emotional flicks, and "quantity" will work for the lengthier productions. "Sweets and chocolatey treats" generally help to win over any resistant viewers like younger children and angstful teens. You can also get those treats typically associated with movies too, like popcorn, Milk Duds, Juji Fruits, and so on.

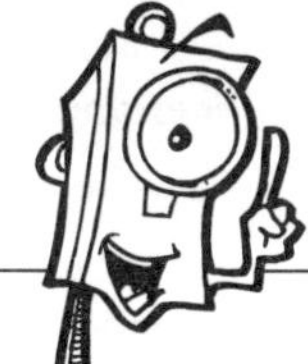

Candid Camera

You will need to always make sure that you have alternative snack options for people with special medical concerns like non-sugar for diabetics, low-salt for high blood pressure, and low-calorie items for dieters.

Here are a few of Joy's snack suggestions that are perfect for video screenings:

- For the creamy snacks: frozen yogurts, low-fat puddings, fruit smoothies.
- For the quantity snacks: air-popped or low-fat microwave popcorn, pretzels, baby carrots, and salsa.
- Sweets and chocolatey treats: strawberries with chocolate syrup for dipping, ice pops, lollipops, Hershey Kisses, bite-size Milky Way Lights.

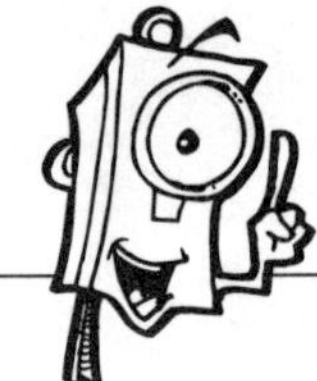

Candid Camera

There are several high-quality/low-cost home theater receivers on the market, and like anything else in the world of electronics, the prices are always falling. Check out entry-level models from Onkyo, Pioneer, and Kenwood to name a few. Check out *Sound and Vision Magazine* (www.soundandvisionmag.com) for the latest prices and reviews.

Equipped for Success

The next thing on your list of pre-screening considerations is to figure out if your home equipment has the beef to satisfy a larger than average crowd. First, take a close look at your TV set. Is it big enough for everyone to see what's going on? You've spent long hours putting your video together, the last thing you want to do is downplay your work on a substandard TV. If you're stuck with a smaller screen… no problem. Just break your audience up into groups and have multiple showings. We did this at a friend's wedding after-party. One hundred twenty people came back to the house and all were dying to see the bachelor party video. Unfortunately, we were stuck with a tiny 14-inch TV in a room that could not hold much more than 15 people. So, we premiered the video about 10 times, and everyone got to see it!

The next big concern is audio. Many of the newer TV sets come with beefy speakers that deliver room-filling stereo sound. But if you have a smaller TV or if you're planning a big screening you can easily take it a step further if you're willing to get your home stereo into the action. Make sure that your stereo receiver has one auxiliary, or any other input available. If your stereo is capable of surround sound, then you're already set up for optimal presentation style audio even though your home videos are not mixed in surround sound.

Connecting everything is as easy as attaching a camcorder to your TV. All you need is a pair of RCA cables (red and white for right and left audio channels). Simply connect the output of your VCR or TV set into your stereo's input and you're ready for action.

Getting Your TV Ready for Action

There are several things that you can do to optimize your TV set's performance and make sure that it will give you years of trouble-free service:

- **Clean the screen!** Dust, dust and more dust! It's a way of life here in New York City and other parts of the world. Since TV screens are a source of static electricity, that means they will collect dust faster than other furniture and appliances in your home. Always check with your owner's manual on the best method of cleaning.
- **Watch out for extra light.** Your TV set itself is a very strong source of light. If you've ever fallen asleep with the television on, you can wake up in the middle

of the night thinking that it's morning! If you are having a screening, try dimming or turning off bright lights in the room to prevent unnecessary glare on your screen. Also, try and position your TV away from windows or bright floor lamps.

- **Wiggle the cables.** If you're having a reception problem, try jiggling the cables behind your set to test if the problem gets better or worse. If you see interference on screen while jiggling, disconnect all the cables and then reconnect them again as tight as possible.
- **Adjust picture controls.** Before a screening, you may want to adjust the contrast, brightness, and sharpness controls to get the optimum picture. Also, don't be a stranger to these buttons while watching regular TV. Sometimes a slight adjustment can make a big difference in the clarity and color of your picture.
- **Adjust the level of your audio long before your audience takes a seat.** There's nothing worse than fumbling with the volume knob at the very beginning of your show when the crowd's attention can be gained or lost at the drop of a hat.

Keeping the Crowd Quiet

Everything's in place; your video is about to premiere. Your heart's pumping loudly and the adrenaline begins to seep its way into your bloodstream. It's going to be a great moment. Your footage has been carefully shot, the script was creatively written, and all of your edits have been carefully thought out. Now, the show is underway, and everything's going perfect, until ... Your wife fires her first of many questions at you. Then your little cousin and his sister begin to brawl. Then your grandmother asks your mom to pass the carrots and dip.

One step short of your viewers falling asleep on you, talking during your show can be a frustrating and insulting experience. This is especially true of the people who question every shot and every line of dialogue. By the time the question is asked and answered, more vital information is missed. This leads to more questions and before you know it, the show's over, bub.

There's not really much you can do about this except to ask your audience not to speak during the show or to wait to ask questions until it's over. People will usually understand and take this into advisement.

There's actually a neat post-production trick you could try. At the beginning of a motion picture in a theater, a title card usually pops up asking the audience to refrain from unnecessary noise and talking during the movie. You can easily make up a similar title card using a character generator, or titler, and flash it at the top of your movie. You're guaranteed to get a good chuckle, and your point has been subtly administered.

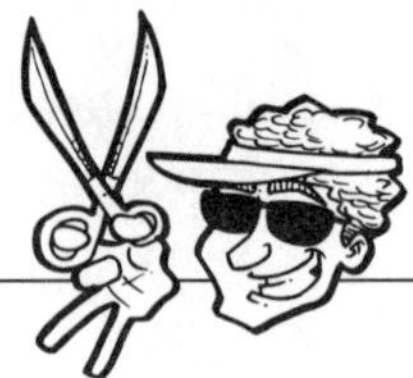

Director's Cut

If you find that people are continuously asking questions, interrupting, or losing interest, you can assume that there may be an inherent problem with some aspect of your video. If possible, watch your audience's reaction throughout and take note where they are attentive and where their eyes glaze over. Then ask yourself why. Consider re-editing or applying your newfound knowledge to future videos.

One major point you should also keep in mind: Don't take the whole screening experience too seriously! Especially if you are a beginner, keep in mind that it takes years to perfect the craft of making home movies that people want to watch. Have fun and experiment! Your first forays into home video don't necessarily have to be *Gone with the Wind* or even *The Blair Witch Project.*

The Least You Need to Know

- Home videos are a great way for your and other people to relive their memories and have a good laugh. The trick is breaking the home video stereotype in order to get others to watch.
- If you don't think about your audience in advance, your audience isn't going to think much of your videos.
- It's important to consider audience comfort and convenience when you set up a screening for your videos.
- The right equipment can make a big difference in your video presentation.
- Ask your audience to reserve comments until the show is over. Once someone interrupts, others are quick to chime in!

Chapter 24

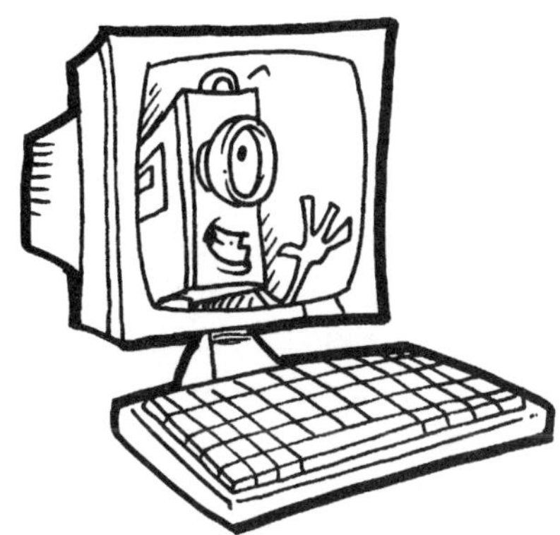

Multimedia Madness: Alternative Methods of Distributing Your Video

In This Chapter

- Video, computers, and you
- Shooting for multimedia
- Video on the Internet
- Your videos on CD-ROM
- A look ahead with multimedia

Sick and tired yet of making a million and one dubs of your videos for all of your friends and family? Maybe it's time to consider the digital route in video circulation. These days it's easier and less expensive than ever to transfer your videos onto the hard drive of your computer. And once the video is in your computer, there are a million and one different things that you can do with it, including the potential to share your videos with a globally connected audience.

Welcome to a new world where multimedia is the next big thing, and all it takes to hop in on the ground floor is a camcorder, computer, a connection to the Internet, and a few other low-cost digital tools. Computers have taken over the world and have changed the way we handle many of our everyday tasks. It was just a matter of time before computers forever changed the way we do home video.

Video, Computers, and You

Computers have forever impacted many aspects of your life, including the way you entertain yourself, do your banking, writing, communicating, shopping, traveling, and scheduling to name a few. In the 1980s, computers virtually replaced the typewriter, and soon after, the desktop publishing industry was born. Books, magazines, and scores of other printed materials were now all being formatted, laid out, and printed on new and powerful PCs. As computing capacity grew, developers set their sights on video. Apple was the first to give it a whirl with their release of Quicktime 1.0 that wasn't initially well received. But after a while, they got it right, and the rest is history.

Now, a large percentage of all video editing, both amateur and professional, is done on the computer via nonlinear editing software. And the growth continues. Software is often updated at least once a year, and computer systems get faster on a weekly basis.

The big buzzword of the 90s is multimedia and recently it has become a convenient and affordable way to enjoy and distribute your home videos. This is especially true as personal computers continue to find their way into homes, businesses, and classrooms. Add to the mix the explosive growth of the Internet and the ever-dropping prices of multimedia tools like CD-ROM burners and video capture cards, and you've got the makings of a new revolution in home video.

Whether you have a Windows machine, a Mac, or any other type of computer, the ability to produce multimedia content from your home videos is easier than ever. In fact, most new computers have multimedia capabilities bundled in with the system. This includes

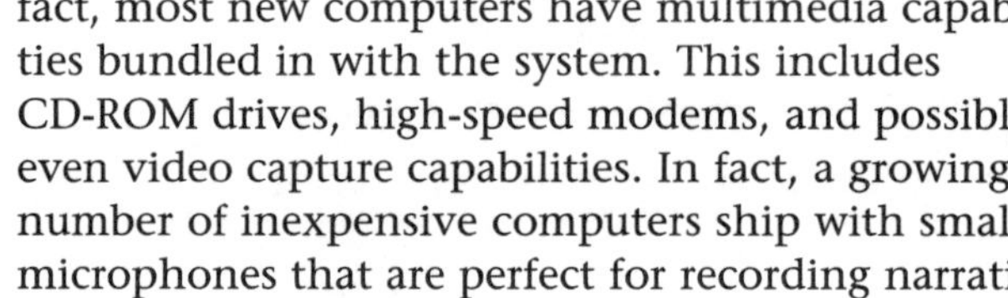

CD-ROM drives, high-speed modems, and possibly even video capture capabilities. In fact, a growing number of inexpensive computers ship with small microphones that are perfect for recording narration in your programs.

Blurred Word

CD-ROM burners are enhanced CD-ROM players that are also capable of recording music or data onto recordable CD-ROMs. Burners are widely available to consumers and have fallen significantly in price since their introduction several years ago. Untrue to its name, there is no smoke or fire that takes place when "burning" a CD!

Adding Fuel to the FireWire

As I've mentioned before, the most exciting recent development in the world of home video is the invention of FireWire (IEEE 1394/i.LINK). This high-speed protocol port is quickly becoming a new standard for everything from scanners to hard drives and in the video market, camcorders. Now, with a FireWire-equipped Windows PC or Mac, getting first-generation, digital video into your computer is as easy as transferring a file.

In fact, there are computers hitting the market with just one purpose in mind: video editing with FireWire and a MiniDV camcorder. Most notably, Apple just released a version of their popular iMac computer called "iMac DV" that ships with FireWire and a nonlinear editing package called "iMovie."

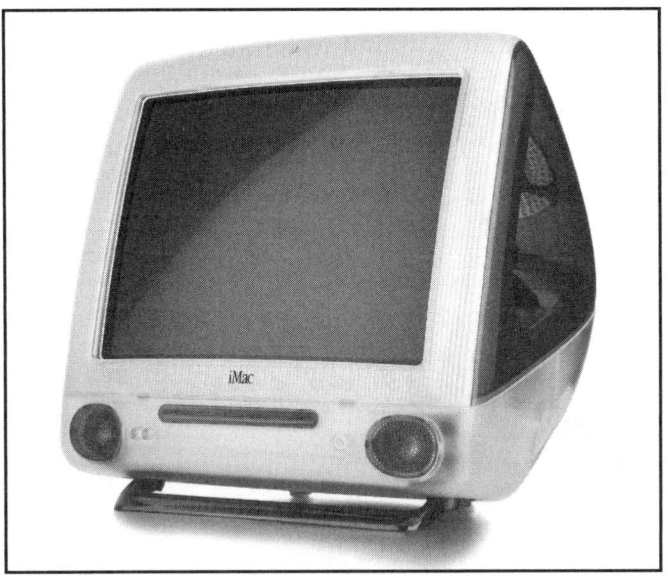

Apple's iMac DV.

(Courtesy of Apple Computer, Inc.)

The Act of Turning Your Videos into X's and O's

If you haven't made the jump just yet to FireWire, you may remember from the nonlinear editing chapter, working with analog video on your computer involves transferring it from your camcorder or VCR to a hard drive. This can be done using a video capture card that allows you to "digitize" your video into your computer by turning the analog signal into digital information. Once the video is in your computer you need nonlinear editing software to create programs and other multimedia content like audio and video clips.

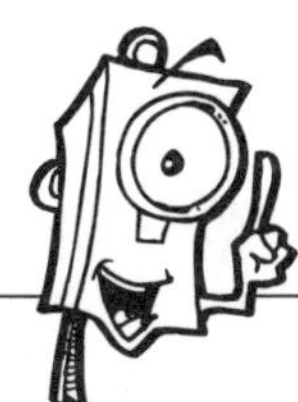

Candid Camera

Once the digitized video is in your computer, you have random access to any part of it. This allows you to instantly scroll or jump back and forth from the beginning of a video/audio clip to the end without having to wait for the winding of a VCR or camcorder.

Without overwhelming you with a million details, it is important to understand that once you digitize video, it lives on your hard drive in a specific file format, depending on the hardware and software that you're using. The most common file formats are QuickTime, AVI and MPEG. It's good to have a basic understanding of the different video file formats since you must know which one your audience will be able to play back on their computers.

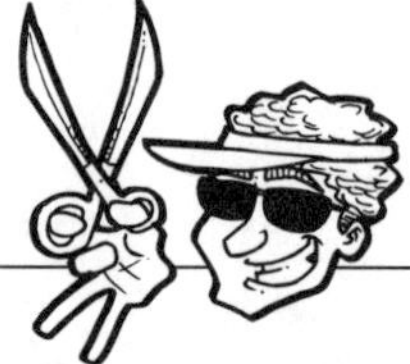

Director's Cut

Media Cleaner Pro is a relatively inexpensive software package that does an excellent job of converting between the most common video file formats. In addition, it provides some color correction, audio and video compression, and other goodies for preparing your final masterpiece for multimedia distribution. You can reach them at www.terran-int.com or 1-800-577-3443.

One of your goals when dealing with digitized video is to work at the highest quality that you can. When you're all finished, you want to save your high-quality version on CD-ROM or videotape, and then squeeze it all down to a file size that's suitable for playing on other's computers. Their computers may not be as well equipped as yours to handle the stress of digital video. Making a squeezed-down version of your original movie is kind of like using the "save as" command in a word processing program. The original is put safely away on your hard drive while a new (smaller) file is created.

Several things are compromised when you make a smaller version of your project that you might plan to play back over the Internet, CD-ROM, or even transfer via e-mail. The first thing that usually is thrown into the fire is frame rate. Full motion video is played back at 30 frames per second (29.97 to be exact). This means that each second, 30 pictures flash by, each one a little different than the next. These differences lay the foundation for motion on the screen. Decreasing the rate to 15 frames per second gives you half the temporal information. In many cases on the Internet, frame rates are very low to accommodate the limited bandwidth that most users have access to through their modem connection. By decreasing the frame rate, you can significantly shrink the size of your file before you distribute it. By lowering the frame rate to 15 frames per second (F.P.S.), you will reduce the file size by 50 percent. By sticking to multiples of 30 F.P.S., you avoid forcing the computer to calculate new frames. In other words, the computer is just cutting away and not adding anything to the movie. I suggest using frame rates of 15, 10, or 6. But you should be careful because when you go too low, it has the potential to make the video look very choppy and simply awful.

Size Does Matter

The next step in making video clips more viable for multimedia is to shrink them down from their original size. Depending on the system, a standard television image on your computer measures 640 × 480 pixels in size. (Or 720 × 480 for MiniDV.) This means that there are 640 pixels (the smallest element of your image) across by 480 pixels vertically. This is equivalent to a full screen image on your TV set.

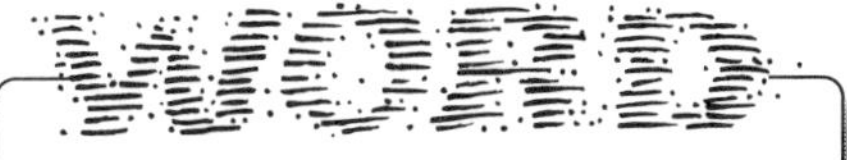

Blurred Word

Pixels are the smallest part of a computer-generated image. They are usually square or rectangular in shape.

With technology as it is right now, there are several things we can do to make the movies smaller and more playable. If computers keep evolving at their present fiery pace, pretty soon you'll be able to experience the same quality on your computer that you do on your TV set!

Today, most video clips distributed via multimedia are only 320 × 240 pixels in size. This is one quarter the size of 640 × 480. I've even seen some movie trailers on the Web that are only 160 × 120 pixels.

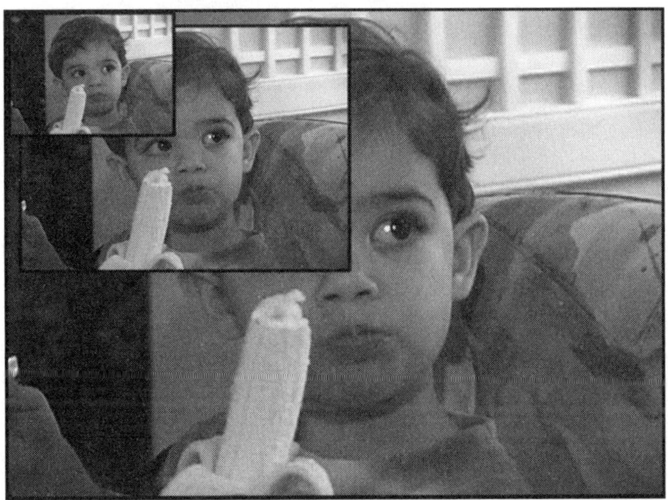

Image sizes: 160 × 120, 320 × 240, 640 × 480 (full screen).

Watching video this small takes much of the impact away from the original footage. Scenic nature shots and far away action shots can be almost completely washed out in the tiny little box. I've found that close up shots work best for multimedia.

I recently downloaded and watched the trailer for *Star Wars: The Phantom Menace.* While I got a basic idea of the story line and the way things were going to look in the theater, it seemed silly to promote such a visually stunning movie in such a small frame. When I finally watched the movie in the theater, it was a completely different experience.

Many multimedia players can blow up the video twice the size or even fill the screen. This may look better, but depending on your system, it may affect playback performance causing you to "drop frames" (stammering playback). It's important to understand that the resolution is not the same as if it was recorded full screen. The blow-up image looks softer, blurrier, and grainier because the pixels are doubled or averaged to fill the screen.

These free, downloadable handy players look like mini VCRs that have little buttons for rewind, fast forward, and frame advance and can be started and stopped at will.

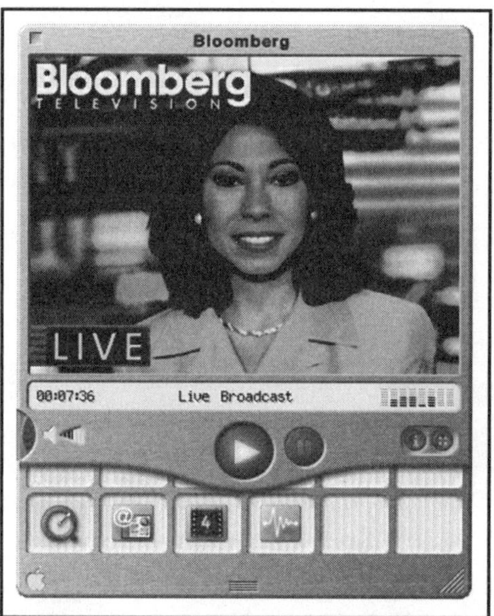

Apple's Quicktime Player (Mac/Windows).

(Courtesy of Apple Computer, Inc.)

Multimedia Is Color Blind

I'll bet George Lucas would have silently cringed if he ever logged on to the Internet and took a look at his new movie trailer. Not only was the action hard to see because the screen was so small, but the color was washed out. This has to do not only with the method of "compression" (see "Crunching the Numbers" later in this chapter) used to make the movie, but also with the capability of your computer monitor to view colors. I was watching the trailer on an older system that could only display 256 colors at a time with a slower processor that was not able to keep up with the frame rate of the trailer.

Full color video in computers is stored as 24 bits (approximately 16 million colors). By lowering the color bit depth to 16 bit (thousands of colors) or 8 bit (256 colors), your file will be much smaller. But there is a trade-off between file size and quality. As you use fewer colors to represent your image, the video will begin to look posterized (see the following figure). Higher bit depths result in better color representation.

Lower bits depths can make an image look murkier than the Mississippi River. Unfortunately, technology dictates that video clips used for multimedia need to be compressed to the max.

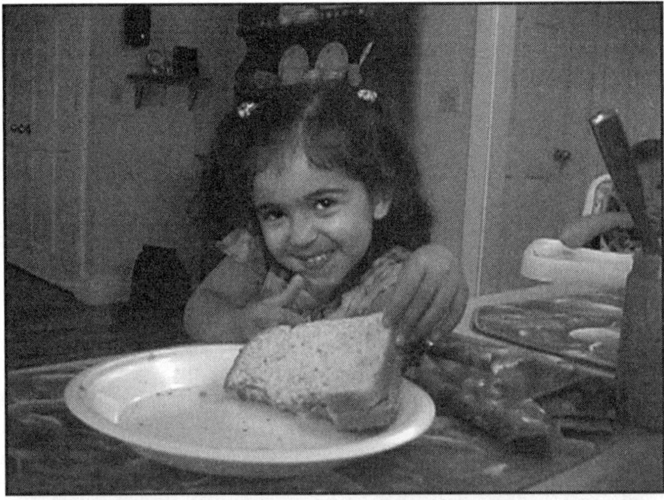

Original image.

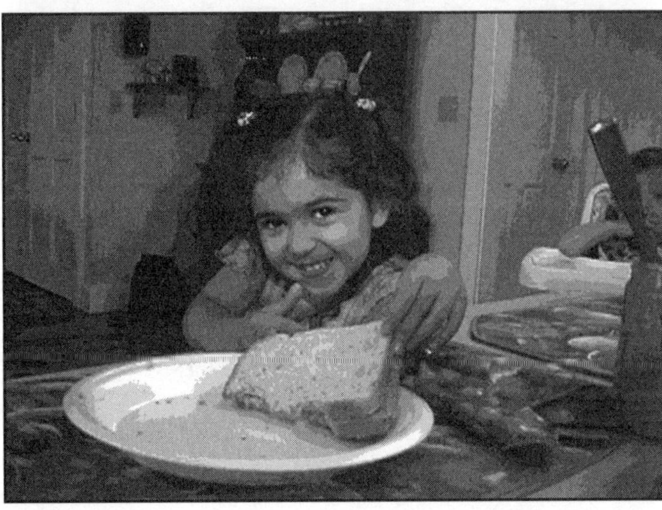

Image represented with too few colors (posterized).

Additionally, if your computer monitor is only able to read 256 colors, for example, then your video's color representation cannot be properly displayed, even before it gets compressed. Most monitors today, however, are capable of designating thousands or even millions of colors to moving video. This means that computer-digitized video can look much like it would on a regular TV set.

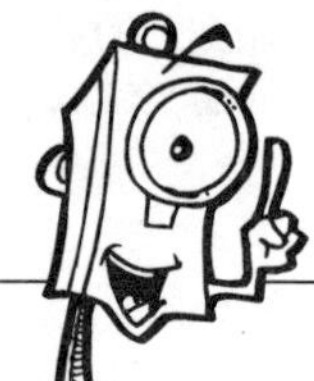

Candid Camera

You must always consider what system your final product will be played back on and create a file compatible with the lowest common denominator. Another option is to create different versions of the movie for different machines. You can make smaller movies for computers with lower performance levels and bigger movies for faster systems.

Crunching the Numbers

The final step in squeezing your video down into a size that's more viable for playback on everyone's computer is to choose a codec (compression/decompression) scheme. Some codecs require additional hardware in order to work, some codecs are better for crunching movies for CD-ROM, some are better for the Internet. It can get a little confusing, so I'd recommend checking out a program like Media Cleaner Pro that does all of the decision making for you. You just answer a few questions about your project, and your movie is made.

It's All in the Shooting

If you think that you might utilize multimedia in your video distribution, then it's important to shoot your video in a certain way. I'm not talking about a brand new video production method, but just a few things to keep in mind while shooting that can enhance your images on the small screen.

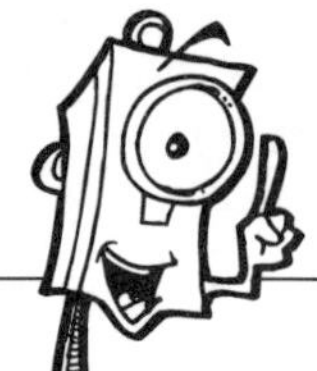

Candid Camera

Shaky video, as you may know by now, can be avoided by using a tripod or any other method of supporting the camera. Excessive zooming in and out can also give your viewers that unsteady feeling.

The first is to pay very close attention to the motion of your video. Here's where shaky home video camera work will really damage your production. Whether it's a fast-paced sporting event or an all-out graduation party, motion must be kept smooth and to a minimum. Decreased image size and frame rates can leave MTV-style video looking like a bunch of still photographs pasted together in a slide-viewer.

Let's say you've got footage of a UFO zipping from one end of the sky to the other, you can forget about uploading it to the Internet. Any extraterrestrial motion will be completely wiped out on the small screen.

Additionally, if you're shooting for multimedia you must take into consideration other potential production problems like lighting and shot selection. Whether you plan to shoot indoors or outdoors, the better your lighting the brighter your colors are going to be. And the brighter your colors are in your source footage, the better your chances of them looking good in the digital domain. If you don't have a lighting kit then you can resort to reflectors or simple household lamps to help you illuminate your scene. It takes just a few minutes to improve your lighting conditions and it can make a world of difference when you play your digitized movies back on your computer.

There's an old adage in computerland called "garbage in, garbage out." It's especially true when you're shooting and editing video for multimedia. If you don't start with a good-looking image, there's very little you can do to enhance it in the post-production process. And when you shrink the movie down to make it multimedia-friendly, it looks even worse thanks to low color representation, low frame rate, and high compression.

Another shooting issue that causes big problems in your final multimedia program or video clip is poor shot selection. If you use wide-angles in many cases the details will be hard to see when the video is transformed for multimedia. Similarly, long shots can be almost impossible to make out. This is especially true if your far away subject is moving. Details and motion can get completely lost in digital compression artifacts.

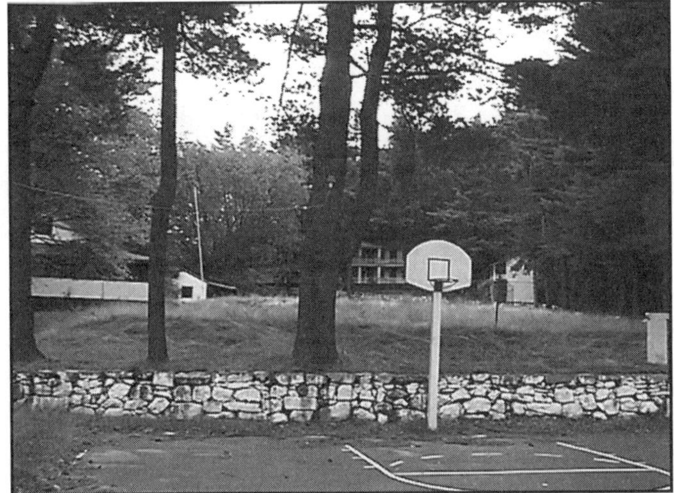

Original footage.

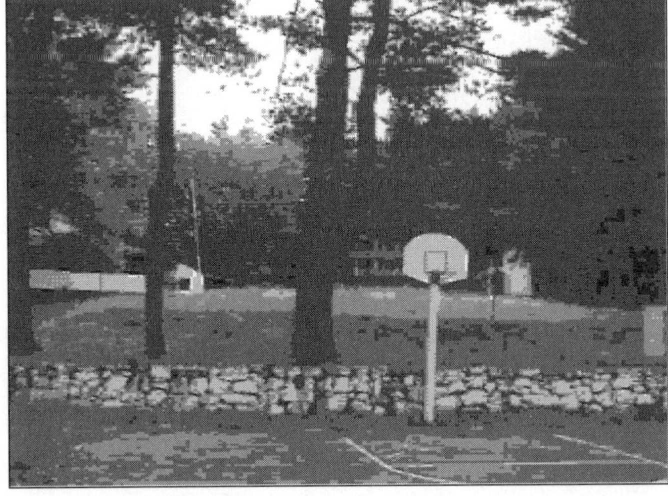

Artifacted footage.

Untangling the Web of Video on the Internet

The Internet is a new and exciting way for you to share your home videos with a worldwide audience. Never before has the general public had such easy access to such a mass method of communication. Now, with video streaming technology, a Web site can become more like a TV station than a home for simple text and graphics.

Video, however, has long been available on the Internet for downloading in the form of QuickTime, AVI (video for Windows) and MPEG. After downloading the entire file onto your hard drive, you could then watch the video back on your computer. Web surfers far and wide rushed to watch every video available on the Net, until they read the "estimated download time remaining" display in their Web browsers. Because video files were relatively large, (commonly 1 to 10 megabytes) they were taking hours and hours to download. Why wait when you can just pop on a TV set and get instant gratification?

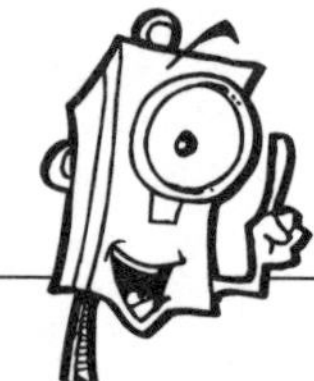

Candid Camera

Since computer configurations vary widely, the founding fathers of digital video tried to create only a few video file formats that work with all different computing platforms, hardware and software. These formats include QuickTime, AVI, and MPEG. You can guarantee that more are on the way, however.

Full Stream Ahead!

Streaming technology has taken the "wait" out of Internet video. Streaming is simply the ability to watch the video clip on your computer without having to first download it. This means that you don't have to wait for the entire file to be copied onto your hard drive for you to play it.

Not too long ago streaming video was a technical fantasy. Now, it is popping up all over the Internet. Even beginner Web sites can have streaming video. All you need to see streaming video over the Web is a streaming-video program, like Quicktime 4 or RealNetworks G2, that adds functionality to Web browsers like Netscape and Microsoft Internet Explorer. You can download a copy for free at www.real.com.

With the slow speed of most people's Internet access, streaming video is often lower quality than the larger, less-compressed files that you can download and watch when the file transfer is complete. As technology advances, this will be less of an issue. We're already starting to see Internet access moving from phone lines to cable TV lines that are allowing people to connect at ever-increasing speeds. Also, some broadcast and cable networks are starting to offer TV shows that are designed for and distributed via the Web. You can check out some of these programs at www.atomfilms.com

www.broadcast.com

www.SHO.com

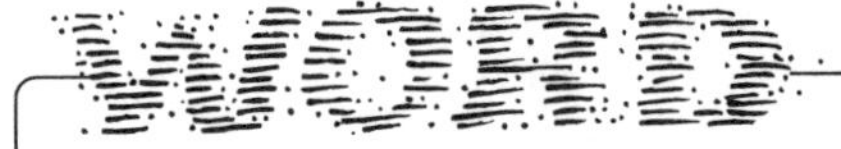

Blurred Word

A **domain name** is a Web address that you can type into a Web browser giving your computer specific directions to the desired Web site on the Internet. Domain names end in ".com" and ".net" for commercial sites, ".edu" for educational sites, and ".org" for organizations.

A Web Site to Call Your Own

Setting up your own Web site is easy to do and can serve as a home-base for your video programs. Internet access and Web hosting companies are a dime a dozen, all you have to do is a little value shopping to find the best deal. I've seen Web hosting for as little as $10 a month. On America Online and various other places on the Internet, you can set up a Web site for free. If you plan to take advantage of web streaming technology, however, make sure that the hosting company is capable of handling streaming media on its Web sites. Otherwise, if you plan to make your video available for downloading first, just about any web hosting service will do.

Here are a few companies that offer low-price Web hosting and make setting up a Web site a snap by setting up your site, registering your domain name, and maintaining your site once it's set up:

- www.wazzu.com
- www.earthlink.com
- www.netcom.com
- www.networksolutions.com
- www.mindspring.com
- www.aol.com
- www.tripod.com

More Multimedia Madness

Before the Internet ever dreamed of harboring video, CD-ROMS were in action as the multimedia delivery method of choice. Even as the Web gains ground as a viable video choice, CD-ROMs are still a low-cost and highly accessible way to distribute home movies. In fact, CD-ROMS are about $1.00 a piece. That's a lot cheaper than spinning off VHS dubs!

Web video and CD-ROM video are similar in that you still need to apply all sorts of compression and file shrinking to squeeze everything onto one disk. And since a recordable CD-ROM can hold up to 650 megabytes of information, you can really pack a whole lot of programming onto one disk.

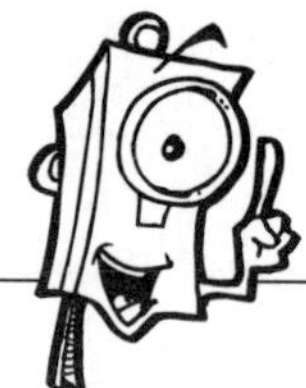

Candid Camera

A recordable CD-ROM disk can hold up to 650 megabytes of information. The best part is that they only cost about $1.50 in any computer or office supply store.

I've had a CD-ROM burner in my video arsenal for several years, and it has always been my favorite way to distribute video that I produce. And with the falling price of CD-ROM drives that have "burning" capabilities, just about anyone can start making their own disks.

Besides video playback, CD-ROMS can also hold 650 megabytes of data. Using the same CD-ROM burner, you can choose to record regular computer files onto a blank CD-ROM instead of audio or video files. Because the recordable CD-ROM media are so cheap, this is a perfect solution for backing up a hard drive or archiving any other important data (see Chapter 27, "Preserving Your Home Videos").

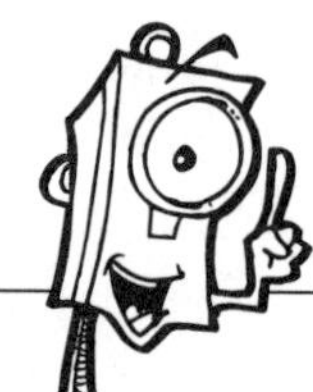

Candid Camera

The other good thing about CD-ROM distribution is that just about every new computer comes standard with a CD-ROM drive. Many of the newest computers also ship with a DVD-ROM drive in the place of a CD-ROM drive. DVD-ROM drives are also capable of reading CD-ROMS.

The Future of Multimedia and Your Home Videos

This is pretty much a wide-open discussion as multimedia is still in its infancy. In just 10 short years we've seen computers evolve from little more than enhanced calculators to mega-machines on steroids. The 400 MHz Macintosh PowerBook that I'm using right now has more computing power than all of my previous computers combined. By the time you read this, 400 MHz computers will long be surpassed by speedier 500, 600, even 700 MHz computers.

Video fits into multimedia's future scheme quite nicely. In fact, the technology is moving faster than it ever has before. DVD-ROM drives are popping up all over the place and DVD burners are just around the corner for the everyday consumer. DVDs are capable of holding up to seven times the amount of information that CD-ROMs can hold, and the next generation of DVD players will be even bigger. The pending introduction of recordable DVD drives will undoubtedly create an explosion in multimedia and instantly create a new home for your videos.

I think that DVD technology is only the tip of the iceberg. Streaming video on the Web is just starting to take off as more and more people utilize the power to reach potential audiences of billions. Looking into the future, I see Web sites that have multiple feeds of streaming video. Right now the satellite TV services have as many as 500+ channels available. Why can't there be that many on the ever-expanding Internet?

One day there may be very few fundamental differences between your computer and TV set. In fact, the two will be fused together into one appliance, like a beefed-up version of WebTV that's capable of Internet access, video conferencing, video on demand, and even E-commerce.

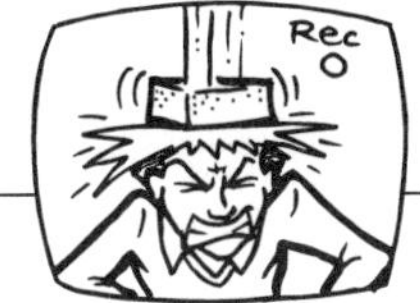

Blooper

Even though there's a certain comfort in building a computer system or a collection of video gear that you are familiar with, the only way to fully benefit from the technological explosion is to upgrade your stuff as often as your budget allows. Part of being an effective beneficiary of technology is to bend with the changes.

Eventually, all of the video-multimedia applications that right now seem like nothing more than fantasy will become part of our everyday lives. Teleconferencing over the Internet will be common, along with the capability to control and view footage from remote video cameras to get the real lowdown on traffic, tropical locations, zoos, even outer space! We'll be able to control the endings in our favorite movies, or even physically participate in them. When it comes to computers and video I'm convinced that anything is possible!

The Least You Need to Know

- Digitizing your videos is the only way to get involved in multimedia.
- Shooting your videos specifically for multimedia can have a big impact on how it looks once it's digitized.
- The Internet is the new frontier for your home videos.
- Multimedia CD-ROMS are a great way to put your videos on display.
- Video and multimedia have a long, prosperous future.

Chapter 25

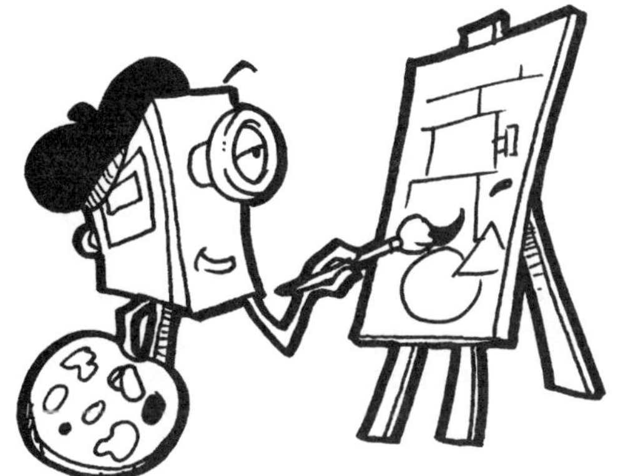

Getting Creative with Your Camcorder

In This Chapter

- Taking your camcorder on a shopping spree
- Choosing a camp and college with camcorder in hand
- Reviewing your performances with personal video footage
- Spy-cam

Let's face it ... the video age has descended upon us, and no longer are camcorders just for shooting birthday parties, weddings, and other fun-filled events. There are a million and one different ways that you can put your camcorder to good use. All it takes is creativity and a little bit of time, and you can introduce video into aspects of your life that you never would have thought of.

In this chapter you'll come across a collection of interesting ways to utilize your camcorder. Most of them I've gathered myself after years of carrying around a video camera. I've also included tips from friends and relatives who, over time, have discovered all sorts of creative camcorder uses. So read on and prepare to use your camcorder in ways you never would have imagined.

Shooting While Shopping

Camcorders are small enough these days to tote around just about anywhere. Ever considered the possibility of taking it along on a shopping spree?

Once you get past the initial silliness of the idea, you'll start to realize that it makes a whole lot of sense. Be it car shopping, clothes shopping, or even house hunting, your camcorder can be an invaluable tool in helping you decide what's right and what's not, especially when you are considering a major purchase.

Here are a few of the benefits of shopping with a camcorder:

- It allows you to consider the item at hand on your own terms in the comfort of your own home. And there's absolutely no pressure from pushy salespeople to deal with.
- You can involve your friends and family in your potential purchase decision by sharing your footage with them. You'd be surprised at how honest people can be in a pre-purchase situation as opposed to a post-purchase situation.
- If you use your camcorder while shopping for a home and eventually purchase one of the ones you've captured on tape, it becomes a neat keepsake to share with your family years down the road.

My brother-in-law Jon proved how useful a camcorder can be on a quest for a new home. He spent an entire afternoon meticulously recording a house he was interested in and took great pains to make sure everybody in his circle of family and friends saw it. For him, it was a vote of confidence when everyone's eyes popped out of their heads at first sight of what appeared to be a mansion and an estate! It also helped to calm the nerves of my sister-in-law Nancy who wasn't sure they were making the right move.

In some of the bigger department stores or shopping centers, however, you might run into a little problem, as many of them don't allow camcorders in their stores. It doesn't hurt to bring it along, and try to get permission to videotape as the need arises.

I find that this camcorder application works best with purchase decisions that I'm going to have to live with for a while. It's also great when my wife can't come along with me, I can share the footage with her, and it's the next best thing to her being there when time is an issue.

Here are some additional expeditions that you can utilize your camcorder on when your money is at stake:

- Gardening and landscaping stores
- Wedding, birthday, anniversary, party locations, and so on
- Computer shopping
- Furniture stores
- Major appliance shopping—dishwasher, refrigerator, washing machine/dryer, and so on
- Major electronics shopping—TV's, stereos, VCRs, and so on

- Sporting goods stores
- Giant discount stores like Home Depot or Costco

The Camcorder-College Connection

Choosing a college for your kids to attend is just as important, if not more important than buying a home. Your camcorder has documented their lives from their first birthday to their graduation now it's time to capture their next big step in the journey to adulthood.

Finding the time to visit a college, however, isn't an easy thing to do. Very often people are forced to cram three or four visits to different schools in just a few days. After a while, the campuses begin to blend together and you begin to forget the highlights of one school as compared to the downsides of another. Color catalogues and University Web sites can only take you so far.

Since New York University is just outside my door, for the sake of this section I decided to tag along for about an hour on a student-led campus tour. It began at the arch in Washington Square Park and took me through one of the dorms. The tour was a wonderful thing, and I learned more about the school in that short time than I learned in the four years that I have lived in the area. We also strolled through the immense library, the student center, several classrooms and lecture centers, the school store, the computer center, and even the physical education center. It was amazing how much ground we covered.

In addition, the students filled me in on college life in general at N.Y.U., and first-hand accounts of the overall classroom environment a potential student will encounter over the next four years. I was also somewhat disturbed to learn during a brief history lesson of Washington Square Park that it was used as a mass burial ground in the late 1800s after a plague ravaged New York City.

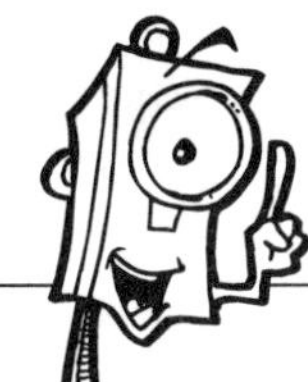

Candid Camera

After seeing the great pain and suffering my wife went through choosing a wedding dress, I realize now that a camcorder could have helped her with the decision making. It would have been great for her to take her time reviewing her choices in private instead of in the store. And just like Alicia Silverstone in the movie *Clueless,* you should never rely on mirrors when you have a Polaroid, or in this case a camcorder at your disposal!

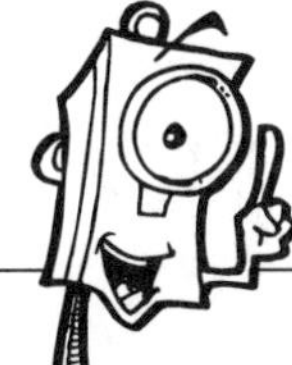

Candid Camera

There's a company called Collegiate Choice Walking Tours (www.collegiatechoce.com) that records the campus tours for you, in their entirety, as you would experience yourself if you were there. On the Web site you'll find a collection of over 330 colleges and universities in the United States, Canada, England, Ireland, and Scotland.

I didn't happen to have a camcorder with me, but if I had been rolling during the tour, it would have been a great refresher in helping to make a decision, especially if I had been overwhelmed with information and details after trips to many other campuses.

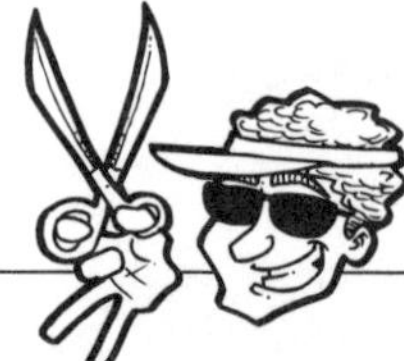

Director's Cut

It is also a good idea to take your camcorder off campus and get a few shots of the surrounding area—where the students live and shop. This can often make the difference between one college or another.

Hello Muddah, Hello Faddah, Hello Camcordah

Perhaps a less intense choice than choosing a college is choosing a day camp or sleepaway camp for your kids. Just like college, you hope that they will spend several years there. But unlike college, your child may decide to attend one camp for as much as ten years or more! And after that, many decide to continue as a waiter or even a counselor.

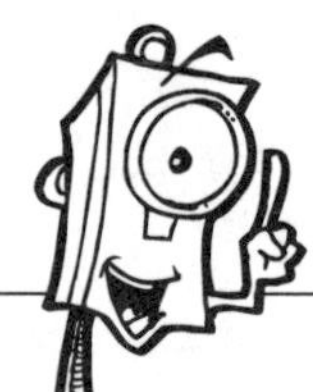

Candid Camera

From my own personal experience I can attest to the importance of choosing the right camp. Not only do I keep in touch with most of my summertime friends, I also met my wife at camp.

If you have the opportunity to browse the American Camping Association (ACA) Web site (www.aca-camps.com) you'll see that there are literally thousands of camps to choose from in just about every state. Many of these camps will send you their own promotional video that they include in their sales presentation kit. But take it from someone who has produced more than one video for sleepaway camps, take the time to visit the camp that you're interested in and shoot your own footage. Promotional camp videos tend to slant towards everything nice and beautiful about a camp and ignore anything that could be viewed as undesirable, like huge boulders on the soccer field or bunks that are propped up with 2 × 4's and cinder blocks.

It's your children's summer at stake here, perhaps the majority of summers for a good chunk of their young lives. Your camcorder is a good way to help you comparison shop for the right camp. Here are a few of the things you should look for in your camcorder's viewfinder:

- ➤ The overall condition of the camp.
- ➤ The surrounding area and scenic beauty.
- ➤ Condition of the athletic facilities and swimming areas.
- ➤ Condition of the bunks.
- ➤ The condition and cleanliness of the toilet and bathing facilities will reveal a lot about the camp.
- ➤ Specialized activities like computers, nature/environmental studies, archery, dance, drama, fencing, fishing, gymnastics, horseback riding, rocketry, and so on.

If you have previewed several camps, a video will help refresh your memory.

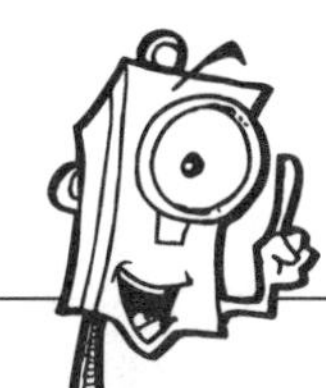

Candid Camera

Your financial situation and the individual needs and skills of your children can also have a big impact on the camp you choose. It pays to take the time to do thorough research and your own video footage can only make the decision easier to make.

The Show Must Go On!

Thanks to a camcorder, now you've got the chance to see what you really look like. Even better, you can watch yourself doing things that you don't often get the opportunity to do, or that you can use practice in like acting, public speaking, or even playing a musical instrument. A self-made videotape gives you the unique opportunity to review your performance in order to make improvements.

Unlike a birthday party or vacation tape, this is personal footage that is shot in the interest of self-improvement. Activities like public speaking and acting can be very nerve-wracking experiences. If you haven't practiced or done it for a while, the mere thought of getting up in front of people is enough to conjure up feelings of panic, even terror. It's more of a mental game than anything else, and a camcorder can help give you the confidence you need to break down the barriers of fear.

Rule #1 in public speaking and acting class: If you're not prepared, you're going to go down in flames. There are very few people in this world who can get up in front of a large crowd, unprepared, and make a smooth and coherent speech.

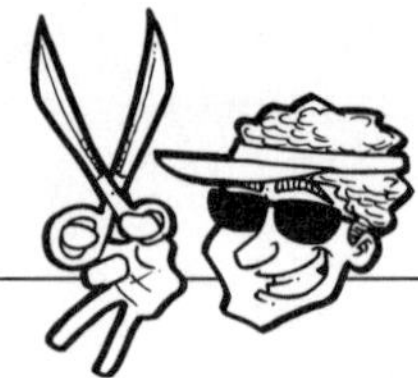

Director's Cut

Jerry Seinfeld said recently during a recent HBO comedy special that people fear public speaking more than they fear death. That means that the majority of people would rather be in the coffin at a funeral than giving the eulogy. Pretty scary, huh?

I hate public speaking (hence, I'm a writer!), but recently I was asked to be the best man at a close friend's wedding. Since he had delivered a perfectly articulate and humorous speech at my wedding, I couldn't just duck out by saying a couple of sentences. So, I broke out the trusty camcorder, and after writing down some thoughts on paper, I practiced the toast over and over again until I felt comfortable with my delivery. At the party, the speech went off without a hitch, and I felt that the practice helped me to sound natural and unrehearsed.

Mount your camcorder on a tripod, or prop it up on a table or shelf and aim it in your direction. With a little practice, you'll be ready to address the masses!

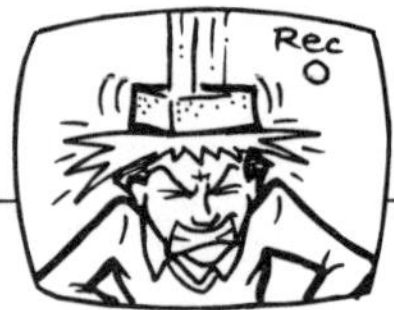

Blooper

If you plan to share your practice footage with others, show it to only one or two people at first. After you're feeling a little more confident, you can start to premiere it in front of larger crowds. This is a great way to gain self confidence and open up doors that you otherwise would never have approached.

Your Camcorder's a Good Sport

Very much along the lines of taping yourself while acting or speaking, you can also tape yourself playing sports in order to help improve your game. Viewing yourself as an outsider on TV can help you pinpoint the subtle nuances in your performance, ultimately making you a better player. It's common practice in the sports world as most athletic teams routinely do this not only for self-improvement, but to study the opponent.

Tennis is an idea sport to videotape, and I thank my tennis-nut of a dad for this example. He always sets a tripod up just slightly past out-of-bounds. Wide angle settings are always good for unsupervised shots. If you can recruit a video-assistant to help get you on tape, call for telephoto shots in order to zoom in on what you're doing.

You can also use a camcorder to tape other activities like skiing, biking, snowboarding, even water-skiing. Just make sure in these extreme conditions to protect your camcorder from the elements.

My friend Dave told me a funny story about how his dad used to drag him out on the golf course to videotape his swing. Golf is the perfect sport to study your technique because a lot of the game relies on the accuracy of your swing. Also, consider taping your children's games and watch them together to give them tips and pointers, just like the big guys and gals do.

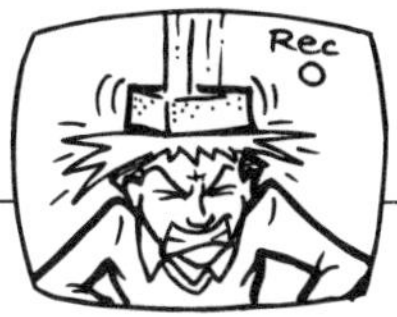

Blooper

If you're taping a sports event, take extra special care not to smack a ball or other object (including a body) into the tripod or mounted camcorder. When a tripod falls, the camcorder usually takes the brunt of the collision.

Snoop-Cam

The small size of camcorders makes them not only easy to carry around, they're also easy to hide! This opens up a world of sneaky surveillance applications that you can pull off yourself.

Unfortunately, video surveillance is the only way that many individuals and small businesses can protect themselves from theft and other various wrongdoings. But before you waste your valuable time hiding a camcorder behind a shelf speaker, make sure you have a compelling reason to do so. Video surveillance can be as simple as propping your camera near a window to monitor activity at the front door. Or you can bury a camcorder in a pile of stuffed animals and hit the record button. The possibilities are endless.

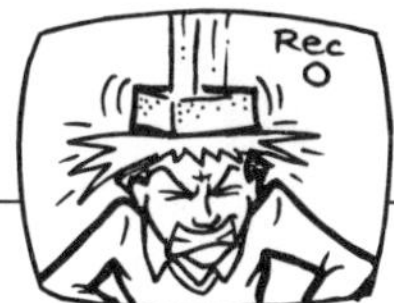

Blooper

You should check with an attorney if you plan to use surveillance video as evidence to criminal activity. Sometimes surveillance video isn't admissible under state or federal regulations.

From a window, you can easily mount a camcorder aimed at your front door. You can even run a cable from your camcorder to your TV set, and instantly be able to switch over if you hear someone knocking. You can also aim it at your driveway, or switch it into wide-angle and get the garage area and the front yard into one shot. Hiding the camcorder should be less of a concern in this case as a visible camera may act as a deterrent to any roving petty criminal or hooligan. Use of such cameras has been known to cut crime in some neighborhoods.

Whenever setting up your shot for Snoop-cam (or Nanny-Cam—see the following page) you should superimpose the date and time and leave it there while the camcorder does its work.

Nanny-Cam

You've probably seen horror videos of abusive and neglectful nannies on various news programs. A few years ago, a friend told me that he and his wife were concerned that the nanny they had hired wasn't spending enough time with the baby. In fact, several people had approached them after observing the nanny in the park practically ignoring their son. So they decided to use their camcorder to find out what was really going on.

One evening, my friend spent a few hours mounting the camera on top of his wall unit. He hid the rig by placing a bath towel over the front of the camcorder, leaving just enough space for a clear shot. Before the Nanny arrived that day, he turned the camera on, pulled the lens back to extreme wide angle, and hit record. Since they knew that they only had approximately two hours of recording time, he and his wife left the apartment early.

While the resulting footage didn't reveal any horrific crime, they did discover that the nanny was spending an incredible amount of time on the phone. Even when the baby was crying, it took her as long as 10 to 15 minutes to come.

Instead of confronting her with the footage, my friend told the nanny that they had to let her go because his wife decided to stop working. Pretty sneaky, but when it's your child's safety at stake, anything's fair game.

Beating the Traffic Cops

Here's a camcorder trick that I attribute fully to my brother-in-law Glenn who has managed to get and beat more New York City parking tickets in one month than most people get in a lifetime.

Sometimes you'll find a ticket on your windshield for no apparent reason. Maybe you were just in the wrong place at the wrong time, or maybe you parked on the site of a fire hydrant that has long since been moved. I believe that the parking police have a secret quota of tickets that they have to meet, but don't quote me on that one!

So Glenn's newest weapon in court is his father's brand new Sony camcorder with a pop-out LCD viewfinder. He's done it at least twice, and so far the judges have not hesitated to take the time to check out his video testimony. He's gone as far as to shoot his watch to give the judge the date and time, then he continues to shoot the entire area surrounding the car, unedited, in search of any hydrants or signs. At this time Glenn is three for three in court with a camcorder. Unfortunately for Glenn, the camcorder method isn't as useful in beating tickets for moving violations!

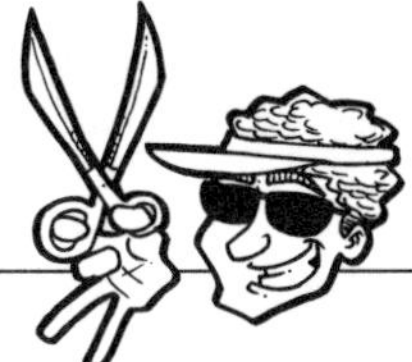

Director's Cut

If you're planning to use video testimony in court, when you are shooting try to avoid starting and stopping your camcorder. Too many starts and stops might cause a judge to think that the footage is edited.

Video Diaries/Journals

What about using your camcorder to record your own personal video diaries or journals? Sounds a little corny, but think about it for a minute. Video diary entries recorded on videotape can be much more informative, entertaining and realistic than written diaries. It's not something that you necessarily have to do every day, but it can be done during special times, vacations, or preparation for a special event like a wedding. You can even use your camcorder to record yourself while studying for an exam. It's really the best way to truly capture the way you're feeling at the time, and upon playback, a neat video-timeline is created as your thoughts and feelings progress with the times.

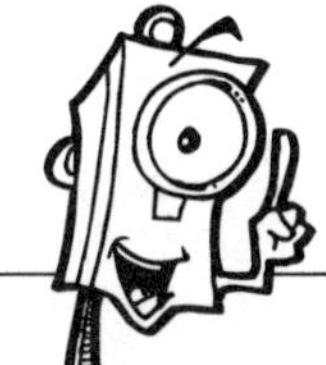

Candid Camera

Don't forget to superimpose the date and time on the video so you'll be able to keep track of your entries.

If keeping a video journal/diary is for you, consider keeping a special tape in your camcorder bag just for this purpose. Make sure it's labeled clearly; you want to keep it separate from your other footage.

I've found that the best way to actually record yourself with a camcorder is to snap the lens into wide-angle mode, and simply turn it around and begin speaking. You can also mount the camcorder on a tripod for a more professional look, but you don't want to spend too much time setting up for recording. The beauty of a video-entry is that it's quick, hassle-free, and simple to do.

A Video Thank-You!

If you don't mind spending some time making a few VHS dubs, consider distributing a video thank-you message the next time you have a party and get lots of gifts. It's a creative, thoughtful alternative to boring thank-you cards that are sold in stationary stores.

The best part of video thank-you messages is that the people you send them to are going to be touched simply by the fact that you went out of your way to do it. This means that you don't have to waste time putting together a slickly edited masterpiece. In fact, you don't really have to edit anything at all. Just record a simple message by yourself or with your family at your side, make straight dubs onto VHS, and then send them out. It's as simple as that!

A Video Birth Announcement

Looking back, I wish that I had taken the time to announce the birth of my son Ben on video rather than on paper. Instead of spending hundreds of dollars on personalized cards, my wife and I could have spend less money on VHS or CD-ROM stock and recorded a neat birth announcement on video. This is a unique way to give your friends and family a firsthand glimpse of your new baby. A photo doesn't compare to live video.

It can be done simply and elegantly. There's no need to include footage in the delivery room, but immediately after is a great time to record a bit when the baby is swaddled from neck to toe in a fresh hospital blanket.

I wouldn't recommend making these types of videos feature-length epics. Aim for two to three minutes with a maximum of about five minutes. It's just enough to give everyone a little teaser and getting them even more excited to visit the baby.

The Least You Need to Know

- A camcorder is an invaluable tool in shopping for anything from a car to college. It allows you to review your choices in the privacy of your own home.
- You can record yourself acting, giving a speech or presentation, and review the footage in order to improve your performance.
- A consumer camcorder is perfect for video surveillance.
- You can use your camcorder to create thoughtful thank-you messages or birth announcements.

Chapter 26

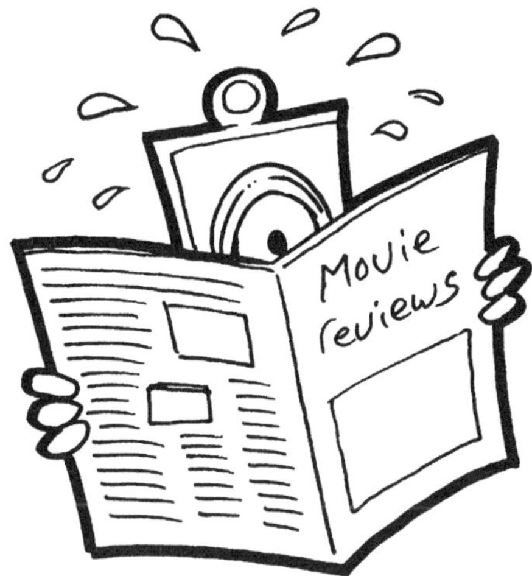

Your Home Videos in the Public Eye

In This Chapter

- Documenting history with home video
- Breaking news is right under your nose
- Call the network!
- Making movies with your camcorder
- Film festivals want your work

There's every reason to believe that a camcorder is one of the most powerful and influential pieces of consumer electronics in human history. Not only are there entire programs being built around home video footage, but news programs often rely on the work of the everyday shooter to supply them with the real scoop.

As camcorder technology continues to develop, the resulting high-quality footage is going to be utilized in more ways than you can possibly imagine. In the near future TV shows aren't the only place you'll see home video having an impact. You'll also see it playing in your local theaters in the form of feature films!

Home Video Is Having a Big Impact

A few weeks ago my wife and I were driving towards the Tappan Zee Bridge in New York. Off in the distance I noticed a single engine plane flying curiously low. As we began to cross the bridge, we both started to become panicky because from our angle, it looked like the plane was on a collision course with the bridge. I quickly asked my wife to grab my camcorder, which was in the back somewhere. While my wife fumbled to get it, I looked up again to see that the plane was coming in way too close for comfort. I noticed that a few of the cars around me began to slow down as well in anticipation of a crash. My wife pulled the camcorder out of the case and powered it up just as the plane buzzed past the bridge. Whew! From where we were, it looked like the plane's wing just missed scraping a pillar.

As I continued into the city with a huge sense of relief, my mind wandered into some truly unsettling thoughts. What would have happened if, by some horrible misfortune, the plane collided with the bridge? First and foremost, it would have been a horrifying disaster, and countless people, including my family, could have been injured or even killed. If, by some twist of fate, we escaped harm and if my wife managed to capture the entire event on tape, you can guarantee that the entire planet would be viewing her footage quicker than you can say "Coming up at 11."

Horrible disasters, historical events, and countless other happenings that have an impact on the public are captured and globally distributed every day thanks to amateur videographers just like yourself. The proliferation of high-quality consumer camcorders broadens the potential view of local and network television. From natural disasters to murders, fires and car crashes, there's a good chance that someone's going to be there with a camcorder to catch the action. Luckily, the day we drove over the bridge it wasn't an earth-shattering event that my wife recorded. It was just some show-off who decided it would be funny to buzz the Tappan Zee Bridge and give hundreds of drivers like myself a heart attack!

But there have been simple home videos that have had a great impact on society. The Rodney King beating footage was shot by someone who just happened to have a camcorder within reach. Most people will never forget the consequences of that little video-clip. Not only did it spark the L.A. riots, but it also led to more violence that was captured on video. And don't forget perhaps one of the most famous pieces of home video in human history, the Zapruder film of the John F. Kennedy assassination.

Similarly, there have been scores of natural disasters captured on camcorders that give the world an idea of what it's like to be in the path of destructive forces like flooding or a tornado. Intense video often spurs an intense and widespread call for action, often leading to multi-million dollar relief efforts. Additionally, severe storm videos also help scientists gain a better understanding of the weather and help them figure out methods of early predictions that can save lives.

Developing a Nose for Breaking News

How would you like to see your camcorder footage broadcast on your local news? Even better, how would you like to see your stuff on national or even international newscasts?

Being in the right place at the right time is only part of the breaking news business. You've got to have the right equipment at your disposal, and you've got to be able to get to it fast. When I think about it, the plane incident on the Tappan Zee Bridge was actually the first time that I ever found myself in the path of potential breaking news. A newsworthy event is hard to come by and even harder to capture on tape. That's why they're so attractive to people in the television news business. In fact, it's probable that you will never have the opportunity to shoot something that TV stations might be interested in. Or, you could find yourself aiming your camcorder at the first UFO landing on the White House lawn. You never know.

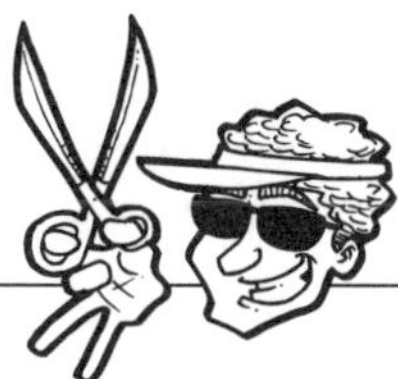

Director's Cut

Before you throw yourself into the path of breaking news, consider some of the footage that you'd be after. Murders, fires, car crashes, and armed robberies are the bread and butter of newscasts and any scoop on these kinds of stories will play on TV news. Some of these situations, however, can be downright disturbing. Make sure that you're prepared for some potentially grisly sights and be aware you might be putting yourself in the path of danger.

The Right Stuff

If the right moment happens to come your way and you shoot it with your camcorder, it might end up on TV. But if you have just a few extra pieces of video gear handy, your chances improve tenfold that TV news people will look at what you've got.

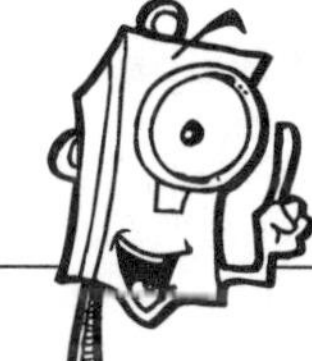

Candid Camera

If you've got a 3-chip MiniDV camcorder, you're in good shape for breaking news. In fact, many TV stations use 3-chip digital camcorders because they're lightweight and shoot amazing quality footage.

First and foremost, it helps to have a high quality camcorder that delivers footage that lives up to the semi-professional or even professional level. Try to have a camcorder that shoots a high-band format like MiniDV, Digital8, SVHS, or Hi8. If shot well, footage from these kinds of camcorders can look very close to the professional cameras that TV stations use.

One of the most useful tools that you can carry in your breaking news video kit is a shotgun light. These inexpensive lights mount on top of many camcorders and have their own separate batteries. Using one helps in low light situations like at the aftermath of a car wreck or a midnight building fire.

A major part of any news story is to hear eyewitnesses talk on camera. If you think you might be in the position to acquire an interview, you'd have the best luck if you plug a handheld microphone into your camcorder. They are reasonably priced and record crisp, clear sound.

Now That You've Found It, How Do You Shoot It?

Here's where all of those fundamentals on shooting better home videos that I've been reiterating throughout the book really come into play. Forget about zooming in and out or panning wildly from side to side, trying to catch any and all movements. Shooting for news should be a smooth and straightforward task.

When you find yourself shooting a news story, you have to quickly figure out the best way to visually tell the story. You want to frame your shots with simple composition so the audience instantly understands what you're trying to convey.

Let's say you've just arrived at the scene of a fire that destroyed a local supermarket. The first thing you want to do is to make contact with authorities on the scene and find out what happened. Then grab a few wide shots, preferably with police cars and fire trucks with flashing sirens in the background. Tight shots work well for news editors, but you have to make sure you have permission to get in close to the scene. After you've covered the main action, look for creative and informative cutaways to help the editor tell the story. A simple shot of a fire hose, open hydrant, or even a bunch of fireman talking about the blaze will work perfectly. If you have time, try to record interviews with police, fire officials, or even the owner of the supermarket.

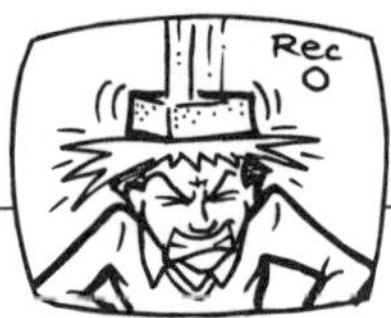

Blooper

If you've arrived on the scene of an accident or some other disaster, tend to the injured before even thinking about shooting video. Think of the reports of crazed cameramen taking pictures while Princess Di lay dying, unattended in her wrecked car. And stay out of the way of the authorities coping with the disaster. By interfering with them, you could unwittingly hinder rescue efforts, and end up a sad addition to the news story yourself.

Will They Really Want It?

If you've been lucky enough to capture a newsworthy event, you're going to be surprised at how quickly it will be snatched up by a TV station. The most important thing to keep in mind is that whatever you decide to do, you must do it quickly!

The first thing on your list is to try and contact the Managing Editor or News Director of your favorite local news. If you can't get anyone on the phone, don't hesitate to tell your story to a news assistant or even an intern. If your story is good enough, the right people will soon find out about it.

If it turns out that they want to buy your footage, don't expect big bucks. At WRGB-TV (Channel 6) in Albany, New York, where I used to work we would give home videographers who gave us footage a "6-shooter" T-shirt and hat! These days I'd be surprised if you'd get more than $50 to $100 for your footage (unless, of course, you've captured something really amazing that instantly gets hurled into the public's face).

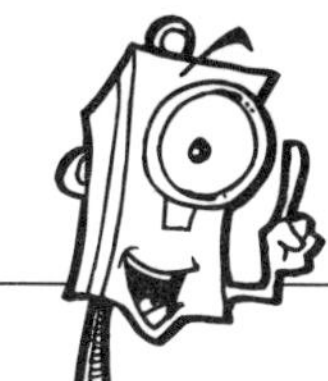

Candid Camera

It's a good idea to gather as much information about the news story as you can. The more information that you can offer the news desk, the less leg work they have to do. This makes your package more attractive to them.

One thing to keep in mind, however, is that you're probably not doing it for the money. Yeah, it would be nice to get some bucks for your hard-earned footage, but it's a great feeling to see your stuff broadcast on TV. And forget about owning the rights after passing the footage along. There's a good chance they'll have you sign ownership away.

Call the Networks: You May Have Something They Want!

Your home videos are invaluable to TV producers for far more than just news. Home videographers have been creating content for entertaining television shows like *America's Funniest Home Videos* and *World's Funniest* for many years. And, as camcorders continue to explode in popularity, the number and quality of these shows are steadily on the rise.

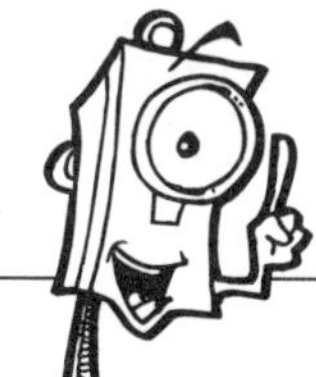

Candid Camera

If you're really serious about catching breaking news, police scanners are perfectly legal and a good way to hone in on any newsworthy action. You can pick up a good police scanner at Radio Shack pretty cheap.

Then there are other shows that rely completely on viewer-submitted footage. And these shows don't necessarily have a happy or funny hook. *Real TV* is a nationally syndicated show by Paramount that features amazing and shocking images that have been captured on camcorder. From daring rescues to crocodile fights, this show tells it the way it really happened.

Similarly, there have been all kinds of other "reality-TV" shows to hit air, some shot with home video equipment, others shot with professional equipment. MTV's *The Real World*, for example, uses professional equipment to capture realistic, everyday occurrences between a carefully selected cast of characters who live together. They use professional production tactics that help them simulate a home video feel. The entire house is a carefully rigged set with microphones, fish-eye cameras, and all sorts of lighting gear. There's even a control room somewhere deep within the house where producers, directors, and story editors monitor the action.

There are also scores of cop dramas on Fox and other networks that utilize camcorders to capture action. They even feature footage that is captured on a dashboard mounted camcorder in a police car. On The Learning Channel, there are two shows, *Paramedics* and *Trauma: Life in the E.R.*, that are entirely shot on Panasonic Mini-DV camcorders. At first glance you'd never be able to tell that these shows were shot with consumer equipment.

If you find yourself with video that you think one of these shows would be interested in, check out the following information:

- **America's Funniest Home Videos**
  Box 4333
  Hollywood, CA 90078
  www.abc.com

  A $3.00 return postage fee in a U.S. money order should be enclosed if the entrant would like the tape returned.
- **World's Most Amazing Videos**
  P.O. Box 933026
  Los Angeles, CA 90093
  www.nbc.com

  Include a money order or check for $3 payable to Nash Entertainment if you would like your videotape returned.

  All submissions become property of Nash Entertainment, Inc.
- **The World's Funniest!**
  P.O. Box 2904
  Toluca Lake, CA 91610-0904
  www.foxworld.com/funniest/
- **Real TV**
  (888) REALTV1
  www.realtv1.com

Movies and Documentaries You Can Shoot with Your Camcorder

Filmmaking is a hugely expensive undertaking. Whether you're shooting on 35mm or 16mm, the film stock itself is expensive, and the developing can send a budget right over the edge. And that's not to mention the making of a film print, film editing, sound editing, and transferring to videotape. Plus, the cameras are incredibly expensive to rent, plus you need to employ and feed scores of people in your crew. A typical film budget usually gets started in the six-figure range and only goes skyrocketing upward from there.

But thanks to low cost and high-quality digital video cameras, a growing circle of filmmakers are foregoing their film cameras for MiniDV camcorders. Even though digital video has a long way to go to catch up with the incredible dynamic range of colors that film is capable of, MiniDV delivers up to 500 lines of vertical resolution which is a force to be reckoned with when you transfer the video to film.

Besides the fact that you can shoot and shoot and shoot and not have to worry about blowing rolls of expensive film, MiniDV camcorders are light and portable, and are great for shooting in low light situations.

It's also becoming quite cost-effective to set up digital editing stations at home using a computer. The footage can easily be transferred from camcorder to computer and back to the camcorder without any noticeable loss in quality. And the audio is CD quality the minute it hits the digital tape.

While 35mm film is still the acquisition medium of choice for movies and probably will continue to be so for a while, a few MiniDV, Hi8 and SVHS films have captured the public's attention and have gone on to be picked up by major distributors. One "home movie" that was so good that it was theatrically released was *The Blair Witch Project*. This film was shot primarily on Hi8 and went on to become one of the most profitable films of all times in relation to how much it cost to make. Two other such films are *The Celebration,* directed by Thomas Vinterberg and *The Cruise* by Bennett Miller. According to the DV Films List on the Internet (www.dvfilmmaker.com), *The Celebration* was shot with the Sony TRV9, and *The Cruise* was shot with the Sony DCR-VX1000. If I look into my crystal ball, I think we'll see more and more films shot on high quality home video equipment in the public eye.

For more on digital filmmaking, here are some Web sites of interest:

- **DV Central**—www.dvcentral.org. A Web site dedicated to digital video (DV).
- **Sony VX-1000 User Group**—http://abruptedge.virtualave.net. Home of the Sony VX-1000 resource group.
- **Canon XL1 Watchdog**—www.mediadesign.net/canondv.htm. A resource center for the Canon XL1.
- **Mac Digital Video Resources**—www.postforum.pair.com. Digital video articles, reviews, discussion boards, and software.
- **Nonlinear Editing Page**—www.nonlinear3.com. A great nonlinear and post-production Web link.
- **Cyber Film School**—www.cyberfilmschool.com. Moviemaking news, reviews, articles, bookstore, software, forums, and links.
- **Digital Cinema**—www.tech-head.com. For anything digital, a great link.

- **Movie Maker Magazine**—www.moviemaker.com. Festival links, production links, call for entries/crew calls, sound clips, classifieds.
- **RES—The Magazine of Digital Filmmaking**—www.resmag.com
- **The DV Filmmaker's Report E-mail Newsletter**—www.dvfilmmaker.com
- **The DV Report E-mail Newsletter**—www.dvreport.com
- **DigiEffects (Cinelook Software)**—www.digieffects.com

Courtesy of The DV Filmmaker's Toolkit—References & Resources Links Page © 1998, 1999 Maxie D. Collier.

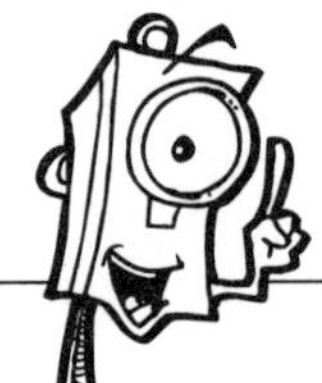

Candid Camera

Most film festivals charge a fee for entering your work. It ranges anywhere from $10 to $100. This can add up quickly if you decide to enter your film into many festivals.

Film Festivals Want Your Videos!

Believe it or not, many film festivals are accepting video entries—especially movies and documentaries that were shot on video. If you've gone through all the trouble of producing and directing your own movie, whatever the length, a film festival is a great way to put your work on display. If your film is chosen to be shown at the festival, it's great fun to attend and very often the director is asked to give a little introduction to the feature. Check out www.filmfestivals.com for a more complete listing of film festivals that accept entries.

The Least You Need to Know

- Home video camcorders are powerful tools in documenting human history.
- Breaking news is only a record button away if you know what to look for and have the right equipment handy.
- More and more network television producers are seeking your home videos.
- A new generation of digital filmmakers are taking advantage of the high quality and low cost of consumer MiniDV camcorders.
- There are tons of film festivals that would be glad to take a look at your video submissions.

Chapter 27

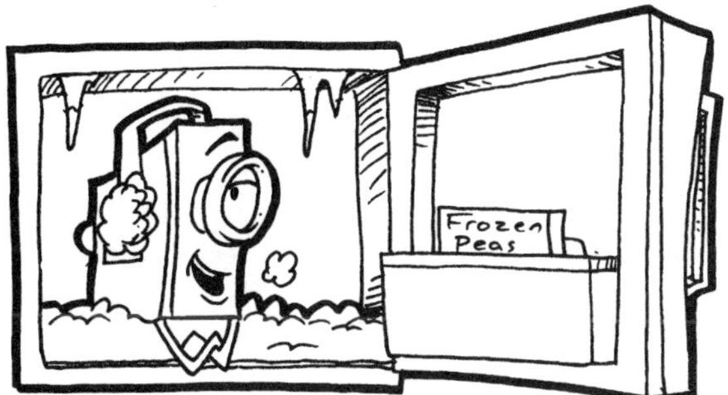

Preserving Your Home Videos

In This Chapter

- The inside scoop on generation loss
- Stopping video degradation in its path!
- Archiving your home videos
- Caring for your videotapes

Shooting and producing home videos can be one of the most satisfying endeavors that you can undertake. Much like other creative hobbies and professions like painting, photography, or even music, making home videos that people really want to see can be very fulfilling and a great way to communicate your thoughts and feelings to others. Taking into account the pure archiving power of history and personal events, video has become the medium of choice for millions of people worldwide.

But the big question is how do you archive the archive? In that I mean how do you preserve your home videos? Unfortunately, at this point in time videos aren't designed to last forever. For many videographers it's a very frustrating thing and that's also why there are still people out there who prefer to shoot on film. Film is considered an "archival" format that means if you take some precautions, it can last a very long time. On the other hand, even if you were to keep your videos on a pillow next to your bed in an air-conditioned room every night, tape has an inherent quality that makes the picture slowly deteriorate. Even the most taken-care-of tapes can lose their picture in anywhere from seven to 15 years. Every single time you play it, there's wear and tear on the videocassette.

There are still things you can do, however, to keep your videos in tip-top shape for as long as possible. You also have the option to transfer your videos to more durable formats, or even more longer lasting media like CD-ROMs.

If you decide to ignore my warnings, however, your videos will forever disappear into a magnetic mish-mash of white snow.

Dubs, Dubs, and More Dubs! The Real Deal on Generation Loss

A colleague at work recently told me a funny story. One afternoon his brother was shopping in New York City and came across a sidewalk table where they were selling videotapes. Some of the titles there caught his eye. *The Devil's Advocate, Flubber, My Best Friend's Wedding,* and *Titanic*. Since *Titanic* had been out in theaters for only a few weeks at the time, he asked the street vendor if it was in fact the James Cameron film. He was assured that it was a perfect copy of an early screening version of the film. That was all he had to hear. He pulled out some cash and bought the tape.

But as luck would have it, when he popped in the tape later that day, he got an unpleasant surprise.

At the very beginning of the tape, there was a lot of grain, grit, and dusty looking layers over what appeared to be people's shadows moving around in the lower third of the screen. He suddenly realized that someone had made this bootleg tape by sneaking a consumer camcorder into a movie theater and recorded the movie by mounting the camera on a tripod!

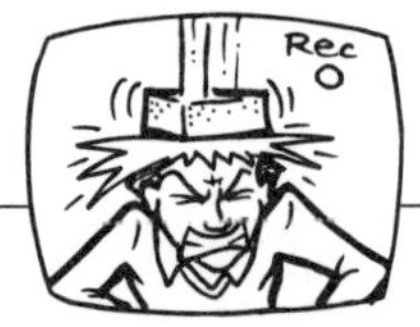

Blooper

In the case of bootlegging, any time you try to record something that was shot on film with a video camera, the results are going to be disappointing. That's because the dynamic range of film is much higher than video. The moral of the story: Stay away from street vendors and video pirates. They'll only take you for a ride! And don't try to do it yourself. It's illegal.

The overall quality of the recording was appalling. The audio could barely be heard, and even worse than that, his brother couldn't make out anything that was going on onscreen. All of the amazing action, special effects, and incredible drama of *Titanic* was washed away in a blur of fuzz and white snow.

The long and short of it is that my friend's brother was the victim of video generation loss, not just theatrical piracy. The street vendors probably used the original camera master only once and started making duplications of duplications and eventually lost track of the copies or sold off the good copies. The original camera master of the bootleg was probably good enough to see what was going on, but after a few generations, the details were lost very quickly.

What happened to my friend's brother on the street happens to home videographers every day. It's especially bad for users of the VHS and 8mm tape formats. After two or three generations, the picture quality decreases incrementally, getting significantly worse with each dub. Generation loss has been plaguing videographers since the inception of video, and professionals and amateurs alike do everything in their power to avoid it. Hi8 and SVHS fare a little better, mainly because you're starting off with higher quality footage (up to 400 lines of resolution as compared to 250 for VHS and 8mm). MiniDV and Digital8 are the best options because they virtually eliminate generation loss by using digital information to transfer video signals back and forth.

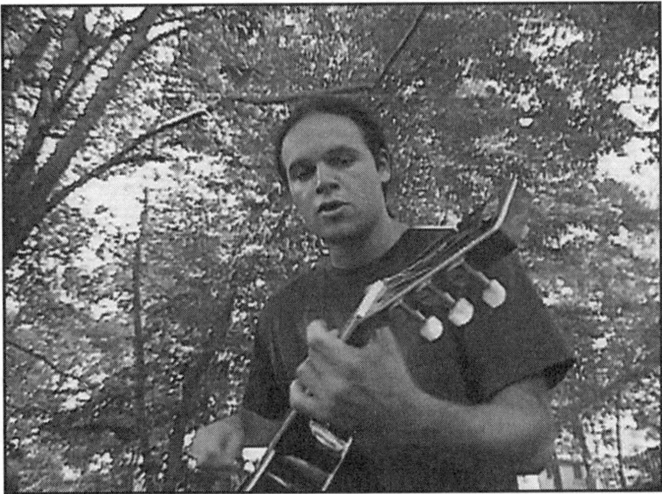

First-generation home video.

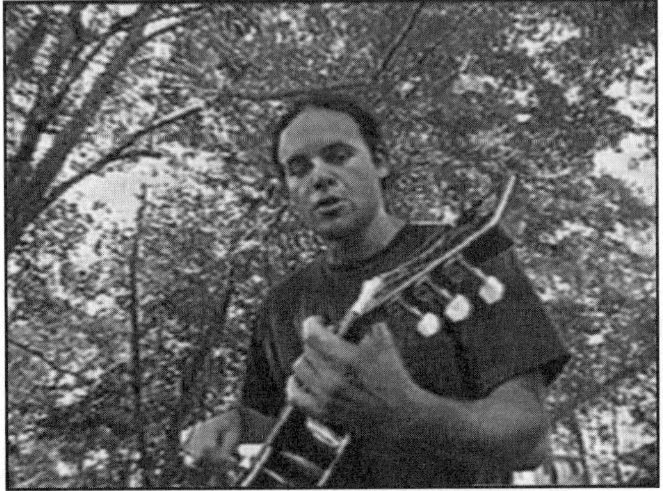

Home video with generation loss.

Nuking the Noise!

What causes generation loss? The first major factor is the introduction of noise into the video signal. We covered this in depth in Chapter 10, "Quiet on the Set!," but noise has equally negative effects on picture as it does on sound. Video noise is defined as any little particle or speck that shows up on screen that is not a part of the video signal. Every video recording contains some noise, and each time you make a dub, the noise gets worse and worse. In your videos too much noise can cause graininess, spotting or washed out colors.

Splitting Signals

One of the other factors that causes generation loss is that the signal becomes weaker and weaker as you copy down from the original recording.

Here are a few recommendations for preventing generation loss. When working with the analog formats:

1. Always work with the highest quality settings and the fastest tape speed (SP).
2. Light your videos as well as you can with lamps you have available or a professional lighting kit.
3. If your original raw footage is going to be used in linear editing, make any and all dubs from the master. First generation copies usually look fine.
4. Don't make dubs from dubs if you can avoid it.
5. When nonlinear editing, use the highest quality video setting your system can handle.
6. Always use a fresh tape when creating edit masters.
7. If possible, upgrade your analog camcorder/editing setup to MiniDV.

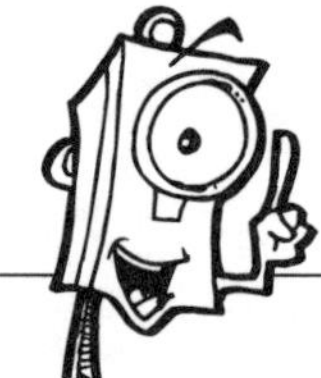

Candid Camera

If you're using an S-video cable (Y/C), the luminance and chrominance are broken up, thus resulting in less negative effects from generation loss. This is a better way to go than a composite (yellow RCA) connection, which combines the luminance and chrominance.

It's All About Edges

One of the best ways to tell the quality of a video picture is the sharpness of the edges of your images. Edges separate anything on screen that have different colors or contrasts. Edges are effected by the high frequencies of a video signal and rapidly lose generation as you make dubs. The edges wear away until eventually you're left with blurry images.

Pruning the Video Generation Family Tree

Generation loss is the spoiler of all videos. From home videos to TV shows, the people behind the scenes bend over backwards to keep generation loss to a minimum. Whether it's linear editing, nonlinear editing, or simply making dupes for friends and family, most consumer video tapes are susceptible to generation loss at one stage or another. MiniDV is the light at the end of the generation loss tunnel, however, but until everyone can afford the technology, a few simple precautions can keep your videos looking as clean as a whistle.

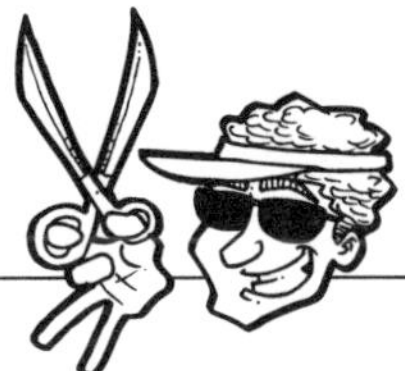

Director's Cut

"When I bought my MiniDV camcorder and editing deck for my home setup, I did a little generation loss test just to see what would happen. I shot a piece of test footage and using FireWire, I dubbed back and forth 10 times. I was stunned when I realized that the tenth generation footage looked exactly the same as the first generation!"
—John Bardsley, Independent Writer/Producer/Editor

It's All in the Equipment

If video quality is important to you, then the best way to help prevent the evils of generation loss is to invest in the best equipment that you can afford. If you can swing a 3 CCD MiniDV camcorder, you're going to be ecstatic with the results.

MiniDV, Hi8, and SVHS all are good options if you're looking for equipment to minimize generation loss. This is especially true since all of these formats have high signal-to-noise ratio (S/N). S/N ratios are measured in decibels (dB). The higher the dB level, the better the picture quality. As you step down the video format ladder, VHS and 8MM have comparably low S/N ratios. This leaves your videos much more susceptible to generation loss.

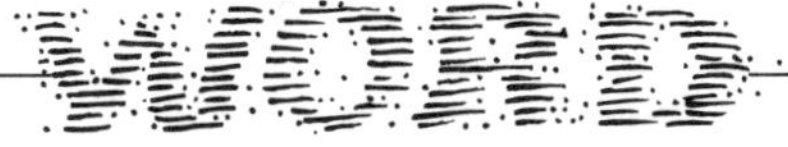

Blurred Word

Signal-to-noise (S/N) ratio is the amount of noise present in the video signal. S/N ratios are usually measured in decibels (dB) and the higher the dB rating, the better the overall picture quality. Low S/N ratios results in poor quality video that is more prone to suffer generation loss. Noise is usually created by interference from other electronic appliances.

Keeping the Extras Out of the Loop

If you can keep external devices and equipment out of your video chain, you'll go a long way in reducing generation loss. This includes video mixers, effects units, and graphic generators. Each one serves a special purpose, but as your video signal passes through, the signal can quickly deteriorate. If you have more than one extra link in the chain your video will suffer significantly before it even leaves home!

This isn't to say that you have to eliminate video extras altogether. Special video devices certainly serve their purpose and spice things up while editing, but if you've got them hooked up even when you don't need them, they can adversely affect your picture. If you're planning a simple edit or just to make dubs with your equipment, disconnect external units from your system. With a little patience you can easily connect and disconnect equipment.

The Shorter the Better

Cable lengths make a real difference when you are wiring video gear together. The longer the cables are, the more susceptible your picture is to degradation due to the noise. Before you buy your cables, take out a tape measure and get as close an estimate as possible for the exact length you're going to need.

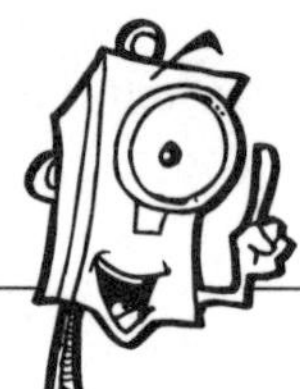

Candid Camera

The more you spend for cables, the better they're going to be. Cheap cables are receptors for noise and other gook that gets in and destroys your picture.

In addition, if you have the option to use S-video (Y/C) cables over the old yellow composite cables (RCA or BNC), go for it. Your picture will not only look better, it will be much more resistant to generation loss.

If you've gone digital, you might have the opportunity to link your equipment with FireWire (IEEE 1394). This is the best way to completely nuke generation loss before it even starts. Each dub that you make will look exactly like the one that came before it.

Don't Make Light of It!

There's actually one thing that you can do during the actual production of your videos to help make them invulnerable to generation loss. The manner in which you light your videos has a lot to do with the overall strength of the picture quality. Most consumer camcorders are optimized for low light situations, but if you lend your camcorder a helping hand in this department, you're going to find that your videos have more viability in the long run. This doesn't necessarily mean that you have to invest thousands of dollars in lighting gear. There are all kinds of things that you can do with household lamps and other lights that you have lying around the house (see Chapter 9, "Cast Some Light on the Matter," for more on this).

There's More Than One Way to Archive Your Footage

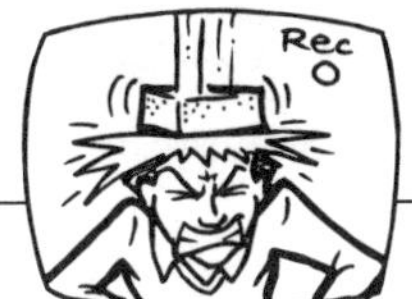

Blooper

In very low-light situations you may notice a grain that is embedded in your picture. When you attempt to make copies of this kind of footage, it degrades a lot quicker than well-lit video.

So far, I've found that the best way to archive my video in a much more permanent format than magnetic tape is to make CD-ROMs of your digitized footage. A few years ago this may not have seemed like a viable option because nonlinear editing gear was exorbitantly expensive. Now, the prices have come down by a factor of ten and just about anyone has access to high quality digitizing and editing gear for their home computers.

The process is relatively easy but it's specific to the kind of nonlinear equipment that you choose. Once you digitize your footage, it is transferred to your hard drive in the form of a digital "file." Just like anything else on your hard drive, you have access to these files and can easily burn them onto CD-ROMs using simple software. The best thing to do is to take your final edited program and combine it into one big file that can then be transferred to a CD-ROM. CD-ROMS can hold up to 650 megabytes of information. So, depending on the quality settings you choose and the image size, you can fit reasonably long programs onto one disk. If you visit your local computer store, there are also CD-ROM authoring programs you can buy (Macromedia Director, for example) that can streamline this process even further. You can even add your own custom multimedia features like graphics, menus, music, and so on.

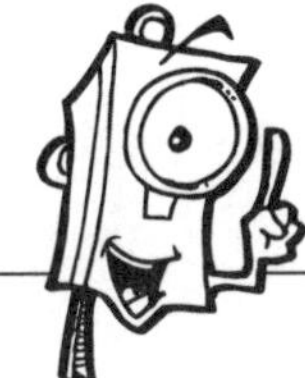

Candid Camera

This is a much disputed point, but I've heard that recordable CD-ROMs have a shelf life of close to 100 years. Some may argue that it's less, but even if they last for only 50 years, it's a lot longer than a videotape will hold images.

If you have the proper software installed, you can even play your videos back right from the CD-ROM. The faster the speed of your computer and CD-ROM drive, the better the video is going to play back on the screen.

The future for this type of storage is exciting. In the not so distant future, recordable DVD-ROMs are going to be making their way into the consumer marketplace. One day you'll be able to store more video on a CD-like disk than you ever imagined, the video will be full screen, and the quality of DVD video blows regular VHS away.

Digital Copy Cat

Another common and effective way to archive your videos is to make digital copies of your analog camcorder footage. This is really convenient if you've recently upgraded from VHS, VHS-C, 8mm, Hi8, and SVHS camcorder to a digital format, and a good way to enjoy your precious footage far into the future.

The only catch here, you need to have a MiniDV/Digital8 that has an analog video input. Right now this can get a bit pricey because only the highest-end MiniDV camcorders have this feature.

If you can manage to swing this one, you can expect a longer shelf life for your tape. That's not to say that digital information doesn't eventually disappear from the surface of your tape, but it takes a lot longer.

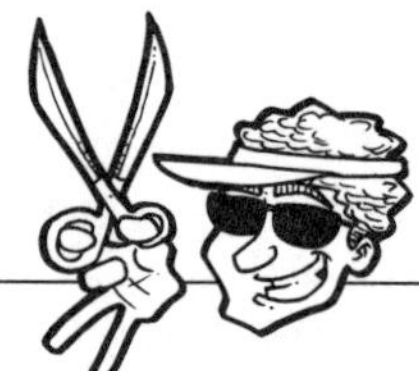

Director's Cut

Sony's new Digital8 format advertises that you can still enjoy your 8mm and Hi8 movies in a new digital camcorder. This is all well and good but your analog tapes are still prone to degradation and unless you make a digital dub, somewhere down the line you can be left with virtually nothing.

Giving Your Videotapes the T.L.C. They Crave

I have a lot of old VHS tapes that I shot back in the mid to late '80s. One day I rounded up my dad, and, together at ABC, we copied much of my old footage over to heavy-duty digital broadcast videotapes. We did this in 1995 so at the time, my footage was only 10 years old. I was shocked to see how much the picture had degraded from just sitting on the shelf. In some cases, the snow and smudges got so bad that the footage was unrecognizable. I was thankful that I did the archiving when I did; otherwise, I may have lost that footage forever. The moral of the story: If possible, make fresh duplicates every couple of years of the home movie footage that's most important to you.

One thing that may have helped save my footage is that I store my videos safely on a shelf in a cool closet. All of my old VHS and Hi8 tapes are also well-protected in hard plastic shells, rather than cardboard sleeves, to keep dust out. Videotapes, like any other delicate possession, should be taken care of in order to increase its longevity. Here are some tips on videotape care that can help make your videos last for a long time:

- Keep your videotapes out of the basement! Moisture and humidity can eat your tapes for lunch. Store them upstairs in a cool, dry place like a hallway closet. The ideal temperature for storing video should never go much below 40 degrees and never much higher than 70 degrees.
- Use the standard recording speed of your VCR. Extended recording times (EP, SLP) will degrade your video before it even sees the light of day.
- Keep your tapes free of dust and dirt. Every now and then, give them a swipe with a lint-free cloth or dusting brush.
- Use the highest quality (most expensive) tapes that you can afford.
- If you make dubs, watch the dubs to avoid putting wear and tear on your edit masters. As you may have already noticed with your existing videotapes, they wear out from repeated viewings.
- Keep the heads clean on your camcorder and VCRs. Excessive internal dust or dirt can easily end up on your tape.
- Always rewind your tapes before you store them.
- Snap off the recording tab immediately after you're done shooting.
- Carefully label your tapes that you plan to store for a long period. Nothing is more frustrating than discovering that you've recorded over precious footage.
- Never leave your tapes in direct sunlight or a hot vehicle.

The Least You Need to Know

- Video degradation over multiple generations can easily be minimized with a few simple precautions.
- CD-ROMs do more than just multimedia. They are a great way to archive your footage as well.
- Take care of your videotapes, and they'll take care of you for a long time to come!

Appendix A

What It Means

assemble editing Selecting raw footage and assembling it in a linear fashion to a master tape.

back lighting Light directed from behind and above your shooting subject. This helps to add dimension to your scene.

beauty shot Any shot that shows off or establishes a person, place or thing.

b-roll Editor's term referring to video that is used for cutaways, l-cuts or to fill in over narration.

byte Unit of digital information that equals one character of text.

camera angle Angle and distance at which the camcorder is pointed at the subject. This could be high, low, wide, telephoto, and so on.

CCD See *Charged Coupled Device.*

CD-ROM Burners Enhanced CD-ROM players that are also capable of recording music or data onto recordable CD-ROMs.

character generators Electronic tools used to create and superimpose titles in your video productions.

Charged Coupled Device (CCD) A silicone chip behind the lens that reads and transforms light rays into moving pictures.

chrominance (C) Part of a video signal that carries the hue and saturation.

codec (compression/decompression) Compression/decompression schemes that help your computer squeeze the huge amount of digital information that is created by capturing video and audio onto your hard drive. The video files are then stretched back out so they can be properly played back.

colored filters Tint the entire video frame any color of the rainbow.

composite When the luminance and chrominance signals are combined into one stream.

contrast The difference between the lightest and darkest portion of a video image.

control track Separate track on a videotape that relays vital information to the VCR or camcorder such as tape speed.

copyright Ownership of a word or piece of music that's registered with the Library of Congress Copyright Office.

cross-fade An audio editing term referring to one audio clip overlapping another and then slowly fading away.

cut The most common transition in video editing, the instantaneous changing from one shot to another. Cuts are considered to be the building blocks of any program.

cutaway shot Any shot that is related to the main action of the scene that offers viewers a different vantage point.

depth of field Portion of video picture in which all objects at different distances from the camcorder appear in focus.

diffusing filters Creates a worn "fuzz" that gives your video a softer look.

Digital Versatile Disk (DVD) Perfect for playing back high-quality video images, DVDs are the same physical size as an audio CD, but capable of storing seven times the amount of information.

digitizing video The process of downloading video from a VCR or camcorder to a computer hard drive for use in nonlinear editing.

director of photography Cameraman and/or lighting designer.

dissolve One of the most common transitions in video editing, when one video or audio source cross-fades into the other. Often used to mark a passage of time in videos, documentaries, or movies.

dolly shot When the camcorder, mounted on a wheeled device, moves towards or away from the subject. Also defined as a camera mount with wheels.

dropouts Occasional white streaks and blips on videotape caused by debris, dust or dirt on the record heads.

dub To duplicate the contents of one videotape to another. Can also apply to adding a sound or a shot to your video.

DVD See *Digital Versatile Disk.*

establishing shot A long shot or wide-angle shot with the purpose of giving the audience a sense of place. Often used at the beginning of a program.

fade in/fade out Increase or decrease in picture brightness at the beginning or end of a segment in your video. The color black is commonly used to dissolve in and/or out of the video.

FireWire (IEEE 1394) A digital transfer protocol that allows you to digitally copy your digital video footage or still-shots from one DV tape to another or from DV tape to your computer's hard drive without any detectable signal loss.

flying eraser heads Mechanism within a VCR or camcorder that allows you to start and stop recording without any distracting glitches.

focal length The distance from the focal point of the lens to the camcorder's imaging surface (CCD).

focal point The exact point in the lens where light converges.

generation loss Overall picture quality degradation resulting from multiple duplication of original footage.

gigabyte Unit of digital information that equals one thousand megabytes.

hard disk array Hard drive configuration where two separate drives are "striped" together so the computer sees it as one larger hard drive that's fast enough to capture digital video.

high fidelity (hi-fi) The method of recording a second, or stereo track underneath the video track of videocassettes, achieving "Super-Stereo" sound.

high key Lighting design that is bright and evenly lit.

i.LINK™ Sony's name for "FireWire" (IEEE 1394).

Internet domain name World Wide Web address that you can type into a web browser giving your computer specific directions to the desired web site on the Internet. Domain names end in .com and .net for commercial sites, .edu for educational sites, and .org for organizations.

iris Tiny opening in the lens of a camcorder that regulates the amount of light striking the CCD (Charged Coupled Device).

jump cut An abrupt or inappropriate edit that results in disrupted continuity in your program. Sometimes used purposely to move action forward.

key lighting The brightest light illuminating the front of your subject. In the three-point lighting scheme, the key light is responsible for setting the mood, defining the form and the overall appearance of the subject.

keying A special video effect that allows you to superimpose one video source over another. Commonly used in titling.

lavalier microphones Tiny microphones that clip on to subject's clothes close to the mouth for super-clean audio.

LCD See *Liquid Crystal Display.*

l-cut Editing technique in which a soundbite has been partially covered by a different related video shot.

Liquid Crystal Display (LCD) A liquid-filled TV screen composed of tiny crystals that, when excited by electricity, help form moving video images.

long shot A shot that takes place far enough away from the action to help reveal overall location. When videotaping people, it usually includes full standing height. (See also *establishing shot.*)

low key Lighting design that is relatively dark, creating a dramatic, moody feel.

low lux Any low light condition.

luminance (Y) Part of a video signal that carries black and white and brightness information.

master tape Videotape that contains selected raw footage.

medium shot When videotaping people, this is considered to include half of their standing height.

megabyte Unit of digital information that equals a million bytes.

monitor Any TV or professional video monitor used to watch the playback or live footage from a camcorder, computer, or deck in an editing setup.

natural light Usually refers to sunlight, either indoors or outdoors.

needledrop licenses Allows you to use a copyrighted work on a per-use basis. Usually refers to music usage in a video production.

neutral-density (ND) filters Filters that reduce the intensity of light passing through the lens without altering the colors.

NTSC TV signal standard used primarily in North America and Japan with 525 lines of definition functioning at 30 frames per second.

omni-directional microphones Microphones that record sound from every direction.

outtake Footage that is not included in the final edited program.

PAL TV signal standard used primarily in Europe with 625 lines of definition.

pan Camera move that follows the action of the shot horizontally from left to right.

pedestal The physical movement of both the camcorder and shooter from a high vantage point to a low, or the other way around.

pixel Smallest part of a computer-generated image. Often rectangular in shape.

point of view (P.O.V.) Camera angle that allows viewers the first-hand perspective of actress or actor.

polarizing filters Block unwanted glare and reflections while sharpening the video clarity.

post-production Stage in video production that takes place after shooting. Editing, sound mixing, sweetening, and special effects commonly take place in post-production.

pre-roll Playback of a pre-selected portion of edited program before an edit point.

processing amplifier (procamp) Allows you to adjust the color and other subtle video properties on the fly.

program auto exposure Automatic dial-settings that adjust the camcorder's shutter and/or iris for special shooting situations.

progressive scan CCD Special CCD (Charged Coupled Device) that scans 60 full frames per seconds as opposed to interlaced (or half) frames.

prosumer equipment Camcorders and other gear that are marketed towards semi-professional and professional videographers seeking near-professional quality at a fraction of the price.

recordable CD-ROM disk Special recordable CD-ROM that can hold up to 650 megabytes of information.

rendering Frame by frame process of recreating video that has been altered by a transition, filter or effect using nonlinear editing software.

rule of thirds Rule of shot composition in which screen is divided into thirds vertically and horizontally, and key elements are evenly placed into these nine areas.

scene transition Video editing term in which one video scene ends and the next one begins.

script Any written or thought-out instructions on shooting, dialogue, acting direction, narration, audio, lighting and camera movement.

signal-to-noise ratio (S/N) The ratio of noise interference as opposed to the picture strength of video.

SMPTE timecode The system of assigning each video frame with a number that's based on a 24-hour clock. SMPTE stands for Society of Motion Picture and Television Engineers.

S/N See *signal-to-noise ratio.*

soundbite Spoken words or phrases by on-camera subject.

source deck Either a camcorder or VCR, used to playback raw footage in an editing situation.

source tape Videotape that contains the raw footage for editing.

special effects filters Distort reality by passing video through different reflective patterns and shapes.

sync The timing signal that is crucial in keeping various video signals electronically coordinated.

take A single camcorder shot or scene. In recording narration, every time the announcer reads the same thing over again is called a take.

talent Anyone who appears on-camera, narrates, or acts in your home videos.

three-point lighting Technique in which three lights work in conjunction with one another to provide a three-dimensional, shadow-free image.

time base corrector External box or internal circuitry inside your VCR that synchronizes the timing of multiple video sources.

time code A series of eight numbers marking the hours, minutes, seconds, and frames of a videotape.

tracking shot A moving (dolly) shot that follows a subject from one place to another.

tripod Three-legged apparatus in which a camcorder can be attached and stabilized.

truck shot The physical movement of both the shooter and camcorder from side to side in a straight line. The camcorder is usually mounted on a wheeled device.

U/V (ultraviolet) filters Common, low priced filters that protect the lens from the effects of ultraviolet light. They are also used to protect the lens from dust, dirt and scratches.

video cassette recorder (VCR) Consumer or professional device capable of playing and recording video.

volume unit meter (VU) Measures the strength of an audio signal with a bouncing needle or LED.

white balance Adjustment that determines how your camcorder "sees" and records colors based on the white-light level of the scene that you're shooting.

zoom When a camcorder's lens is shifted from its deepest wide-angle setting to extreme telephoto.

Appendix B

Recommended Reading

Here are some helpful home video resources.

Books

Ayan, Jordan E. *Aha!: 10 Ways to Free Your Creative Spirit and Find Your Great Ideas.* Crown Publishing, 1997.

Browne, Steven E. *Nonlinear Editing Basics: Electronic Film and Video Editing.* Focal Press, 1998.

Desposito, Joseph, and Kevin Garabedian. *Complete Camcorder Troubleshooting and Repair.* Howard W. Sams & Co., 1998.

Foster, Jack. *How to Get Ideas.* Berrett-Koehler Publishing, 1996.

Gyure, George A. *Start and Operate a Profitable Videotaping Business Using Your Camcorder.* Amherst Media, 1996.

Herrell, Adrienne L., and Joel P. Fowler *Camcorder in the Classroom: Using the Videocamera to Enliven Curriculum.* Prentice Hall College Division, 1997.

Jones, Frederick. *Desktop Digital Video Production.* Prentice Hall, 1998.

Ohanian, Thomas A. *Digital Nonlinear Editing: Editing Film and Video on the Desktop.* Focal Press, 1998.

Pohlmann, Ken C. *Principles of Digital Audio.* McGraw-Hill, 1995.

Rodriguez, Robert. *Rebel Without a Crew: Or How a 23-Year-Old Filmmaker with $7,000 Became a Hollywood Player.* Plume, 1996.

Sherman, Sharon R. *Documenting Ourselves: Film, Video, and Culture.* University Press of Kentucky, 1998.

Soifer, Rosanne. *Music in Video Production.* Focal Press, 1997.

Camcorder, Home Video, and Editing Magazines

Camcorder & Computer Video
805-644-3824

A great mag for camcorder shopping and info on nonlinear editing systems.

DV
www.dv.com
415-905-2200

Higher end mag on digital video, audio, and animation (3D).

New Media
www.newmedia.com
650-573-5170

Focus is on multimedia—Internet, CD-ROM, DVD, and so on. Good information on nonlinear editing and digital video.

Sound and Vision
www.soundandvisionmag.com
212-767-6000

Tons of useful information on stereos, home theater systems (including TVs, VCRs, DVD players), and even camcorders.

Videomaker
www.videomaker.com
530-891-8410

Everything you could possibly want to know about home video.

Videography
www.videography.com
212-378-0400

Popular magazine in the video industry. Great information on camcorders, post production, and digital video.

Digital Filmmaking Web Sites

Canon XL1 Watchdog
www.mediadesign.net/canondv.htm

Cyber Film School
www.cyberfilmschool.com

DigiEffects (Cinelook Software)
www.digieffects.com

Digital Cinema
www.tech-head.com

DV Central
www.dvcentral.org

The DV Filmmaker's Report (E–Mail Newsletter)
www.dvfilmmaker.com

The DV Report E-mail Newsletter
www.dvreport.com

Mac Digital Video Resources
www.postforum.pair.com

Movie Maker Magazine
www.moviemaker.com

Nonlinear Editing Page
www.nonlinear3.com

RES The Magazine of Digital Filmmaking
www.resmag.com

Sony VX-1000 User Group
http://ironman.linkport.com/~mediablitz/

Courtesy of The DV Filmmaker's Toolkit—References & Resources Links Page © 1998, 1999 by Maxie D. Collier.

Internet Resources for Weather Forecasting

Accuweather, Inc.
www.accuweather.com/weatherf/index_corp

America Online, Inc.
www.aol.com/mynews/weather/home.adp

CNN Interactive Weather
www.cnn.com/WEATHER/

EarthWatch, Inc.
www.earthwatch.com/

Excite, Inc.
www.excite.com/weather/

Intellicast
www.intellicast.com/

Lycos, Inc.
http://weather.lycos.com/

Massachusetts Institute of Technology
www.mit.edu/weather

MSNBC
www.msnbc.com/news/WEA_Front.asp

National Weather Service, NOAA
www.nws.noaa.gov/

The New York Times Co.
www.nytimes.com/partners/weather/

Unisys Weather
http://weather.unisys.com/

USA TODAY, a Division of Gannett Co., Inc.
www.usatoday.com/weather/wfront.htm

The Weather Channel Enterprises, Inc.
www.weather.com/twc/homepage.twc

The Weather Underground, Inc.
www.wunderground.com/

WeatherNex
http://cirrus.sprl.umich.edu/wxnet/

Yahoo!
http://weather.yahoo.com/

Additional Web Sites and Internet Resources

Here are some more links for you ...

Search Engines

www.excite.com

www.infoseek.com

www.lycos.com

www.metacrawler.com

www.thunderstone.com

www.yahoo.com

Web Site Hosting

www.aol.com

www.earthlink.com

www.mindspring.com

www.netcom.com

www.networksolutions.com

www.tripod.com

www.wazzu.com

Additional Web Sites

www.acacamps.com

www.backstage.com

www.collegiatechoice.com

www.m-w.com

www.real.com

www.soundandvisionmag.com

Camcorder and Accessory Manufacturers

Here are companies that sell or distribute camcorders and video accessories. Wherever possible, Internet links are included.

Major Camcorder Manufacturers

Canon U.S.A., Inc.
1-800-828-4040
www.canon.com

Hitachi America, Ltd.
650-583-7647
www.hitachi.com

JVC of America
973-315-5000
www.jvc-america.com

Panasonic Broadcast & Television Systems Company
1-800-528-8601
www.panasonic.com/pbds

Panasonic Consumer Electronics Co.
1-800-211-7262
www.panasonic.com/video

Sharp
Video Division at Sharp Electronics Corporation
Sharp Plaza, Mahwah, NJ 07430
1-800-BE-SHARP
www.sharp-usa.com

Sony Corporation
www.sony.com

Tripod Manufacturers

Benbo (distributed by Tifen Co.)
21 Jet View Dr.
Rochester, NY 14624
716-328-7800
www.saundersphoto.com

Bogen Photo Corp.
565 East Crescent Ave.
Ramsey, NJ 07446-0506
201-818-9500
www.bogenphoto.com

Cartoni USA
2755 Alamo St., Suite 103
Simi Valley, CA 93065
1-888-227-8664/805-520-6086
www.cartoni.com

Gitzo S.A. (distributed by Bogen Photo Corp.)
565 East Crescent Ave.
Ramsey, NJ 07446-0506
201-818-9500
www.gitzo.com

Linhof (distributed by H.P. Marketing Corp.)
(Professional tripods)
16 Chapin Rd.
Pine Brook, NJ 07058
1-800-735-4373
www.linhof.net

MSE-Matthews Studio Equipment, Inc.
2405 Empire Ave.
Burbank, CA 91504
818-843-6715
www.matthewsgrip.com

Miller Fluid Heads (USA) Inc.
216 Little Falls Rd.
Cedar Grove, NJ 07009-1231
973-857-8300
www.miller.com.au/products.htm

Sachtler Corp. of America
55 N. Main St.
Freeport, NY 11520
516-867-4900
www.sachtler.com

Slik Corp. (distributed by ToCAD America, Inc.)
300 Webro Rd.
Parsippany, NJ 07054-2882
973-428-9800
www.slik.com

Velbon Tripod Co. (a division of Hakuba U.S.A)
10621 Bloomfield St., Ste. 39
Los Alamitos, CA 90720
1-800-423-1623
www.velbon.com

Vinten, Inc.
709 Executive Blvd.
Valley Cottage, NY 10989
914-268-0100
www.vinten.com

Lens Accessory Manufacturers

Adorama Camera, Inc.
42 W. 18th St.
NY, NY 10011
1-800-223-2500
www.adorama.net/default.tpl

Canon U.S.A, Inc.
1 Canon Plaza
Lake Success, NY 11042
1-800-828-4040
www.usa.canon.com

Century Precision Optics (A Tinsley Co.)
11049 Magnolia Blvd.
N. Hollywood, CA 91601
1-800-228-1254
www.centuryoptics.com

Kenko Co., Ltd. (distributed in the U.S. by THK Photo Products, Inc.)
2360 Mira Mar Ave.
Long Beach, CA 90815
1-800-421-1141
www.thkphoto.com

Minolta Corp.
101 Williams Dr.
Ramsey, NJ 07446
1-800-808-4888
www.minolta.com

Raynox
150 20th St.
Brooklyn, NY 11232
1-800-943-2000
www.digitaletc.com

Rosco Laboratories, Inc.
52 Harbor View
Stamford, CT 06902
1-800-767-2669
www.rosco.com

Sakar International, Inc.
195 Carter Dr.
Edison, NJ 08817
732-248-1306

Schneider Optics, Inc.
285 Oser Ave
Hauppauge, NY 11788
1-800-645-7239
www.schneideroptics.com

Sony Consumer Electronics, Inc.
One Sony Dr.
Park Ridge, NJ 07656
1-800-222-7669
www.sony.com

Tiffen Manufacturing Corporation
90 Oser Ave.
Hauppauge, NY 11788-3886
1-800-645-2522
www.tiffen.com

Lighting Equipment Manufacturers

Anton Bauer, Inc.
14 Progress Dr.
Shelton, CT 06484
1-800-422-3473
www.antonbauer.com

Arriflex Corp.
617 Route 303
Blauvelt, NY 10913
914-353-1400
www.arri.com

Beseler
1600 Lower Rd.
Linden, NJ 07036
908-862-7999
www.beseler-photo.com

Bogen Photo Corp.
565 E. Crescent Ave.
Ramsey, NJ 07446-0506
201-818-9500
www.bogenphoto.com

Cine 60
630 E. 9th Ave. (second floor)
New York, NY 10036
212-586-8782

Frezzi Energy Systems/Frezzolini Electronics, Inc.
7 Valley Street
Hawthorne, NJ 07506
1-800-345-1030
www.frezzi.com

Hahnel USA
N7653 650th St.
Beldenville, WI 54003
715-273-7799
http://hahnel-usa.com/index.html

Jasco Products Co.
3111 N.W. 122nd St.
Oklahoma City, OK 73114
1-800-654-8483
www.jascoproducts.com

Lowel-Light Manufacturing
140 58th St.
Brooklyn, NY 11220-2515
1-800-334-3426
www.lowel.com

NRG Research, Inc.
233 Rogue River Hwy. Bldg.#144
Grant Pass, OR 97527
1-800-753-0357
www.nrgresearch.com

Photoco, Inc.
4347 Cranwood Parkway
Cleveland, OH 44128
1-800-955-5505

Photoflex, Inc.
333 Encinal St.
Santa Cruz, CA 95060-2132
1-800-486-2674
www.photoflex.com

Smith Victor Corp.
301 North Colfax St.
Griffith, IN 46319
1-800-348-9862

Vanguard USA, Inc. (subsidiary of Guardforce Corp.)
9157 E. M-36
Whitmore Lake, MI 48189
1-800-875-3322
www.vanguardusa.com

Microphone Manufacturers

AKG Acoustics, U.S.
1449 Donelson Pike
Airpark Business Centre 12
Nashville, TN 37217
615-360-0499
www.akg-acoustics.com

Audio-Technica U.S., Inc.
1221 Commerce Dr.
Stow, Oh 44224
330-686-2600
www.audio-technica.com

Azden Corp.
147 New Hyde Park Rd.
Franklin Square, NY 11010
516-328-7500
www.azdencorp.com

Beyerdynamic Sales USA
56 Central Avenue
Farmingdale, NY 11735
516-293-3200
www.beyerdynamic.com

Nady Systems, Inc.
6701 Shellmound St.
Emeryville, CA 94608-1023
510 652 2111
www.nadywireless.com

Samson Technologies Corp.
P.O. Box 9031
Syosset, NY 11791-9031
516-364-2244
www.samsontech.com.

Sennheiser Electronic Corp.
1 Enterprise Dr.
Old Lyme, CT 06371
860-434-9190
www.sennheiserusa.com

Shure Brothers, Inc.
222 Hartrey Avenue
Evanston, IL 60202-3696
847-866-2200
www.shure.com

Sony Electronics, Inc.
3300 Zanker Rd.
San Jose, CA 95134
1-800-222-7669
www.sel.sony.com/SEL

Telex Communications, Inc.
9600 Aldrich Ave. South
Minneapolis, MN 55420
612-884-4051
www.telex.com

Camcorder Bag Manufacturers

Ambico (a division of Recoton Corp.)
2950 Lake Emma Rd.
Lake Mary, FL 32746-6240
www.recoton.com

Beseler
1600 Lower Rd.
Linden, NJ 07036
908-862-7999
www.beseler-photo.com

Domke (distributed by The Saunders Group)
21 Jet View Dr.
Rochester, NY 14624
716-328-7800
www.saundersphoto.com

Lowepro USA, Inc. (a division of DayMen Photo Marketing, Ltd.)
3171 Guerneville Rd.
Santa Rosa, CA 95401
707-575-4363
www.lowepro.com

M. Billingham & Company Ltd. (distributed by Leica Camera, Inc.)
156 Ludlow Ave.
Northvale, NJ 07647
1-800-222-0118
www.billingham.co.uk/

Pelican Products, Inc.
23215 Early Ave.
Torrance, CA 90505
1-800-473-5422
www.pelican.com

Photoflex, Inc.
333 Encinal St.
Santa Cruz, CA 95060
1-800-486-2674
www.photoflex.com

PortaBrace/K & H Products, Ltd.
Box 249
North Bennington, VT 05257
802-442-8171
www.portabrace.com

Tamarac, Inc.
9240 Jordan Ave.
Chatsworth, CA 91311
1-800-662-0717
www.tamarac.com

TENBA Quality Cases Ltd.
50 Washington St.
Brooklyn, NY 11201
718-222-9870
www.tenba.com

ZERO Halliburton (distributed by ToCAD America, Inc.)
300 Webro Rd.
Parsippany, NJ 07054-2882
973-428-9800
www.tocad.com/zero.html

Camcorder Batteries

Aardvark Batteries & Accessories
www.aardvarkbat.com
1-888-883-4937

Atbatt.com
www.atbatt.com
1-877-4AT-BATT

The Battery Bank
www.batterybank.com
1-800-229-9449

Batteries Direct
www.batteriesdirect.com
1-888-320-1212

Go Battery
www.gobattery.com
1-888-GO-Battery

E-Battery
http://e-battery.com
1-877- BATT2GO

MJM Electronic
www.mjmelectronic.com
1-888-226-4606

Mail-Order Companies for Camcorders and Video Gear

Abe's of Maine
(718) 998-6650

Adorama
1-800-223-2500
E-mail: adorama@aol.com

Armato's
1-800-628-6801
www.armatos.com

B & H Photo/Video/Pro Audio
1-800-947-9925
www.bhphotovideo.com

Beach Camera
1-800-634-1811
www.beachcamera.com

Berger Bros. Camera and Video Exchange
1-888-262-4160
www.berger-bros.com

Camera Sound
1-800-477-0022
www.camerasound.com

Camera World
1-800-729-8933
www.cameraworld.com

CCI Camera City, Inc.
1-800-837-8623
www.ccicameracity.com

DV Direct
1-888-383-8366
www.dvdirect.com

Elite Video
1-800-468-1996
www.elitevideo.com

Family Photo & Video
1-800-899-7468
E-mail: familyph@aol.com

Marine Park
1-800-448-8811

Tri-State Camera & Video
E-mail: tscamvid@aol.com

Worldwide Video Enterprises
1-800-617-4686
www.buydig.com

Internet Resources for Purchasing Camcorders and Video Gear

http://1-1-800-electro.com/index2sony.html

http://focuscamera.com/

www.888camcorder.com/camcorder.htm

www.audiovideo.com

www.bid.com

www.camcorder.com

www.camcorders4sale.com/

www.cameraworld.com/

www.circuitcity.com/

www.electronics4sale.com

www.1mall4all.com/digital_eye.htm

www.planet3000.com/

www.shopunet.com/

www.supremevideo.com/

www.videodiscovery.com

www.virtual-electronics.com/

www.wolfcamera.com

Script-Writing Software

ComedyWriter
Story development
Ideascapes

IdeaFisher™
Story development
Idea Fisher Systems, Inc.

Fiction Master
Story development
The Writepro Corporation

Final Draft™
Script processing
B.C. Software

FirstAid for Writers
Story development
The Writepro Corporation

Movie Magic™ Dramtica Pro
Story development
Screenplay Systems, Inc.

Movie Magic™ Screenwriter
Script processing
Screenplay Systems, Inc.

Plots Unlimited
Story development
Ashleywilde Publishers

ScriptThing™
Script processing
Scriptperfection Enterprises

Scriptware®
Script processing
Cinovations, Inc.

ScriptWizard™
Script processing
Warren and Associates

SideBySide™
Script processing
Simon Skill

Storybuilder
Story development
Seven Valleys Software

StoryCraft
Story development
Storycraft

Three By Five
Story development
B.C. Software, Inc.

Write a Blockbuster
Story development
Truby's Writers Studio

Write Pro®
Story development
The Writepro Corporation

Writer's Blocks
Story develoment
Ashley Software

A Zillion Kajillion Rhymes & Cliches
Rhyming dictionary/cliche thesaurus

Teleprompter Companies

Audio Video Design, Inc.
709-J Silver Palm Ave.
Melbourne, FL 32901
1-800-749-7266
www.avd-prompt.com

Autocue, Inc. (QTV)
104 East 25th St.
NY, NY 10010
212-460-9050
or
5919 W 3rd St., Suite 1A
LA, CA 90036
323-936-6195
www.qtv.com

Bay Coast Group, Inc.
3665 East Bay Dr., Suite 204-174
Largo, FL 33773
1-800-806-1994
www.baycoast.com

Electronic Script Prompting
6129 Western Ave.
Clarendon Hills, IL 60514
630-887-0346
www.prompting.com

Listec Video
707 Chillingworth Dr.
West Palm Beach, FL 33409
561-683-3002
http://listec.com

Magic Teleprompting, Inc.
1390 Waller St.
San Francisco, CA 94117
1-800-646-6244
www.magicscroll.com

Marietta Design Group, Inc.
1000 Whitlock Ave., Suite 320
Marietta, GA 30064
770-514-9552
www.mariettadesign.com

Mirror Image
2189 Abraham Ln.
Oshkosh, WI 54904
920-232-0220
www.teleprompters.com

The Orator Company, Inc.
55 Pepper Tree Rd.
Chula Vista, CA 91910
1-800-565-7504
www.the-orator.com

Q Systems
1333 Eighth Ave.
San Diego, CA 92101
1-800-538-9301
www.qsystemswest.com

Stewart Instruments, Inc.
PO Box 11929
Prescott, AZ 86304
520-778-6988
www.si-inc.com/prompter/

Tekskil Industries, Inc.
108-15290
103 A Ave.
Surrey, BC
Canada, V3R7A2
1-877-835-7545
www.tekskil.com/index.html

When Things Go Wrong

The following organizations can help you resolve mail-order and Internet-related conflicts when purchasing camcorders and video gear.

Consumer Fraud Information

Council of Better Business Bureaus, Inc.
4200 Wilson Blvd., Suite 800
Arlington, VA 22203-1804
703-276-0100
Fax: 703-525-8277
www.bbb.org

National Consumers League
1701 K Street, NW, Suite 1201
Washington, D.C. 20006
202-835-3323
Fax: 202-835-0747
www.nclnet.org

National Fraud Information Center
1-800-876-7060
www.fraud.org

United States

Direct Marketing Association
Mail Order Action Line
1120 Avenue of the Americas
New York, NY 10036-6700
212-768-7277
Fax: 212-302-6714
www.the-dma.org

Federal Trade Commission
600 Pennsylvania Avenue, NW
Washington, D.C. 20580
202-326-2222
www.ftc.gov

U.S. Postal Service
www.usps.gov

Canada

Canadian Marketing Association
1 Concorde Gate
Toronto, Ontario M3C 3N6
416-391-2362
Fax: 416-441-4062
www.the-cma.org

Royal Canadian Mounted Police
www.rcmp-grc.gc.ca

Strategis: Industry Canada
Government of Canada Business Information Site
(includes Office of Consumer Affairs)
1-800-328-6189
http://strategis.ic.gc.ca

Where to Show Your Home Videos

Here are some possible avenues for showing your videos.

TV Shows That Want Your Home Videos!

America's Funniest Home Videos
Box 4333
Hollywood, CA 90078
www.abc.com

A $3.00 return postage fee in U.S. money order should be enclosed if the entrant would like the tape returned.

Real TV
1-888-REALTV1
www.realtv1.com

If *Real TV* airs your story, they will pay the normal license fees: a minimum of $250. Or more, if the footage is truly exceptional.

The World's Funniest!
P.O. Box 2904
Toluca Lake, CA 91610-0904
www.foxworld.com/funniest/

World's Most Amazing Videos
P.O. Box 933026
Los Angeles, CA 90093
www.nbc.com

Include a money order or check for $3 payable to Nash Entertainment if you would like your videotape returned. All submissions become property of Nash Entertainment, Inc.

Film Festivals Want Your Home Videos!

AFI Los Angeles International Film Festival
2021 North Western Avenue
Los Angeles, CA 90027
213-856-7707
Fax: 213-462-4049
E-mail: afifest@afionline.org
http://afionline.org

This festival is held annually in fall.

Arizona State University Art Museum Short Film & Video Festival
Tenth Street & Mill Avenue
Tempe, AZ 85287-2911
602-965-2787
Fax: 602-965-5254
(Contact: John D. Spiak)
E-mail: spiak@asu.edu
http://asuam.fa.asu.edu/filmfest/main.htm

This festival is held annually in spring.

Carolina Film & Video Festival
P.O. Box 26170
University of North Carolina at Greensboro
Greensboro, NC 27402
336-334-5360
Fax: 336-334-5039
(Contact: Jenny Rescigno)
E-mail: cfvf.uncg.edu
http://cfvf.cjb.net

This festival is held annually in late winter.

Chicago Underground Film Festival
3109 N. Western Ave.
Chicago, IL 60618
773-327-FILM
E-mail: info@cuff.org
www.cuff.org

This festival is held annually in summer.

CineMart
P. O. Box 21696
3001 AR Rotterdam
The Netherlands
(011) (31) 10 4118080
Fax: (011) (31) 10 4135132
(Contact: Ido Abram)
E-mail: iffr@luna.nl
www.iffrotterdam.nl

This festival is held annually in winter.

Hamptons International Film Festival
3 Newtown Mews
East Hampton, NY 11937
516-324-4600
Fax: 516-324-5116
(Contact: Bruce Feinberg)
E-mail: hiff@hamptonsfest.org
www.hamptonsfest.org/

This festival is held annually in fall.

Hollywood Black Film Festival
USC School of Cinema
310-348-3944
(Contact: Tanya Kersey-Henley, Executive Director)
E-mail: Hollywood Black Film Festival@blacktalentnews.com
www.hbff.org

This festival is held annually in winter.

Hollywood Film Festival
433 N. Camden Drive, Suite 600
Beverly Hills, CA 90210
310-288-1882
Fax: 310-475-0193
(Contact: Carlos de Abreu)
E-mail: awards@hollywoodawards.com
http://hollywoodfestival.com/

This festival is held annually in summer.

Human Rights Watch International Film Festival
The Ritzy Cinema
Brixton Oval, Coldharbour Lane
Bixton, London SW2 1JG
(44-171) 737-2121
Fax: (44-171) 733-2229
(Contact: John Anderson, Associate Director)
E-mail: andersj@hrw.org
www.hrw.org/iff

This festival is held annually in winter.

iREVlation Independent Film Festival
P.O. Box 135
South Fremantle, WA 6162 Australia
(61) 8 9336 2482
Fax: same
(Contact: Richard Sowada, Festival Director)
E-mail: dakota@omen.net.au
www.omen.net.au/~dakota/riff.htm

This festival is held annually in winter.

Irish Reels Film & Video Festival
911 Media Arts Center
117 Yale Ave.
Seattle, WA 98109
206-523-1579
(Contact: Caroline Cumming, Program Director/Fidelma McGuin, Festival Director)
E-mail: caroline@manicmedia.com
www.911media.org/events/irishreels/

This festival is held annually in winter.

Maine Jewish Film Festival
Portland, Maine
207-799-5953
(Contact: David Connerty-Marin, Director)
E-mail: dcmarin@nlis.net
http://uahc.org/me/bethaam/mjff.html

This festival is held annually in winter.

New Directors/New Films
The Film Society of Lincoln Center
70 Lincoln Center Plaza, Fourth Floor
New York, NY 10023
212-875-5610
Fax: 212-875-5636
(Contact: Richard Pena/Sara Bensman)
E-mail: sbensman@filmlinc.com
www.filmlinc.com/ndnf/ndnf.htm

This festival is held annually in early spring.

New York International Independent Film & Video Festival
175 5th Avenue, #2334
New York, NY 10010
212-777-7100
Fax: 212-387-0873
E-mail: filmfest@bway.net
www.nyfilmvideo.com

This festival is held three times a year in winter, spring, and fall.

New York Underground Film Festival
341 Lafayette, #236
New York, NY 10012
212-252-3845
Hotline: 212-252-EVIL
E-Mail: festival@nyuff.com off

This festival is held annually in late spring.

Portland International Film Festival
Northwest Film Centre
1219 SW Park Avenue
Portland, OR 97205
503-221-1156
Fax: 503-294-0874
(Contact: Bill Foster)
E-mail: info@nwfilm.org
www.nwfilm.org

This festival is held annually in winter. Only short subjects are considered.

Rotterdam International Film Festival
P. O. Box 21696
3001 AR Rotterdam
The Netherlands
(011) (31-10) 411-8080
Fax: (011) (31-10) 413-5132
(Contact: Simon Field)
E-mail: iffr@luna.nl
www.iffrotterdam.nl

This festival is held annually in winter. Short subjects and feature-length films are considered.

Santa Barbara International Film Festival
1216 State St., #710
Santa Barbara, CA 93101
805-963-0023
Fax: 805-962-2524
(Contact: Rhea A. Lewis)
E-mail: info@sbfilmfestival.com
www.sbfilmfestival.com

This festival is held annually in late winter. Films and screenplays are considered.

South by Southwest (SXSW) Film Festival
P.O. Box 4999
Austin, TX 78765
512-467-7979
Fax: 512-451-0754
(Contact: Nancy Schafer)
E-mail: sxsw@sxsw.com
www.sxsw.com

This festival is held annually in late winter.

Sundance Film Festival
P. O. Box 16450
Salt Lake City, UT 84116
801-328-3456
Fax: 801-575-5175
(Contact: Geoff Gilmore)
E-mail: sundance@xmission.com
www.sundance.org

This festival is held annually in winter. Short subjects and feature-length films are considered.

Telluride IndieFest!
P.O. Box 860
Telluride, CO 81435
970-728-2629
Fax: 970-728-6254
E-mail: indiefest@usa.net
www.telluridemm.com/indifest.html

This festival is held annually in late fall.

Toronto International Film Festival
2 Carlton Street, Suite 1600
Toronto, Ontario M5B 1J3
Canada
416-967-7371
Fax: 416-967-9477
(Contact: Piers Handling)
E-mail: tiffg@torfilmfest.ca
www.bell.ca/filmfest

This festival is held annually in late summer.

Index

Symbols

D

E

F

M

N

O

P–Q

R

S

T

U–V

W

X–Y–Z

White Balance Card

With your camcorder in manual White Balance mode, point the lens of your camcorder at this card and hit the White Balance button.

tear here

The Complete Idiot's Reference Card

Camcorder Features You Can't Live Without

- Image Stabilization
- Manual Focus
- Manual White Balance
- Manual Exposure
- Date and Time
- Color Viewfinder

Video Magazine and World Wide Web Resources

www.videomaker.com—Videomaker Magazine
www.soundandvisionmag.com—Sound and Vision Magazine
www.dv.com—Digital Video Magazine
www.videography.com—Videography Magazine
www.newmedia.com—New Media Magazine
www.resmag.com—Res Magazine
www.elitevideo.com
www.bhphotovideo.com
www.dvcentral.org
www.dvfilmmaker.com
www.sony.com
www.canon.com
www.panasonic.com/video
www.jvc-america.com
www.sharp-usa.com
www.hitachi.com

On-Location Essentials

Spare Batteries: Both for the camcorder, lights, and your audio mixer, clip-on and wireless lavalier microphones.

Spare Videotapes: This is the last thing you want to run out of!

Extension Cords/Power Strips/Adapters: Wrap them around your arms and legs if you run out of carrying space.

Spare Light Bulbs: On a bad day, these can blow as often as once an hour. On a good day, you'll definitely blow at least one.

Spare Camcorder: If you've got one, bring it. Even if you're shooting with a Mini-DV camcorder and you have a Hi8 as a backup, you never know when you're going to need it. It's better to have Hi8 footage than no footage at all!

Gaffer's/Duct/Electrical Tape: These are great to have in your bag of tricks the day of the shoot. You can tie down wires to increase safety on the set; you can even hide a lavalier microphone with the stuff. There's not a movie set in the world that doesn't have at least 30 rolls of Gaffer's tape lying around.

Toolkit: No matter what you're shooting, indoors or outdoors, bring a toolkit. If something breaks, you can pull out a screwdriver and needle-nose pliers and fix it.

Battery Charger A/C Power Supply: If you're shooting indoors and there are outlets available, there's no reason to rely on batteries unless you plan to be moving around a lot.

Videotape Care

- Keep your videotapes out of the basement! Moisture and humidity can eat your tapes for lunch. Store them upstairs in a cool, dry place like a hallway closet. The ideal temperature for storing video should never go much below 40 degrees and never much higher than 70 degrees.
- Use the standard recording speed of your VCR. Extended recording times (EP, SLP) will degrade your video before it even sees the light of day.
- Keep your tapes free of dust and dirt. Every now and then give them a swipe with a lint-free cloth or dusting brush.
- Use the highest quality (most expensive) tapes that you can afford.
- Keep the heads clean on your camcorder and VCRs. Excessive internal dust or dirt can easily end up on your tape.
- Always rewind your tapes before you store them.
- Snap off the recording tab immediately after you're done shooting.
- Carefully label your tapes that you plan to store for a long period. Nothing is more frustrating than discovering that you've recorded over precious footage.
- Never leave your tapes in direct sunlight or a hot vehicle.

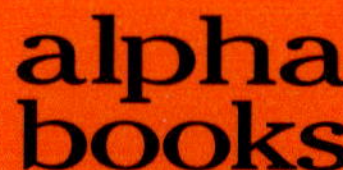